子連れ狼

LONE WOLF AND CUB

子連れ狼

story
KAZUO KOIKE

art
GOSEKI KOJIMA

DARK HORSE COMICS

translation
DANA LEWIS

lettering & retouch
DIGITAL CHAMELEON

cover artwork
FRANK MILLER with **LYNN VARLEY**

publisher
MIKE RICHARDSON

editor
MIKE HANSEN

assistant editor
TIM ERVIN-GORE

consulting editor
TOREN SMITH for **STUDIO PROTEUS**

book design
DARIN FABRICK

art director
MARK COX

Published by Dark Horse Comics, Inc. in association
with MegaHouse and Koike Shoin Publishing Company.

Dark Horse Comics, Inc.
10956 SE Main Street, Milwaukie, OR 97222
www.darkhorse.com

First edition: February 2001
ISBN: 1-56971-507-6

1 3 5 7 9 10 8 6 4 2

Printed in Canada

To find a comics shop in your area, call the
Comic Shop Locator Service toll-free at 1-888-266-4226

LANTERNS FOR THE DEAD

子連れ狼

By KAZUO KOIKE
& GOSEKI KOJIMA

VOLUME

6

A NOTE TO READERS

Lone Wolf and Cub is famous for its carefully researched re-creation of Edo-Period Japan. To preserve the flavor of the work, we have chosen to retain many Edo-Period terms that have no direct equivalents in English. Japanese is written in a mix of Chinese ideograms and a syllabic writing system, resulting in numerous synonyms. In the glossary, you may encounter words with multiple meanings. These are words written with Chinese ideograms that are pronounced the same but carry different meanings. A Japanese reader seeing the different ideograms would know instantly which meaning it is, but these synonyms can cause confusion when Japanese is spelled out in our alphabet. *O-yurushi o* (please forgive us)!

LONE WOLF AND CUB

TABLE OF CONTENTS

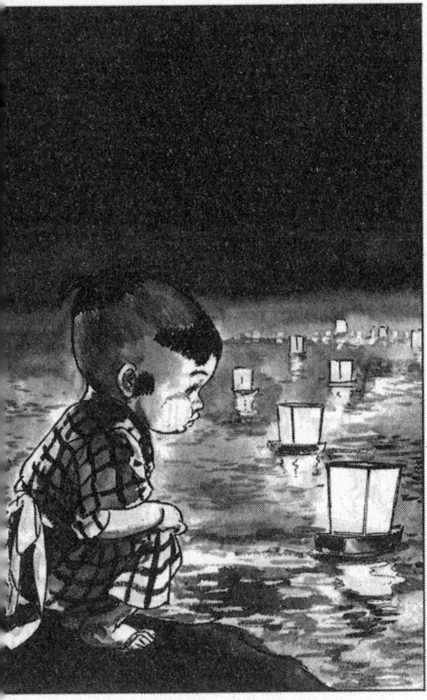

the twenty-ninth

Floating Spirits

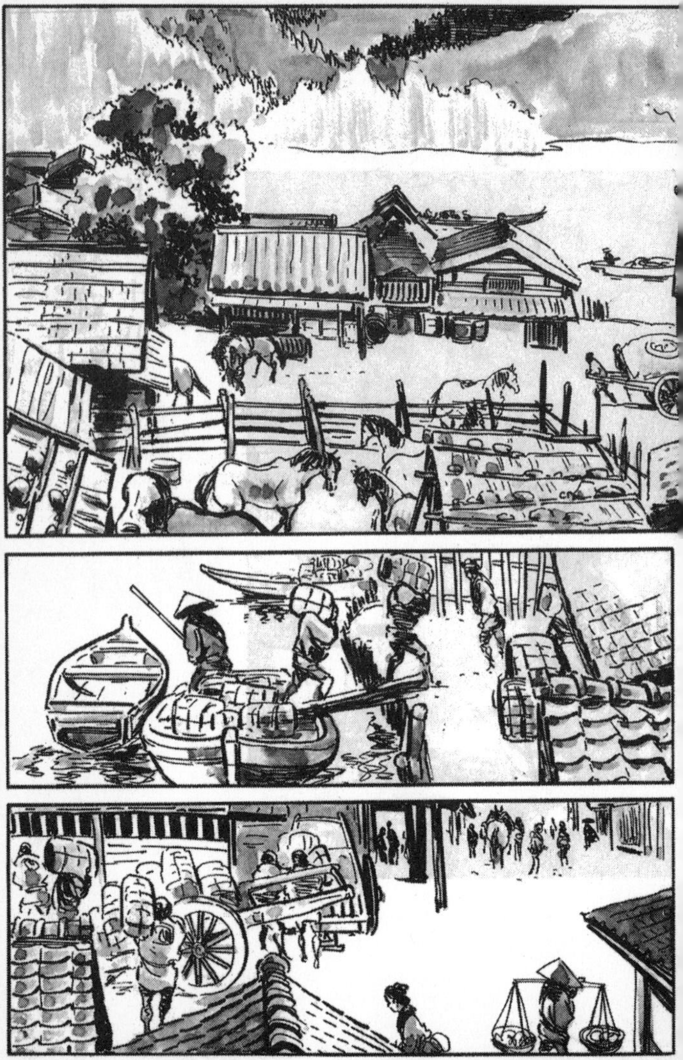

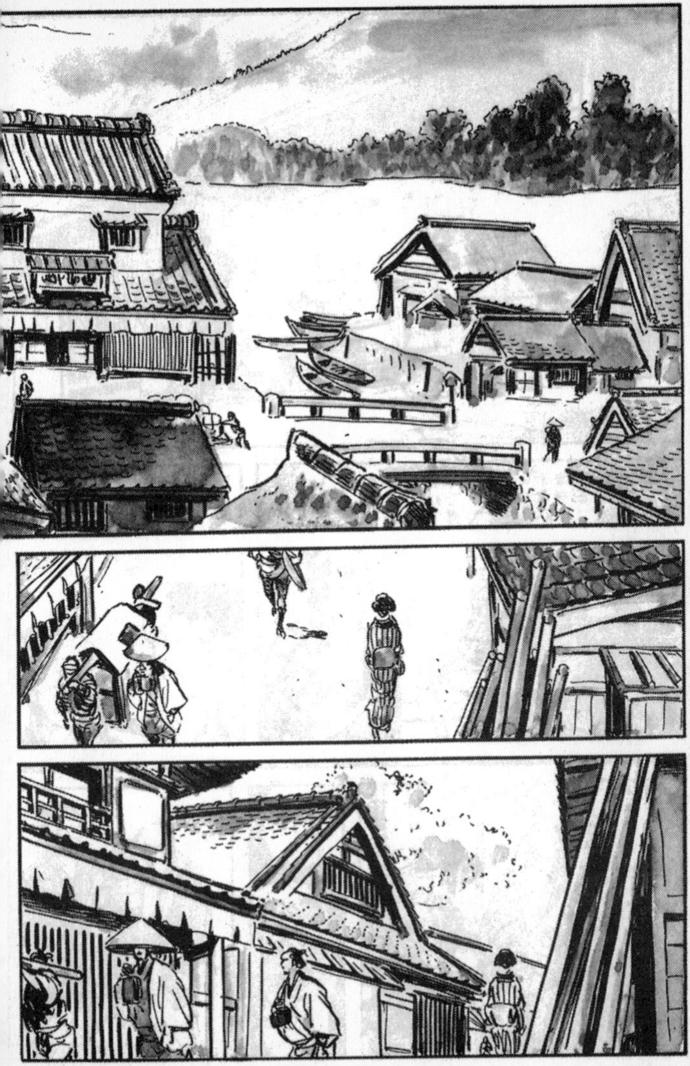

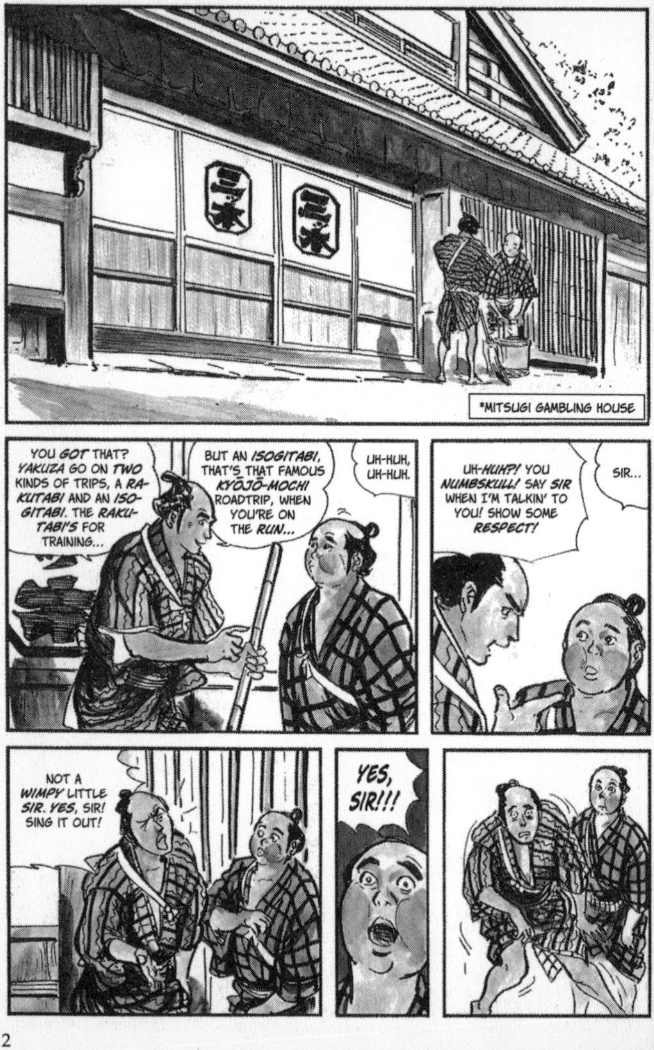
*MITSUGI GAMBLING HOUSE
YOU GOT THAT? YAKUZA GO ON TWO KINDS OF TRIPS, A RAKUTABI AND AN ISOGITABI. THE RAKUTABI'S FOR TRAINING...
BUT AN ISOGITABI, THAT'S THAT FAMOUS KYŌJŌ-MOCHI ROADTRIP, WHEN YOU'RE ON THE RUN...
UH-HUH, UH-HUH.
UH-HUH?! YOU NUMBSKULL! SAY SIR WHEN I'M TALKIN' TO YOU! SHOW SOME RESPECT!
SIR...
NOT A WIMPY LITTLE SIR. YES, SIR! SING IT OUT!
YES, SIR!!!

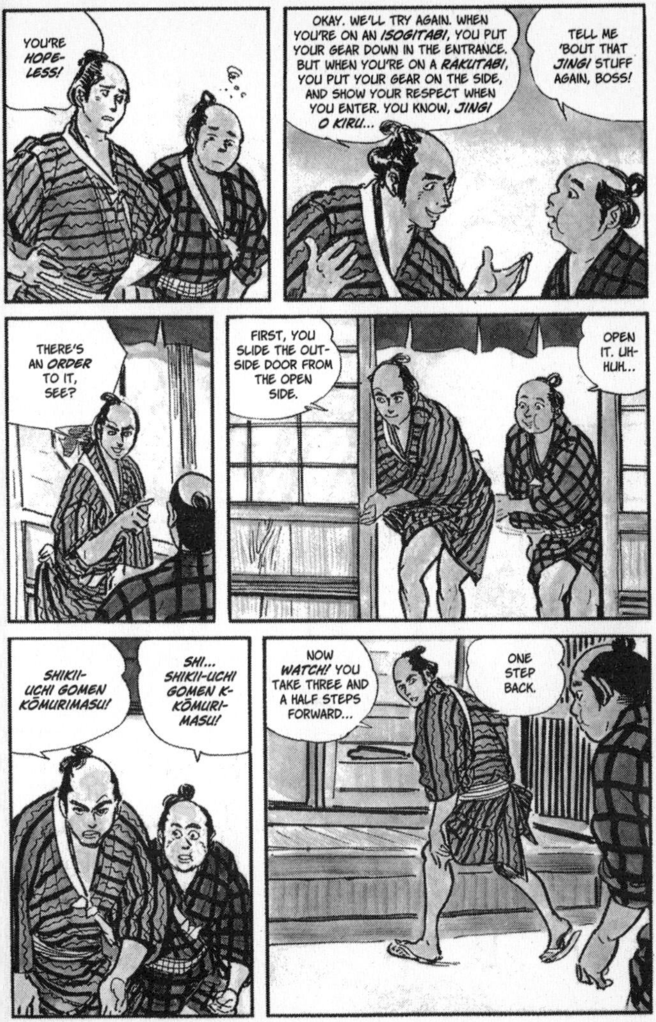
YOU'RE HOPE-LESS!
TELL ME 'BOUT THAT JINGI STUFF AGAIN, BOSS!
OKAY. WE'LL TRY AGAIN. WHEN YOU'RE ON AN ISOGITABI, YOU PUT YOUR GEAR DOWN IN THE ENTRANCE. BUT WHEN YOU'RE ON A RAKUTABI, YOU PUT YOUR GEAR ON THE SIDE, AND SHOW YOUR RESPECT WHEN YOU ENTER. YOU KNOW, JINGI O KIRU...
THERE'S AN ORDER TO IT, SEE?
FIRST, YOU SLIDE THE OUT-SIDE DOOR FROM THE OPEN SIDE.
OPEN IT. UH-HUH...
SHIKII-UCHI GOMEN KŌMURIMASU!
SHI... SHIKII-UCHI GOMEN K-KŌMURI-MASU!
NOW WATCH! YOU TAKE THREE AND A HALF STEPS FORWARD...
ONE STEP BACK.

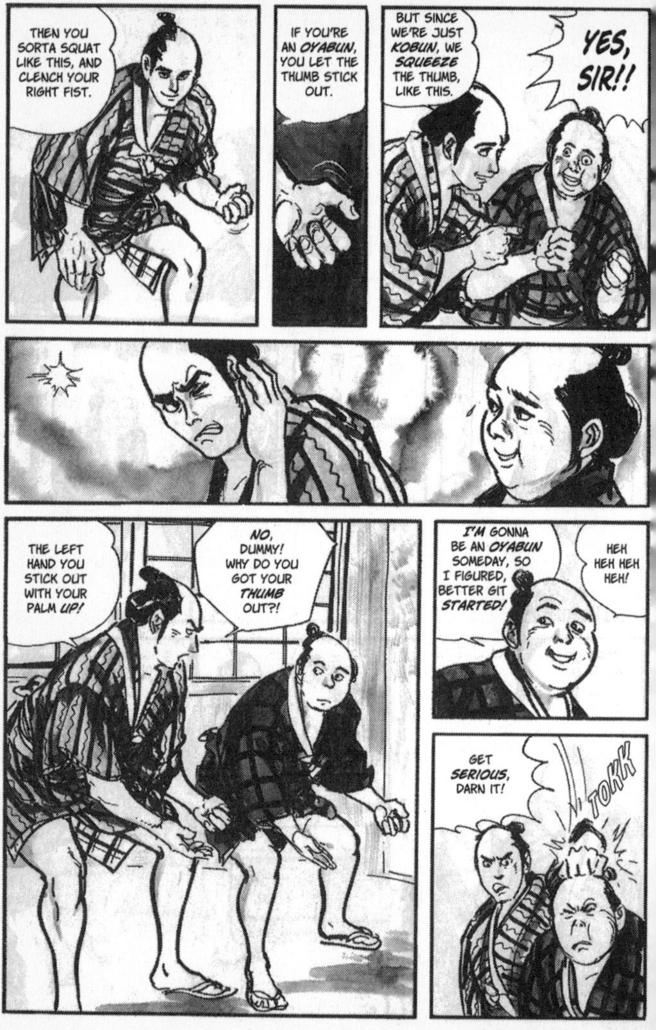
THEN YOU SORTA SQUAT LIKE THIS, AND CLENCH YOUR RIGHT FIST.
IF YOU'RE AN *OYABUN*, YOU LET THE THUMB STICK OUT.
BUT SINCE WE'RE JUST *KOBUN*, WE *SQUEEZE* THE THUMB, LIKE THIS.
YES, SIR!!
THE LEFT HAND YOU STICK OUT WITH YOUR PALM *UP!*
NO, DUMMY! WHY DO YOU GOT YOUR *THUMB* OUT?!
I'M GONNA BE AN *OYABUN* SOMEDAY, SO I FIGURED, BETTER GIT *STARTED!*
HEH HEH HEH HEH!
GET *SERIOUS*, DARN IT!
TOKK

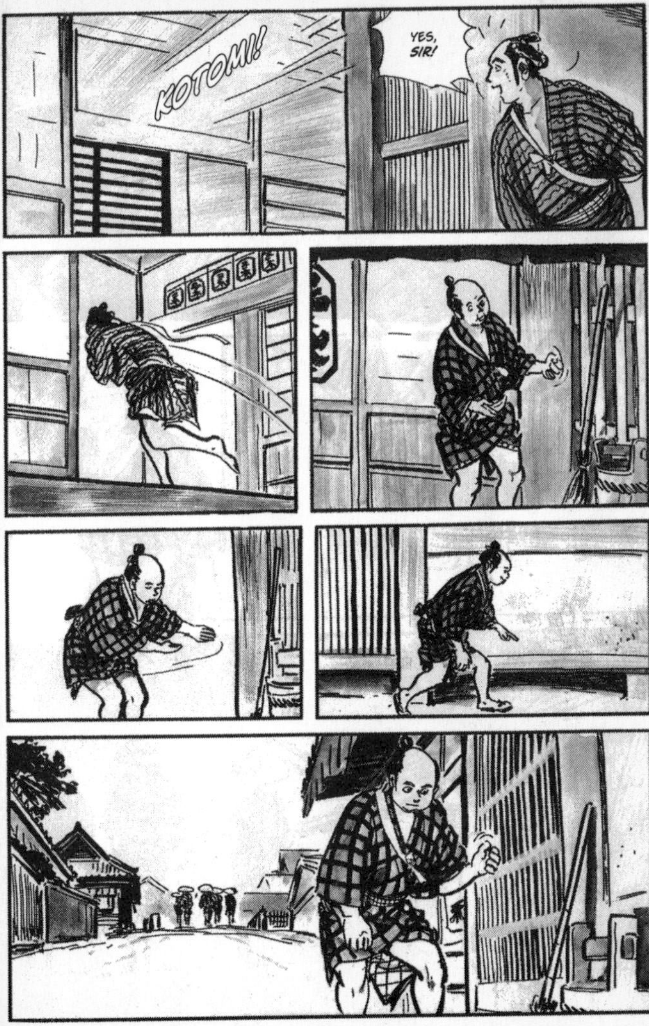
KOTOMI!
YES, SIR!

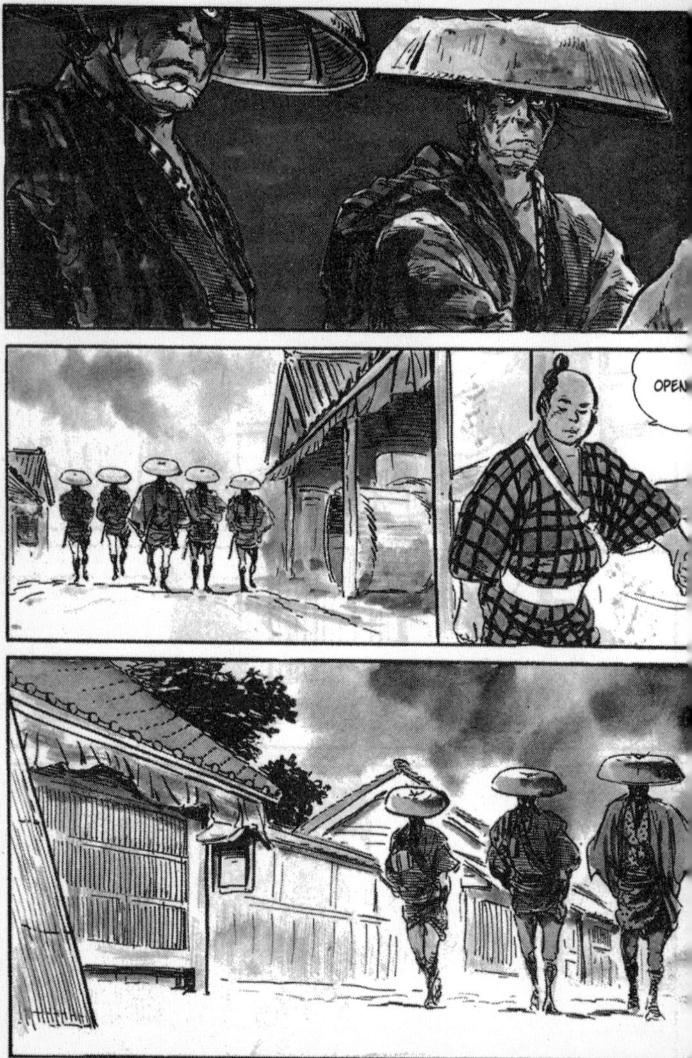
OPEN

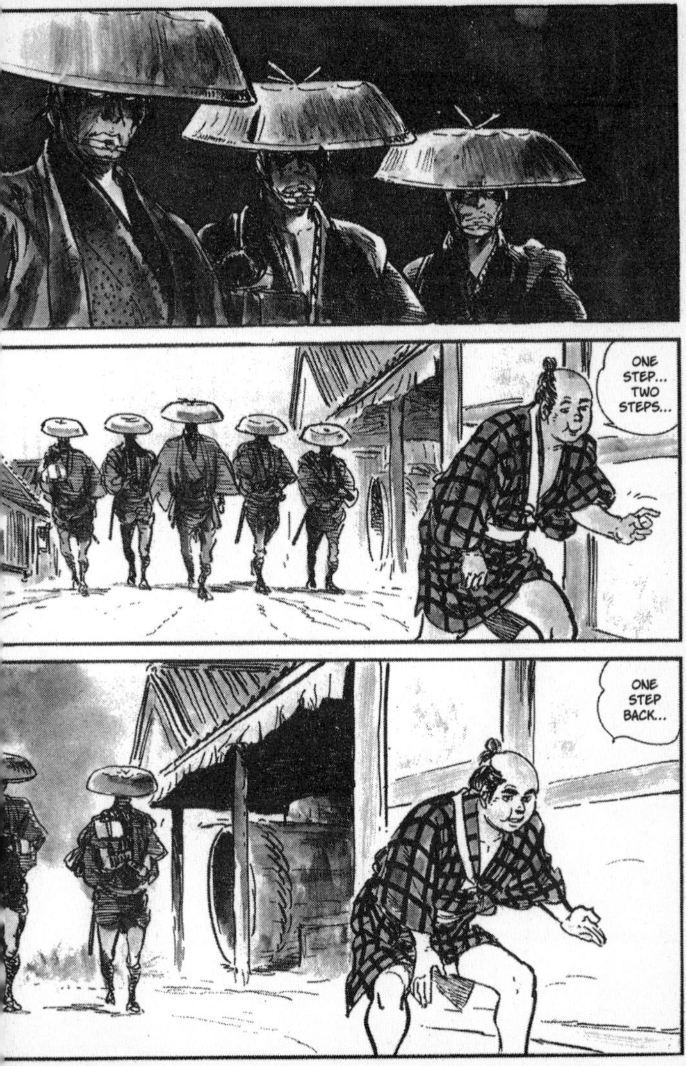
ONE STEP... TWO STEPS...
ONE STEP BACK...

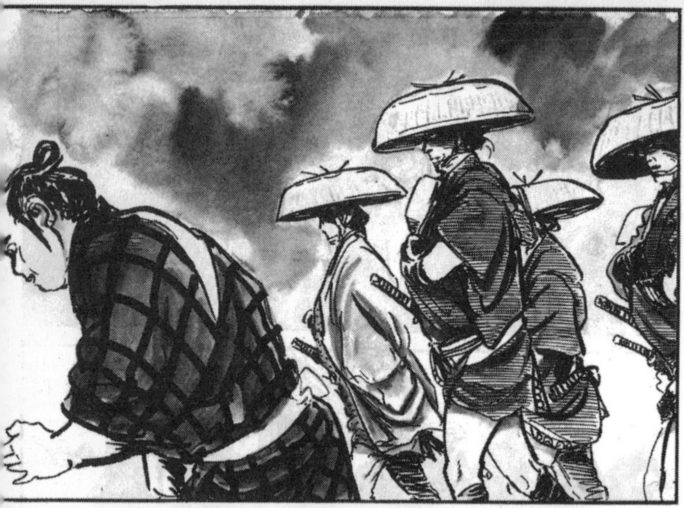

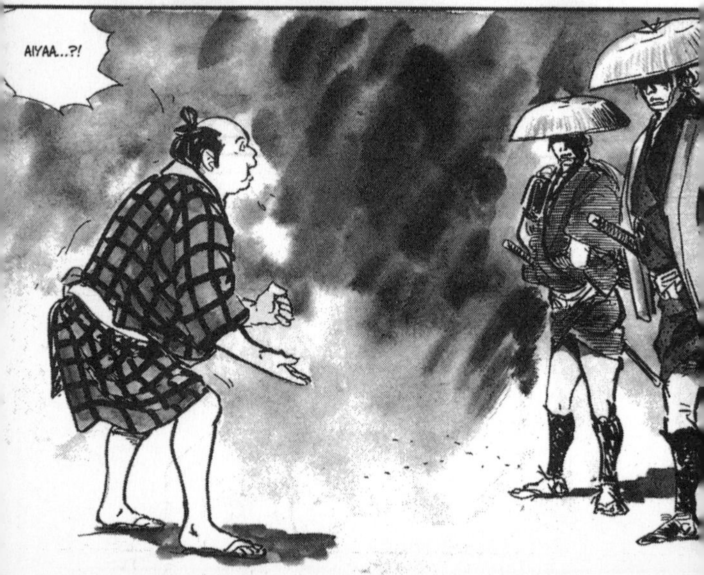
AIYAA...?!

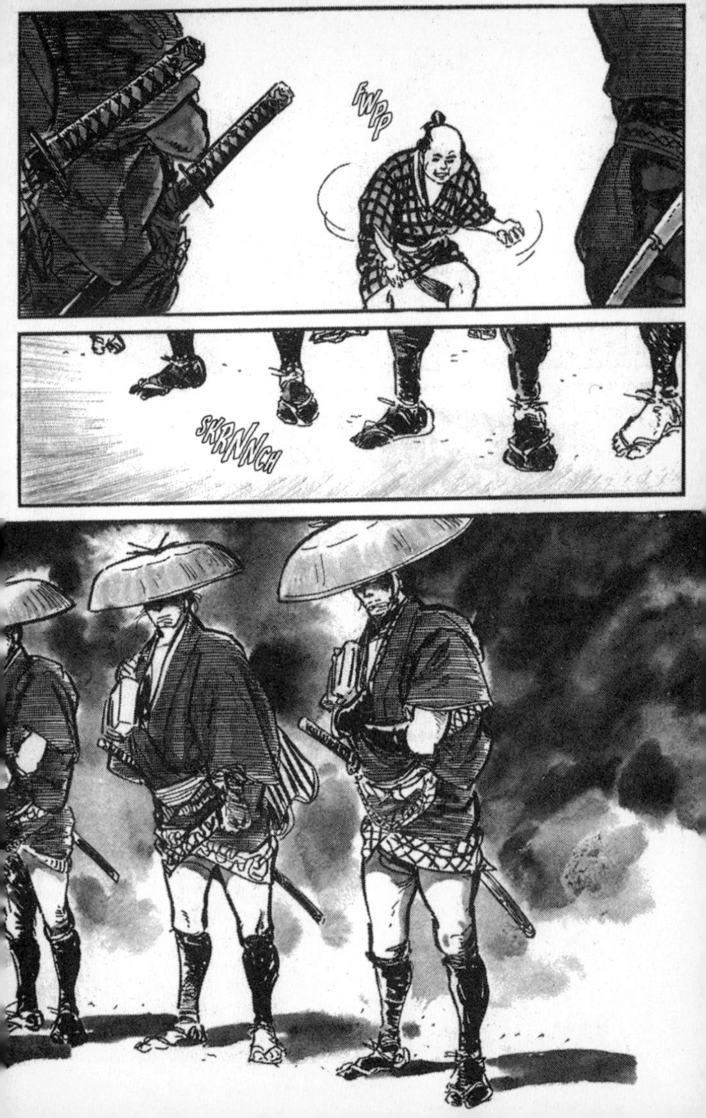
FWPP
SKRNNCH

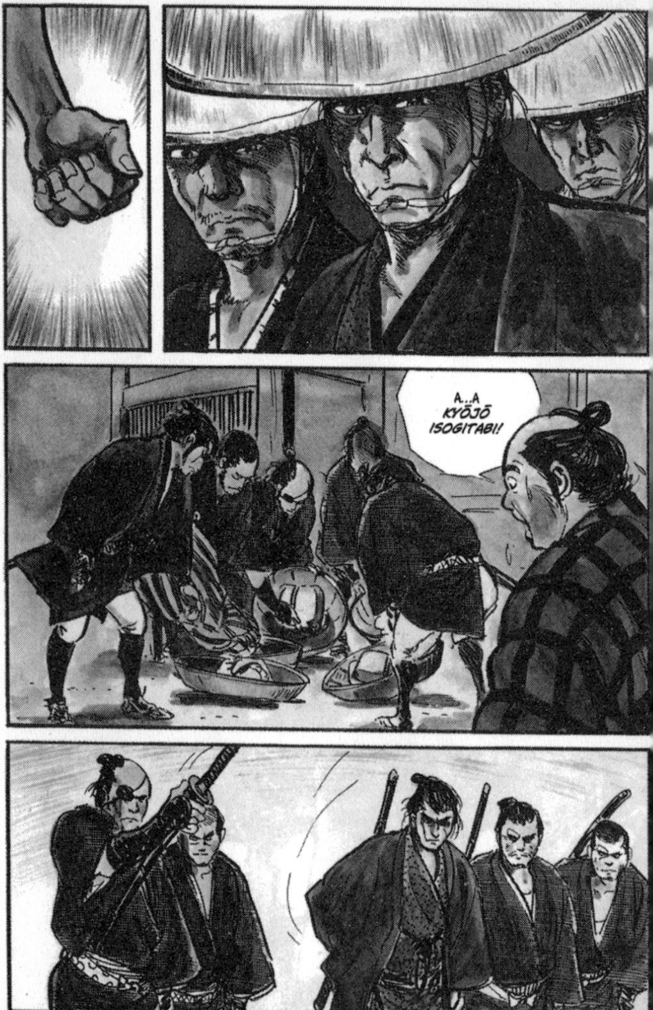
A...A KYŌJŌ ISOGITABI!

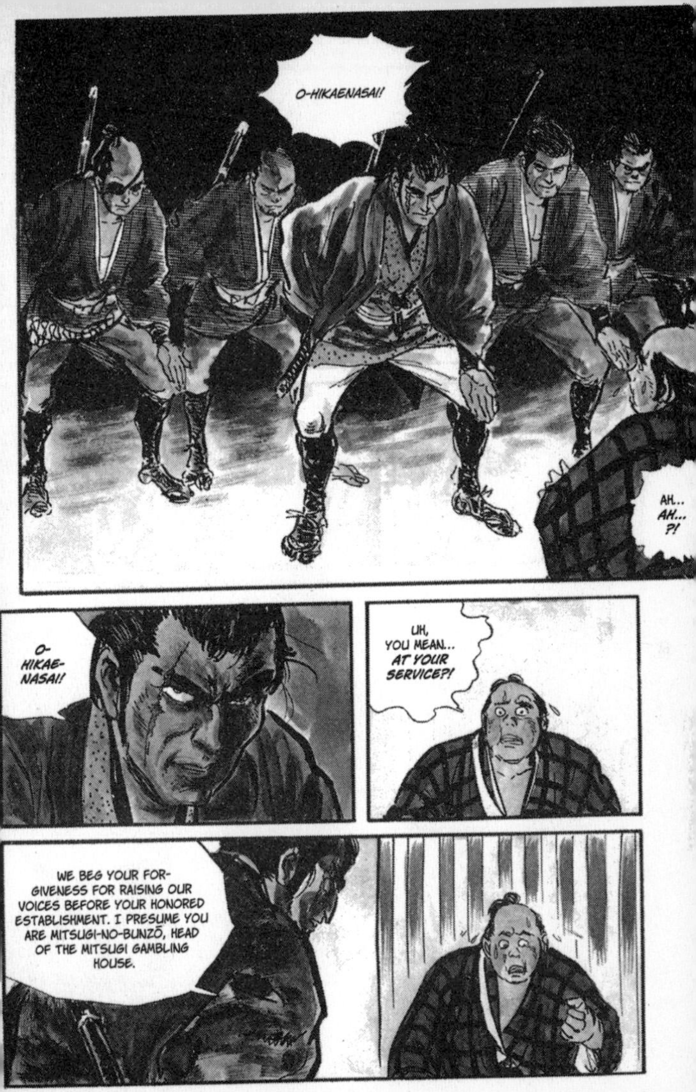
O-HIKAENASAI!
AH... AH... ?!
O-HIKAE-NASAI!
UH, YOU MEAN... AT YOUR SERVICE?!
WE BEG YOUR FOR-GIVENESS FOR RAISING OUR VOICES BEFORE YOUR HONORED ESTABLISHMENT. I PRESUME YOU ARE MITSUGI-NO-BUNZŌ, HEAD OF THE MITSUGI GAMBLING HOUSE.

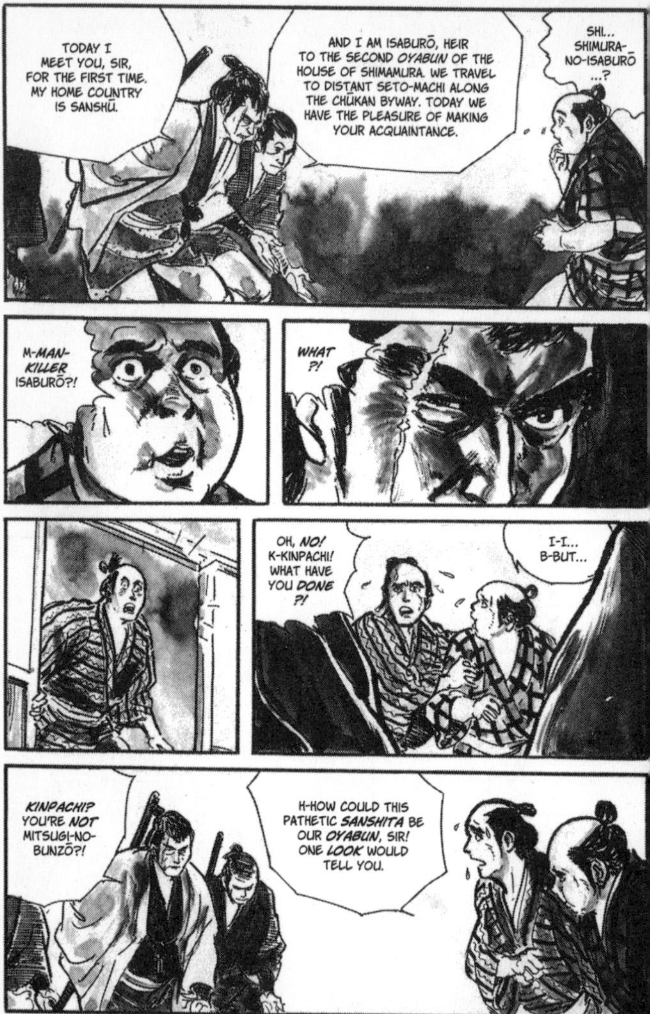
TODAY I MEET YOU, SIR, FOR THE FIRST TIME. MY HOME COUNTRY IS SANSHŪ.
AND I AM ISABURŌ, HEIR TO THE SECOND *OYABUN* OF THE HOUSE OF SHIMAMURA. WE TRAVEL TO DISTANT SETO-MACHI ALONG THE CHŪKAN BYWAY. TODAY WE HAVE THE PLEASURE OF MAKING YOUR ACQUAINTANCE.
SHI... SHIMURA-NO-ISABURŌ ...?
M-*MAN-KILLER* ISABURŌ?!
WHAT ?!
OH, *NO!* K-KINPACHI! WHAT HAVE YOU *DONE* ?!
I-I... B-BUT...
KINPACHI? YOU'RE *NOT* MITSUGI-NO-BUNZŌ?!
H-HOW COULD THIS PATHETIC *SANSHITA* BE OUR *OYABUN*, SIR! ONE *LOOK* WOULD TELL YOU.

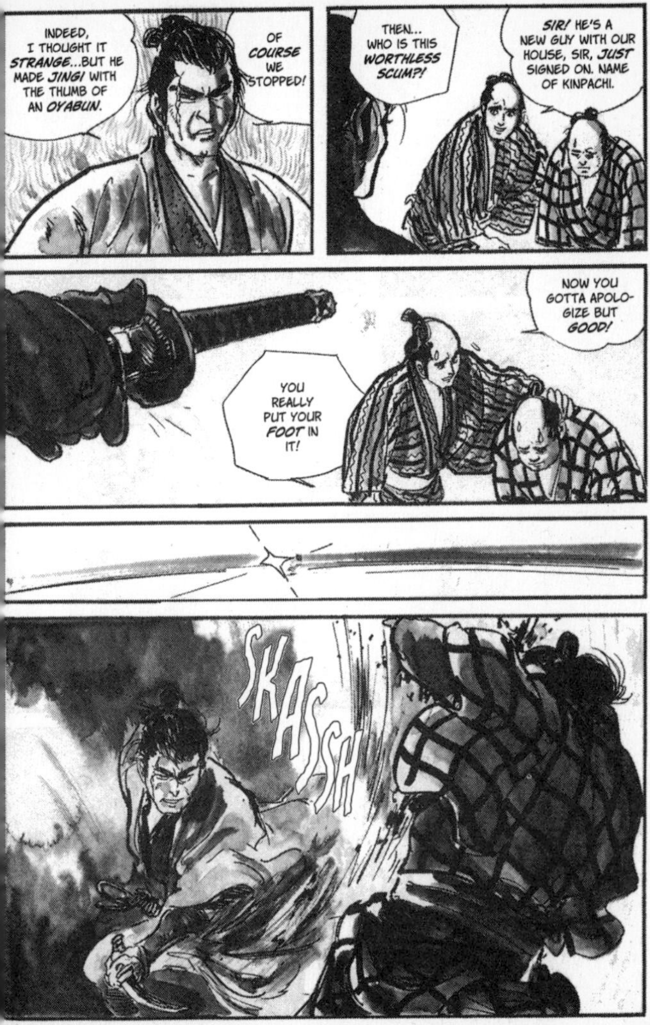
INDEED, I THOUGHT IT STRANGE...BUT HE MADE JINGI WITH THE THUMB OF AN OYABUN.
OF COURSE WE STOPPED!
THEN... WHO IS THIS WORTHLESS SCUM?!
SIR! HE'S A NEW GUY WITH OUR HOUSE, SIR, JUST SIGNED ON. NAME OF KINPACHI.
YOU REALLY PUT YOUR FOOT IN IT!
NOW YOU GOTTA APOLOGIZE BUT GOOD!
SKASSH

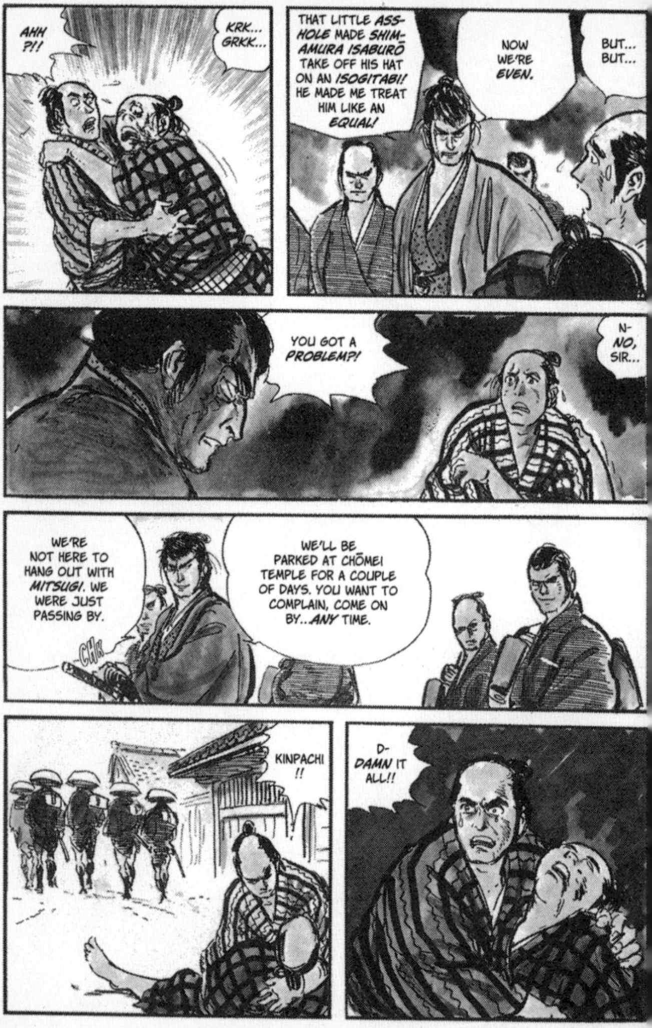
AHH ?!!
KRK... GRKK...
THAT LITTLE ASS-HOLE MADE SHIM-AMURA ISABURŌ TAKE OFF HIS HAT ON AN ISOGITABI! HE MADE ME TREAT HIM LIKE AN EQUAL!
NOW WE'RE EVEN.
BUT... BUT...
YOU GOT A PROBLEM?!
N-NO, SIR...
WE'RE NOT HERE TO HANG OUT WITH MITSUGI. WE WERE JUST PASSING BY.
CHK
WE'LL BE PARKED AT CHŌMEI TEMPLE FOR A COUPLE OF DAYS. YOU WANT TO COMPLAIN, COME ON BY...ANY TIME.
KINPACHI !!
D-DAMN IT ALL!!

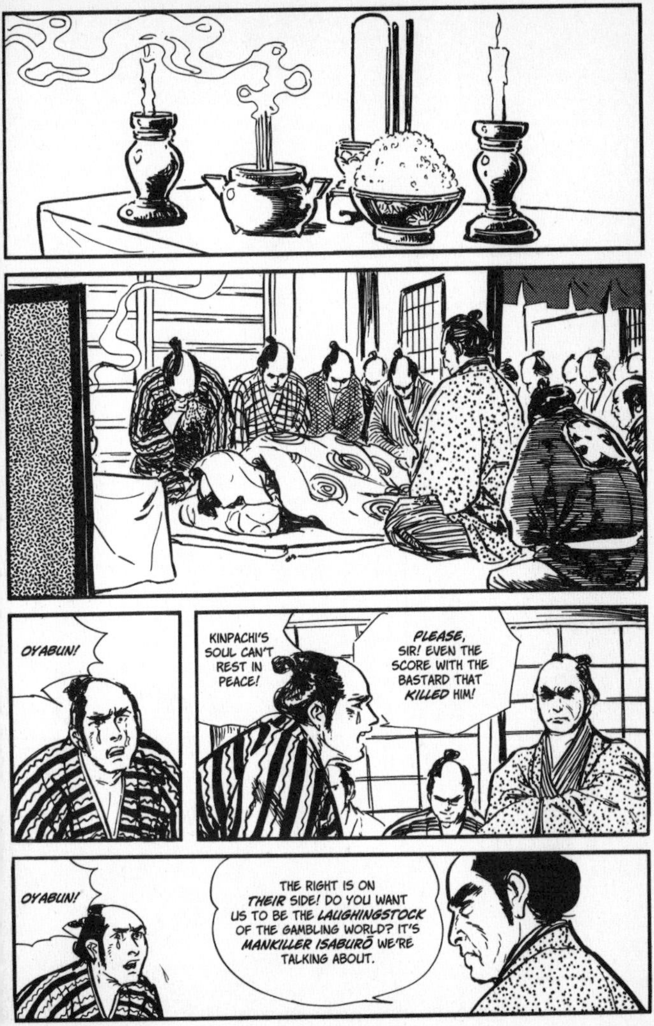
OYABUN!
KINPACHI'S SOUL CAN'T REST IN PEACE!
PLEASE, SIR! EVEN THE SCORE WITH THE BASTARD THAT KILLED HIM!
OYABUN!
THE RIGHT IS ON THEIR SIDE! DO YOU WANT US TO BE THE LAUGHINGSTOCK OF THE GAMBLING WORLD? IT'S MANKILLER ISABURŌ WE'RE TALKING ABOUT.

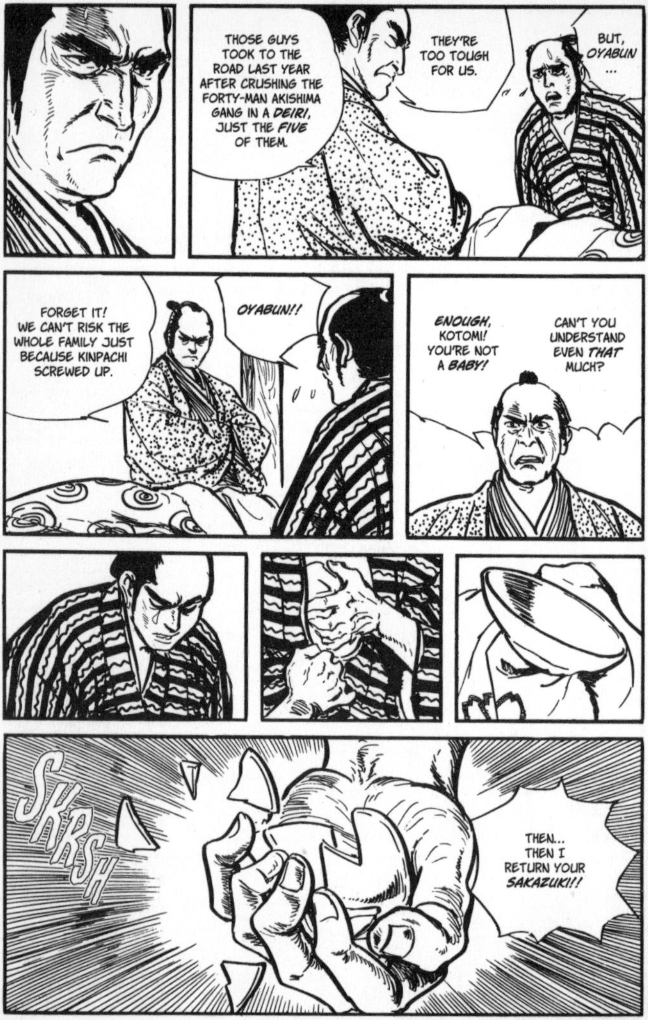
THOSE GUYS TOOK TO THE ROAD LAST YEAR AFTER CRUSHING THE FORTY-MAN AKISHIMA GANG IN A *DEIRI*, JUST THE *FIVE* OF THEM.
THEY'RE TOO TOUGH FOR US.
BUT, *OYABUN* ...
FORGET IT! WE CAN'T RISK THE WHOLE FAMILY JUST BECAUSE KINPACHI SCREWED UP.
OYABUN!!
ENOUGH, KOTOMI! YOU'RE NOT A *BABY!*
CAN'T YOU UNDERSTAND EVEN *THAT* MUCH?
SKRSH
THEN... THEN I RETURN YOUR *SAKAZUKI!!*

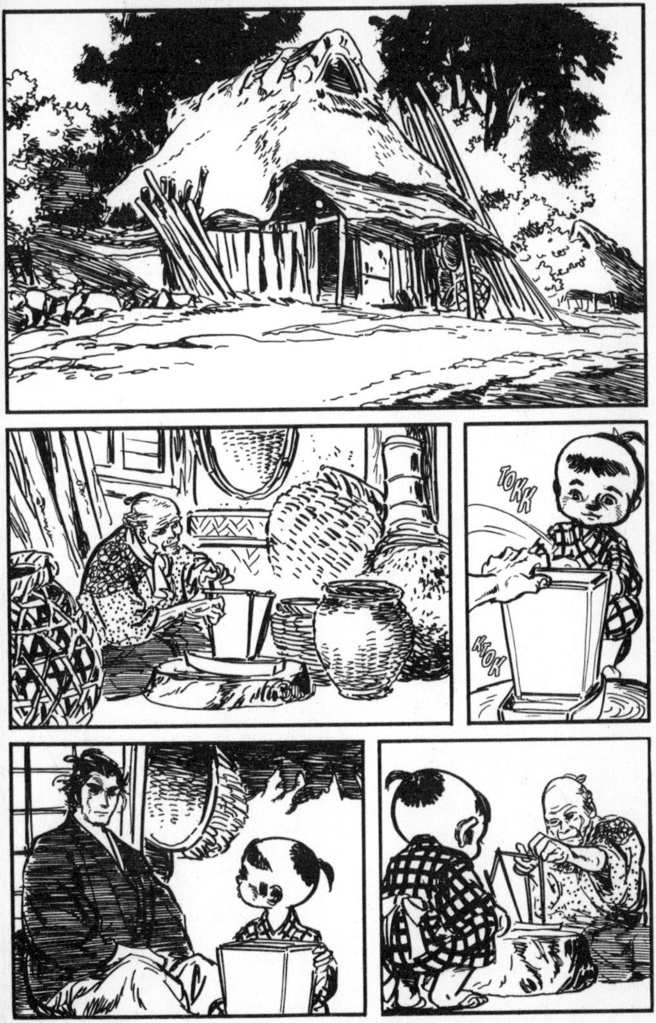
TOKK
KTOK

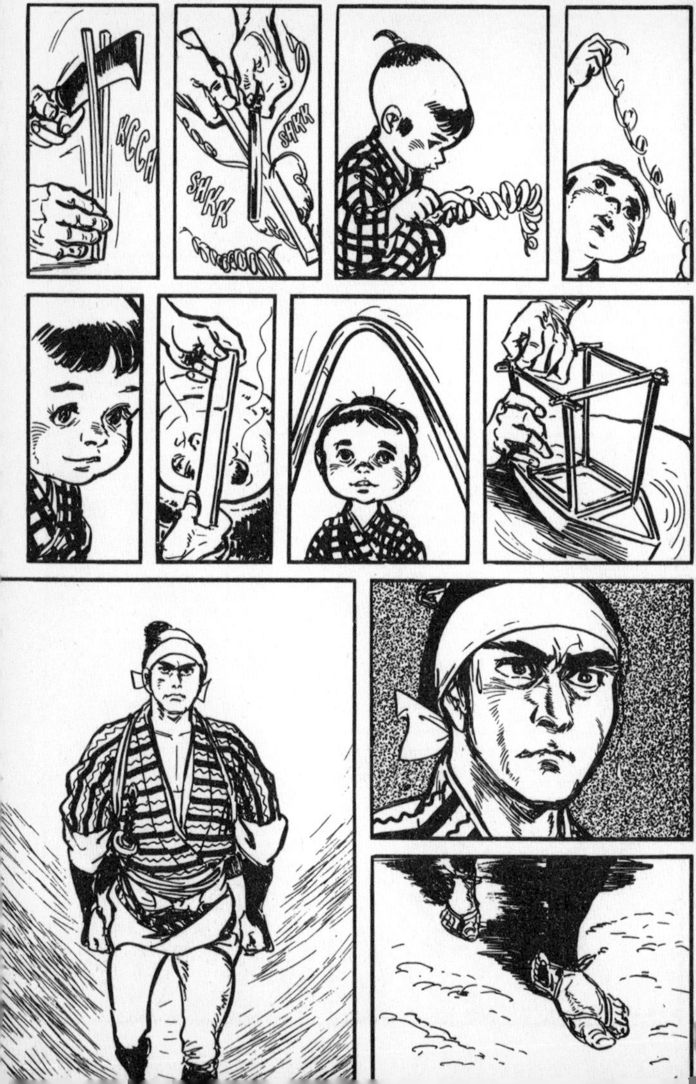
KCCH
SHKK
SHKK

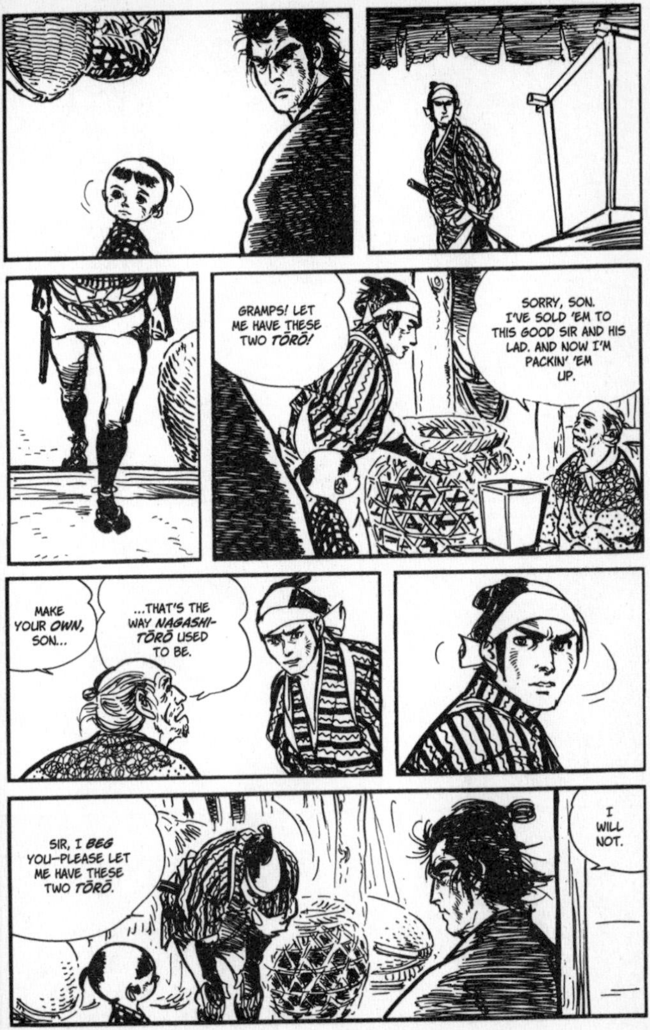
GRAMPS! LET ME HAVE THESE TWO *TŌRŌ!*
SORRY, SON. I'VE SOLD 'EM TO THIS GOOD SIR AND HIS LAD. AND NOW I'M PACKIN' 'EM UP.
MAKE YOUR *OWN,* SON...
...THAT'S THE WAY *NAGASHI-TŌRŌ* USED TO BE.
SIR, I *BEG* YOU—PLEASE LET ME HAVE THESE TWO *TŌRŌ.*
I WILL NOT.

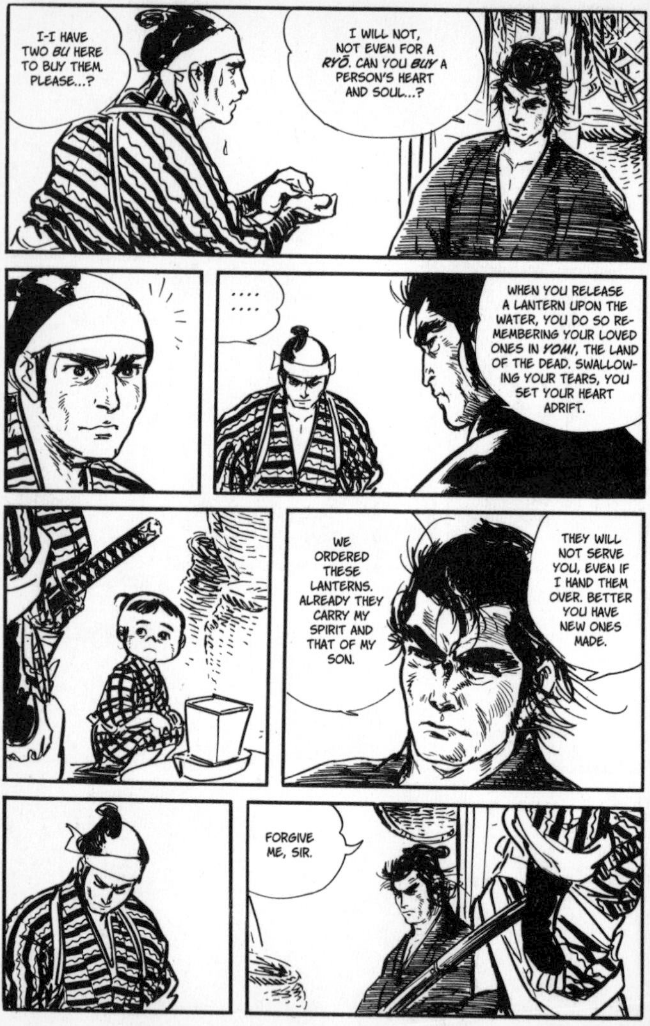
I-I HAVE TWO *BU* HERE TO BUY THEM. PLEASE...?
I WILL NOT, NOT EVEN FOR A *RYŌ*. CAN YOU *BUY* A PERSON'S HEART AND SOUL...?
....
....
WHEN YOU RELEASE A LANTERN UPON THE WATER, YOU DO SO RE-MEMBERING YOUR LOVED ONES IN *YOMI*, THE LAND OF THE DEAD. SWALLOW-ING YOUR TEARS, YOU SET YOUR HEART ADRIFT.
WE ORDERED THESE LANTERNS. ALREADY THEY CARRY MY SPIRIT AND THAT OF MY SON.
THEY WILL NOT SERVE YOU, EVEN IF I HAND THEM OVER. BETTER YOU HAVE NEW ONES MADE.
FORGIVE ME, SIR.

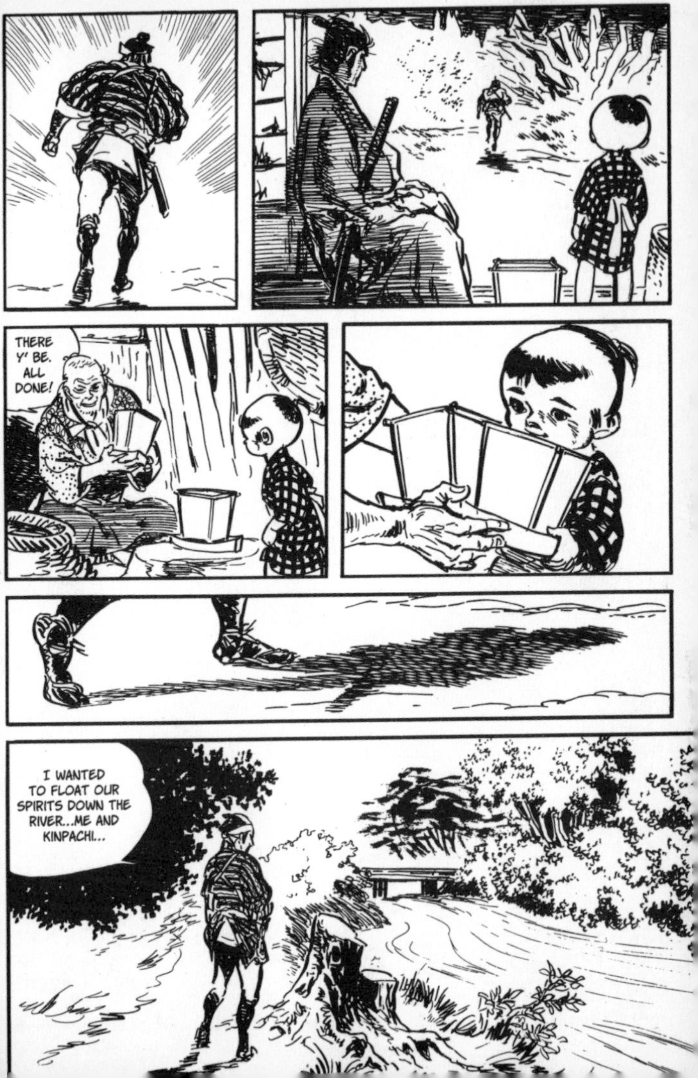
THERE Y' BE. ALL DONE!
I WANTED TO FLOAT OUR SPIRITS DOWN THE RIVER...ME AND KINPACHI...

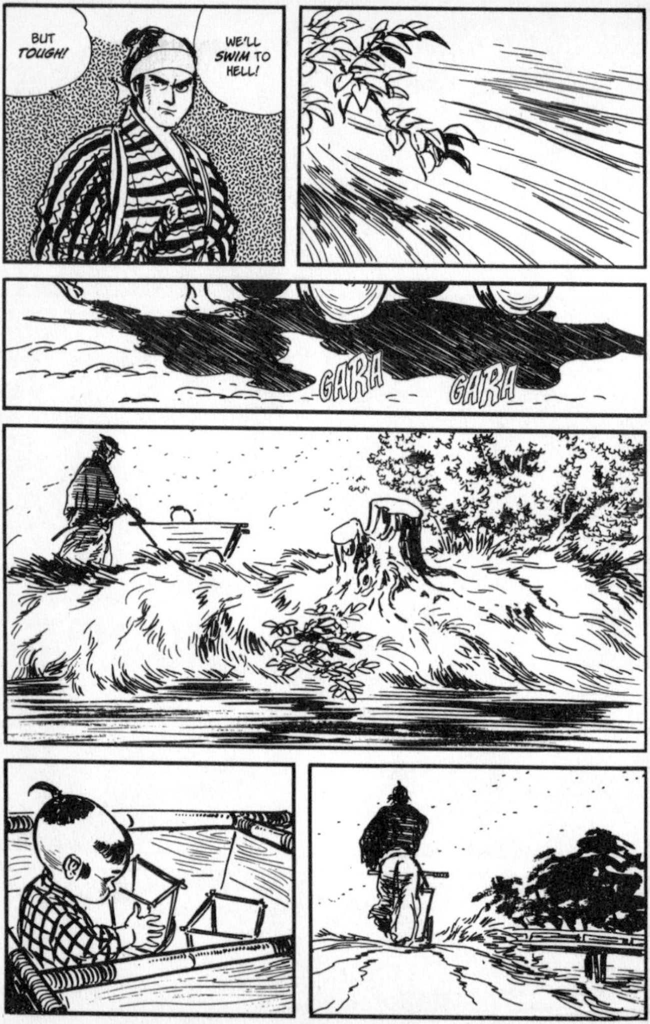
BUT TOUGH!
WE'LL SWIM TO HELL!
GARA
GARA

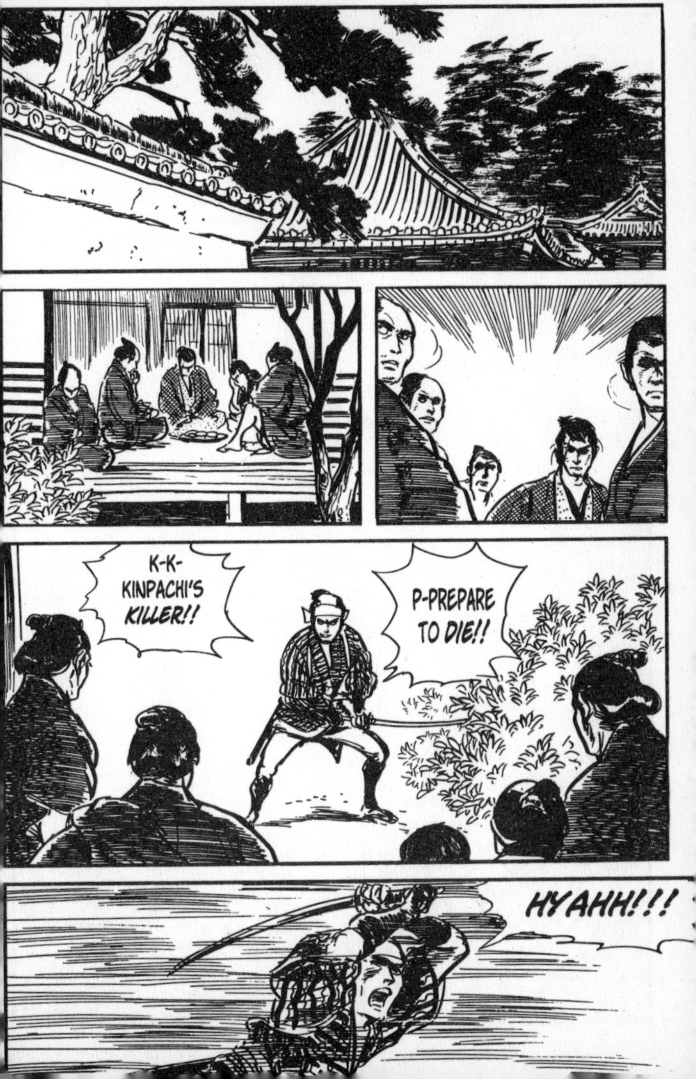
K-K-
KINPACHI'S
KILLER!!
P-PREPARE
TO DIE!!
HYAHH!!!

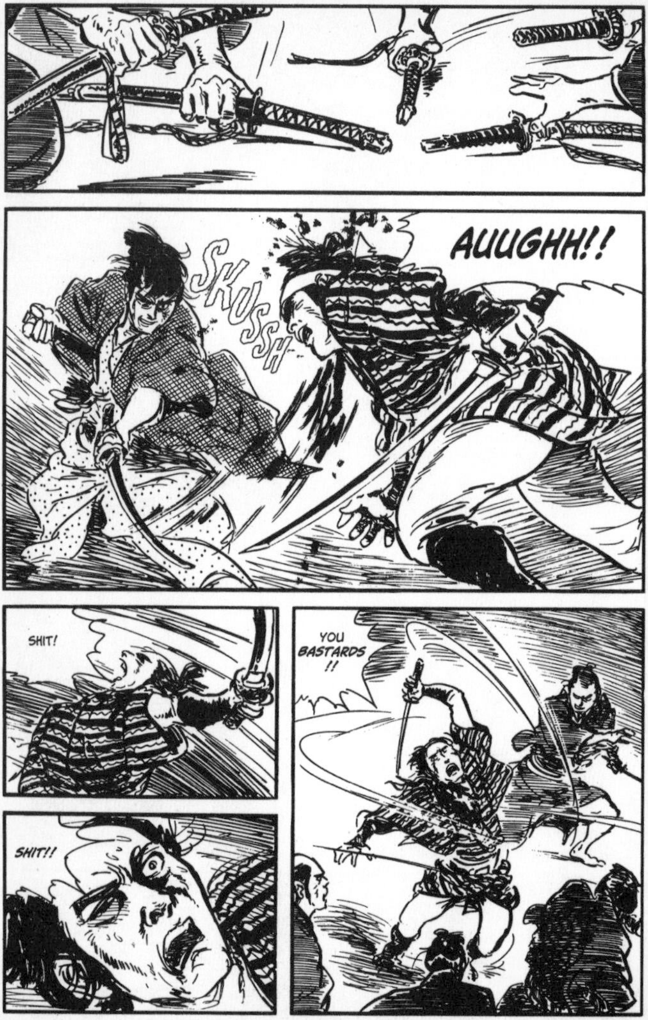
SKUSSH
AUUGHH!!
SHIT!
YOU BASTARDS !!
SHIT!!

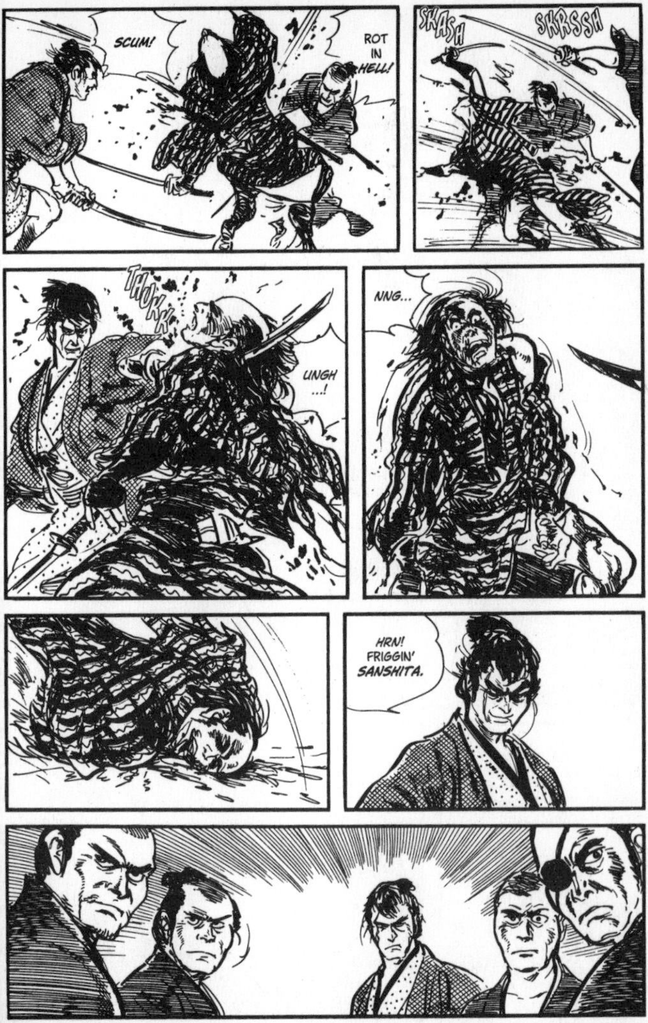
SCUM!
ROT IN HELL!
SKASH
SKRSSH
THUKK
UNGH ...!
NNG...
HRN! FRIGGIN' SANSHITA.

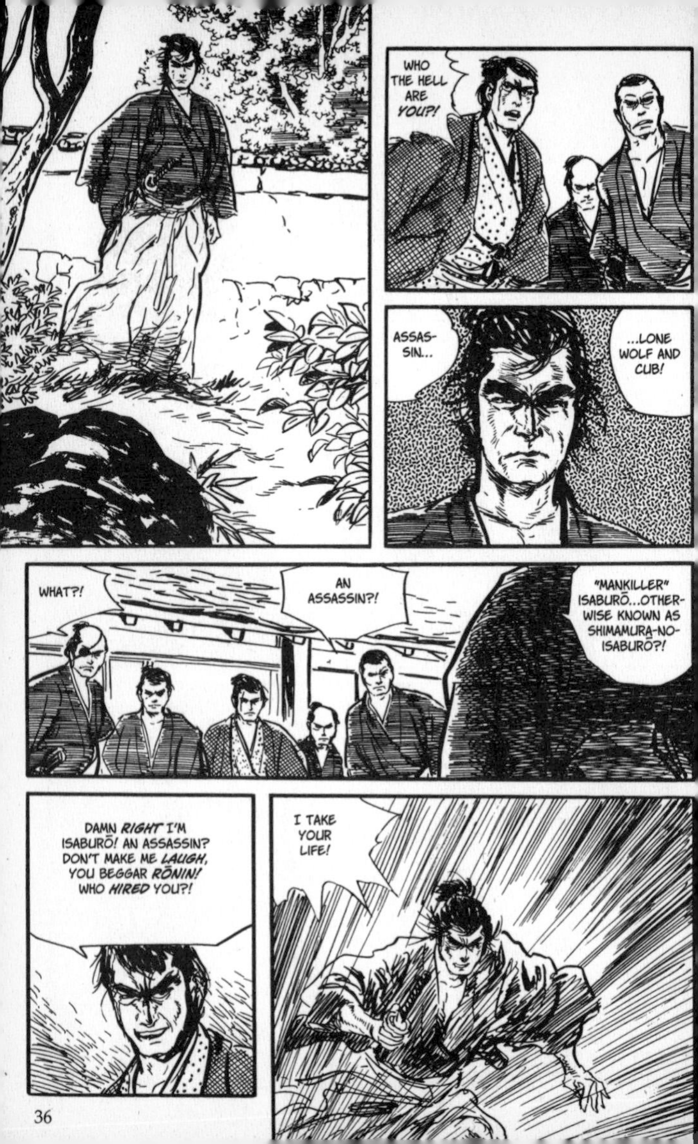
WHO THE HELL ARE YOU?!
ASSAS-SIN...
...LONE WOLF AND CUB!
WHAT?!
AN ASSASSIN?!
"MANKILLER" ISABURŌ...OTHER-WISE KNOWN AS SHIMAMURA-NO-ISABURŌ?!
DAMN RIGHT I'M ISABURŌ! AN ASSASSIN? DON'T MAKE ME LAUGH, YOU BEGGAR RŌNIN! WHO HIRED YOU?!
I TAKE YOUR LIFE!

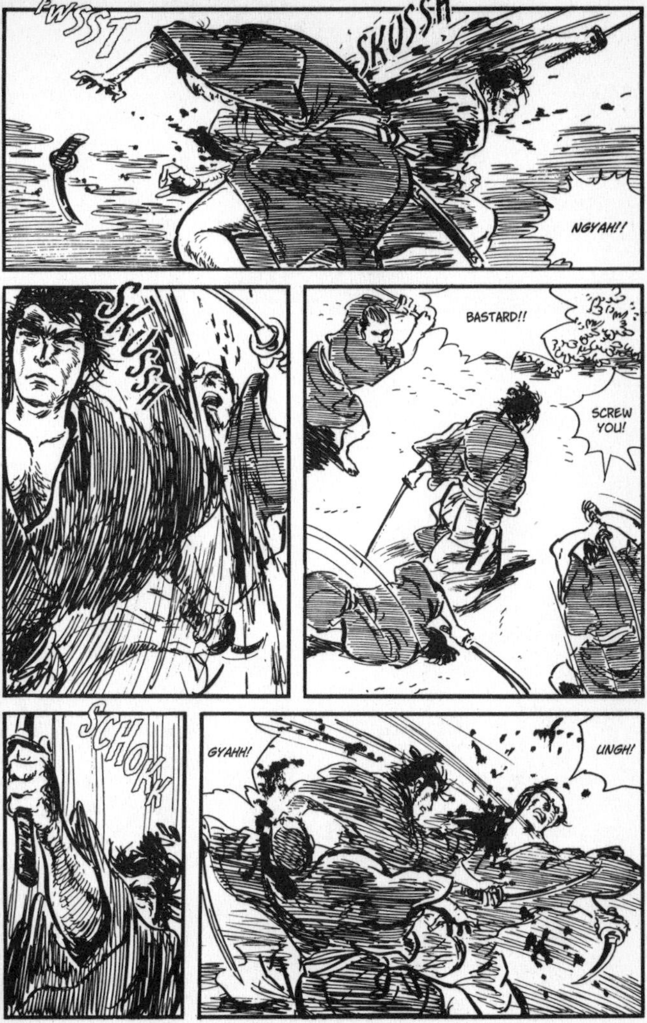
FWSSST
SKUSSH
NGYAH!!
SKUSSH
BASTARD!!
SCREW YOU!
SCHOKK
GYAHH!
UNGH!

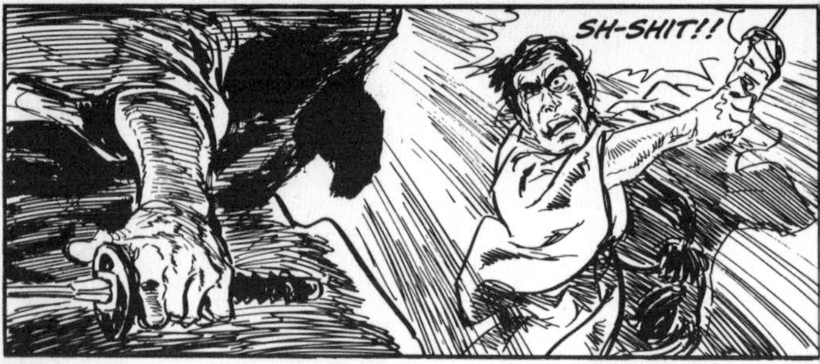
SH-SHIT!!
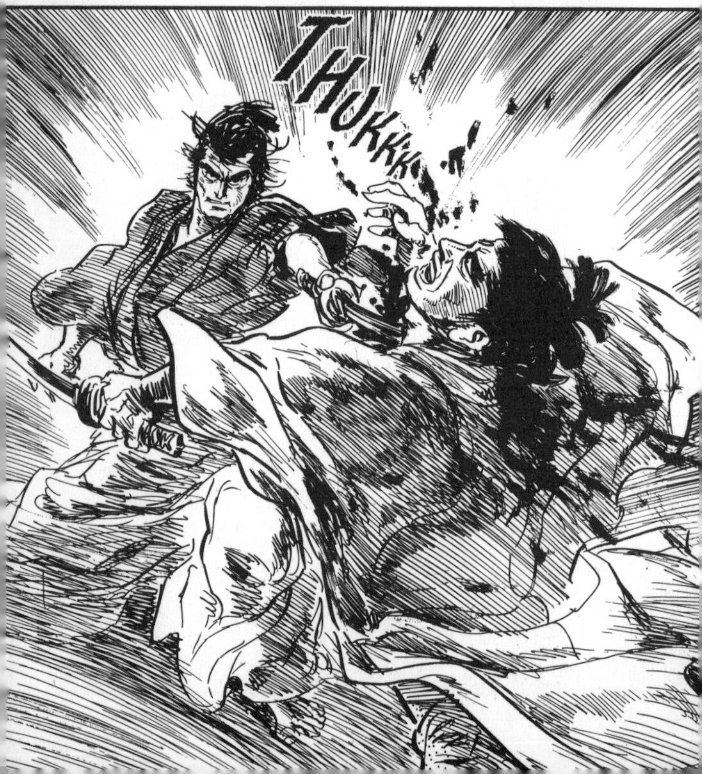
THUKKK

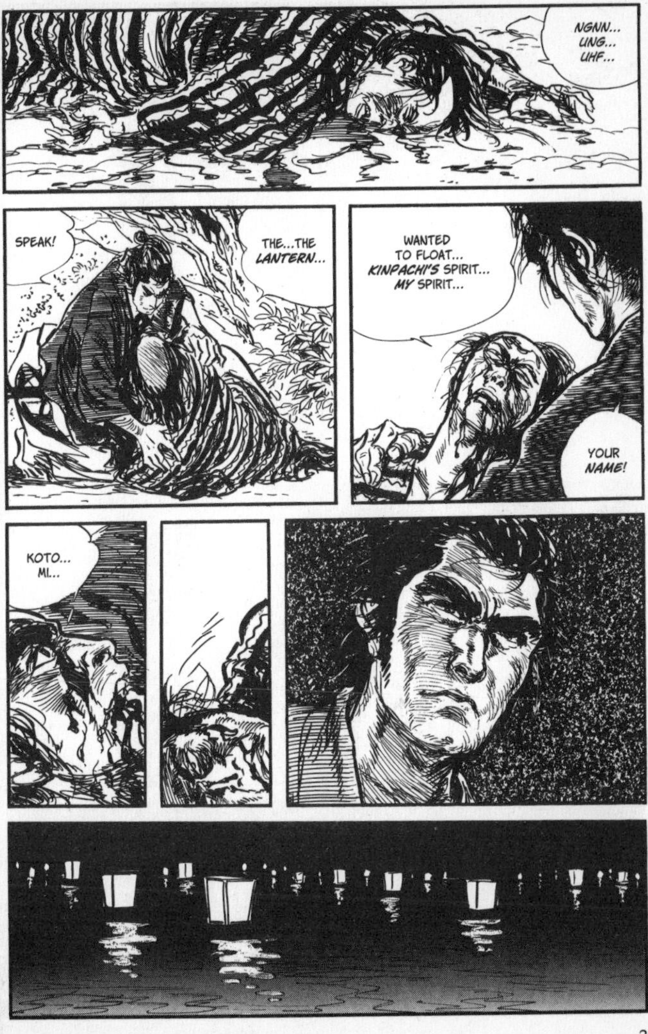
NGNN... UNG... UHF...
SPEAK!
THE...THE LANTERN...
WANTED TO FLOAT... KINPACHI'S SPIRIT... MY SPIRIT...
YOUR NAME!
KOTO... MI...

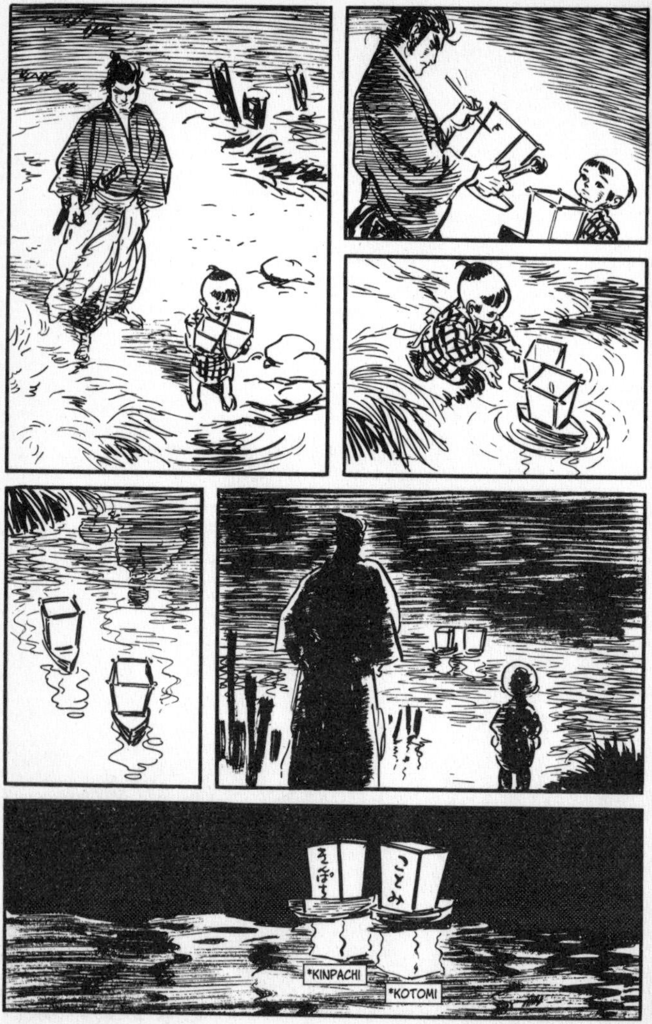
きんぱち
ことみ
*KINPACHI
*KOTOMI

the thirtieth

Deer Chaser

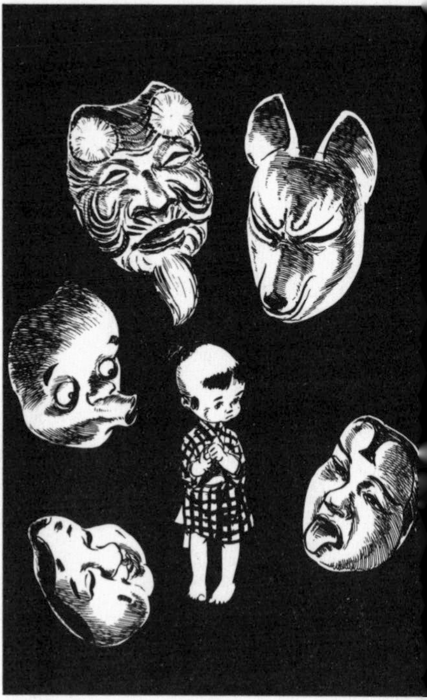

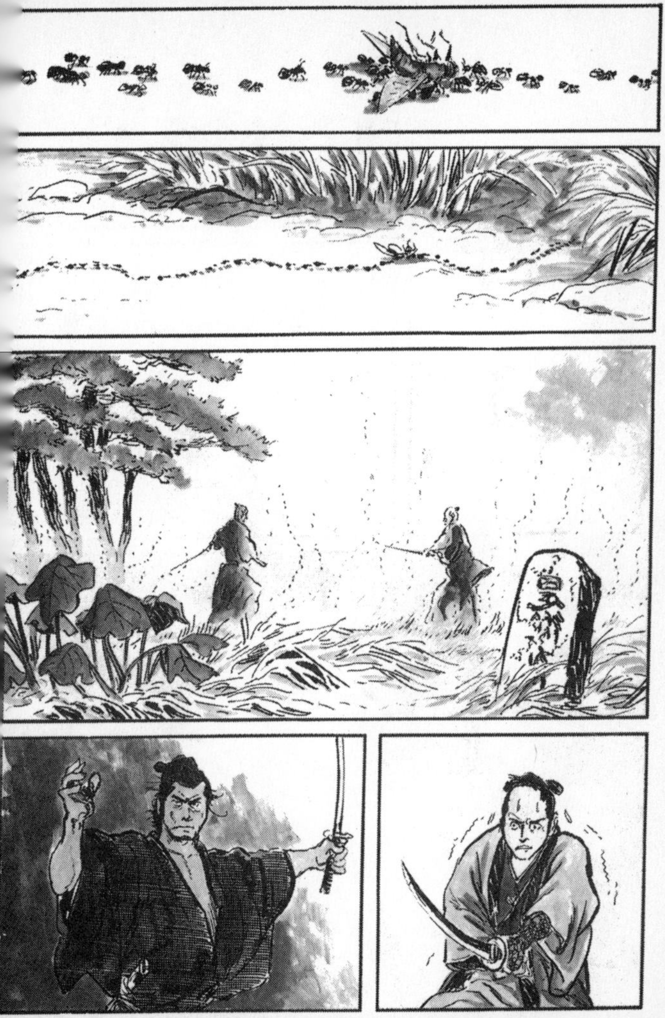

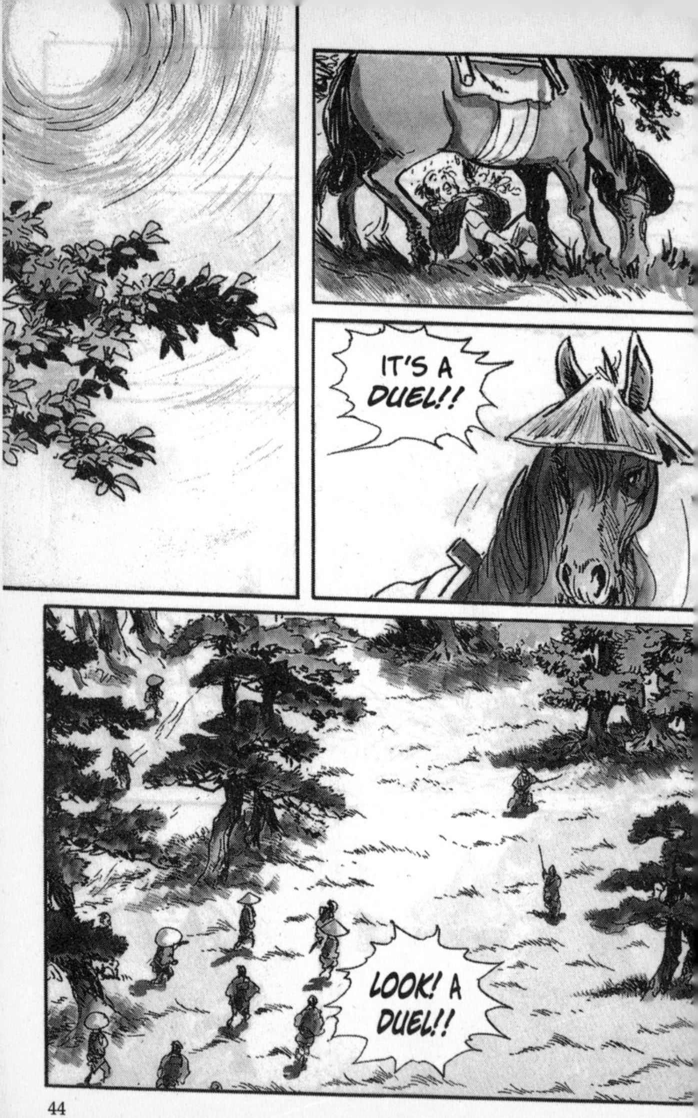
IT'S A DUEL!!
LOOK! A DUEL!!

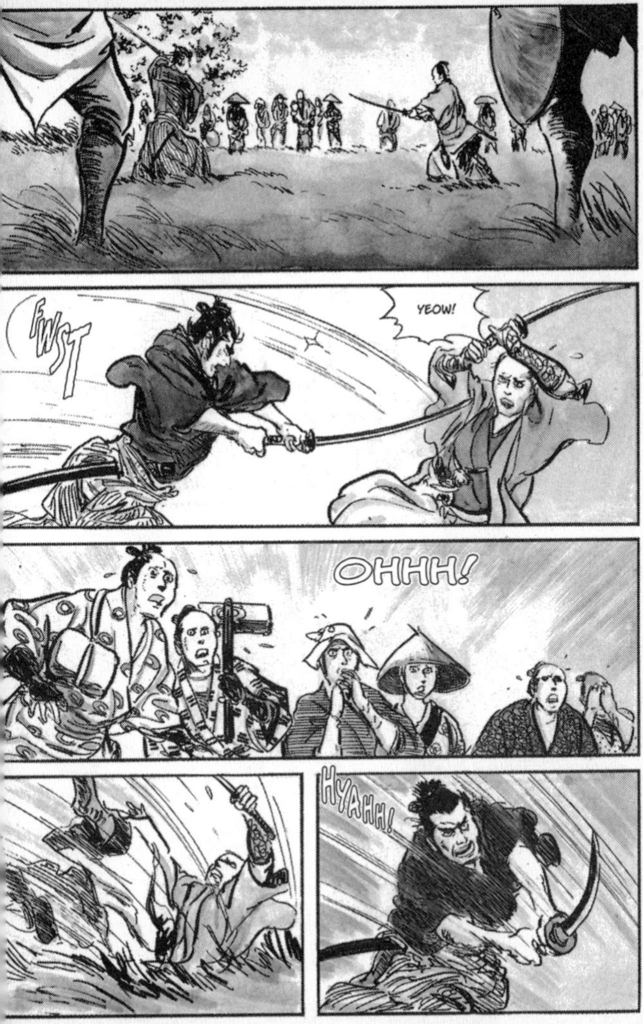
FWST
YEOW!
OHHH!
HYAHH!

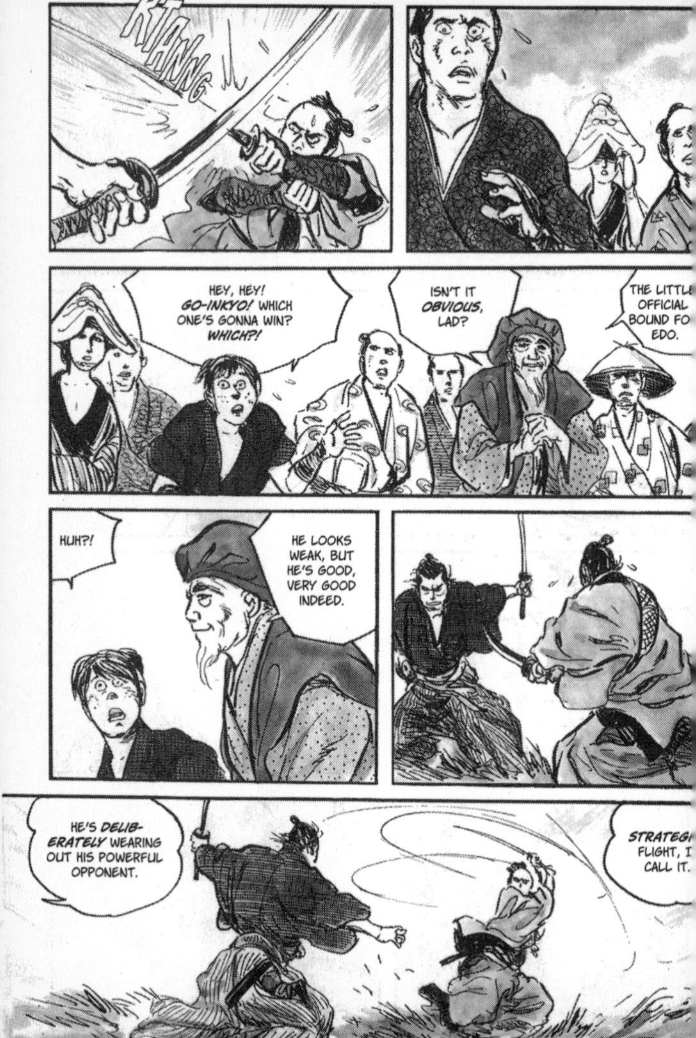
KTANG
HEY, HEY! GO-INKYO! WHICH ONE'S GONNA WIN? WHICH?!
ISN'T IT OBVIOUS, LAD?
THE LITTL OFFICIAL BOUND FO EDO.
HUH?!
HE LOOKS WEAK, BUT HE'S GOOD, VERY GOOD INDEED.
HE'S DELIBERATELY WEARING OUT HIS POWERFUL OPPONENT.
STRATEG FLIGHT, I CALL IT.

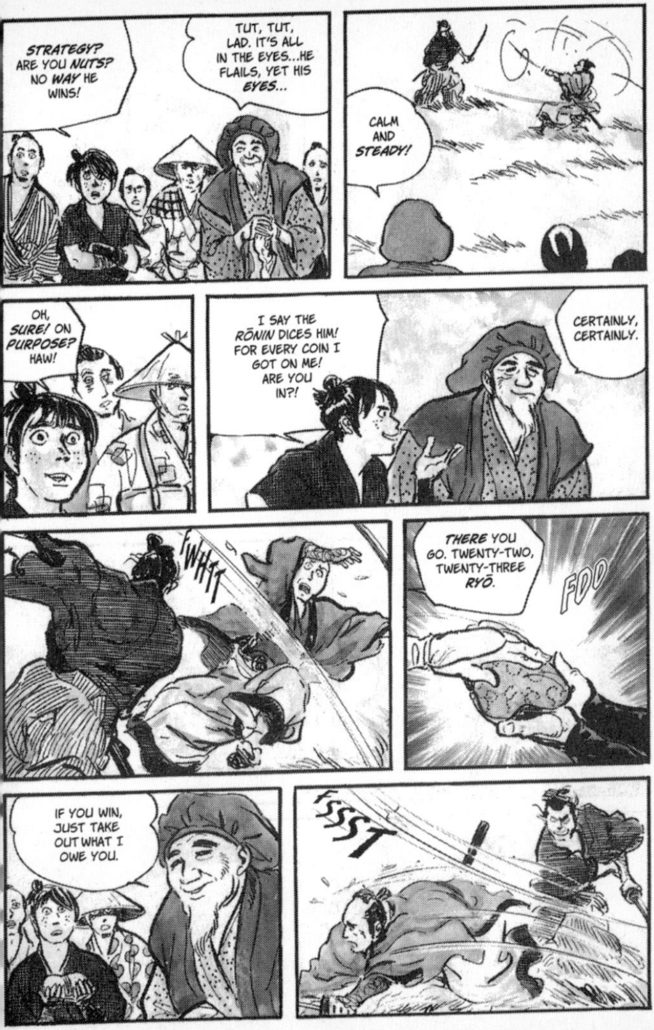
STRATEGY? ARE YOU NUTS? NO WAY HE WINS!
TUT, TUT, LAD. IT'S ALL IN THE EYES...HE FLAILS, YET HIS EYES...
CALM AND STEADY!
OH, SURE! ON PURPOSE? HAW!
I SAY THE RŌNIN DICES HIM! FOR EVERY COIN I GOT ON ME! ARE YOU IN?!
CERTAINLY, CERTAINLY.
WHIT
THERE YOU GO. TWENTY-TWO, TWENTY-THREE RYŌ.
FDD
IF YOU WIN, JUST TAKE OUT WHAT I OWE YOU.
FSSST

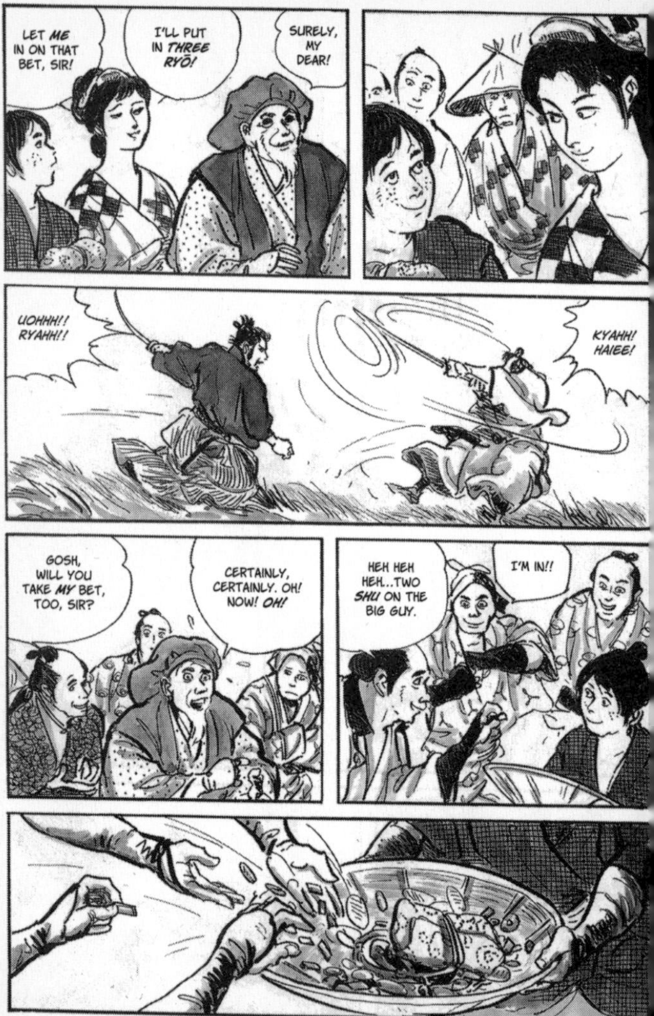
LET *ME* IN ON THAT BET, SIR!
I'LL PUT IN *THREE RYŌ!*
SURELY, MY DEAR!
UOHHH!! RYAHH!!
KYAHH! HAIEE!
GOSH, WILL YOU TAKE *MY* BET, TOO, SIR?
CERTAINLY, CERTAINLY. OH! NOW! *OH!*
HEH HEH HEH...TWO *SHU* ON THE BIG GUY.
I'M IN!!

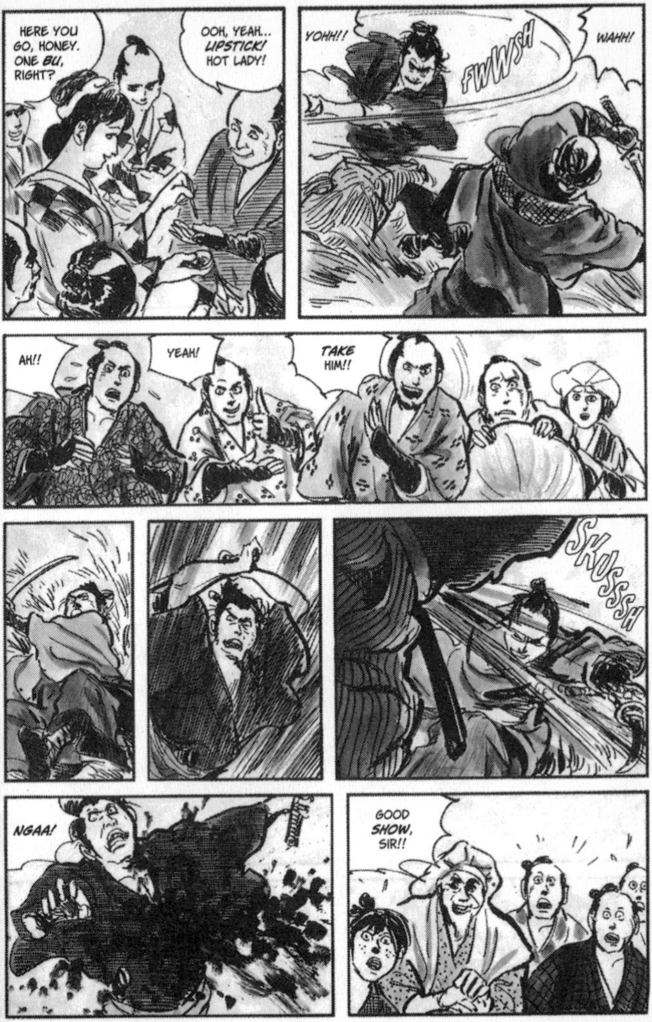
HERE YOU GO, HONEY. ONE BU, RIGHT?
OOH, YEAH... LIPSTICK! HOT LADY!
YOHH!!
FWWSH
WAHH!
AH!!
YEAH!
TAKE HIM!!
SKUSSSH
NGAA!
GOOD SHOW, SIR!!

SKASSH

SKSSH SPLTT

50

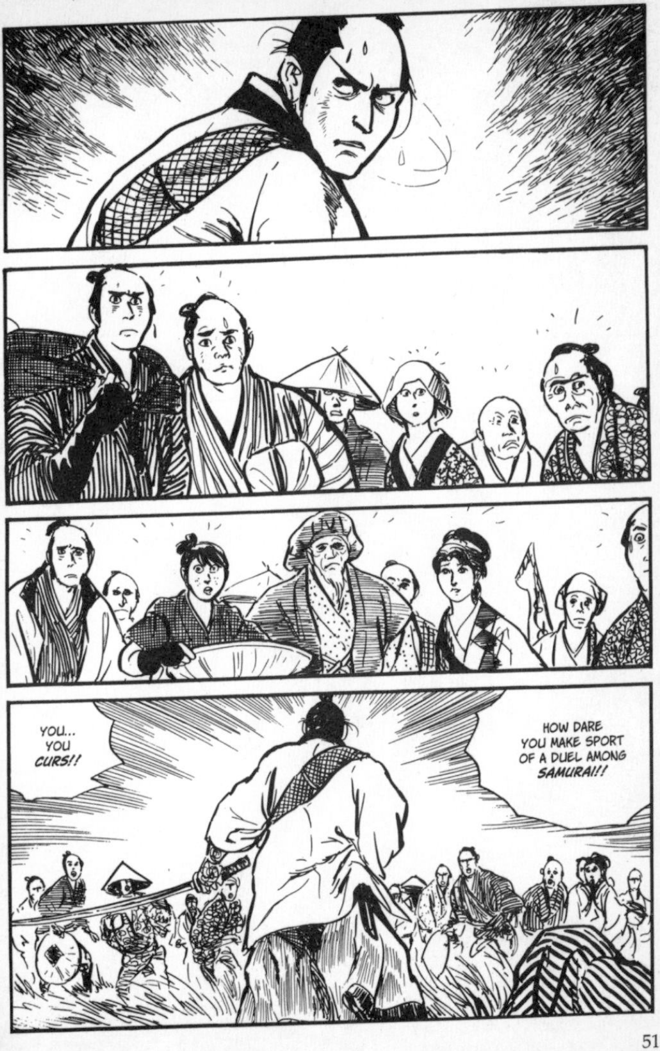
YOU...
YOU
CURS!!
HOW DARE
YOU MAKE SPORT
OF A DUEL AMONG
SAMURAI!!

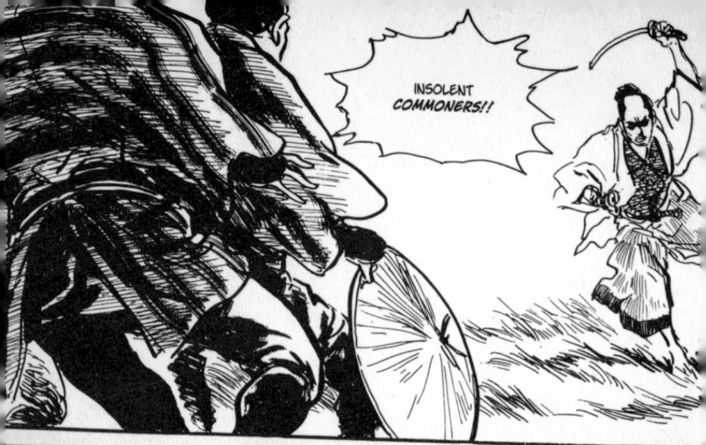
INSOLENT COMMONERS!!
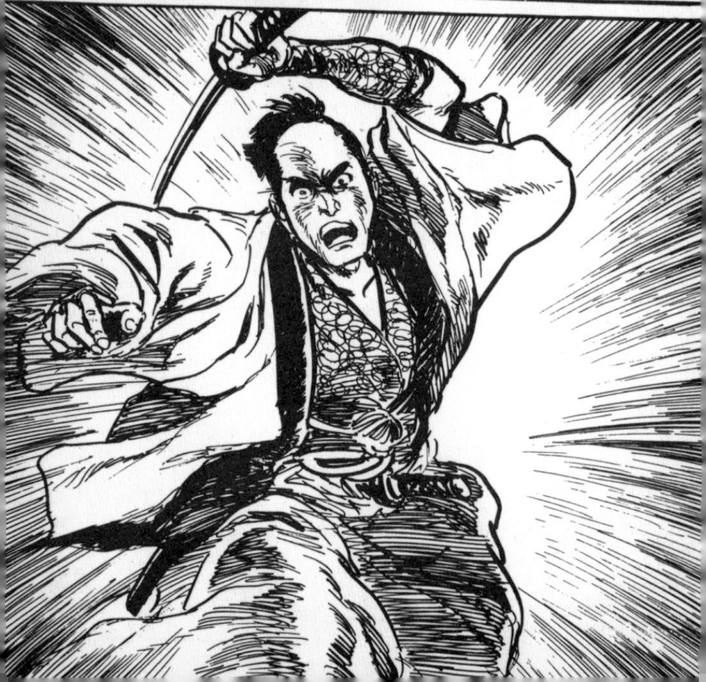

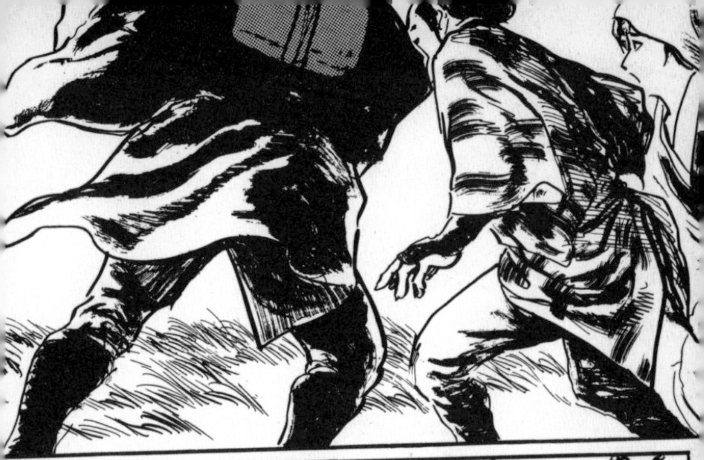
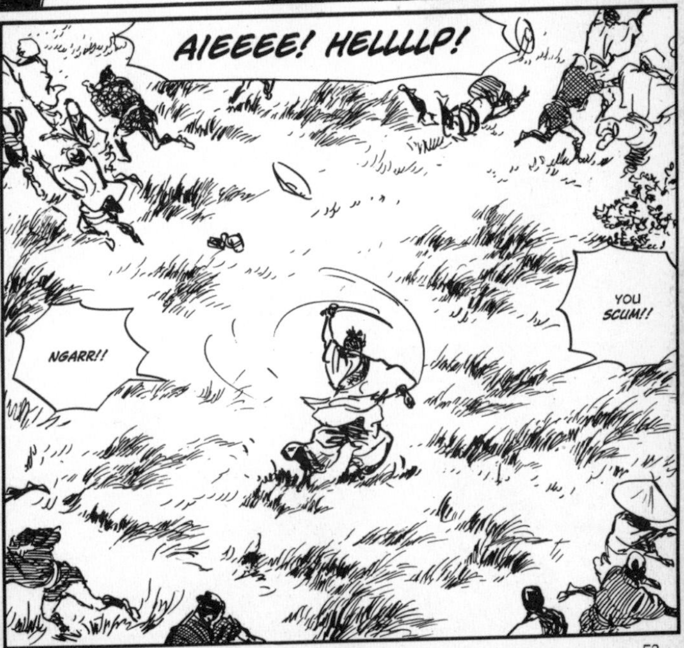
AIEEEE! HELLLLP!
NGARR!!
YOU SCUM!!

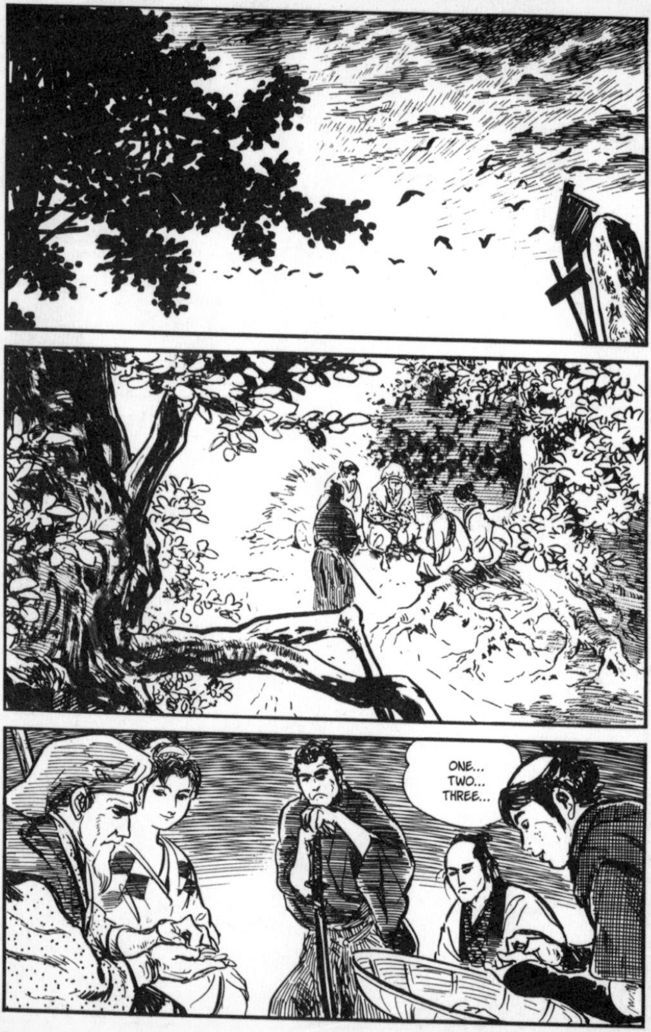
ONE... TWO... THREE...

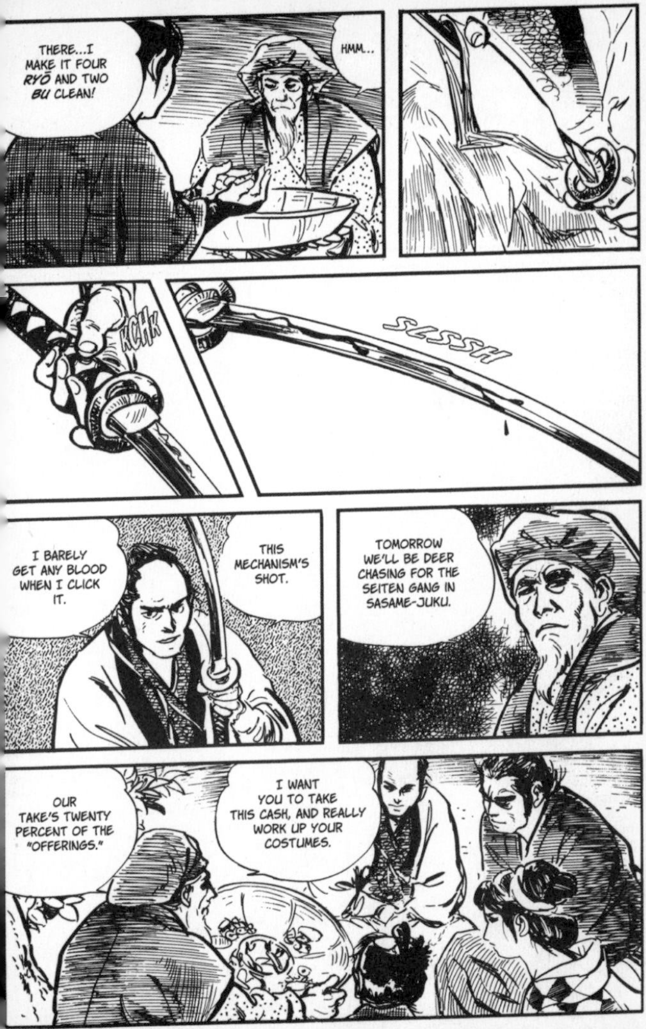
THERE...I MAKE IT FOUR RYŌ AND TWO BU CLEAN!
HMM...
KCHK
SLSSH
I BARELY GET ANY BLOOD WHEN I CLICK IT.
THIS MECHANISM'S SHOT.
TOMORROW WE'LL BE DEER CHASING FOR THE SEITEN GANG IN SASAME-JUKU.
OUR TAKE'S TWENTY PERCENT OF THE "OFFERINGS."
I WANT YOU TO TAKE THIS CASH, AND REALLY WORK UP YOUR COSTUMES.

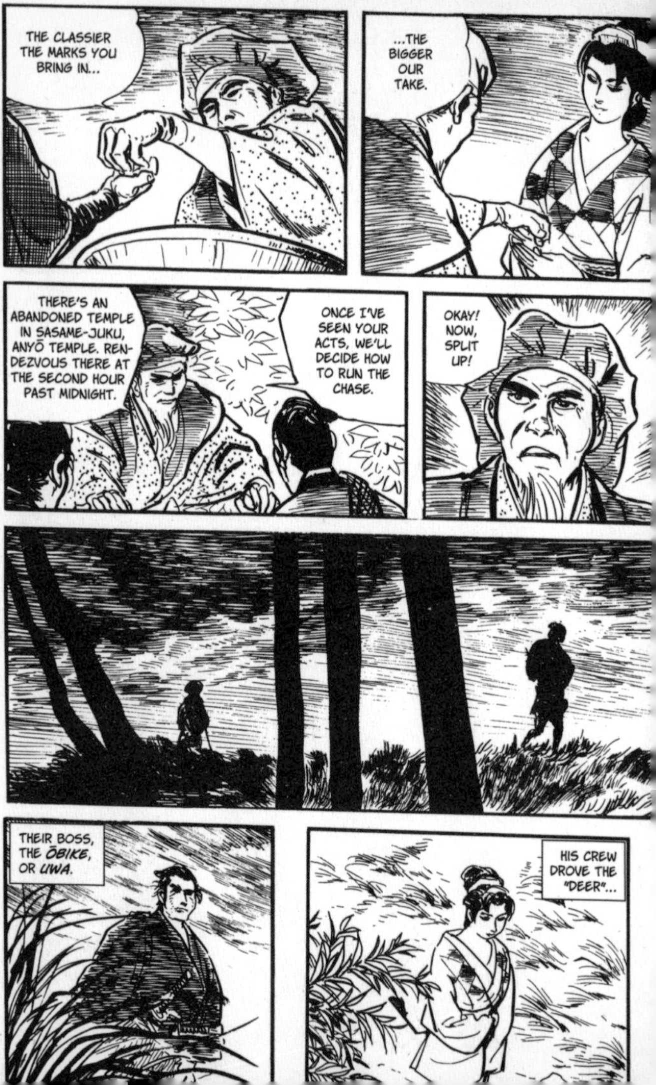
THE CLASSIER THE MARKS YOU BRING IN...
...THE BIGGER OUR TAKE.
THERE'S AN ABANDONED TEMPLE IN SASAME-JUKU, ANYŌ TEMPLE. RENDEZVOUS THERE AT THE SECOND HOUR PAST MIDNIGHT.
ONCE I'VE SEEN YOUR ACTS, WE'LL DECIDE HOW TO RUN THE CHASE.
OKAY! NOW, SPLIT UP!
THEIR BOSS, THE *ŌBIKE*, OR *UWA*.
HIS CREW DROVE THE "DEER"...

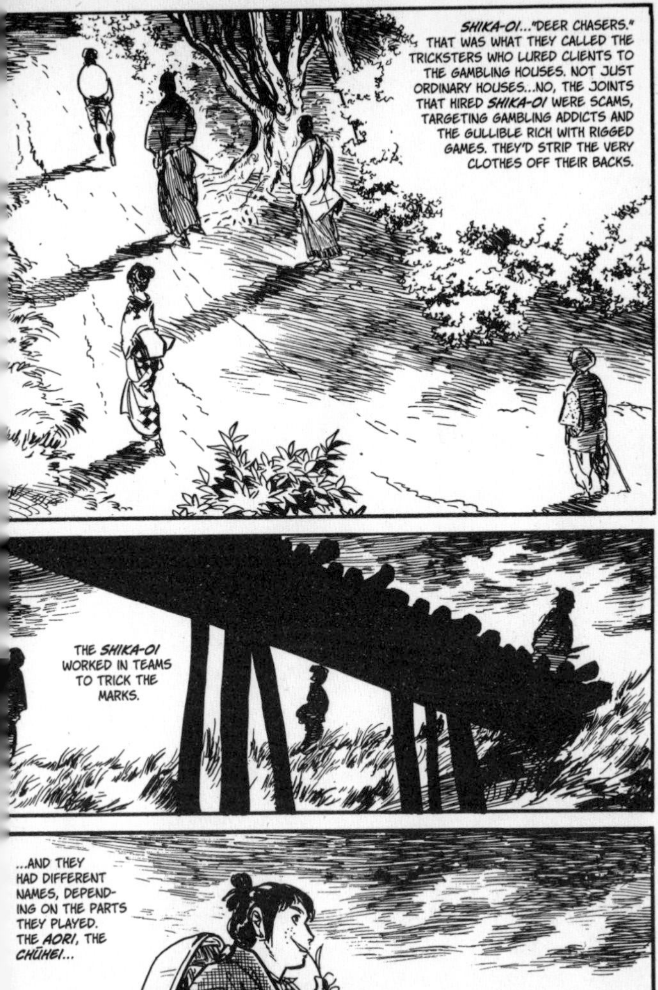
SHIKA-OI..."DEER CHASERS." THAT WAS WHAT THEY CALLED THE TRICKSTERS WHO LURED CLIENTS TO THE GAMBLING HOUSES. NOT JUST ORDINARY HOUSES...NO, THE JOINTS THAT HIRED SHIKA-OI WERE SCAMS, TARGETING GAMBLING ADDICTS AND THE GULLIBLE RICH WITH RIGGED GAMES. THEY'D STRIP THE VERY CLOTHES OFF THEIR BACKS.
THE SHIKA-OI WORKED IN TEAMS TO TRICK THE MARKS.
...AND THEY HAD DIFFERENT NAMES, DEPENDING ON THE PARTS THEY PLAYED. THE AORI, THE CHŪHEI...

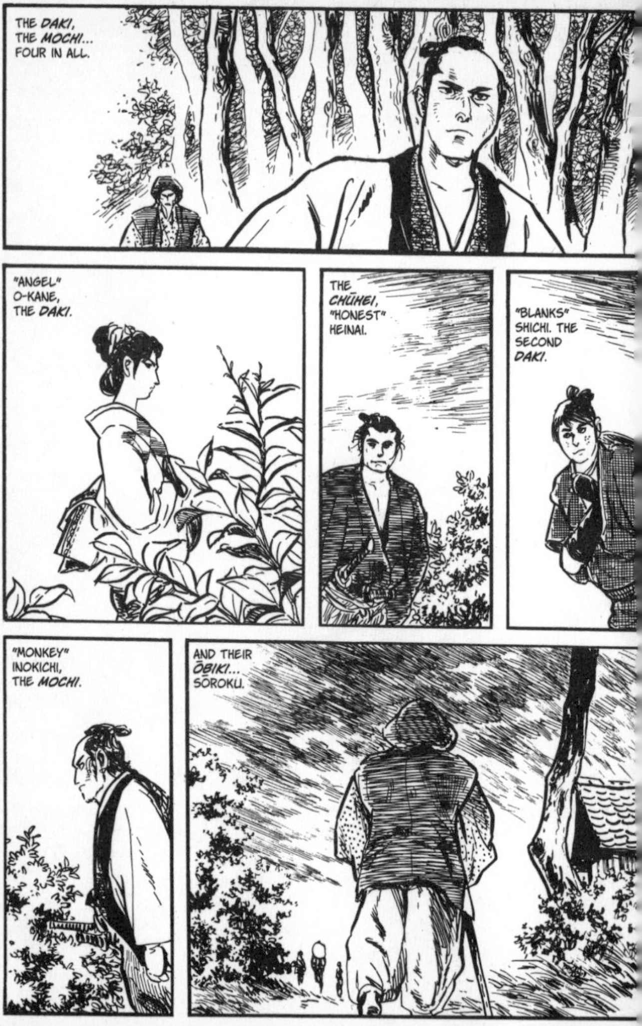
THE *DAKI*, THE *MOCHI*... FOUR IN ALL.
"ANGEL" O-KANE, THE *DAKI*.
THE *CHŪHEI*, "HONEST" HEINAI.
"BLANKS" SHICHI. THE SECOND *DAKI*.
"MONKEY" INOKICHI, THE *MOCHI*.
AND THEIR *ŌBIKI*... SŌROKU.

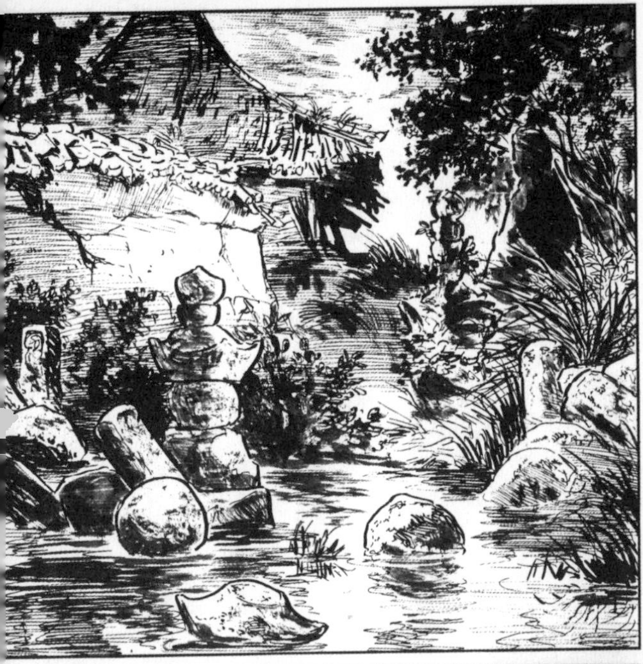

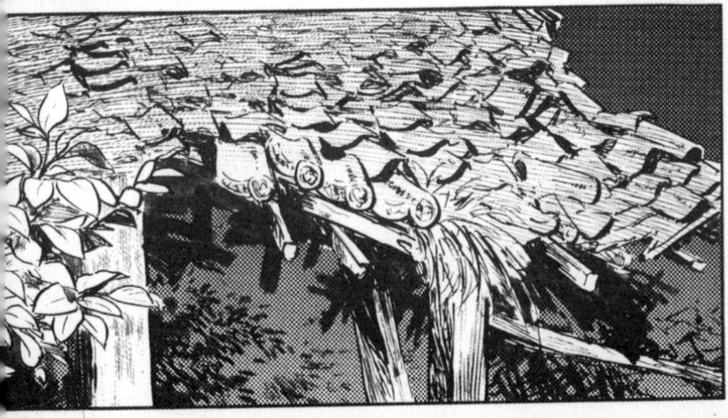

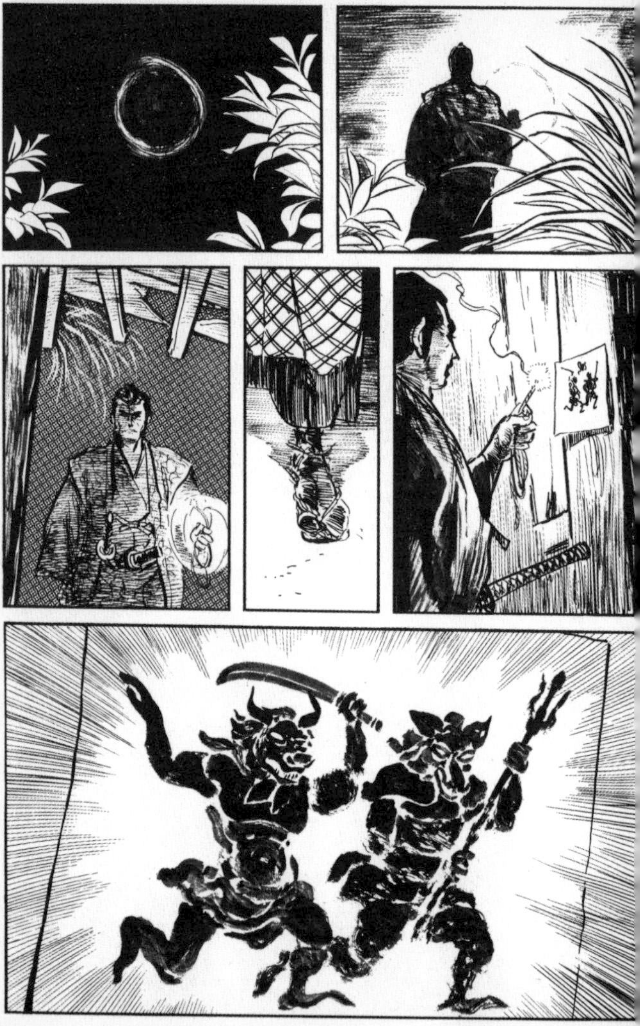

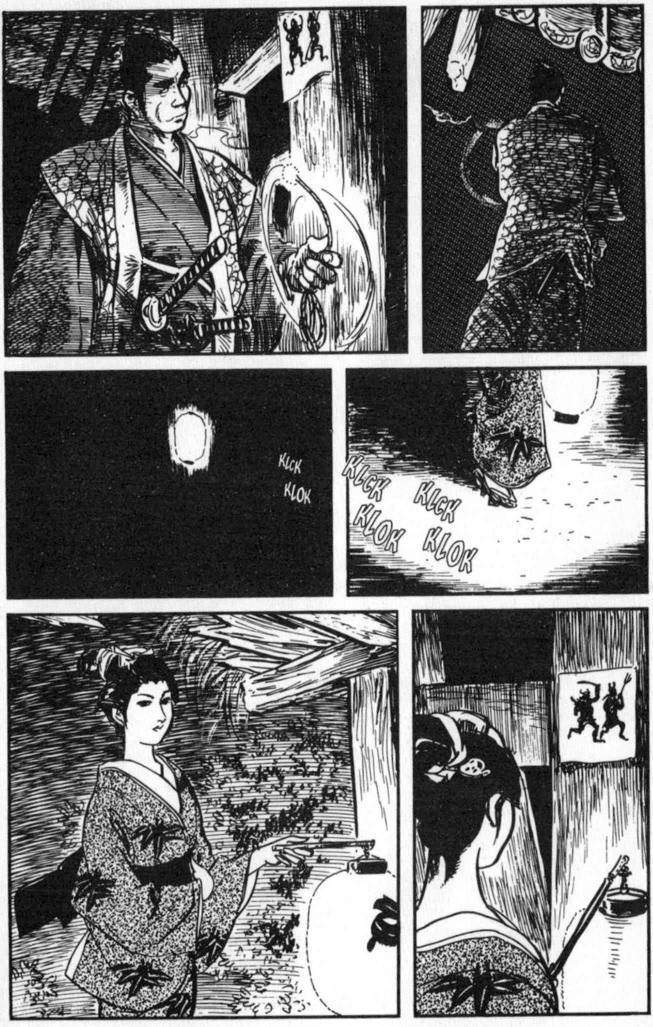
KLCK
KLOK
KLCK
KLOK
KLCK
KLOK

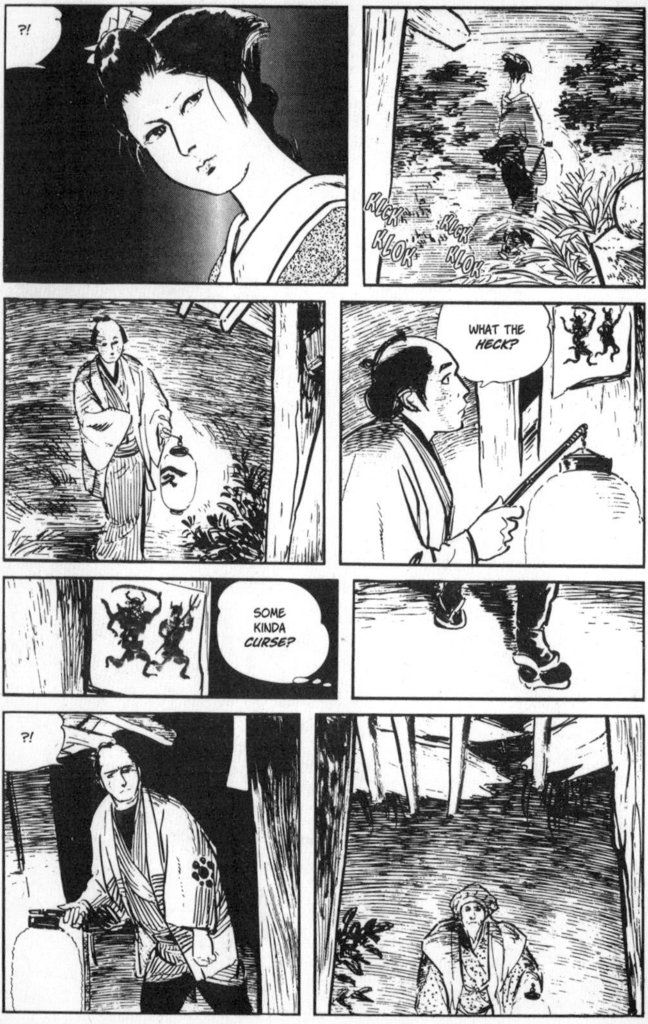
?!
KLICK
KLOK
KLICK
KLOK
WHAT THE HECK?
SOME KINDA CURSE?
?!

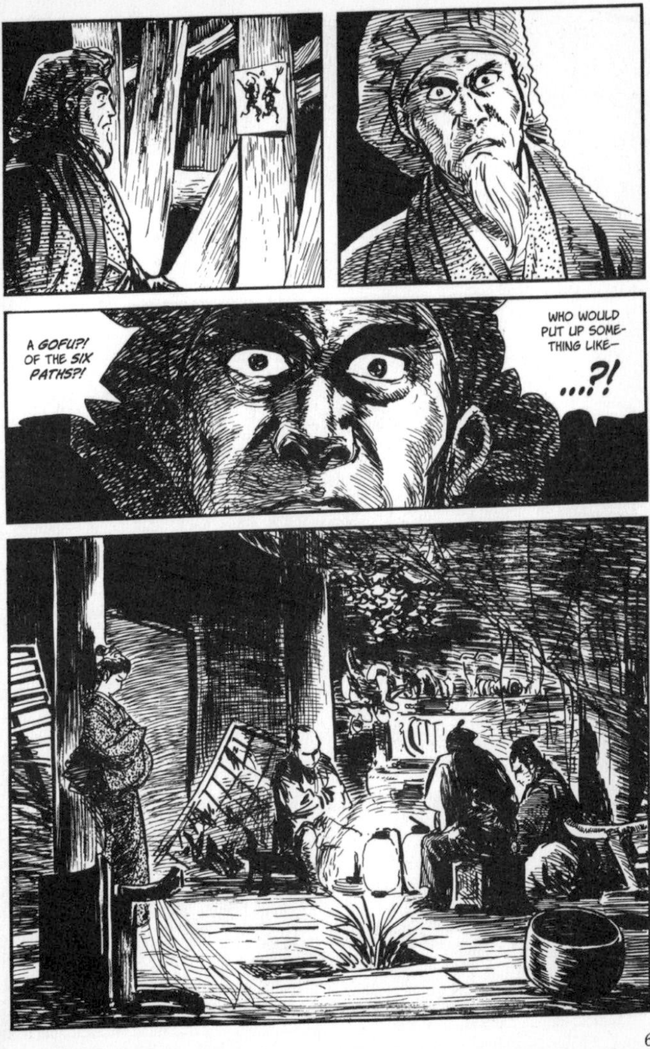
A GOFU?! OF THE SIX PATHS?!
WHO WOULD PUT UP SOME-THING LIKE—
....?!

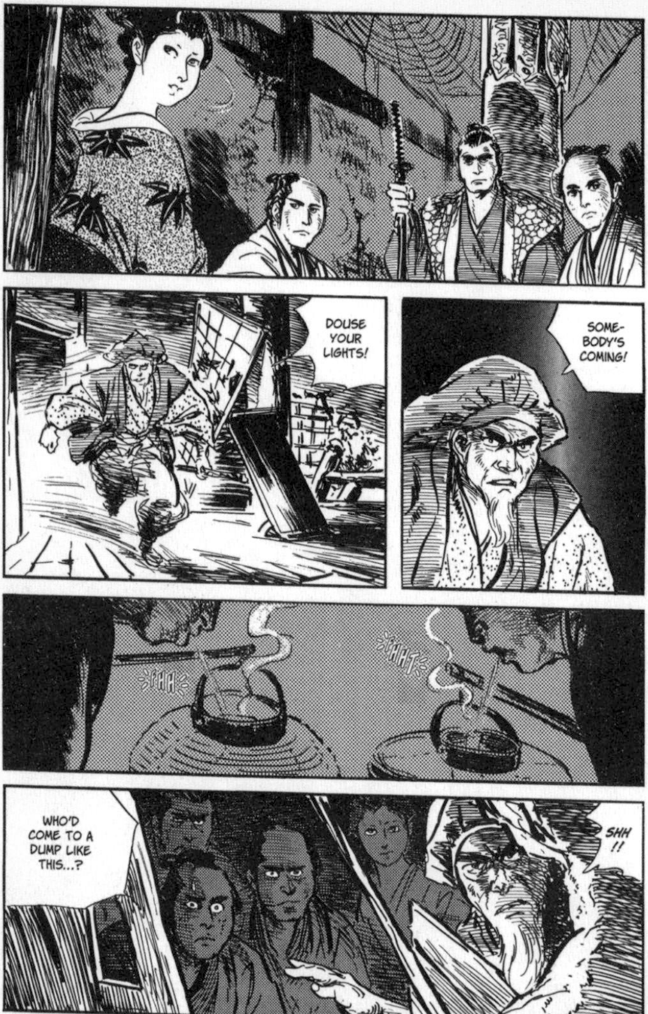
DOUSE YOUR LIGHTS!
SOME-BODY'S COMING!
FSHH
SHHT
WHO'D COME TO A DUMP LIKE THIS...?
SHH !!

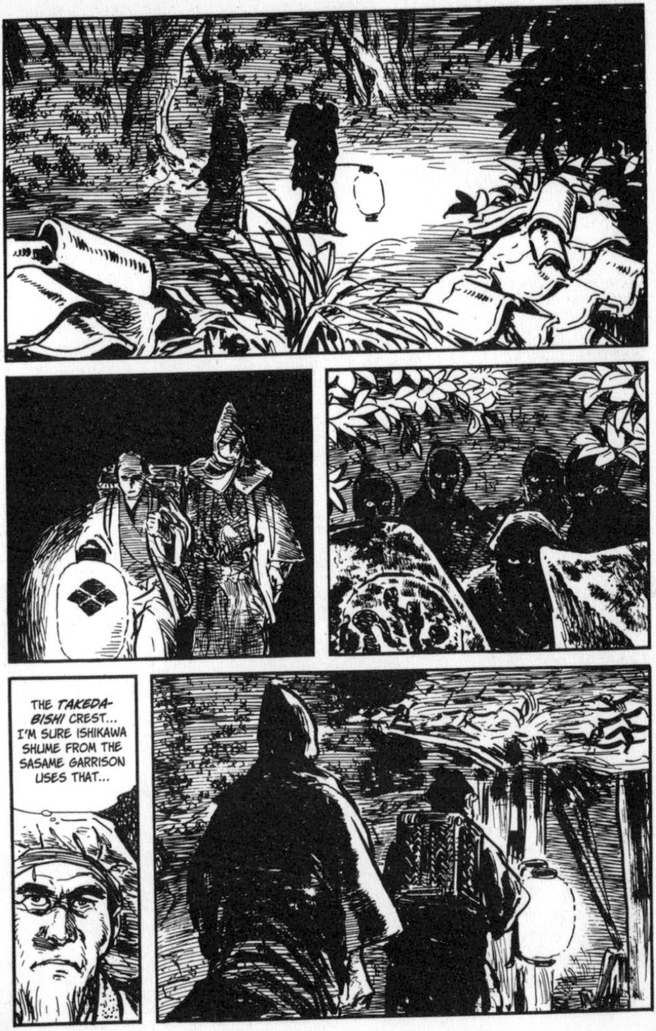
THE *TAKEDA-BISHI* CREST... I'M SURE ISHIKAWA SHUME FROM THE SASAME GARRISON USES THAT...

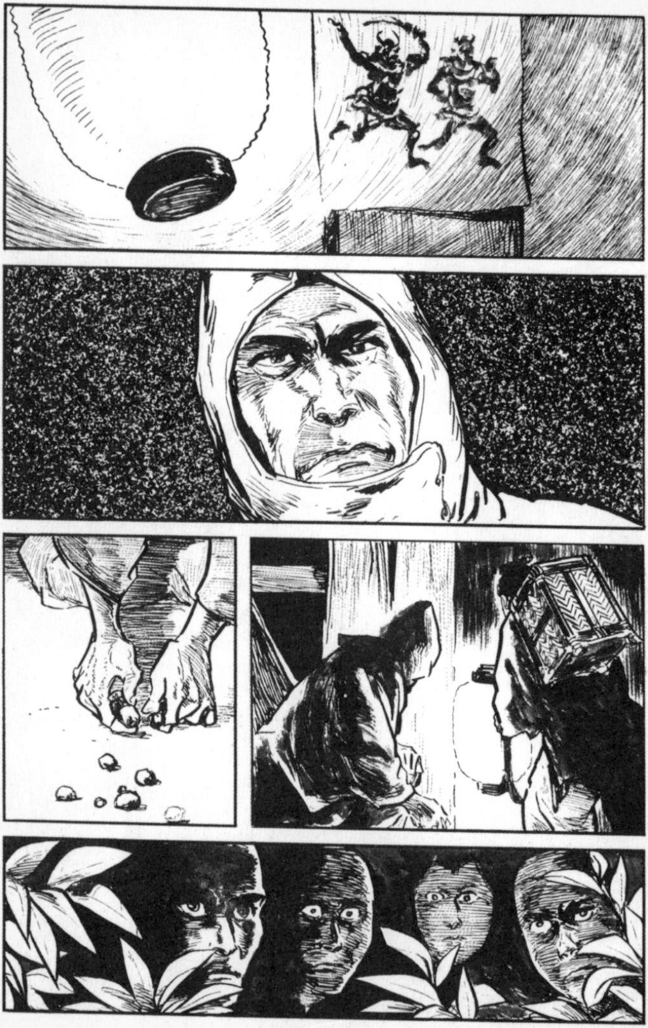

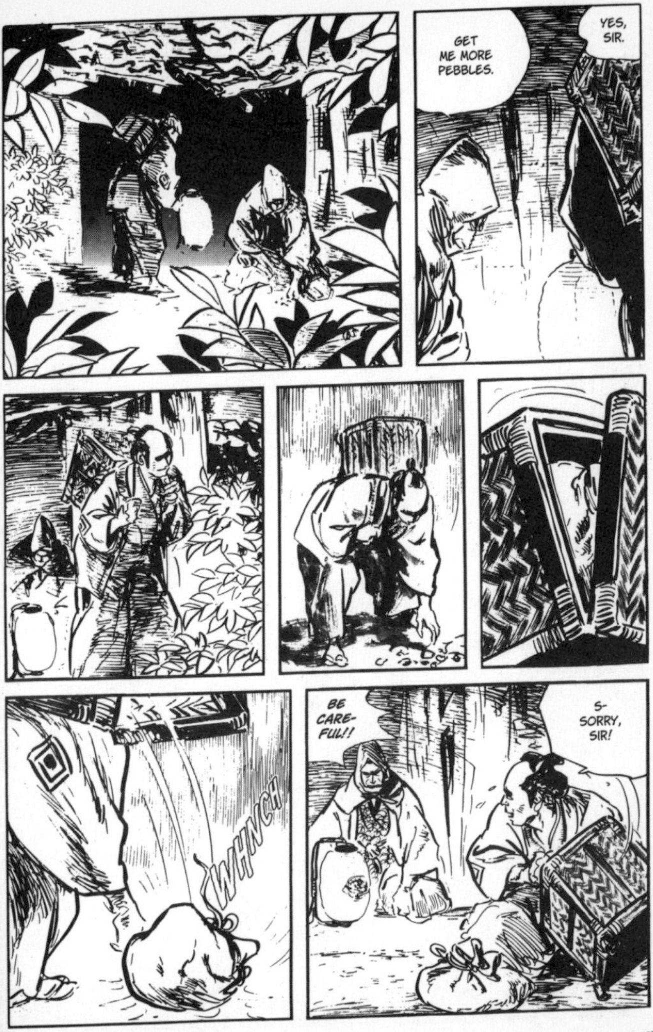
GET ME MORE PEBBLES.
YES, SIR.
WHNCH
BE CARE-FUL!!
S- SORRY, SIR!

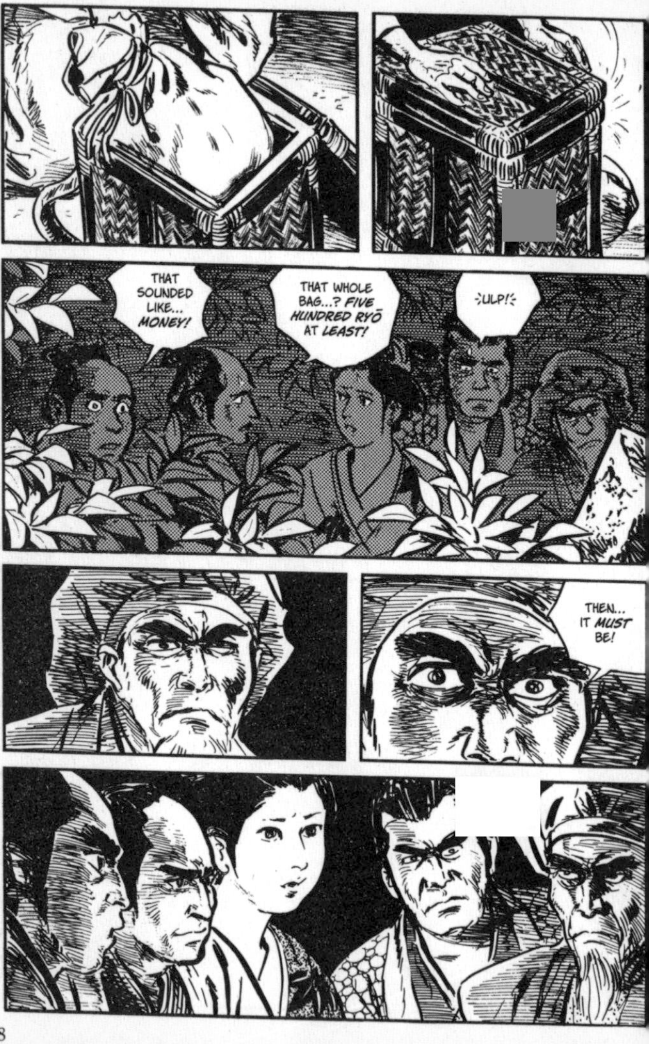
THAT SOUNDED LIKE... MONEY!
THAT WHOLE BAG...? FIVE HUNDRED RYŌ AT LEAST!
ULP!
THEN... IT MUST BE!

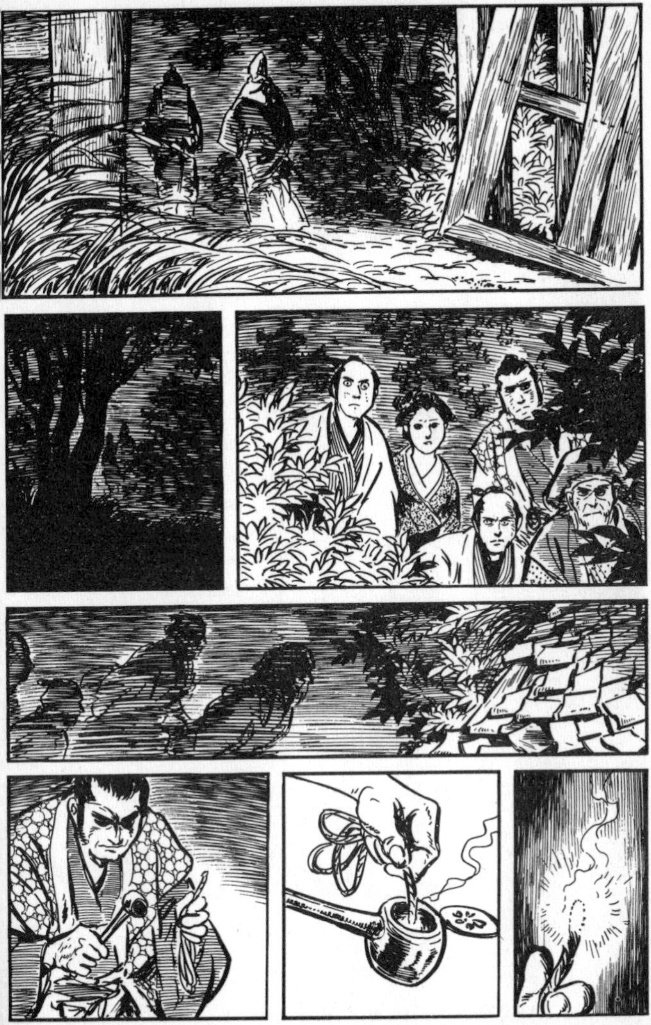

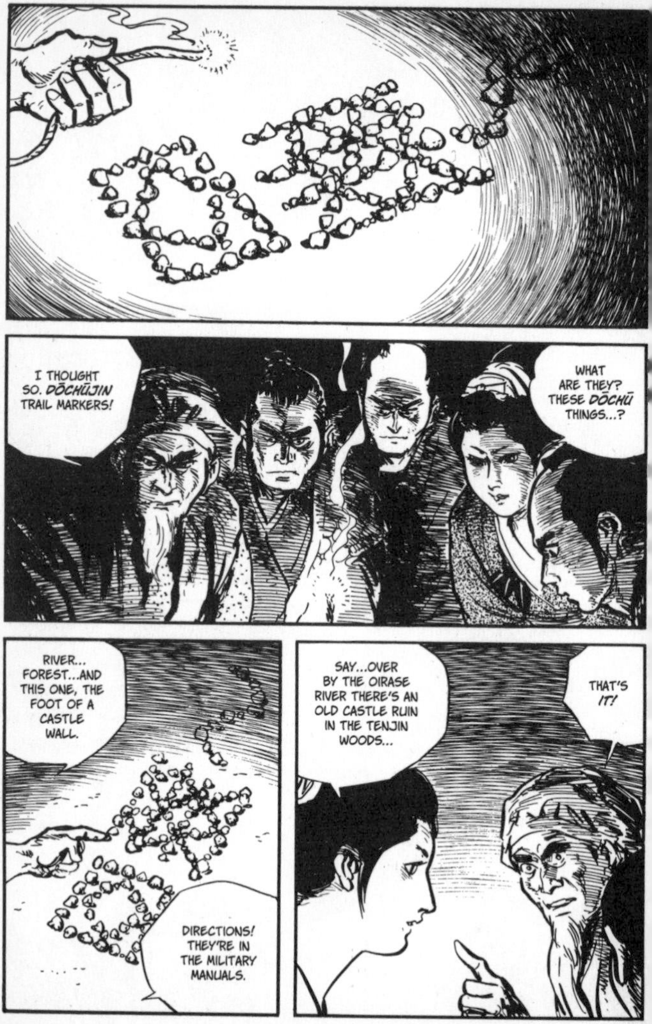

I THOUGHT SO. *DŌCHŪJIN* TRAIL MARKERS!
WHAT ARE THEY? THESE *DŌCHŪ* THINGS...?
RIVER... FOREST...AND THIS ONE, THE FOOT OF A CASTLE WALL.
DIRECTIONS! THEY'RE IN THE MILITARY MANUALS.
SAY...OVER BY THE OIRASE RIVER THERE'S AN OLD CASTLE RUIN IN THE TENJIN WOODS...
THAT'S *IT!*

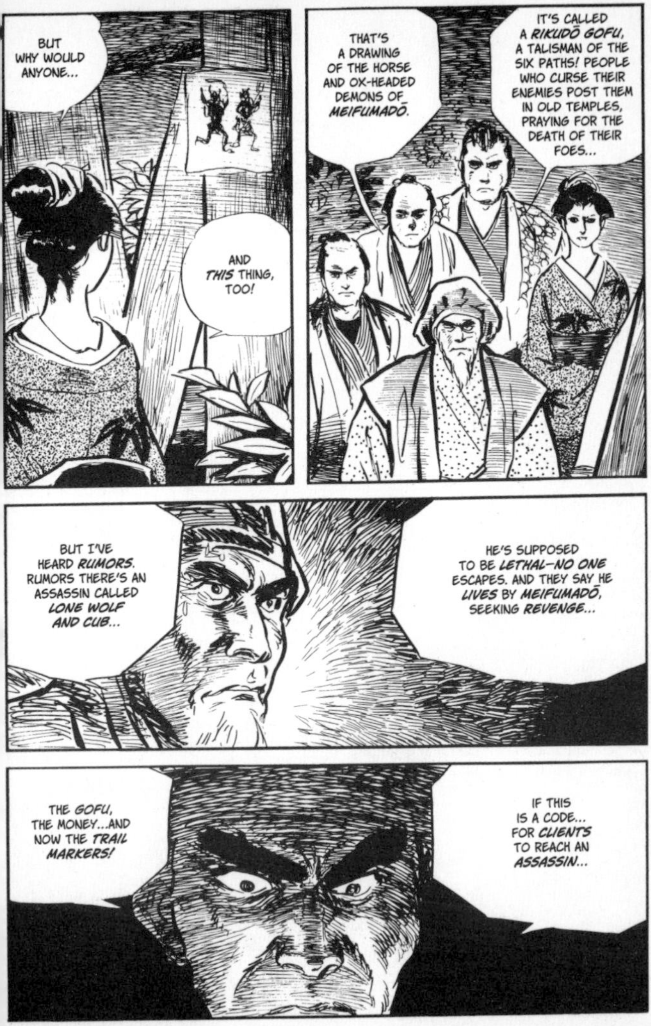
BUT WHY WOULD ANYONE...
AND THIS THING, TOO!
THAT'S A DRAWING OF THE HORSE AND OX-HEADED DEMONS OF MEIFUMADŌ.
IT'S CALLED A RIKUDŌ GOFU, A TALISMAN OF THE SIX PATHS! PEOPLE WHO CURSE THEIR ENEMIES POST THEM IN OLD TEMPLES, PRAYING FOR THE DEATH OF THEIR FOES...
BUT I'VE HEARD RUMORS. RUMORS THERE'S AN ASSASSIN CALLED LONE WOLF AND CUB...
HE'S SUPPOSED TO BE LETHAL—NO ONE ESCAPES. AND THEY SAY HE LIVES BY MEIFUMADŌ, SEEKING REVENGE...
THE GOFU, THE MONEY...AND NOW THE TRAIL MARKERS!
IF THIS IS A CODE... FOR CLIENTS TO REACH AN ASSASSIN...

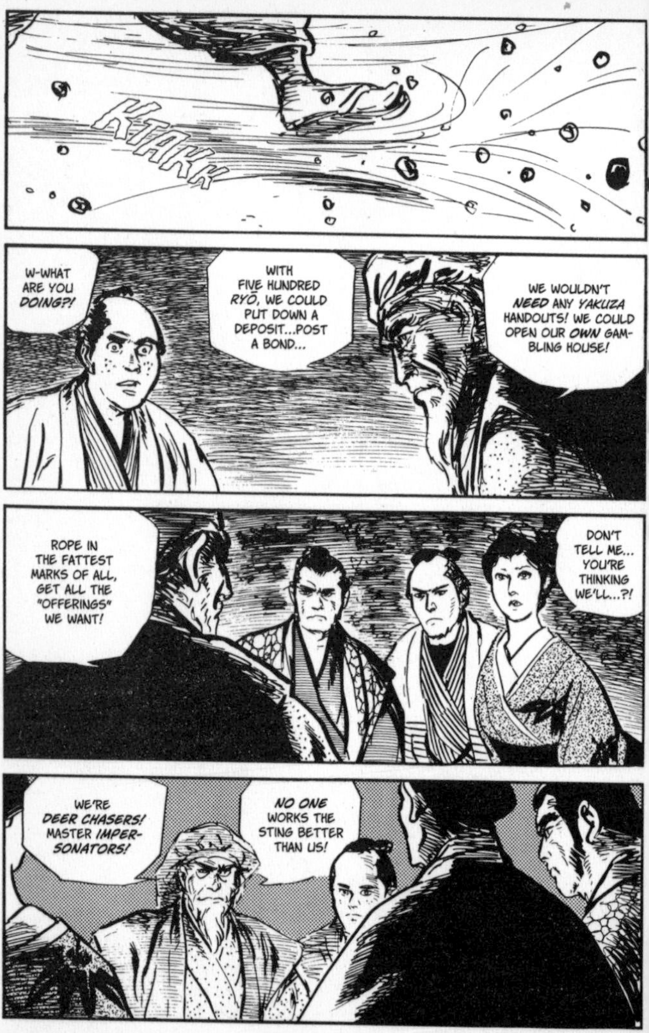
KTAKK
W-WHAT ARE YOU DOING?!
WITH FIVE HUNDRED RYŌ, WE COULD PUT DOWN A DEPOSIT...POST A BOND...
WE WOULDN'T NEED ANY YAKUZA HANDOUTS! WE COULD OPEN OUR OWN GAMBLING HOUSE!
ROPE IN THE FATTEST MARKS OF ALL, GET ALL THE "OFFERINGS" WE WANT!
DON'T TELL ME... YOU'RE THINKING WE'LL...?!
WE'RE DEER CHASERS! MASTER IMPERSONATORS!
NO ONE WORKS THE STING BETTER THAN US!

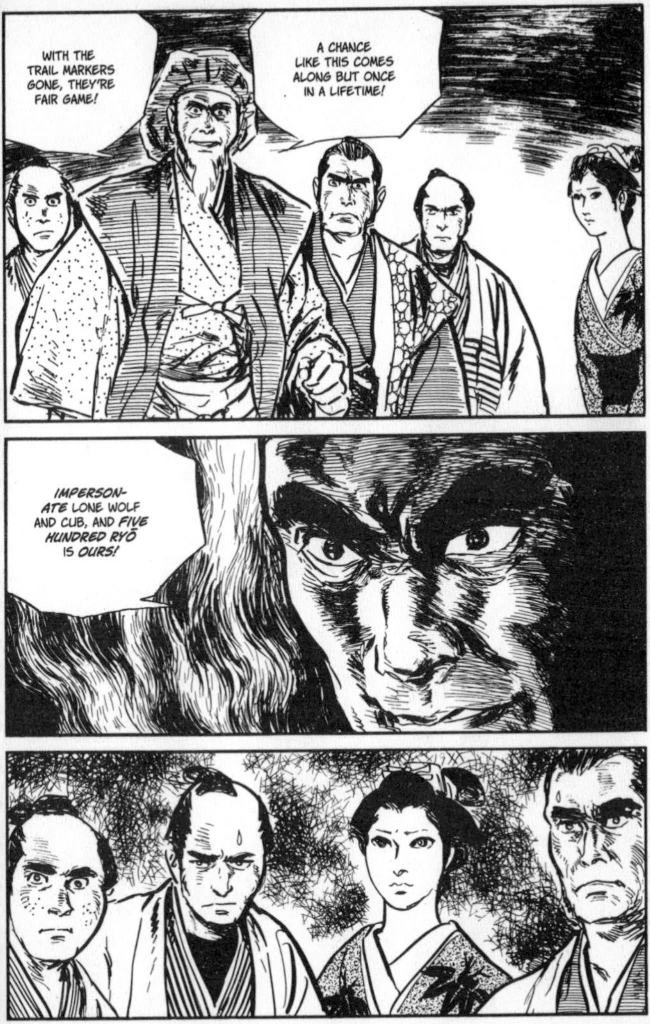
WITH THE TRAIL MARKERS GONE, THEY'RE FAIR GAME!
A CHANCE LIKE THIS COMES ALONG BUT ONCE IN A LIFETIME!
IMPERSONATE LONE WOLF AND CUB, AND *FIVE HUNDRED RYŌ* IS *OURS!*

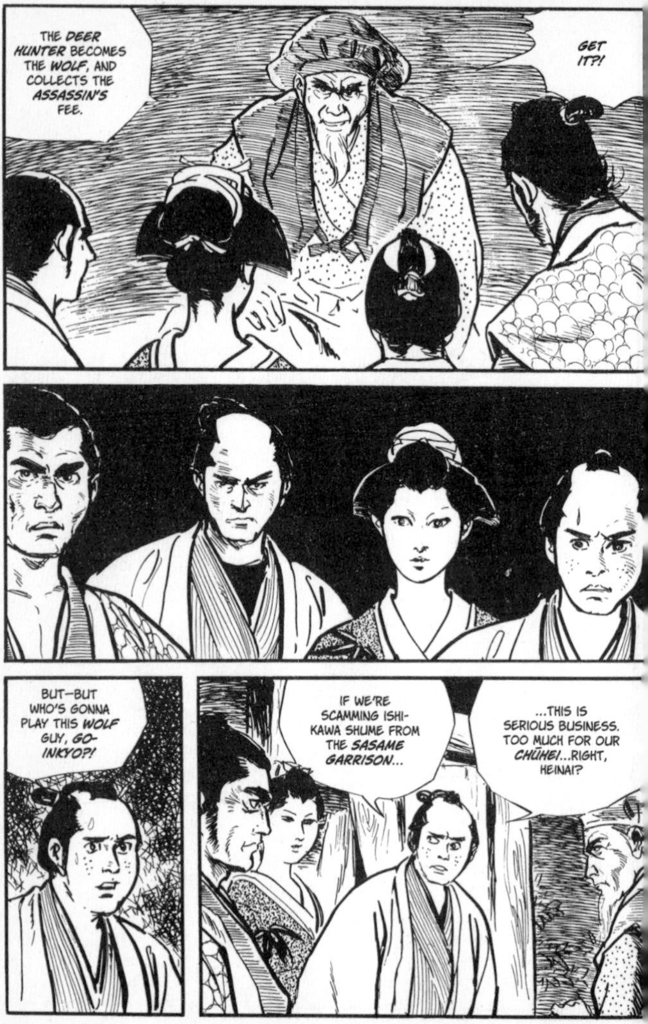
THE *DEER HUNTER* BECOMES THE *WOLF*, AND COLLECTS THE *ASSASSIN'S* FEE.
GET IT?!
BUT—BUT WHO'S GONNA PLAY THIS *WOLF* GUY, *GO-INKYO?!*
IF WE'RE SCAMMING ISHI-KAWA SHUME FROM THE *SASAME GARRISON*...
...THIS IS SERIOUS BUSINESS. TOO MUCH FOR OUR *CHŪHEI*...RIGHT, HEINAI?

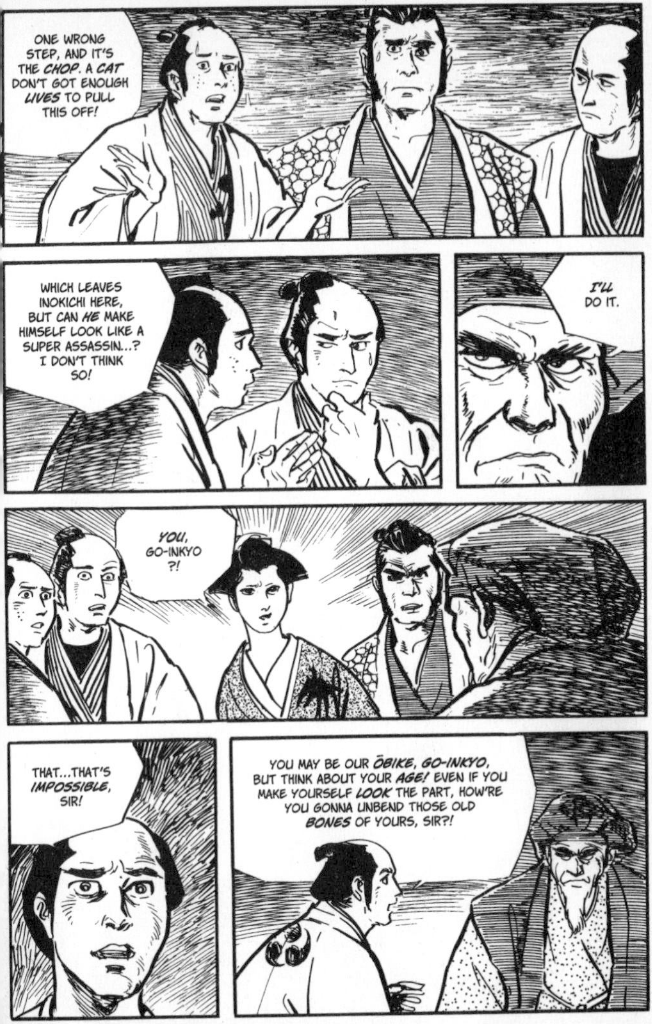
ONE WRONG STEP, AND IT'S THE *CHOP*. A *CAT* DON'T GOT ENOUGH *LIVES* TO PULL THIS OFF!
WHICH LEAVES INOKICHI HERE, BUT CAN *HE* MAKE HIMSELF LOOK LIKE A SUPER ASSASSIN...? I DON'T THINK SO!
I'LL DO IT.
YOU, GO-INKYO ?!
THAT...THAT'S *IMPOSSIBLE*, SIR!
YOU MAY BE OUR *ŌBIKE, GO-INKYO*, BUT THINK ABOUT YOUR *AGE!* EVEN IF YOU MAKE YOURSELF *LOOK* THE PART, HOW'RE YOU GONNA UNBEND THOSE OLD *BONES* OF YOURS, SIR?!

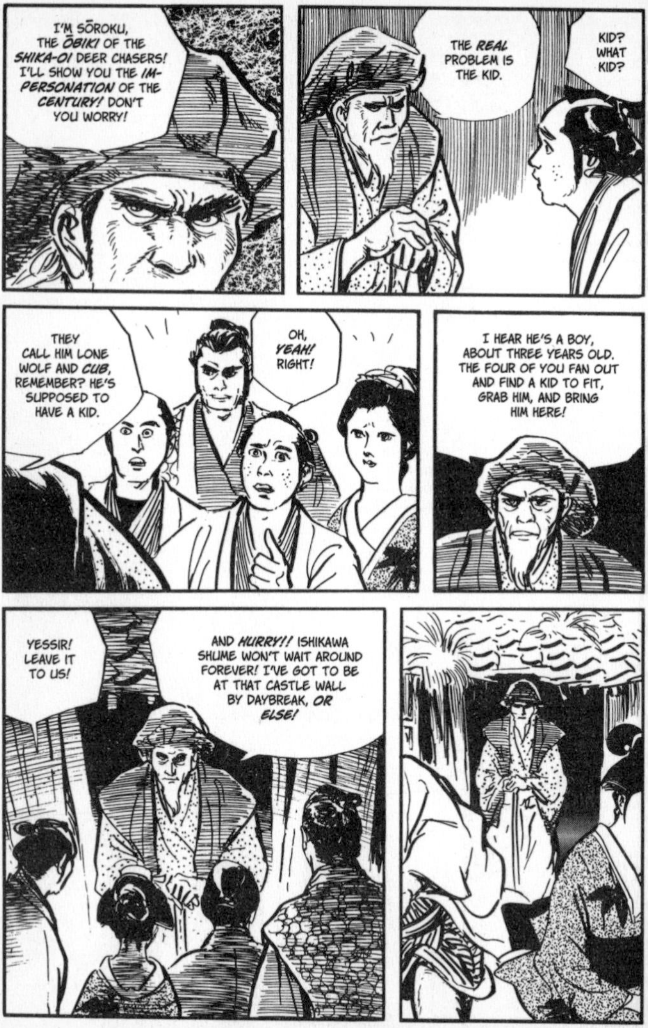
I'M SŌROKU, THE ŌBIKI OF THE SHIKA-OI DEER CHASERS! I'LL SHOW YOU THE IMPERSONATION OF THE CENTURY! DON'T YOU WORRY!
THE REAL PROBLEM IS THE KID.
KID? WHAT KID?
THEY CALL HIM LONE WOLF AND CUB, REMEMBER? HE'S SUPPOSED TO HAVE A KID.
OH, YEAH! RIGHT!
I HEAR HE'S A BOY, ABOUT THREE YEARS OLD. THE FOUR OF YOU FAN OUT AND FIND A KID TO FIT, GRAB HIM, AND BRING HIM HERE!
YESSIR! LEAVE IT TO US!
AND HURRY!! ISHIKAWA SHUME WON'T WAIT AROUND FOREVER! I'VE GOT TO BE AT THAT CASTLE WALL BY DAYBREAK, OR ELSE!

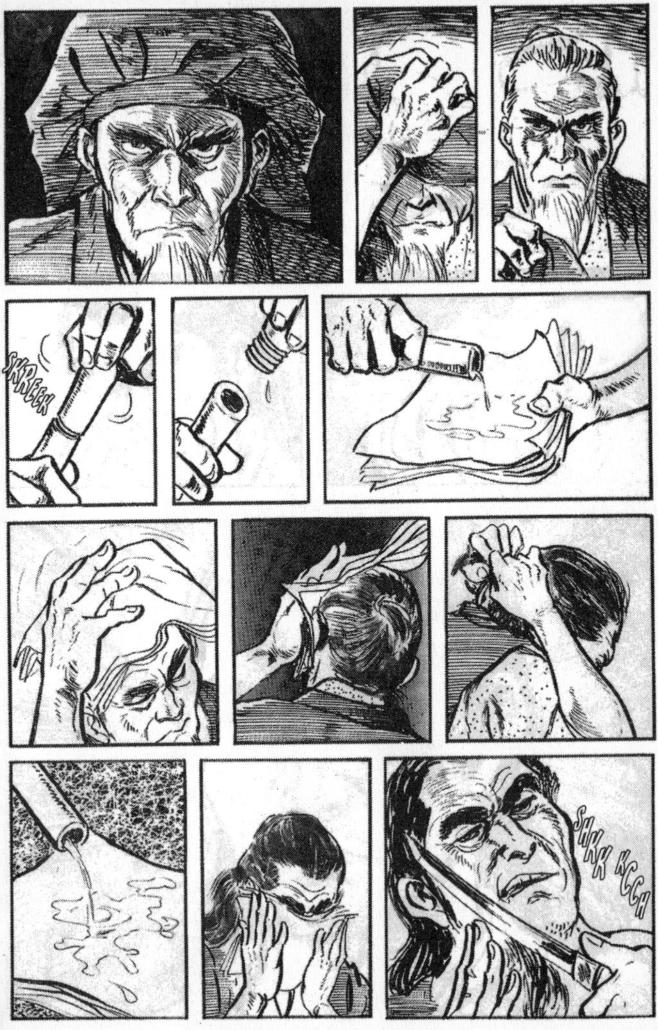
SKREEK
SHKK KCCH

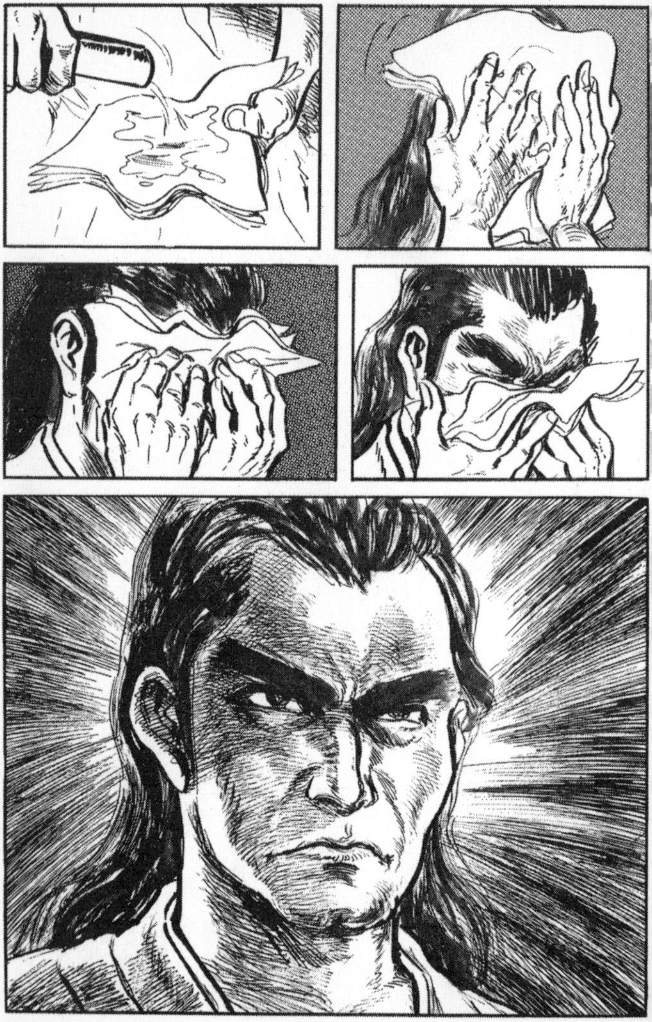

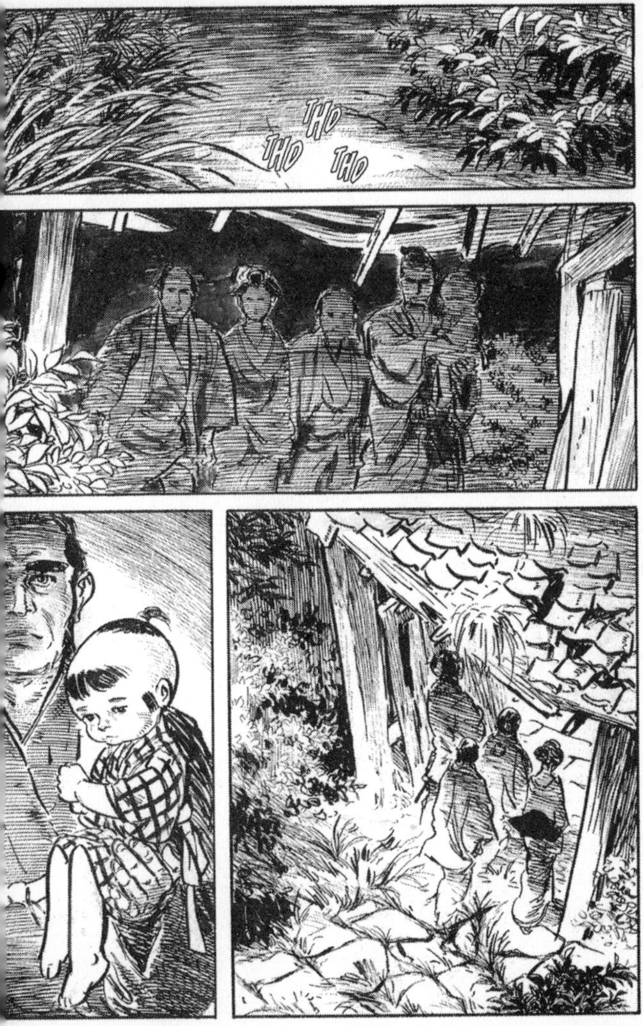
THD
THD
THD

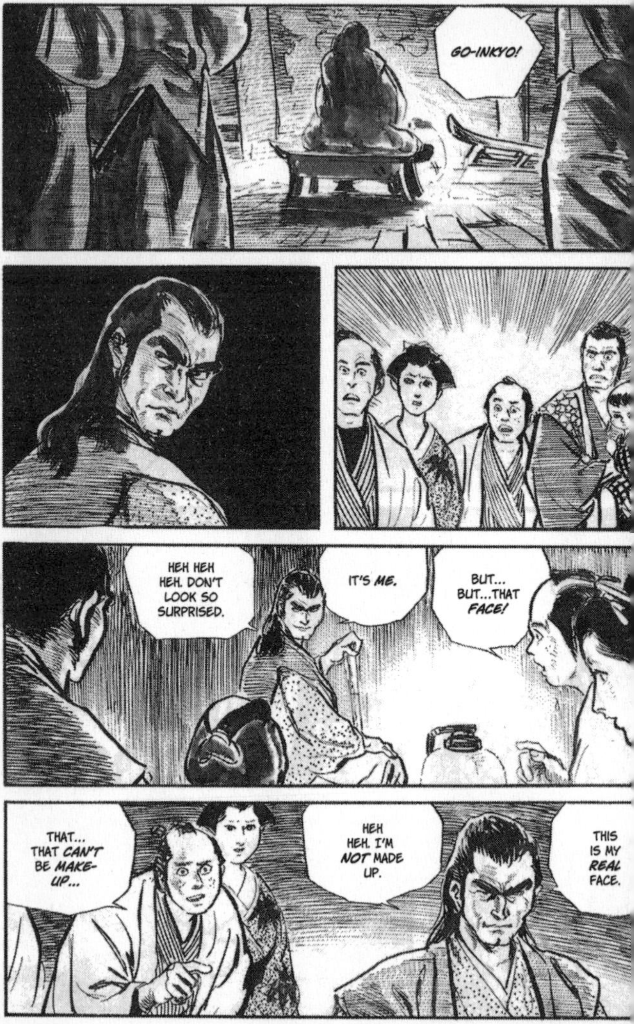
GO-INKYO!
HEH HEH HEH. DON'T LOOK SO SURPRISED.
IT'S *ME.*
BUT... BUT...THAT *FACE!*
THAT... THAT *CAN'T* BE *MAKE-UP...*
HEH HEH. I'M *NOT* MADE UP.
THIS IS MY *REAL* FACE.

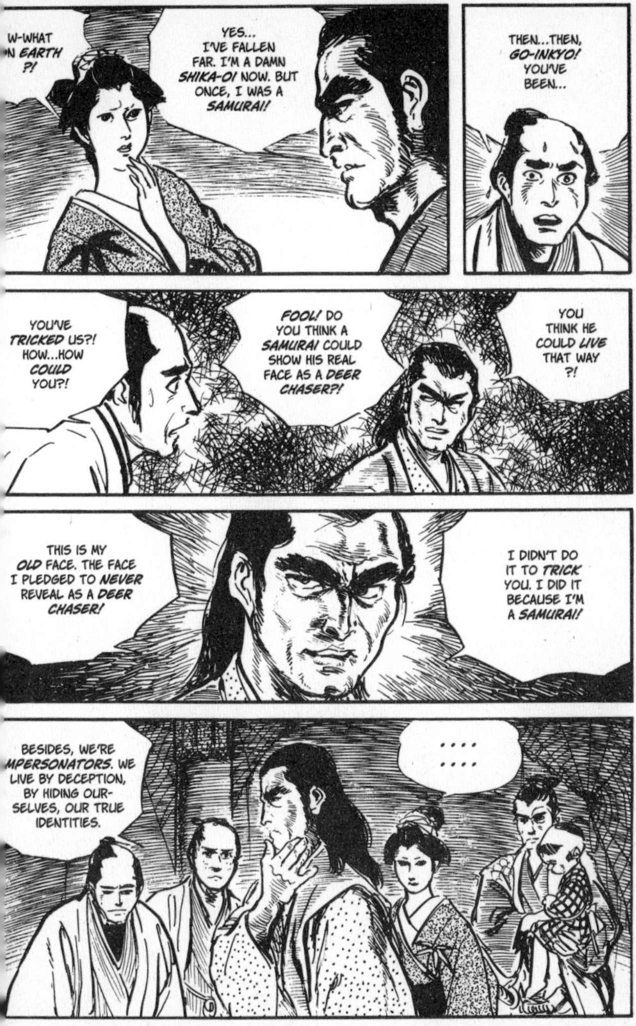
W-WHAT
N EARTH ?!
YES... I'VE FALLEN FAR. I'M A DAMN SHIKA-OI NOW. BUT ONCE, I WAS A SAMURAI!
THEN...THEN, GO-INKYO! YOU'VE BEEN...
YOU'VE TRICKED US?! HOW...HOW COULD YOU?!
FOOL! DO YOU THINK A SAMURAI COULD SHOW HIS REAL FACE AS A DEER CHASER?!
YOU THINK HE COULD LIVE THAT WAY ?!
THIS IS MY OLD FACE. THE FACE I PLEDGED TO NEVER REVEAL AS A DEER CHASER!
I DIDN'T DO IT TO TRICK YOU. I DID IT BECAUSE I'M A SAMURAI!
BESIDES, WE'RE MPERSONATORS. WE LIVE BY DECEPTION, BY HIDING OUR-SELVES, OUR TRUE IDENTITIES.
....
....

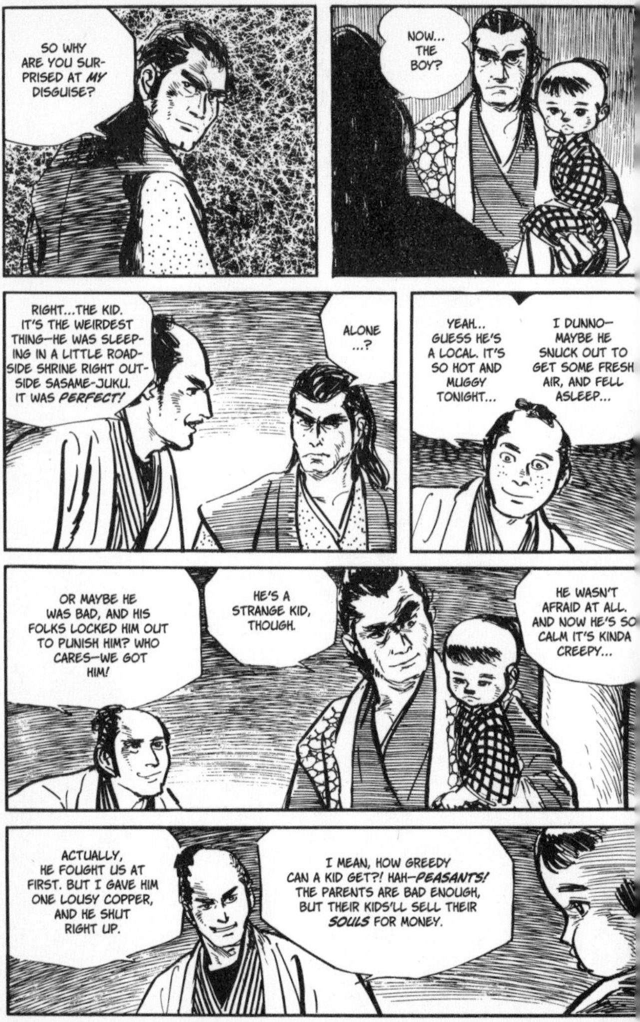
SO WHY ARE YOU SURPRISED AT *MY* DISGUISE?
NOW... THE BOY?
RIGHT...THE KID. IT'S THE WEIRDEST THING—HE WAS SLEEPING IN A LITTLE ROADSIDE SHRINE RIGHT OUTSIDE SASAME-JUKU. IT WAS *PERFECT!*
ALONE ...?
YEAH... GUESS HE'S A LOCAL. IT'S SO HOT AND MUGGY TONIGHT...
I DUNNO— MAYBE HE SNUCK OUT TO GET SOME FRESH AIR, AND FELL ASLEEP...
OR MAYBE HE WAS BAD, AND HIS FOLKS LOCKED HIM OUT TO PUNISH HIM? WHO CARES—WE GOT HIM!
HE'S A STRANGE KID, THOUGH.
HE WASN'T AFRAID AT ALL. AND NOW HE'S SO CALM IT'S KINDA CREEPY...
ACTUALLY, HE FOUGHT US AT FIRST. BUT I GAVE HIM ONE LOUSY COPPER, AND HE SHUT RIGHT UP.
I MEAN, HOW GREEDY CAN A KID GET?! HAH—*PEASANTS!* THE PARENTS ARE BAD ENOUGH, BUT THEIR KIDS'LL SELL THEIR *SOULS* FOR MONEY.

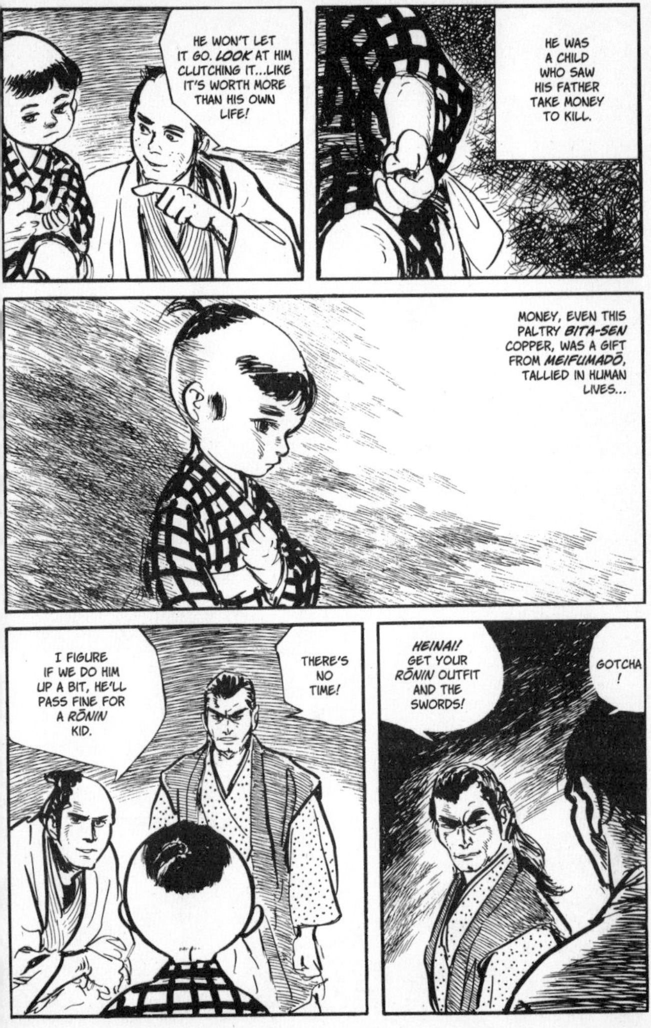
HE WON'T LET IT GO. *LOOK* AT HIM CLUTCHING IT...LIKE IT'S WORTH MORE THAN HIS OWN LIFE!
HE WAS A CHILD WHO SAW HIS FATHER TAKE MONEY TO KILL.
MONEY, EVEN THIS PALTRY *BITA-SEN* COPPER, WAS A GIFT FROM *MEIFUMADŌ*, TALLIED IN HUMAN LIVES...
I FIGURE IF WE DO HIM UP A BIT, HE'LL PASS FINE FOR A *RŌNIN* KID.
THERE'S NO TIME!
HEINAI! GET YOUR *RŌNIN* OUTFIT AND THE SWORDS!
GOTCHA!

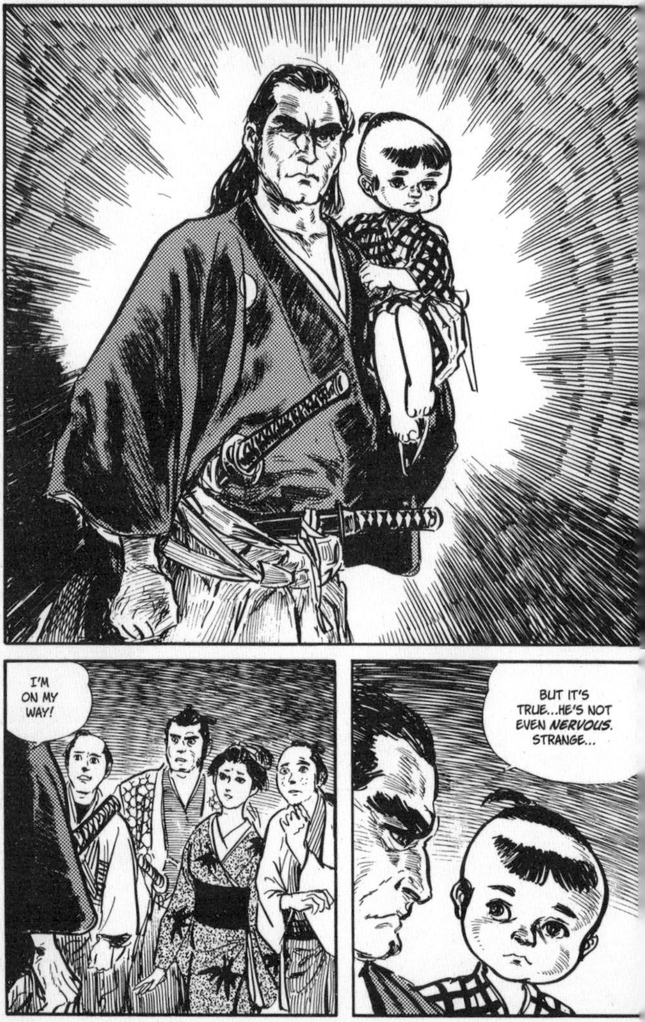
I'M ON MY WAY!
BUT IT'S TRUE...HE'S NOT EVEN *NERVOUS*. STRANGE...

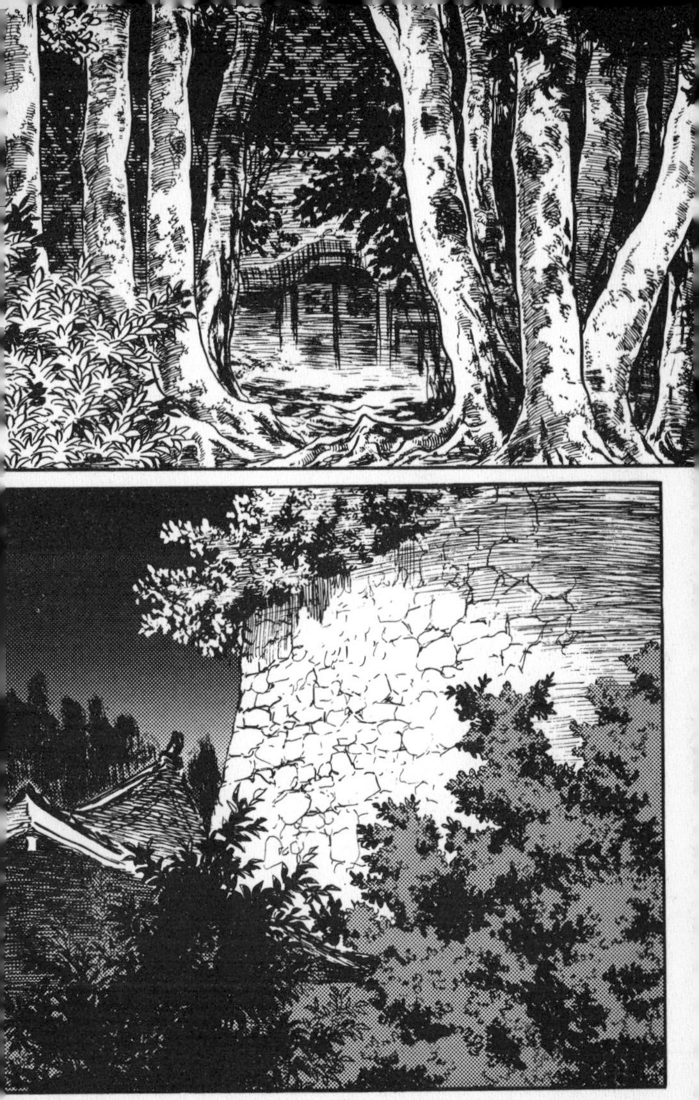

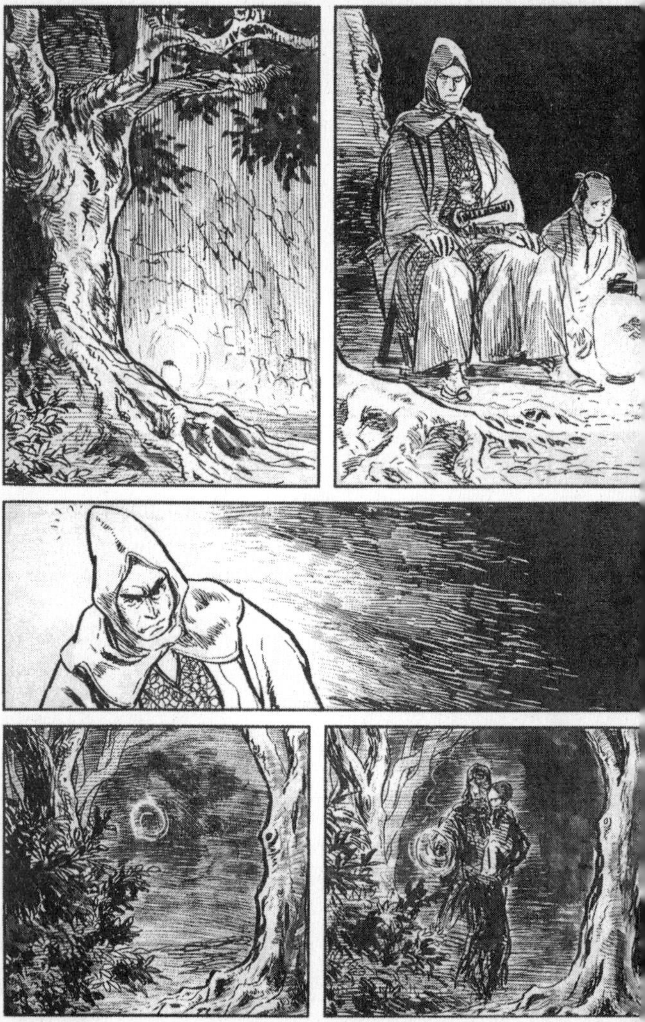

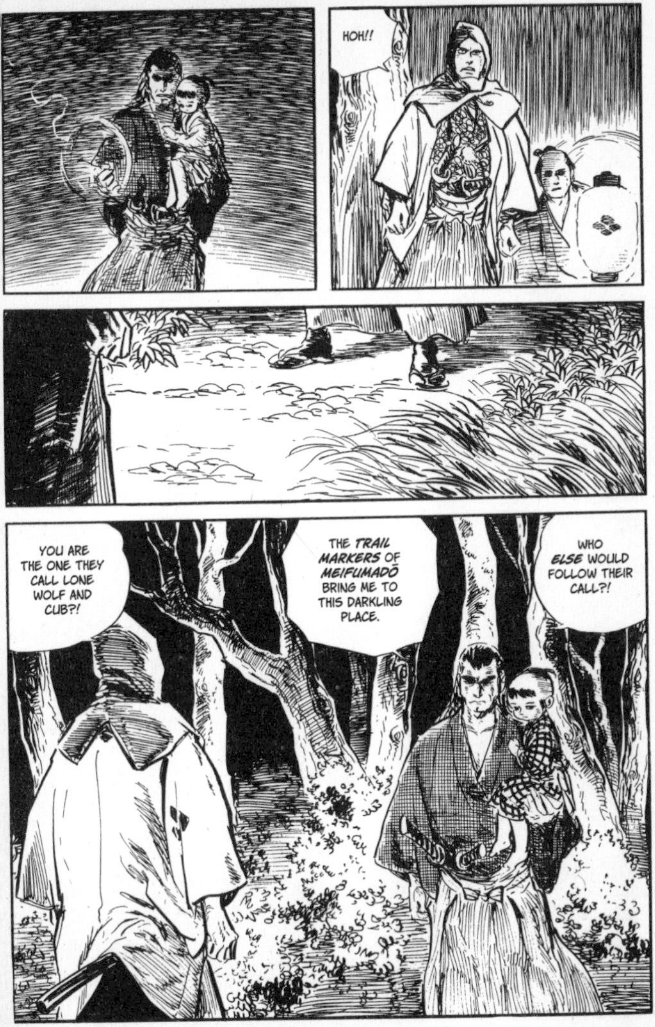
HOH!!
YOU ARE THE ONE THEY CALL LONE WOLF AND CUB?!
THE *TRAIL MARKERS* OF *MEIFUMADŌ* BRING ME TO THIS DARKLING PLACE.
WHO *ELSE* WOULD FOLLOW THEIR CALL?!

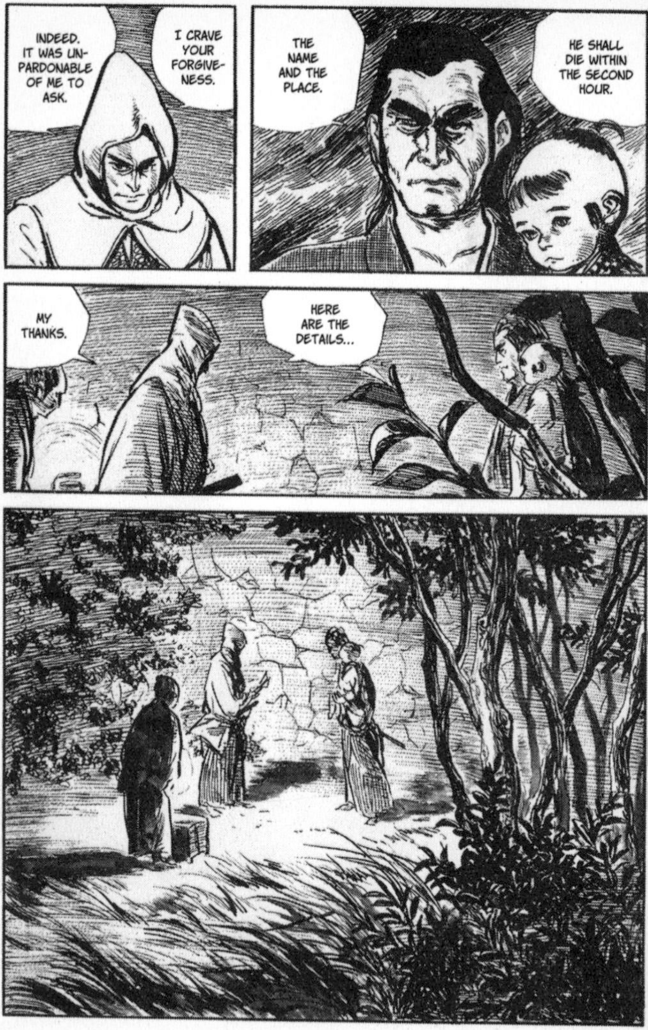
INDEED. IT WAS UN-PARDONABLE OF ME TO ASK.
I CRAVE YOUR FORGIVE-NESS.
THE NAME AND THE PLACE.
HE SHALL DIE WITHIN THE SECOND HOUR.
MY THANKS.
HERE ARE THE DETAILS...

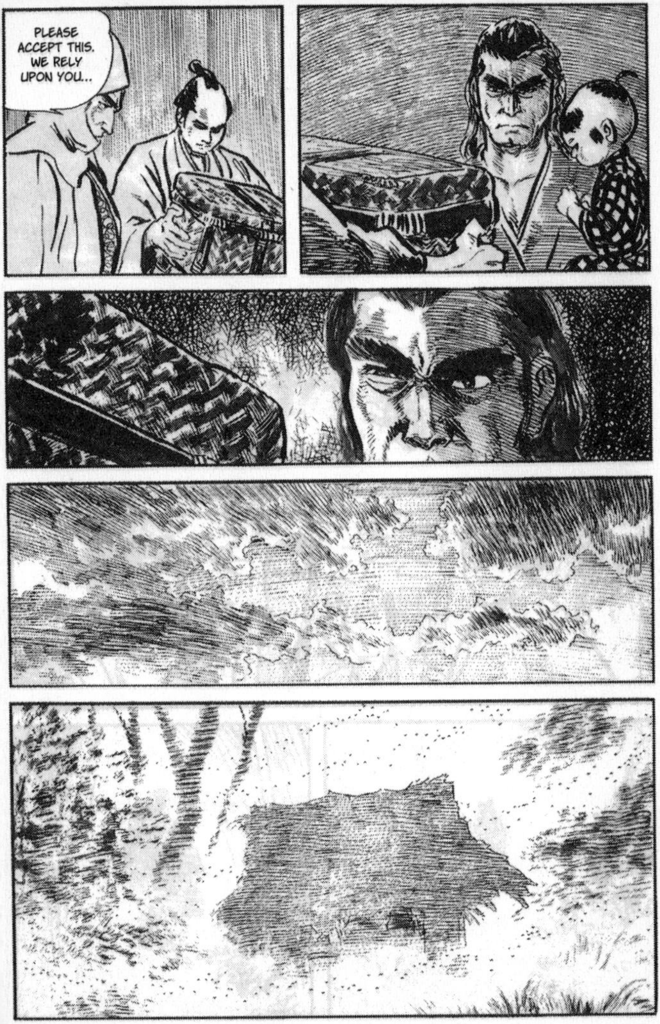
PLEASE ACCEPT THIS. WE RELY UPON YOU...

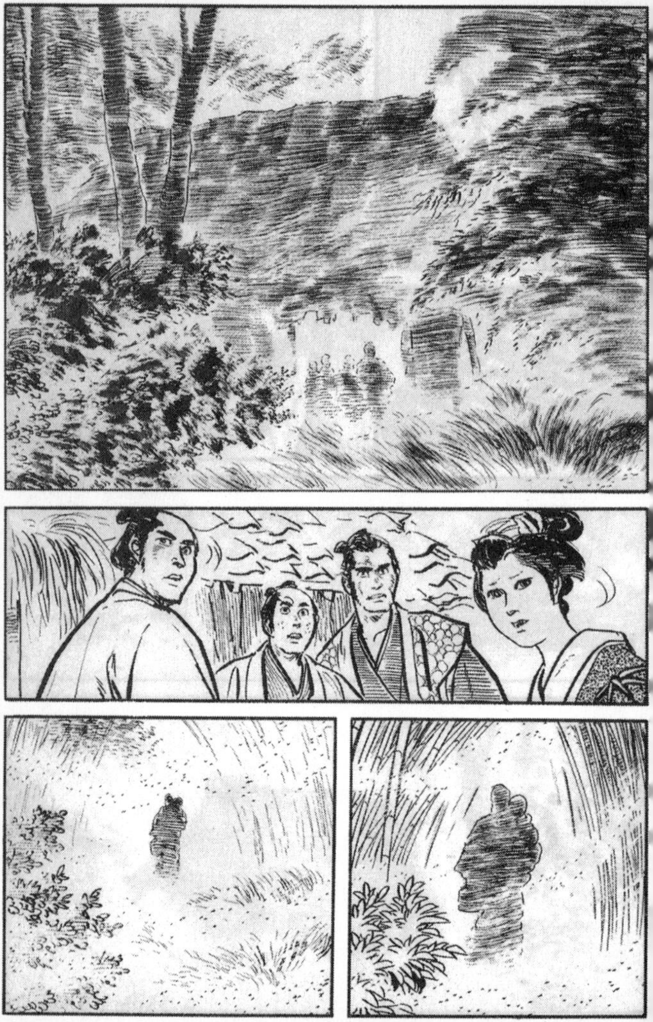

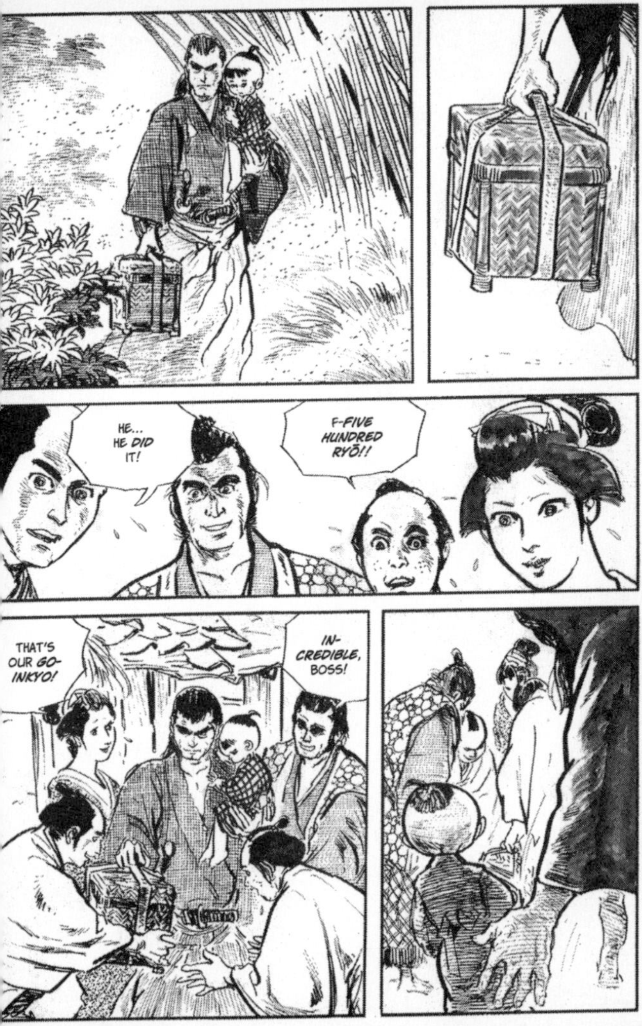
HE... HE DID IT!
F-FIVE HUNDRED RYŌ!!
THAT'S OUR GO-INKYO!
IN-CREDIBLE, BOSS!

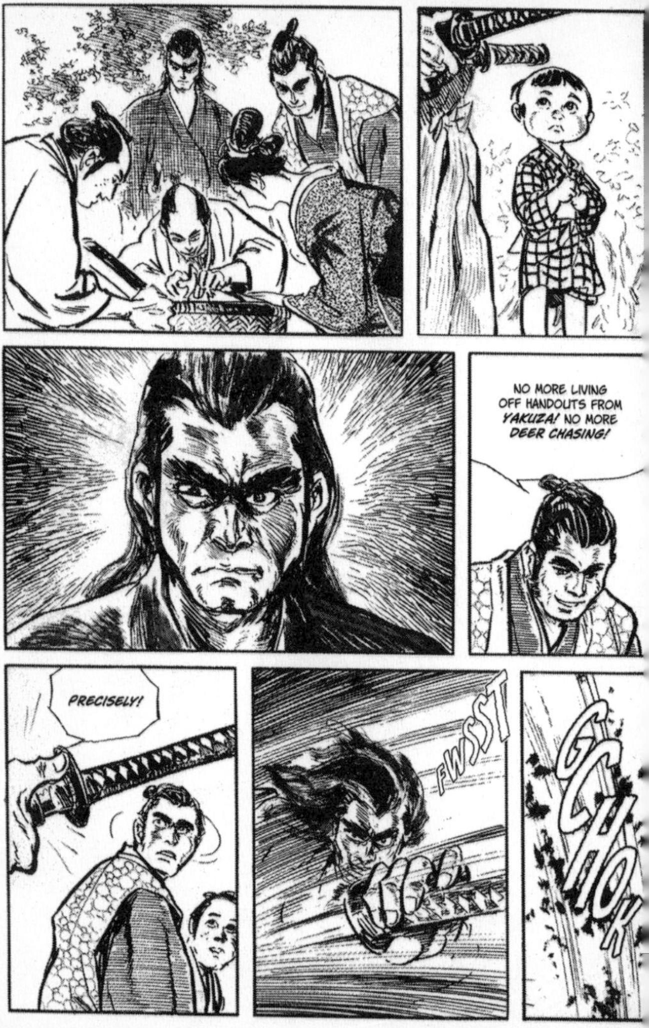
NO MORE LIVING OFF HANDOUTS FROM *YAKUZA!* NO MORE *DEER CHASING!*
PRECISELY!
FWSST
GCHOK

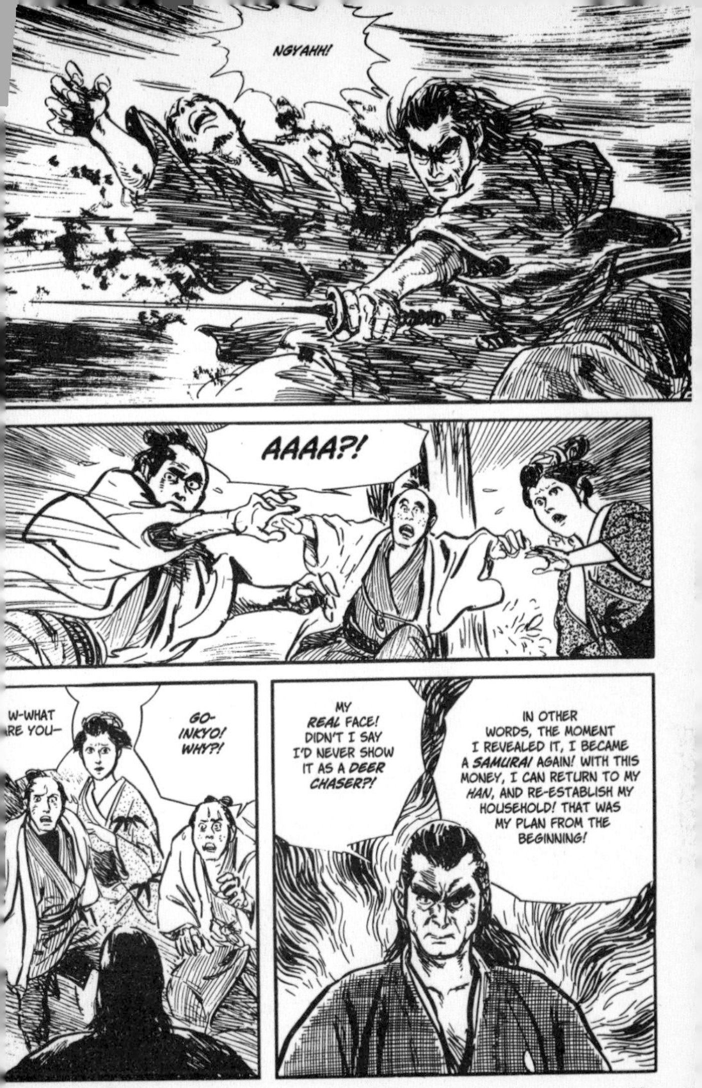
NGYAHH!
AAAA?!
W-WHAT ARE YOU—
GO-INKYO! WHY?!
MY REAL FACE! DIDN'T I SAY I'D NEVER SHOW IT AS A DEER CHASER?!
IN OTHER WORDS, THE MOMENT I REVEALED IT, I BECAME A SAMURAI AGAIN! WITH THIS MONEY, I CAN RETURN TO MY HAN, AND RE-ESTABLISH MY HOUSEHOLD! THAT WAS MY PLAN FROM THE BEGINNING!

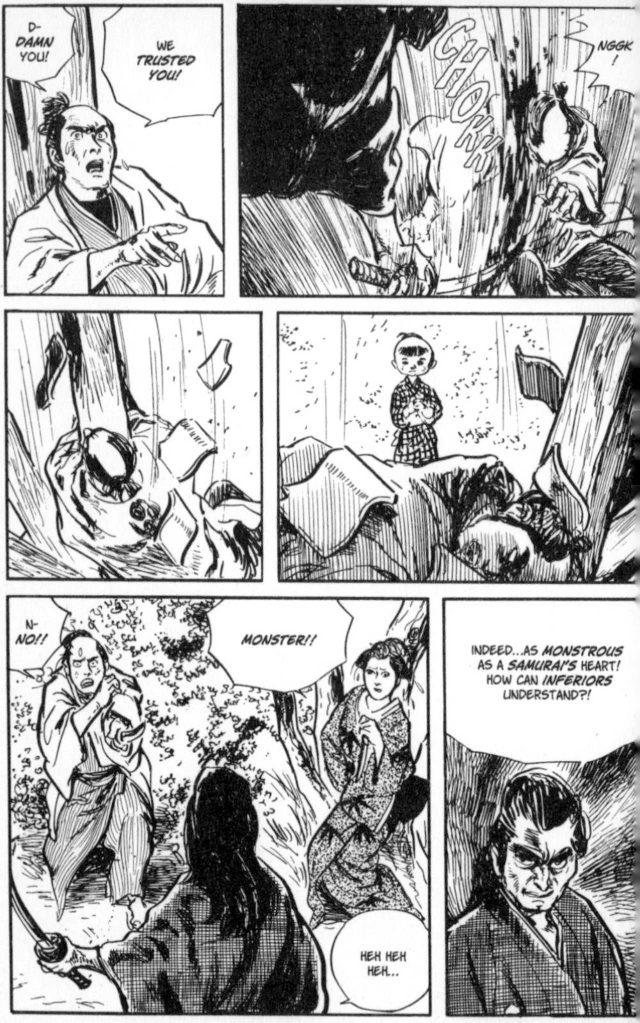
D- DAMN YOU!
WE TRUSTED YOU!
CHOKK
NGGK!
N- NO!!
MONSTER!!
HEH HEH HEH...
INDEED...AS MONSTROUS AS A SAMURAI'S HEART! HOW CAN INFERIORS UNDERSTAND?!

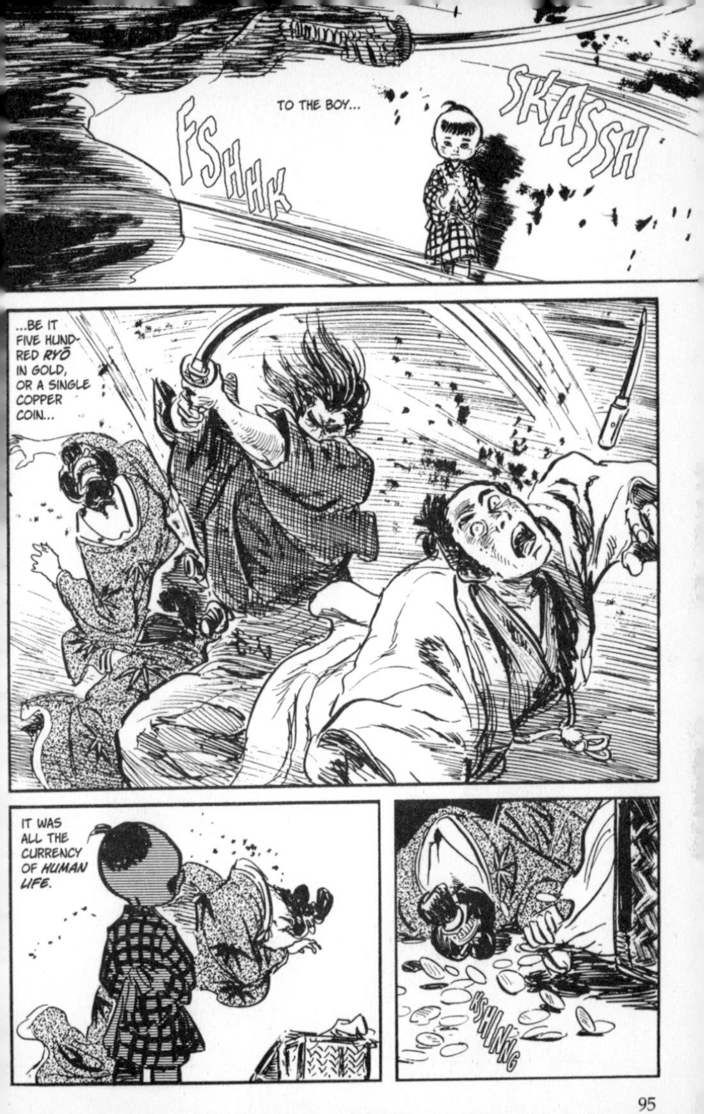
FSHHK
TO THE BOY...
SKASSH
...BE IT FIVE HUNDRED *RYŌ* IN GOLD, OR A SINGLE COPPER COIN...
IT WAS ALL THE CURRENCY OF *HUMAN LIFE*.
KSHINNG

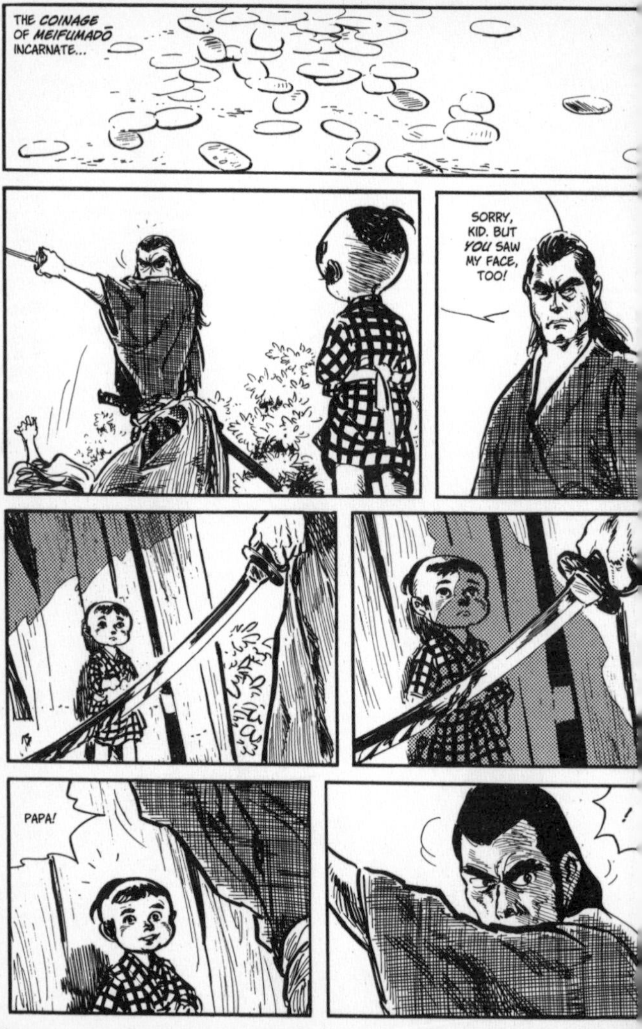
THE *COINAGE* OF *MEIFUMADŌ* INCARNATE...
SORRY, KID. BUT *YOU* SAW MY FACE, TOO!
PAPA!
!

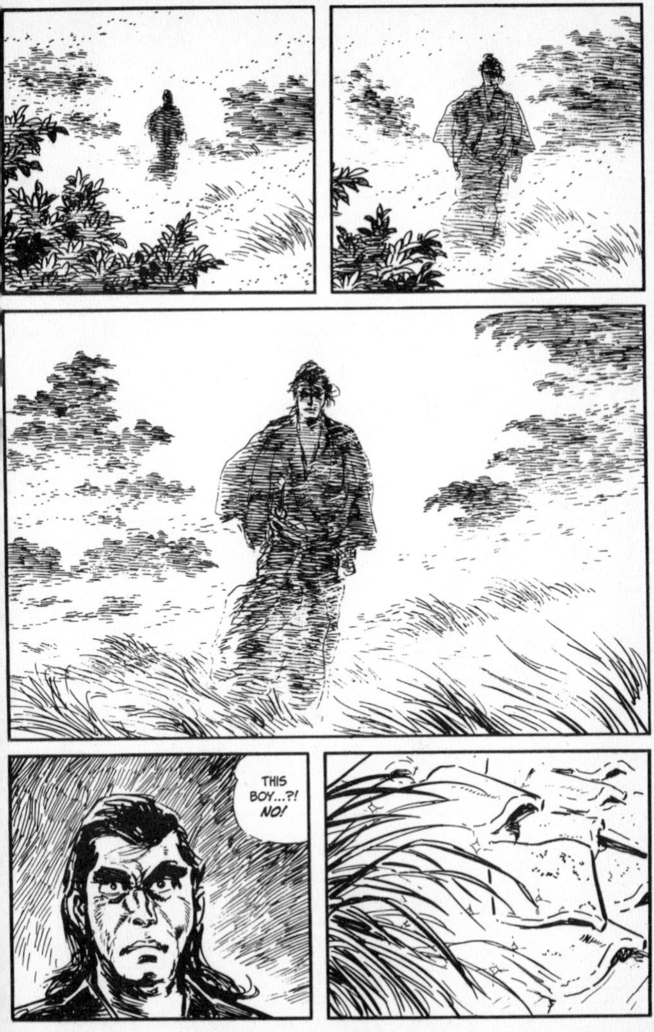
THIS BOY...?! NO!

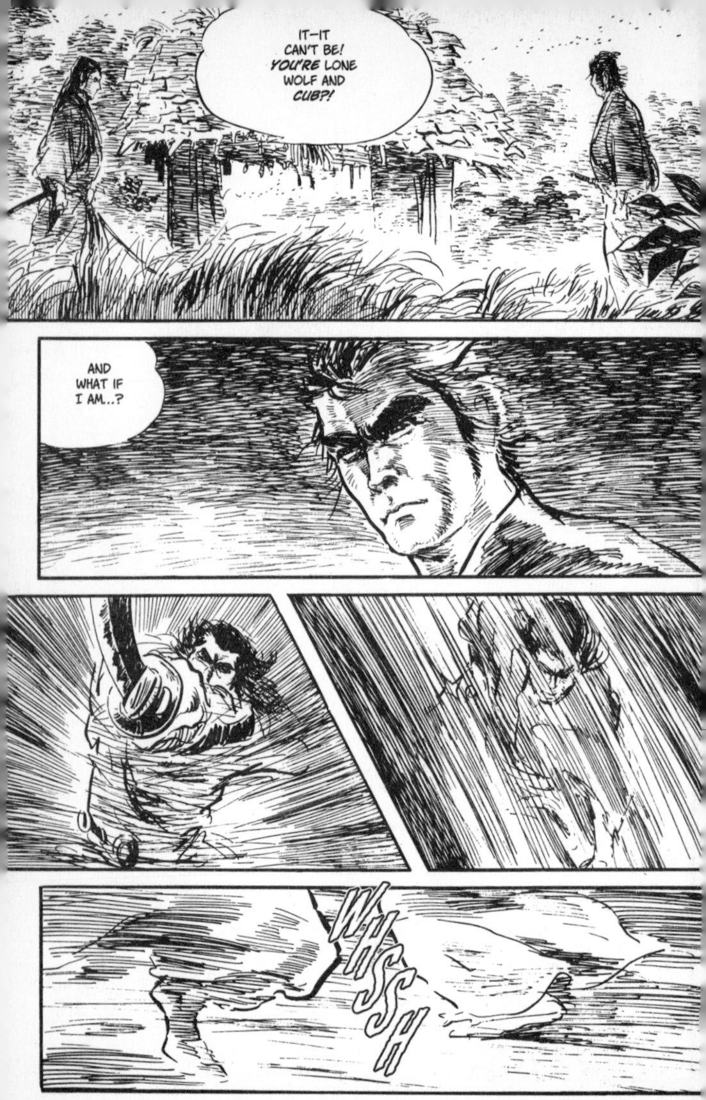
IT—IT CAN'T BE! *YOU'RE* LONE WOLF AND *CUB?!*
AND WHAT IF I AM..?
WHSSH

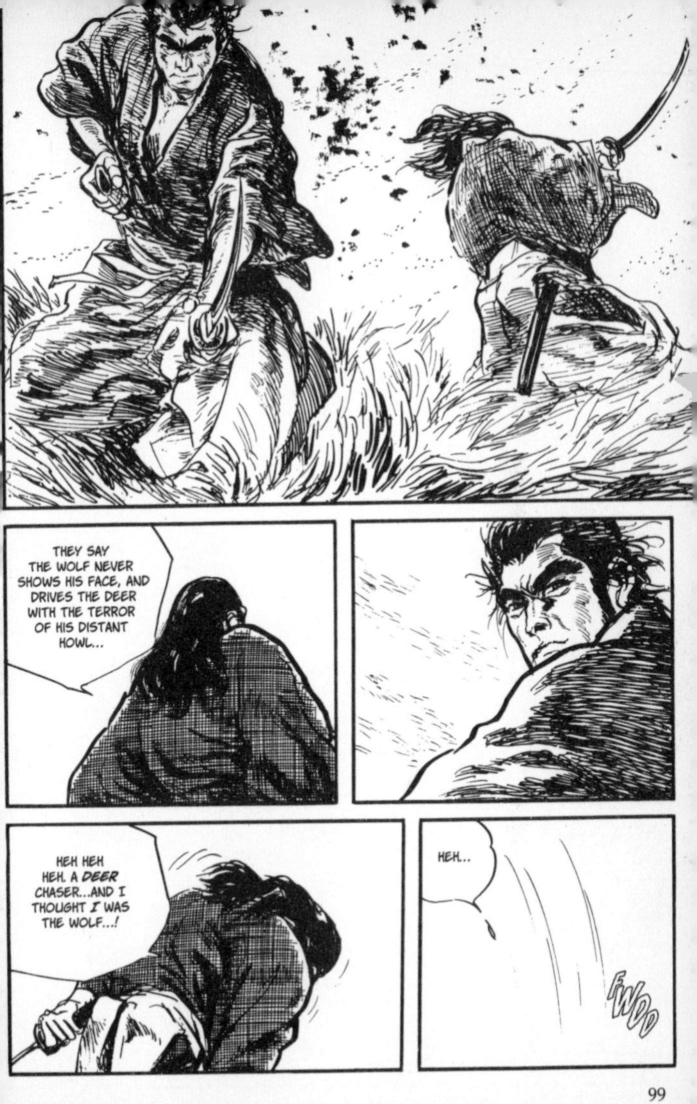
THEY SAY THE WOLF NEVER SHOWS HIS FACE, AND DRIVES THE DEER WITH THE TERROR OF HIS DISTANT HOWL...
HEH HEH HEH. A *DEER* CHASER...AND I THOUGHT *I* WAS THE WOLF...!
HEH...
FWOO

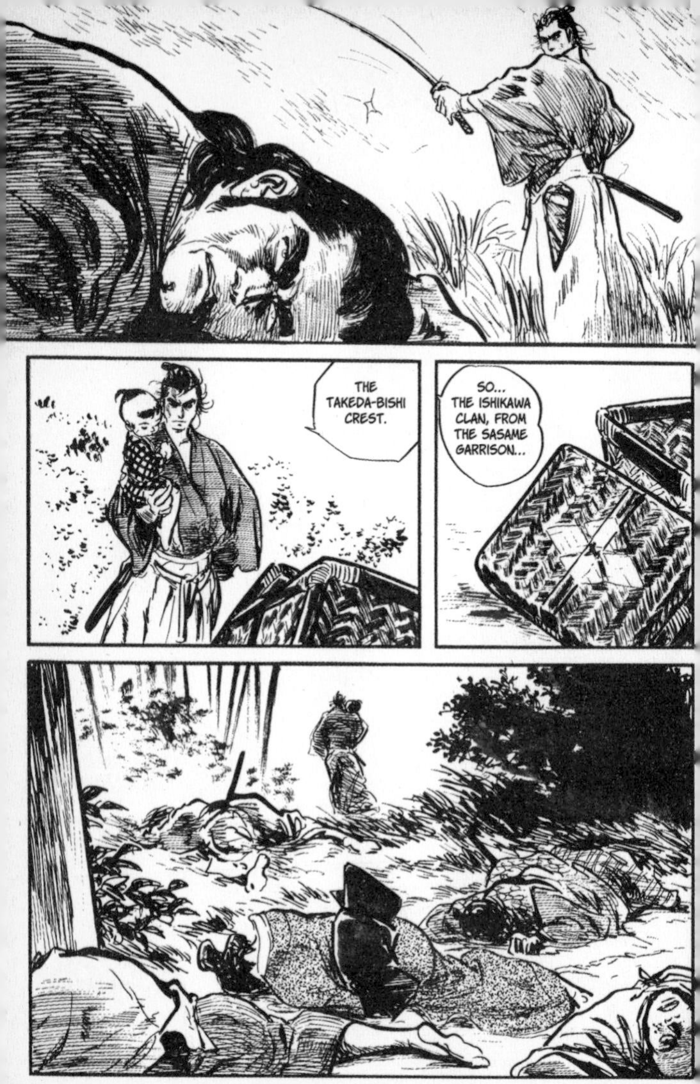
THE TAKEDA-BISHI CREST.
SO... THE ISHIKAWA CLAN, FROM THE SASAME GARRISON...

the thirty-first

Hunger Town

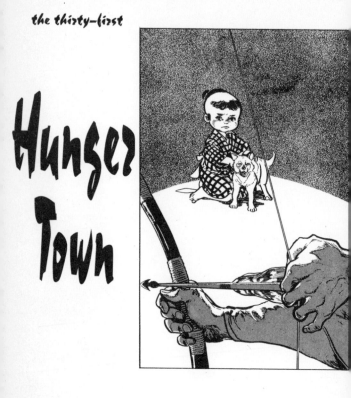

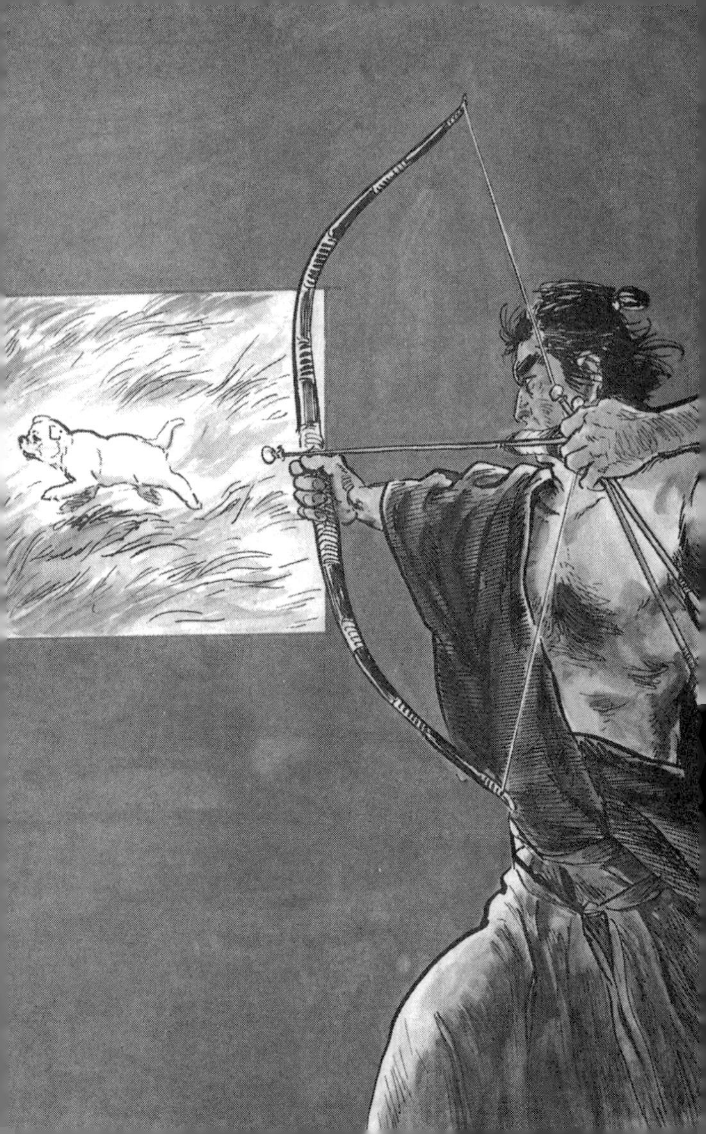

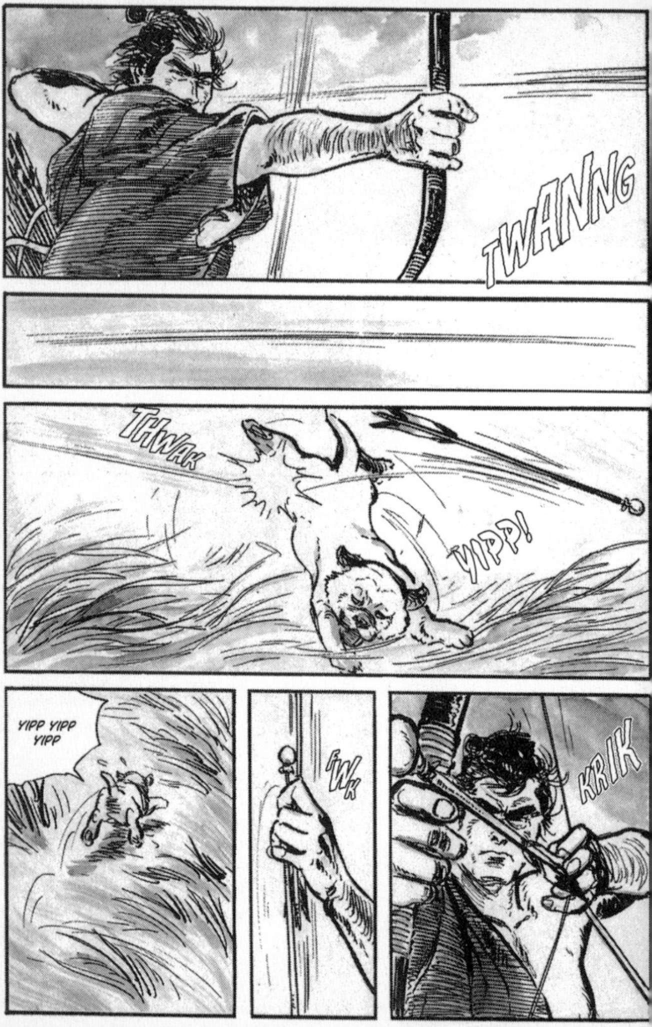
TWANNG
THWAK
YIPP!
YIPP YIPP YIPP
FWK
KRIK

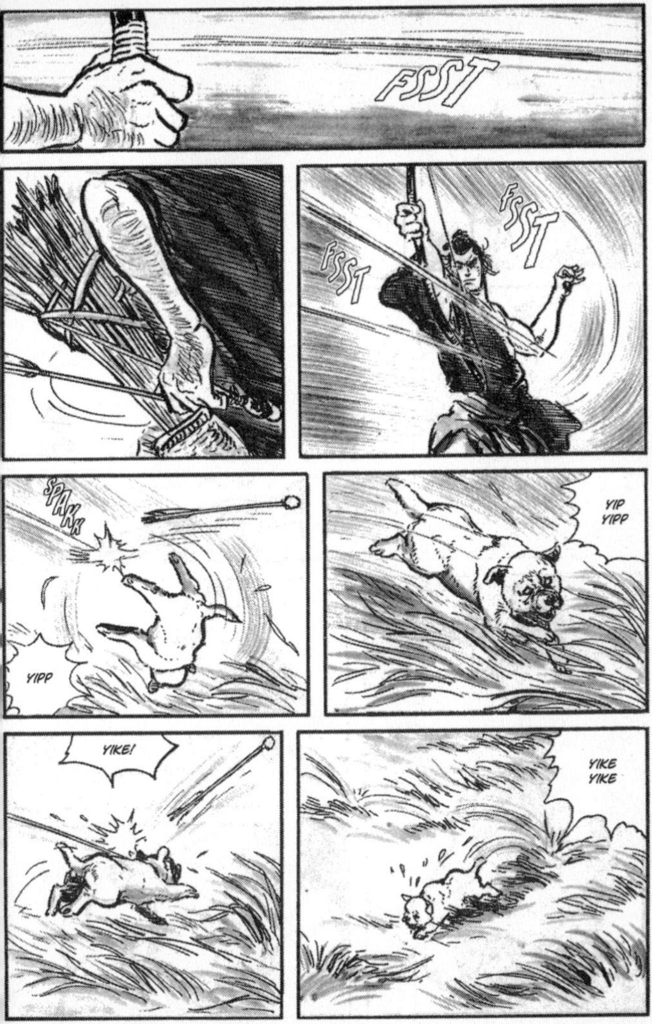
FSST
FSST
FSST
SPAKK
YIPP
YIP YIPP
YIKE!
YIKE YIKE

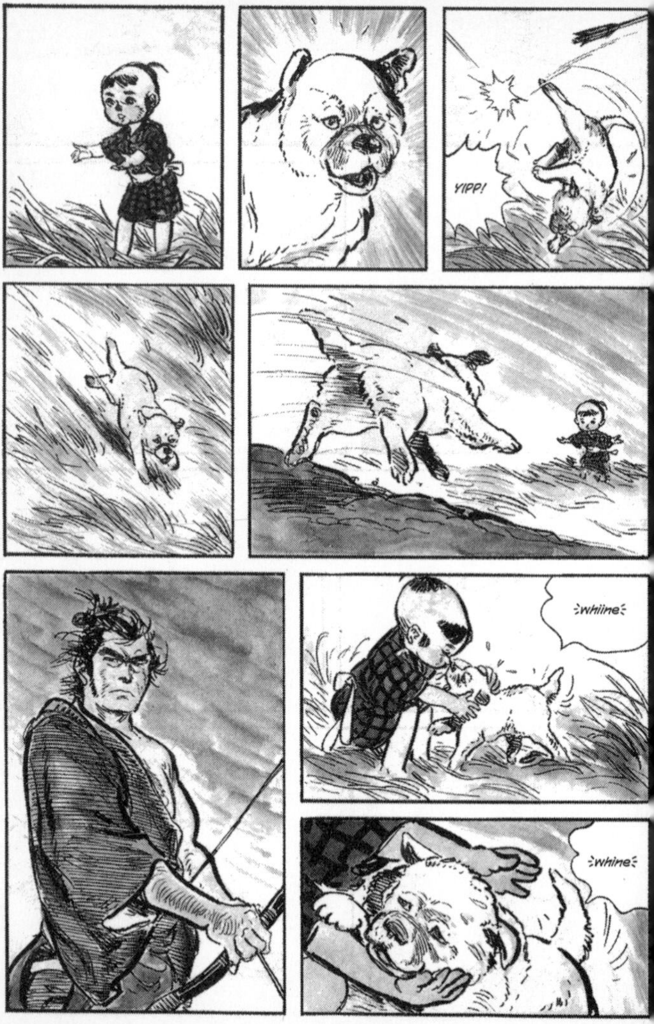
YIPP!
whiine
whine

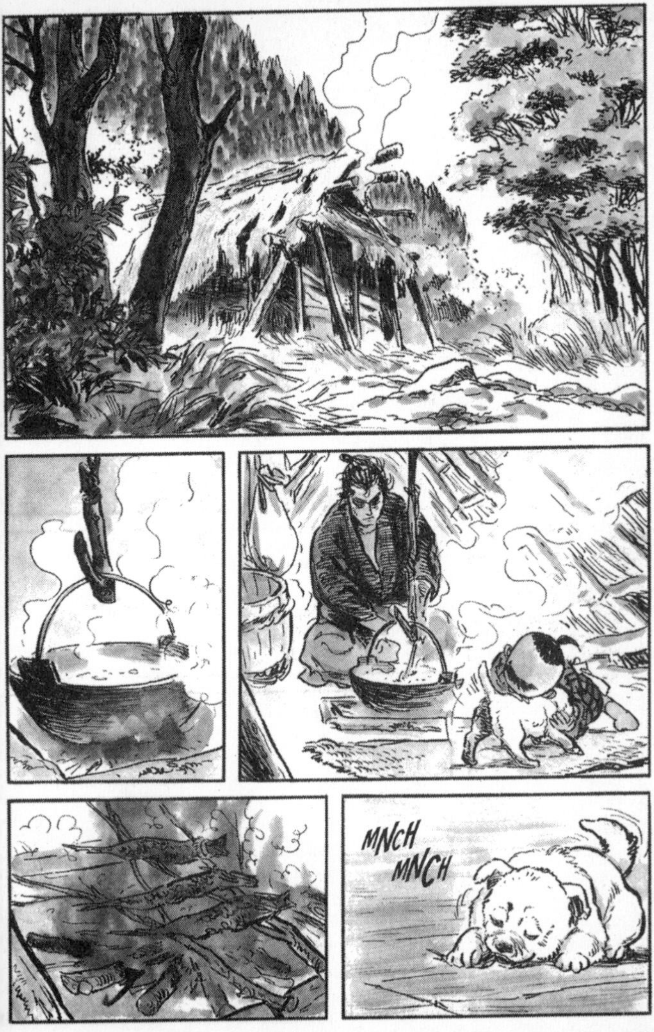
MNCH
MNCH

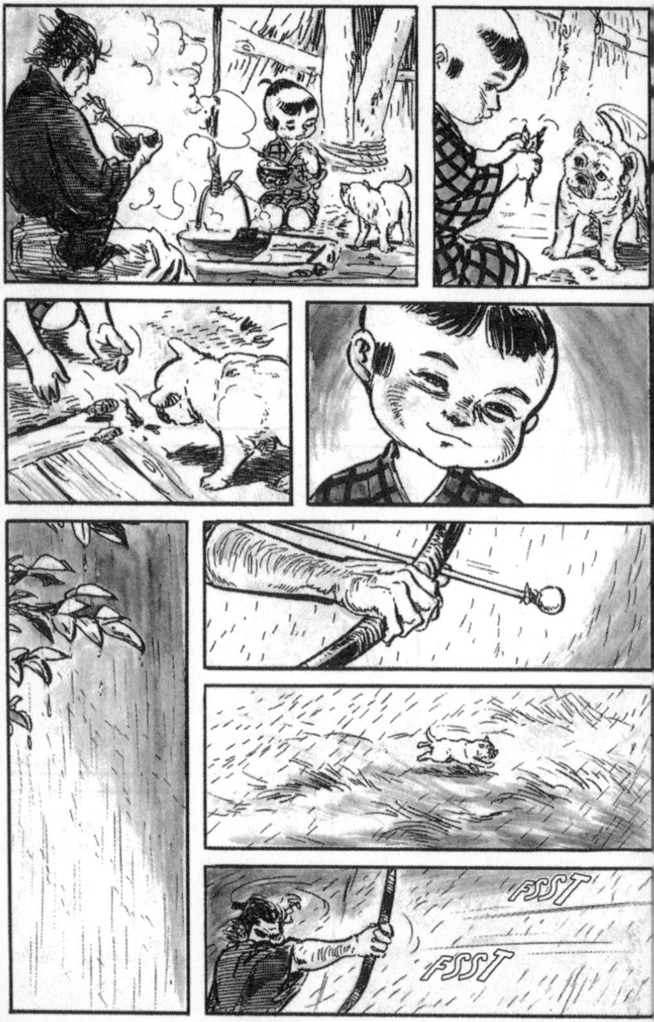
FSST
FSST

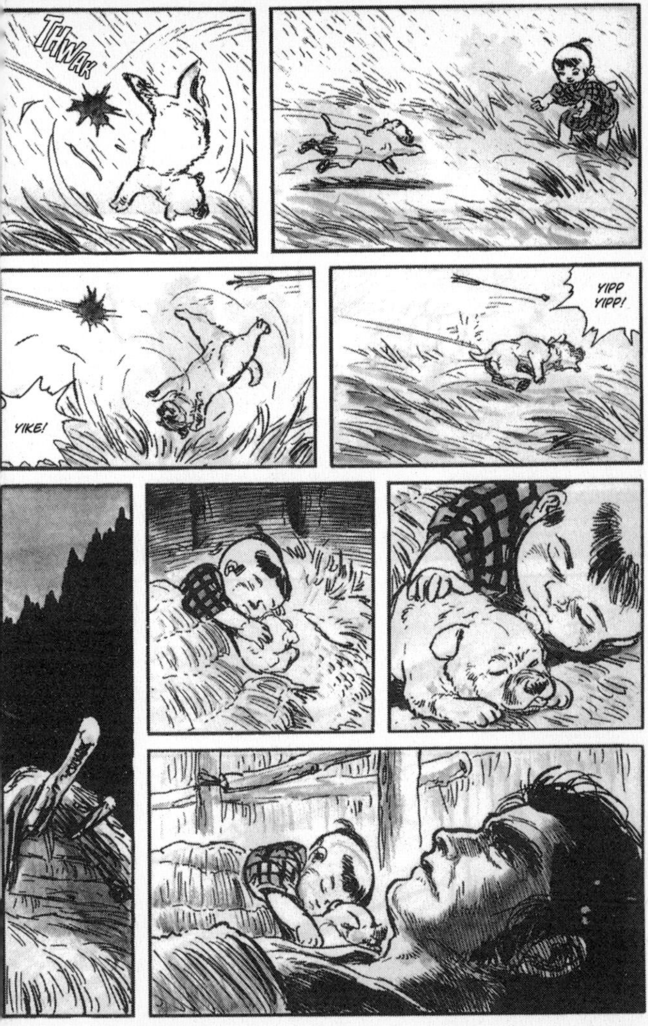
THWAK
YIKE!
YIPP YIPP!

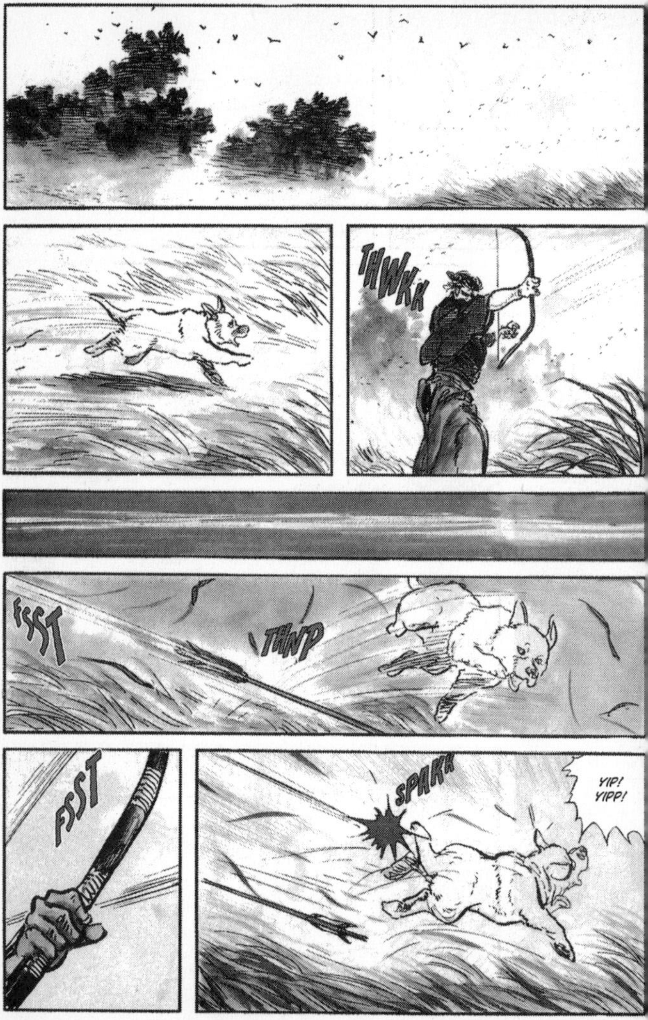
THWKK
FSST
THNP
FSST
SPAKK
YIP! YIPP!

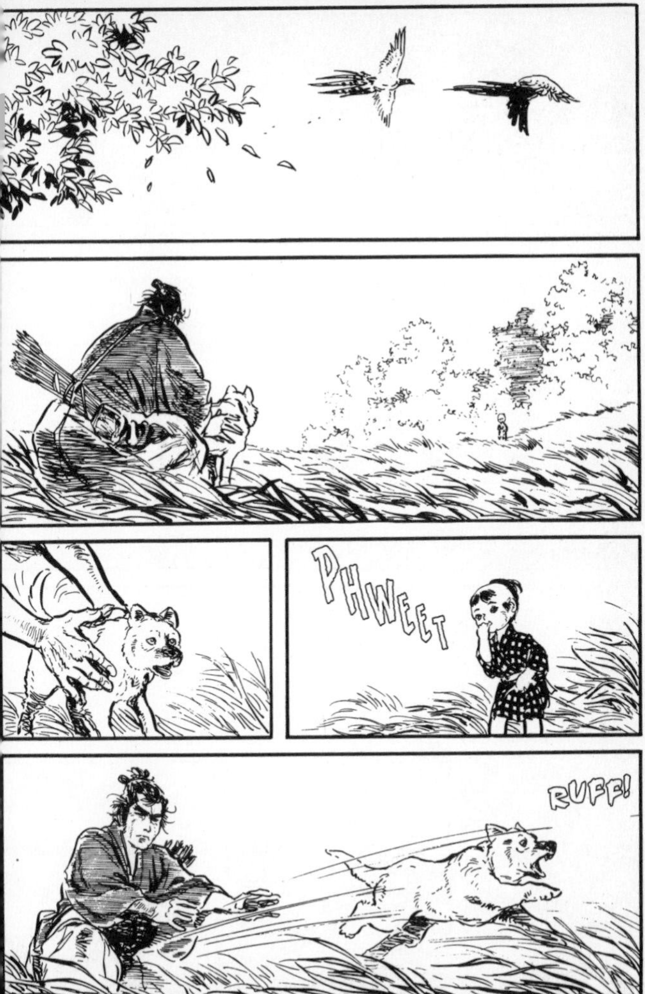
PHWEET
RUFF!

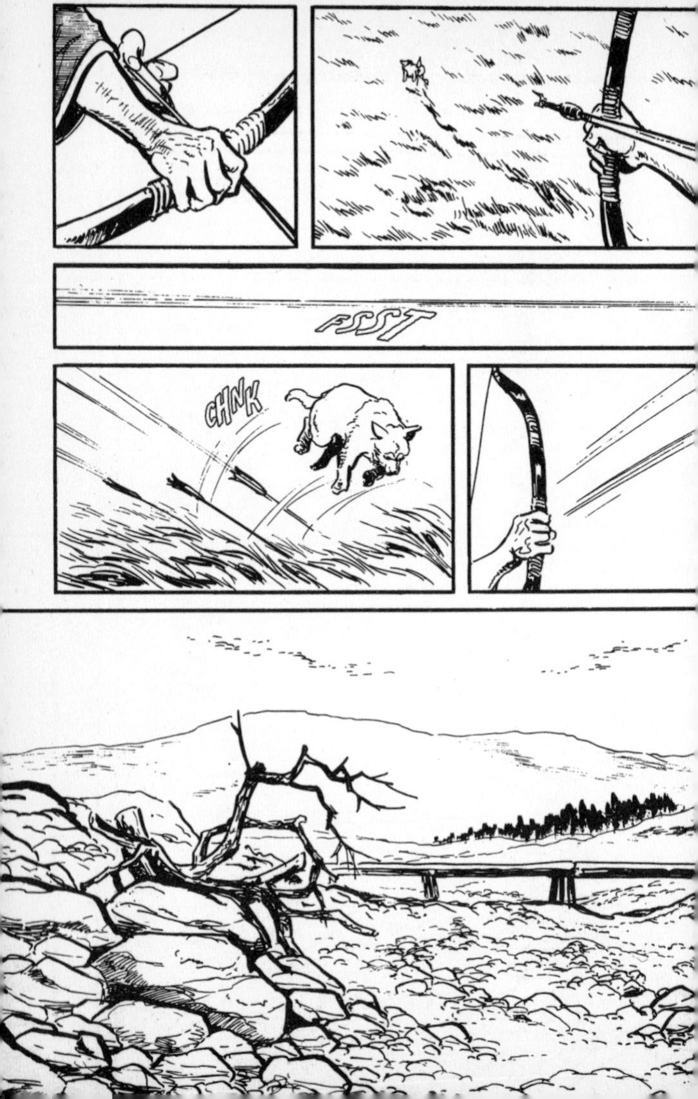
FSST
CHNK

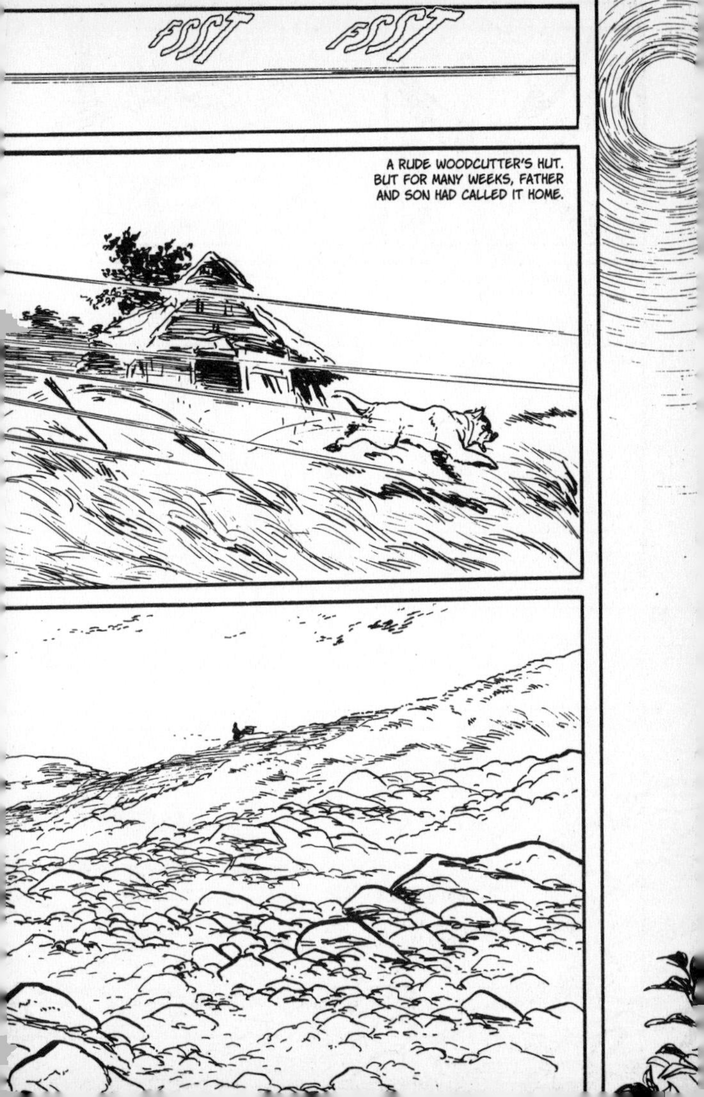
FSST FSST
A RUDE WOODCUTTER'S HUT. BUT FOR MANY WEEKS, FATHER AND SON HAD CALLED IT HOME.

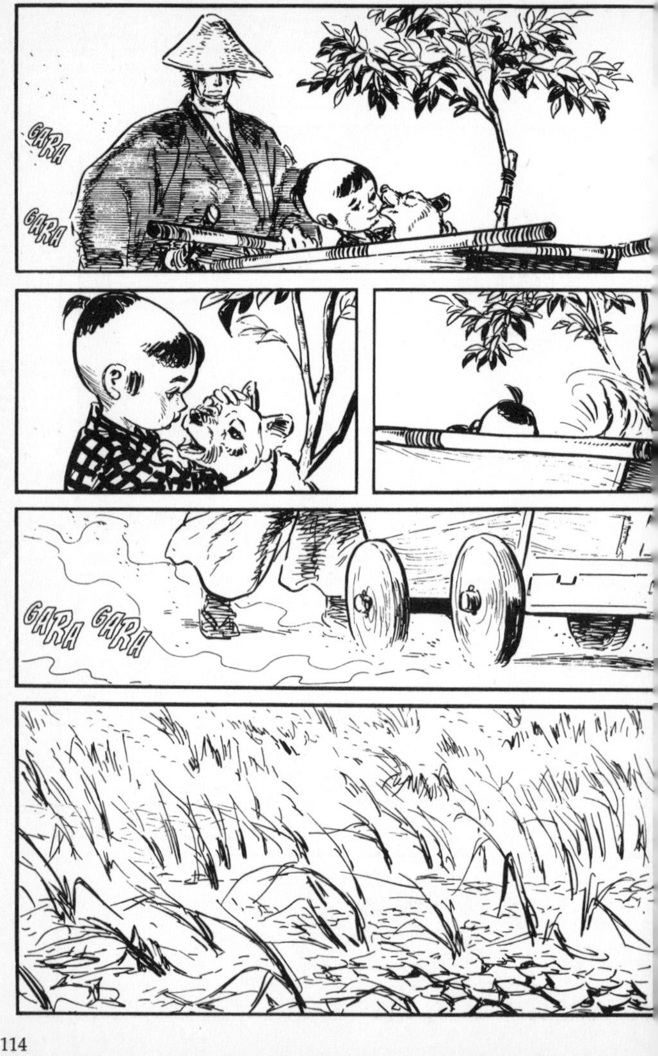
GARA
GARA
GARA
GARA

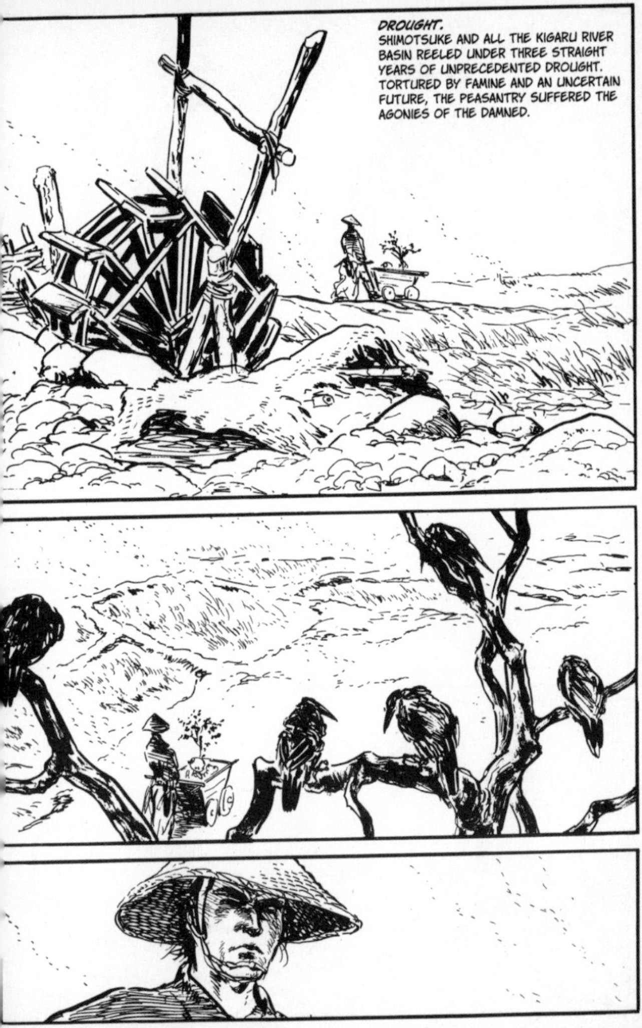
DROUGHT.
SHIMOTSUKE AND ALL THE KIGARU RIVER BASIN REELED UNDER THREE STRAIGHT YEARS OF UNPRECEDENTED DROUGHT. TORTURED BY FAMINE AND AN UNCERTAIN FUTURE, THE PEASANTRY SUFFERED THE AGONIES OF THE DAMNED.

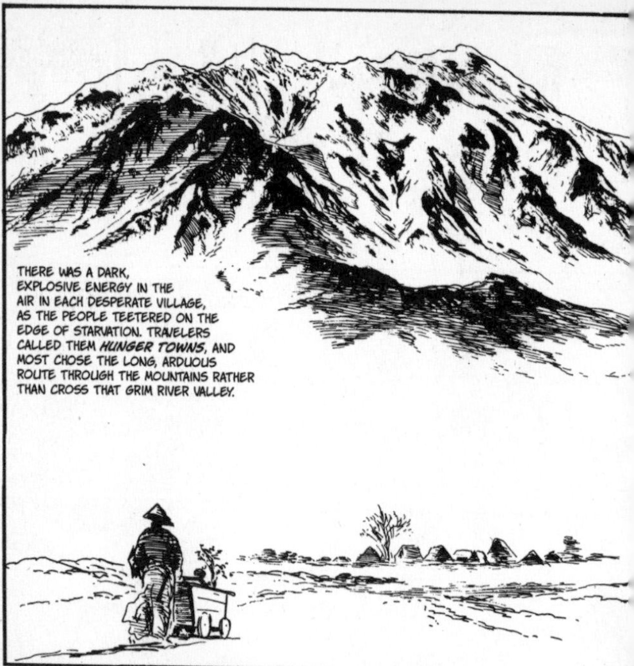
THERE WAS A DARK, EXPLOSIVE ENERGY IN THE AIR IN EACH DESPERATE VILLAGE, AS THE PEOPLE TEETERED ON THE EDGE OF STARVATION. TRAVELERS CALLED THEM *HUNGER TOWNS*, AND MOST CHOSE THE LONG, ARDUOUS ROUTE THROUGH THE MOUNTAINS RATHER THAN CROSS THAT GRIM RIVER VALLEY.

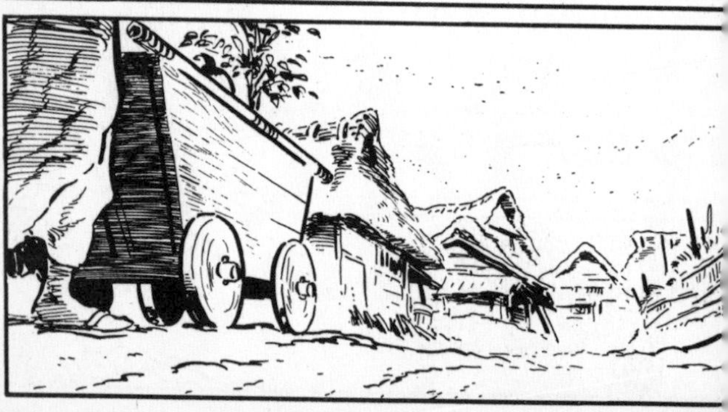

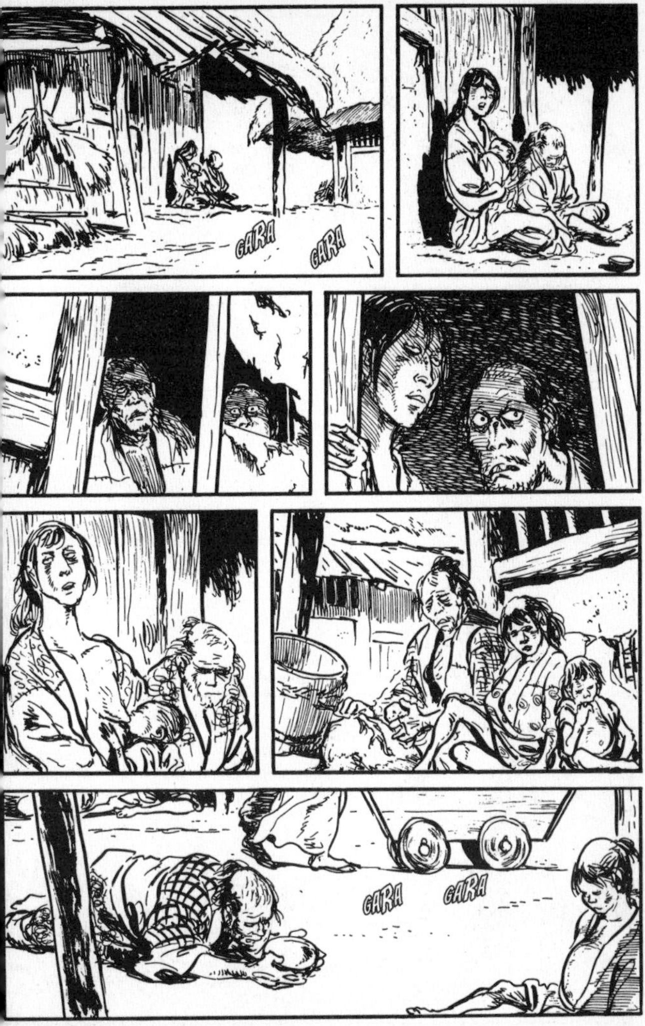
GARA
GARA
GARA
GARA

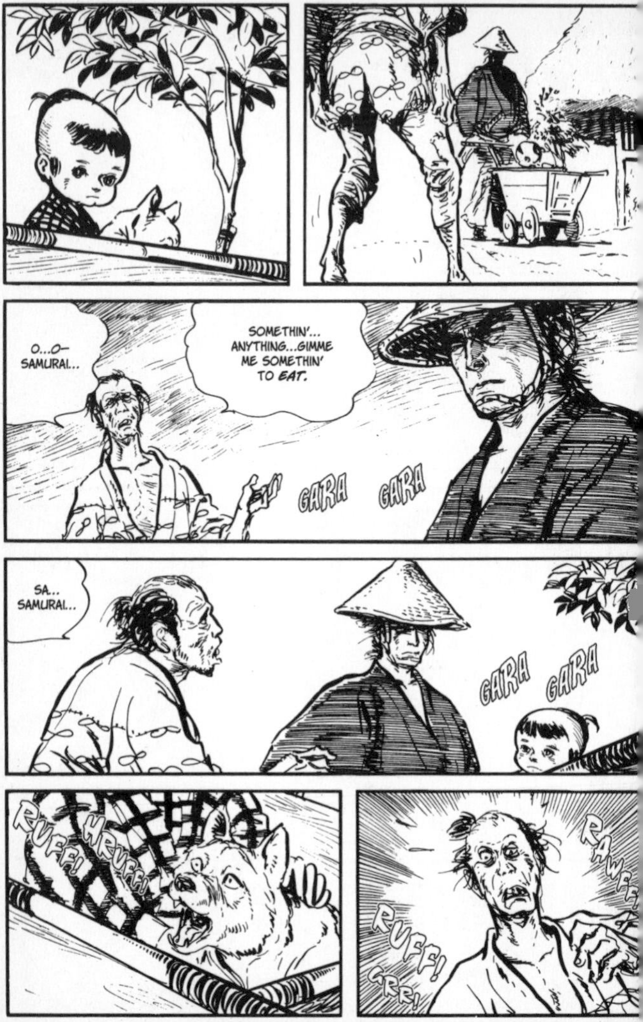
O...O—
SAMURAI...
SOMETHIN'...
ANYTHING...GIMME
ME SOMETHIN'
TO EAT.
GARA
GARA
SA...
SAMURAI...
GARA
GARA
RUFF!
HRUFF!
RUFF!
GRR!

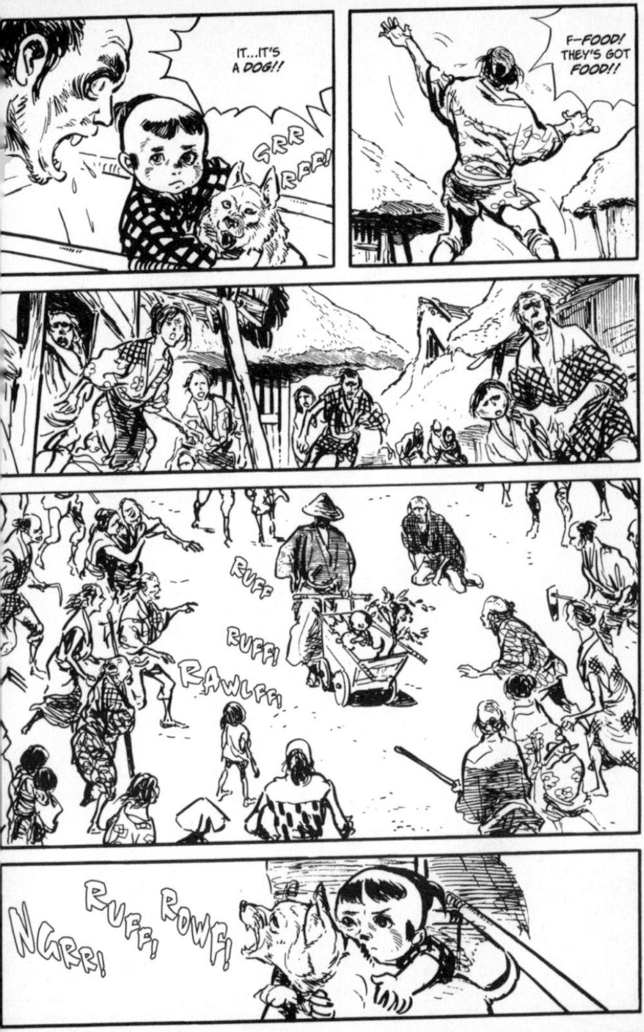
IT...IT'S A DOG!!
GRR
RFF!
F-FOOD! THEY'S GOT FOOD!!
RUFF
RUFF!
RAWLFF!
NGRR!
RUFF!
ROWF!

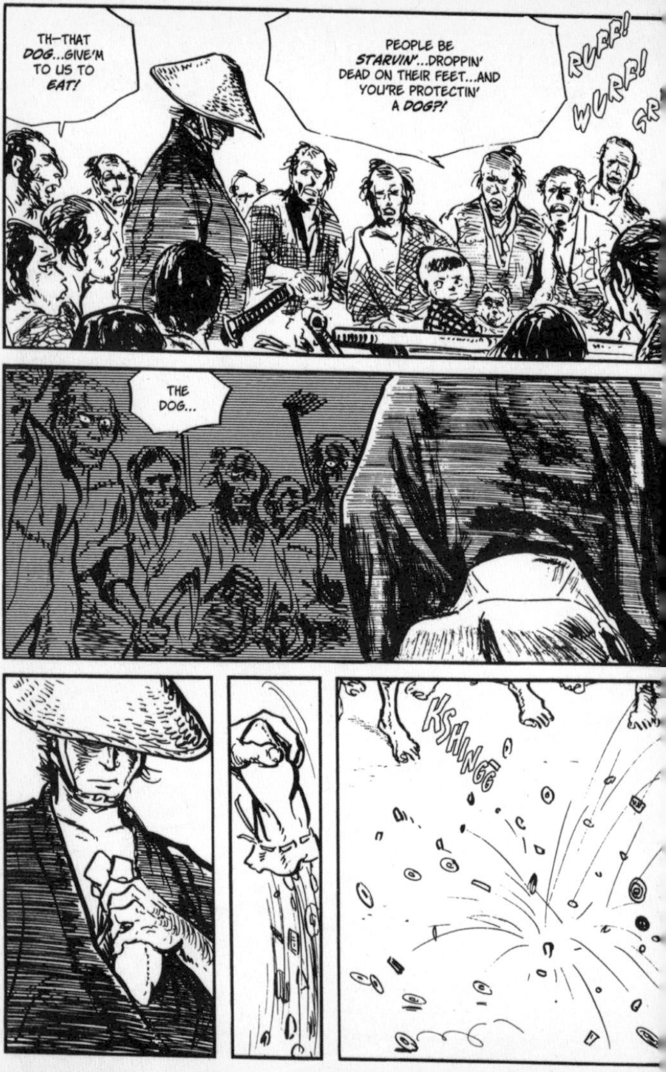
TH—THAT *DOG*...GIVE'M TO US TO *EAT!*
PEOPLE BE *STARVIN'*...DROPPIN' DEAD ON THEIR FEET...AND YOU'RE PROTECTIN' A *DOG?!*
RUFF!
WURF!
GR
THE DOG...
KSHINGG

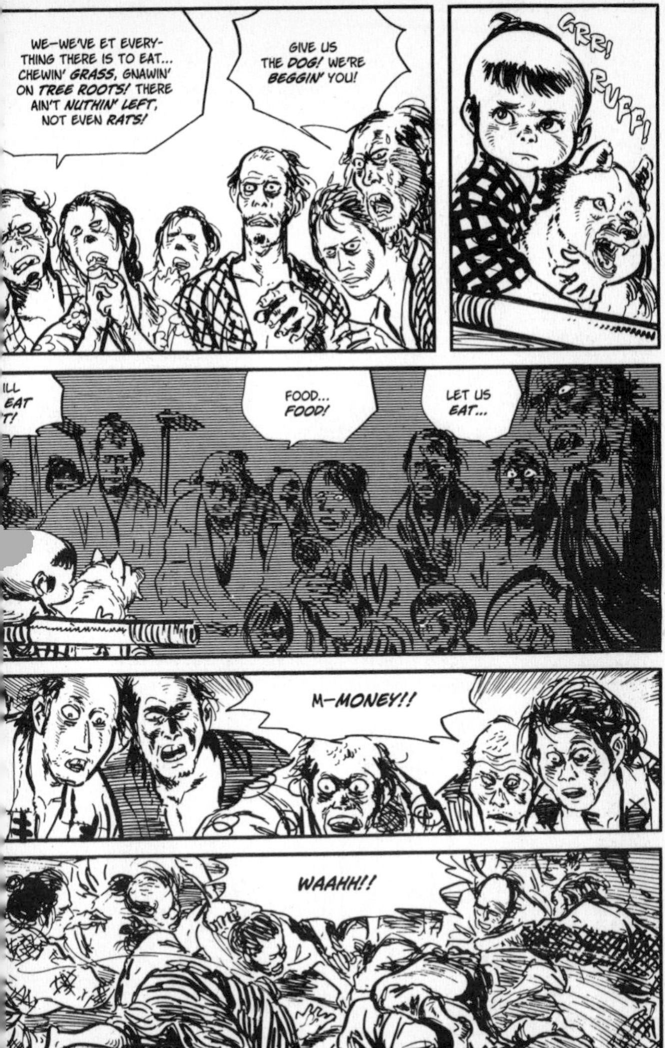
WE—WE'VE ET EVERYTHING THERE IS TO EAT... CHEWIN' *GRASS*, GNAWIN' ON *TREE ROOTS!* THERE AIN'T *NUTHIN' LEFT*, NOT EVEN *RATS!*
GIVE US THE *DOG!* WE'RE *BEGGIN'* YOU!
GRR!
RUFF!
FOOD... *FOOD!*
LET US EAT...
M-*MONEY!!*
WAAHH!!

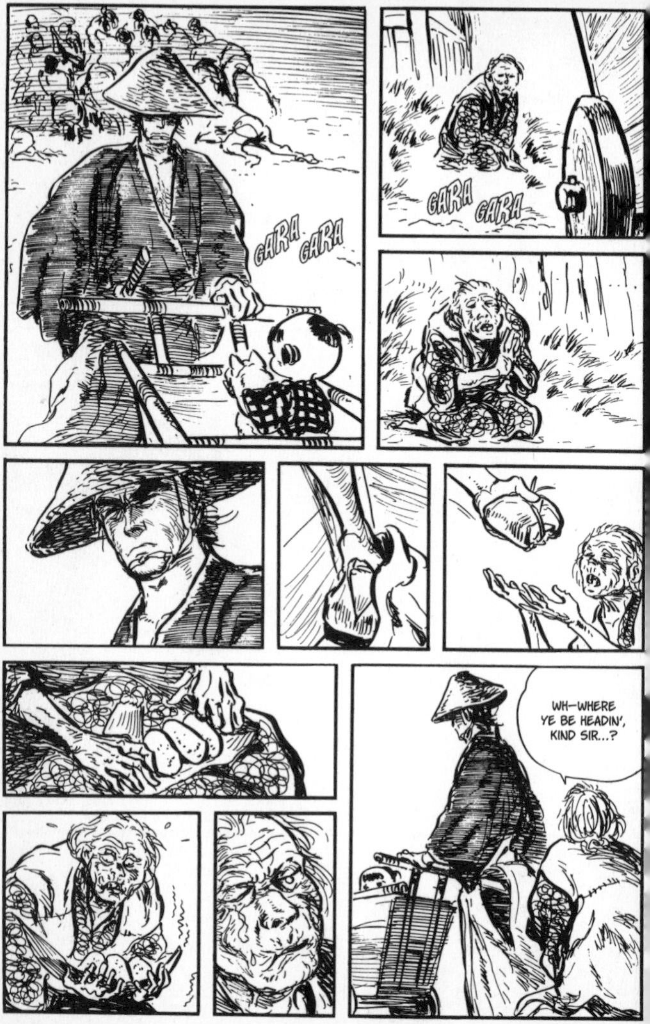
GARA GARA
GARA GARA
WH—WHERE YE BE HEADIN', KIND SIR...?

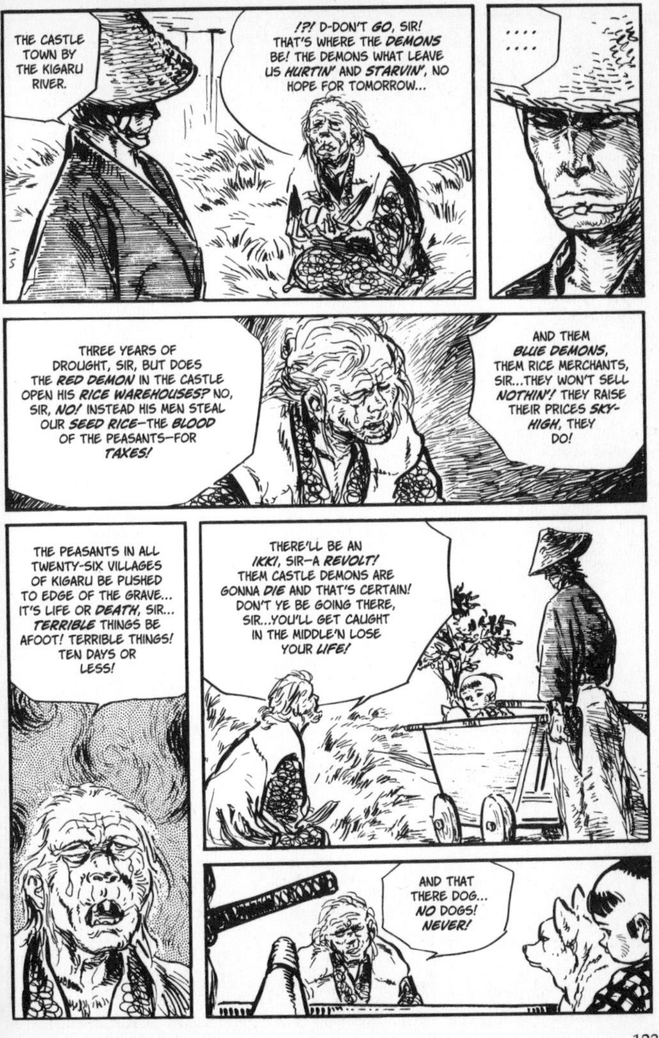
THE CASTLE TOWN BY THE KIGARU RIVER.
!?! D-DON'T GO, SIR! THAT'S WHERE THE DEMONS BE! THE DEMONS WHAT LEAVE US HURTIN' AND STARVIN', NO HOPE FOR TOMORROW...
....
THREE YEARS OF DROUGHT, SIR, BUT DOES THE RED DEMON IN THE CASTLE OPEN HIS RICE WAREHOUSES? NO, SIR, NO! INSTEAD HIS MEN STEAL OUR SEED RICE—THE BLOOD OF THE PEASANTS—FOR TAXES!
AND THEM BLUE DEMONS, THEM RICE MERCHANTS, SIR...THEY WON'T SELL NOTHIN'! THEY RAISE THEIR PRICES SKY-HIGH, THEY DO!
THE PEASANTS IN ALL TWENTY-SIX VILLAGES OF KIGARU BE PUSHED TO EDGE OF THE GRAVE... IT'S LIFE OR DEATH, SIR... TERRIBLE THINGS BE AFOOT! TERRIBLE THINGS! TEN DAYS OR LESS!
THERE'LL BE AN IKKI, SIR—A REVOLT! THEM CASTLE DEMONS ARE GONNA DIE AND THAT'S CERTAIN! DON'T YE BE GOING THERE, SIR...YOU'LL GET CAUGHT IN THE MIDDLE'N LOSE YOUR LIFE!
AND THAT THERE DOG... NO DOGS! NEVER!

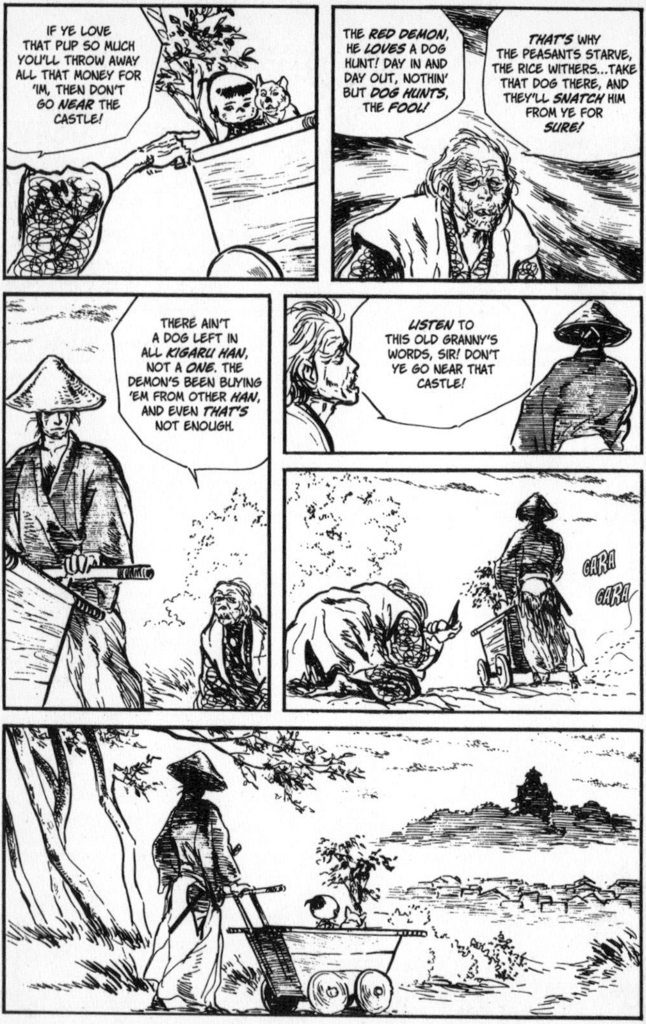
IF YE LOVE THAT PUP SO MUCH YOU'LL THROW AWAY ALL THAT MONEY FOR 'IM, THEN DON'T GO NEAR THE CASTLE!
THE RED DEMON, HE LOVES A DOG HUNT! DAY IN AND DAY OUT, NOTHIN' BUT DOG HUNTS, THE FOOL!
THAT'S WHY THE PEASANTS STARVE, THE RICE WITHERS...TAKE THAT DOG THERE, AND THEY'LL SNATCH HIM FROM YE FOR SURE!
THERE AIN'T A DOG LEFT IN ALL KIGARU HAN, NOT A ONE. THE DEMON'S BEEN BUYING 'EM FROM OTHER HAN, AND EVEN THAT'S NOT ENOUGH.
LISTEN TO THIS OLD GRANNY'S WORDS, SIR! DON'T YE GO NEAR THAT CASTLE!
GARA
GARA

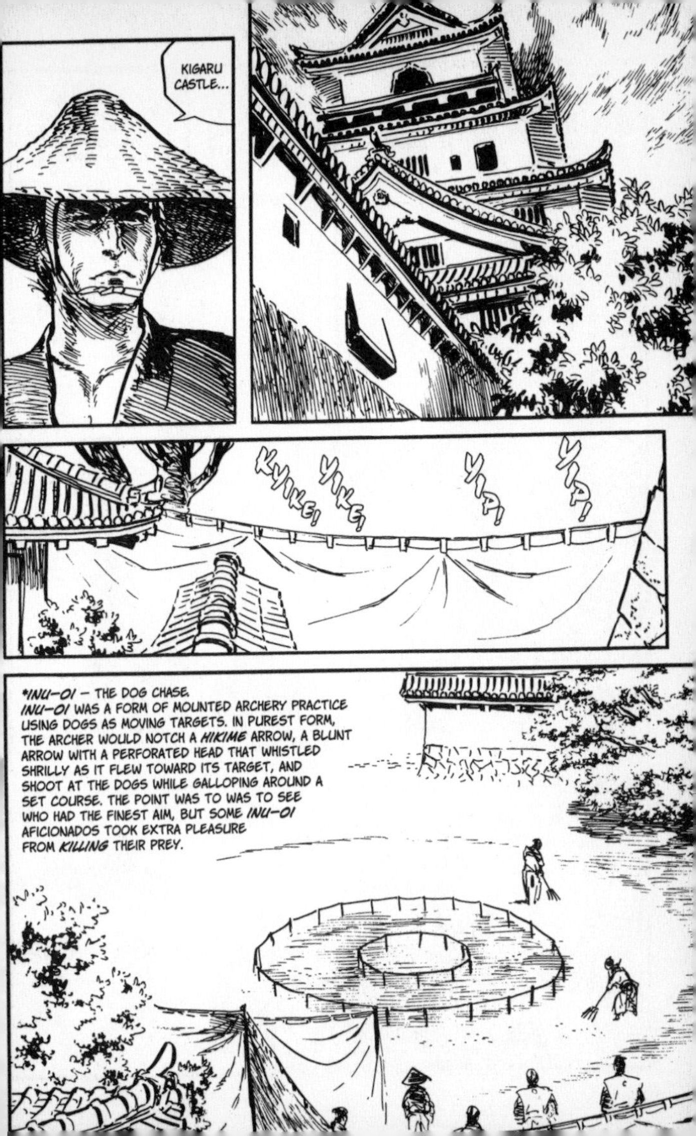
KIGARU CASTLE...
KYIKE, YIKE, YIP! YIP!
*INU-OI – THE DOG CHASE.
INU-OI WAS A FORM OF MOUNTED ARCHERY PRACTICE USING DOGS AS MOVING TARGETS. IN PUREST FORM, THE ARCHER WOULD NOTCH A HIKIME ARROW, A BLUNT ARROW WITH A PERFORATED HEAD THAT WHISTLED SHRILLY AS IT FLEW TOWARD ITS TARGET, AND SHOOT AT THE DOGS WHILE GALLOPING AROUND A SET COURSE. THE POINT WAS TO WAS TO SEE WHO HAD THE FINEST AIM, BUT SOME INU-OI AFICIONADOS TOOK EXTRA PLEASURE FROM KILLING THEIR PREY.

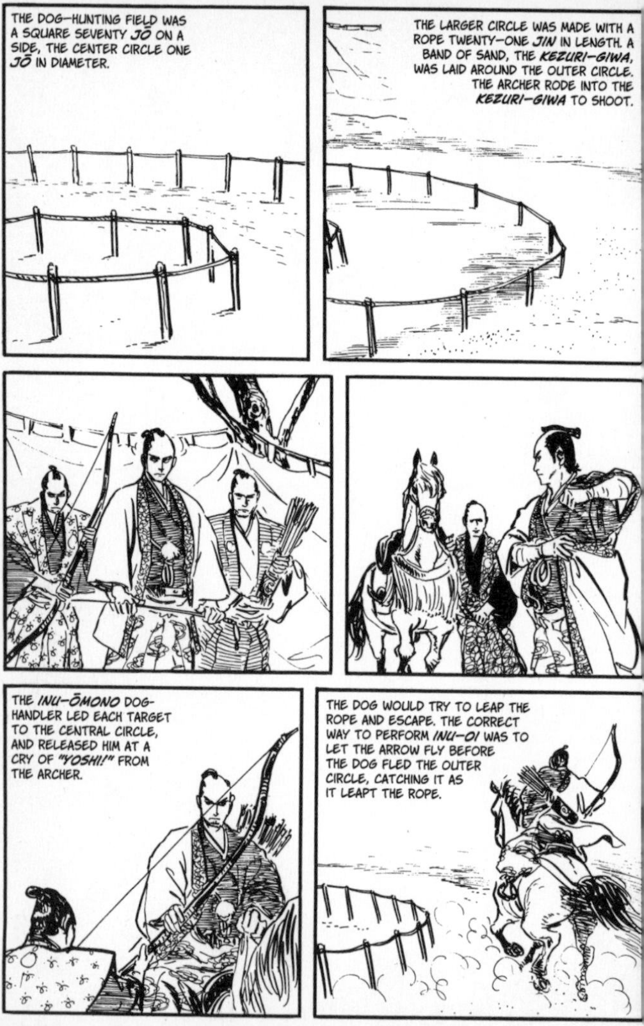
THE DOG-HUNTING FIELD WAS A SQUARE SEVENTY JŌ ON A SIDE, THE CENTER CIRCLE ONE JŌ IN DIAMETER.
THE LARGER CIRCLE WAS MADE WITH A ROPE TWENTY-ONE JIN IN LENGTH. A BAND OF SAND, THE KEZURI-GIWA, WAS LAID AROUND THE OUTER CIRCLE. THE ARCHER RODE INTO THE KEZURI-GIWA TO SHOOT.
THE INU-ŌMONO DOG-HANDLER LED EACH TARGET TO THE CENTRAL CIRCLE, AND RELEASED HIM AT A CRY OF "YOSHI!" FROM THE ARCHER.
THE DOG WOULD TRY TO LEAP THE ROPE AND ESCAPE. THE CORRECT WAY TO PERFORM INU-OI WAS TO LET THE ARROW FLY BEFORE THE DOG FLED THE OUTER CIRCLE, CATCHING IT AS IT LEAPT THE ROPE.

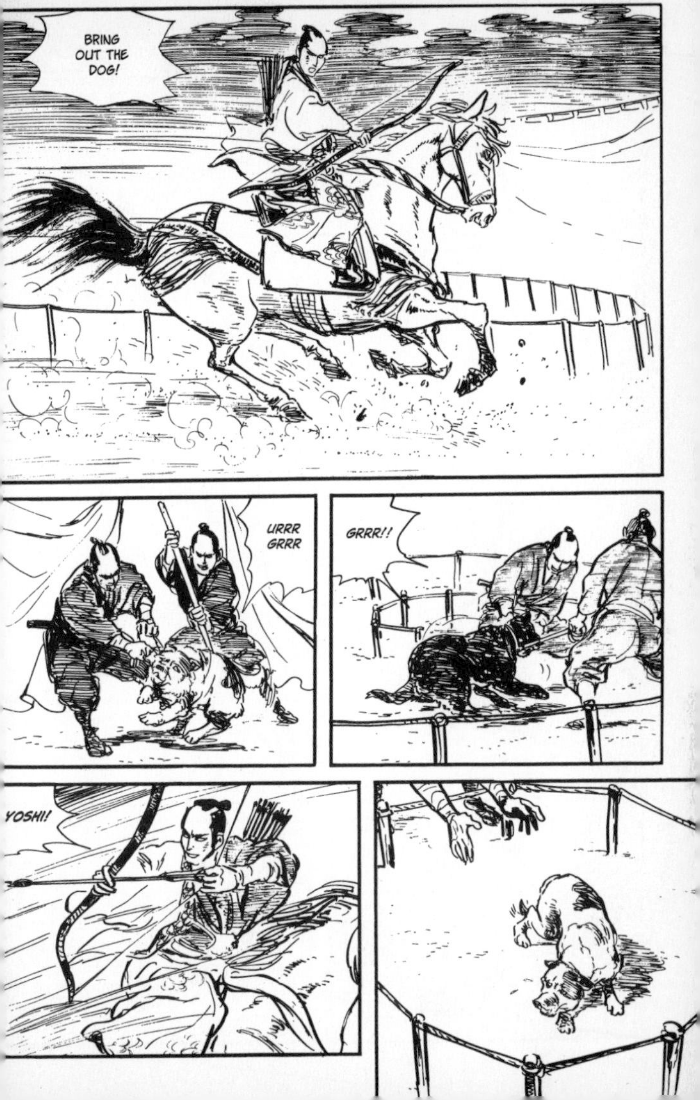
BRING OUT THE DOG!
URRR GRRR
GRRR!!
YOSHI!

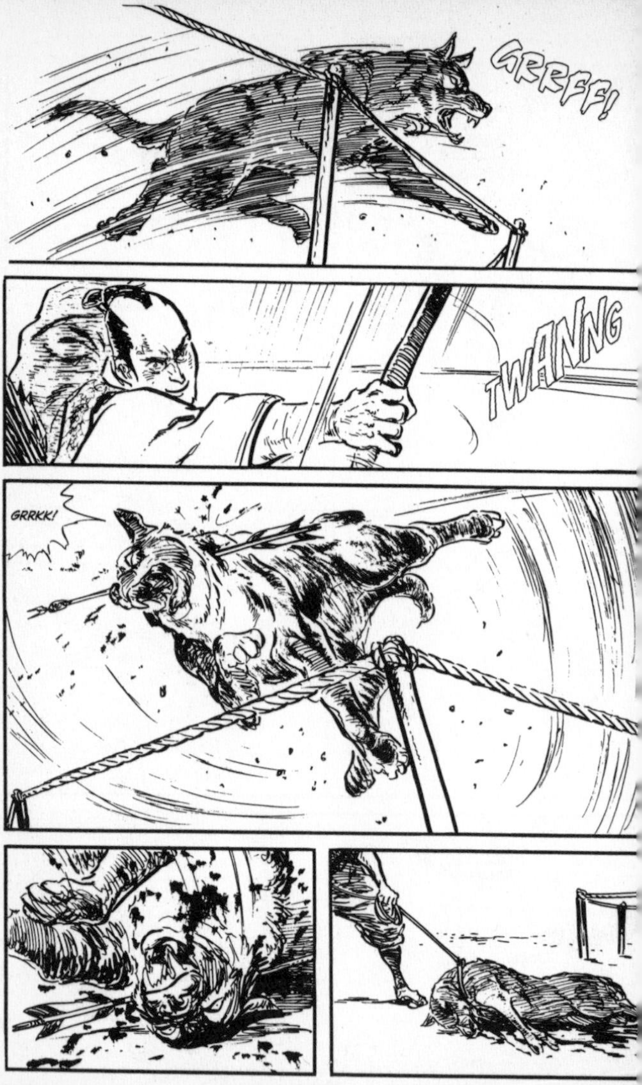
GRRFFF!
TWANNG
GRRKK!

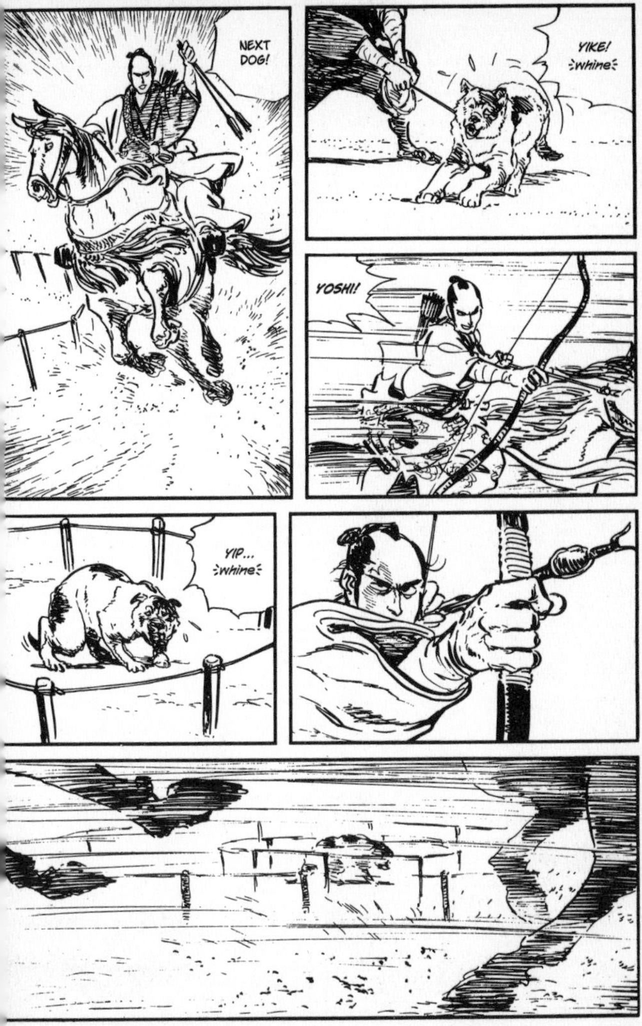
NEXT DOG!
YIKE! whine
YOSHI!
YIP... whine

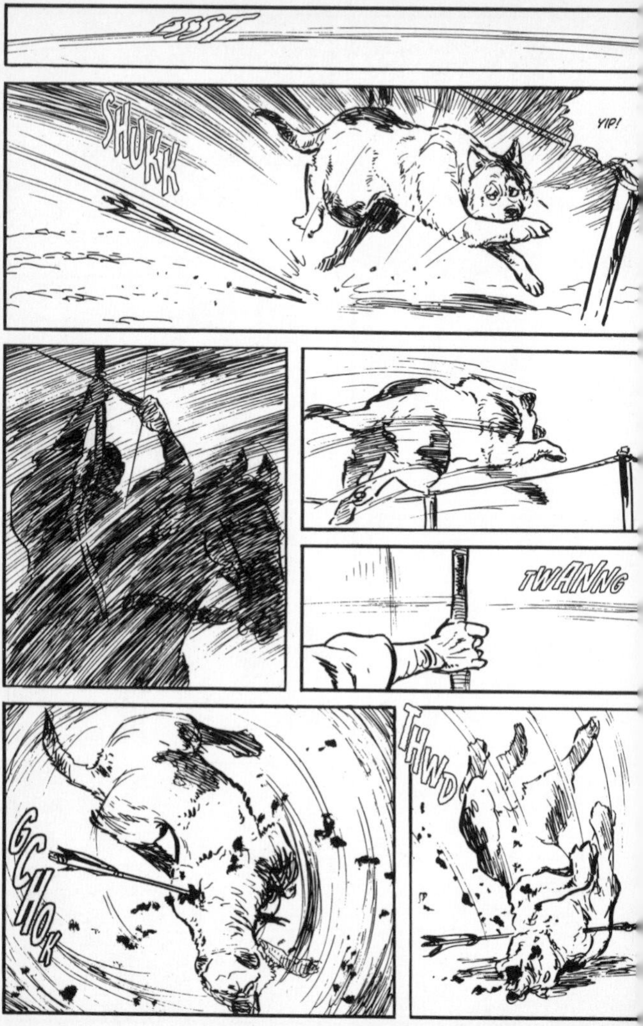

PSST
SHUKK
YIP!
TWANNG
GCHOK
THWD

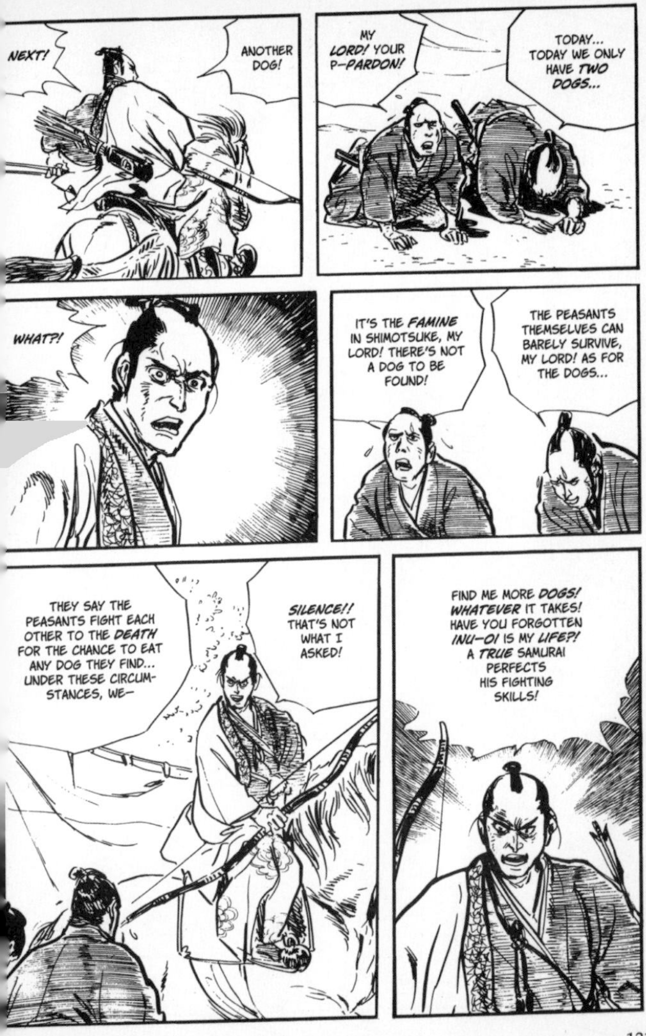
NEXT!
ANOTHER DOG!
MY LORD! YOUR P-PARDON!
TODAY... TODAY WE ONLY HAVE TWO DOGS...
WHAT?!
IT'S THE FAMINE IN SHIMOTSUKE, MY LORD! THERE'S NOT A DOG TO BE FOUND!
THE PEASANTS THEMSELVES CAN BARELY SURVIVE, MY LORD! AS FOR THE DOGS...
THEY SAY THE PEASANTS FIGHT EACH OTHER TO THE DEATH FOR THE CHANCE TO EAT ANY DOG THEY FIND... UNDER THESE CIRCUM-STANCES, WE-
SILENCE!! THAT'S NOT WHAT I ASKED!
FIND ME MORE DOGS! WHATEVER IT TAKES! HAVE YOU FORGOTTEN INU-OI IS MY LIFE?! A TRUE SAMURAI PERFECTS HIS FIGHTING SKILLS!

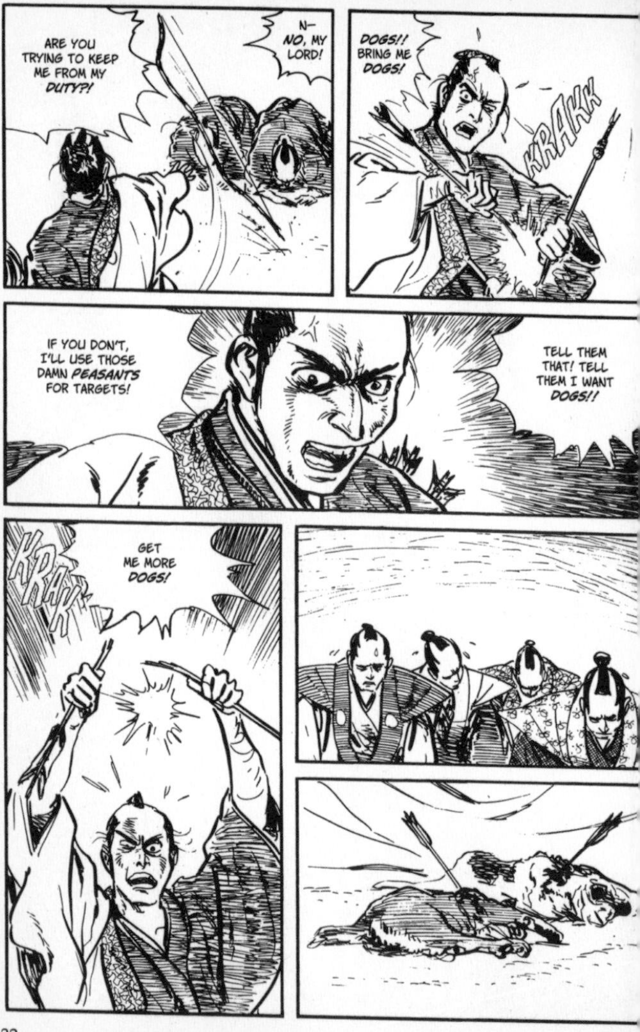
ARE YOU TRYING TO KEEP ME FROM MY DUTY?!
N— NO, MY LORD!
DOGS!! BRING ME DOGS!
KRAKK
IF YOU DON'T, I'LL USE THOSE DAMN PEASANTS FOR TARGETS!
TELL THEM THAT! TELL THEM I WANT DOGS!!
KRAK
GET ME MORE DOGS!

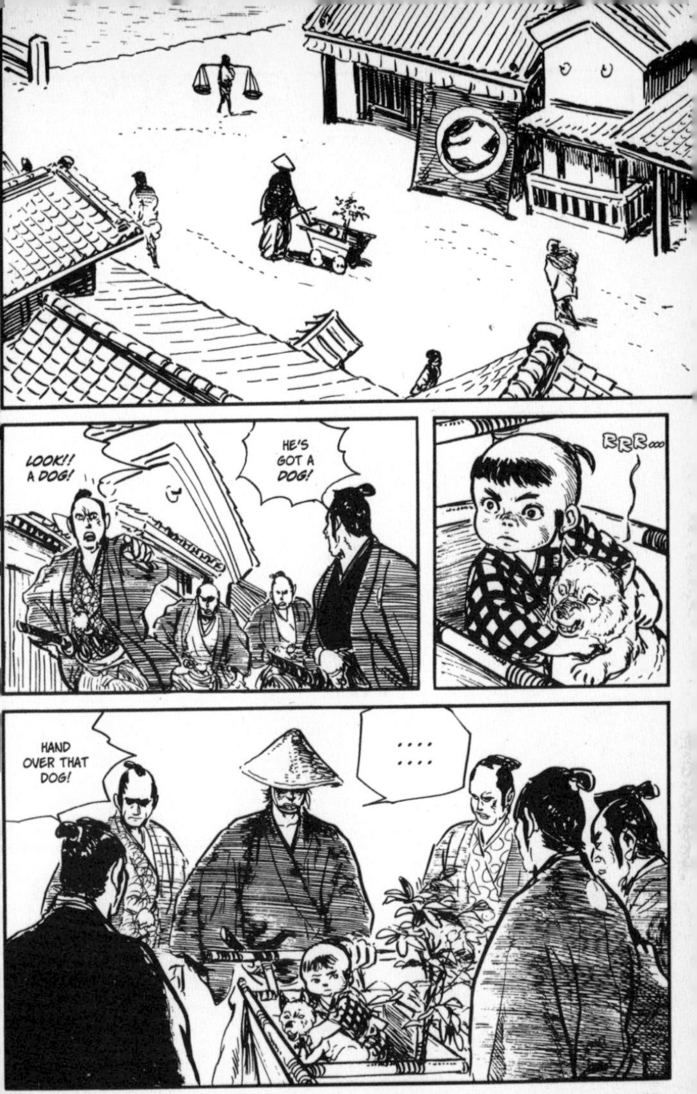
LOOK!! A DOG!
HE'S GOT A DOG!
RRRooo
HAND OVER THAT DOG!
....
....

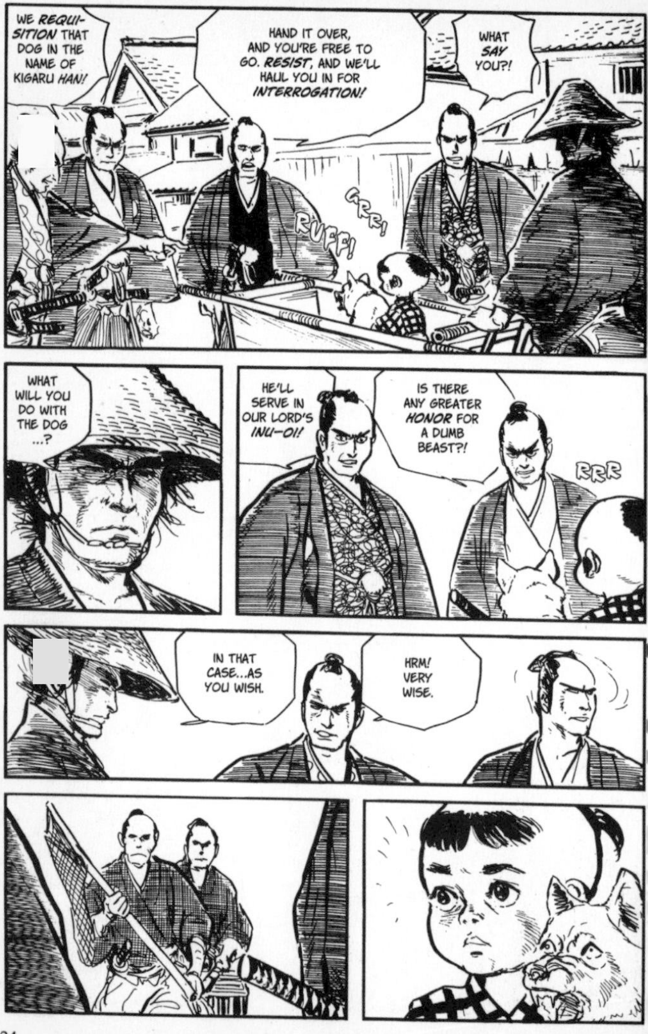
WE REQUISITION THAT DOG IN THE NAME OF KIGARU HAN!
HAND IT OVER, AND YOU'RE FREE TO GO. RESIST, AND WE'LL HAUL YOU IN FOR INTERROGATION!
WHAT SAY YOU?!
GRRR!
RUFF!
WHAT WILL YOU DO WITH THE DOG ...?
HE'LL SERVE IN OUR LORD'S INU-OI!
IS THERE ANY GREATER HONOR FOR A DUMB BEAST?!
RRR
IN THAT CASE...AS YOU WISH.
HRM! VERY WISE.

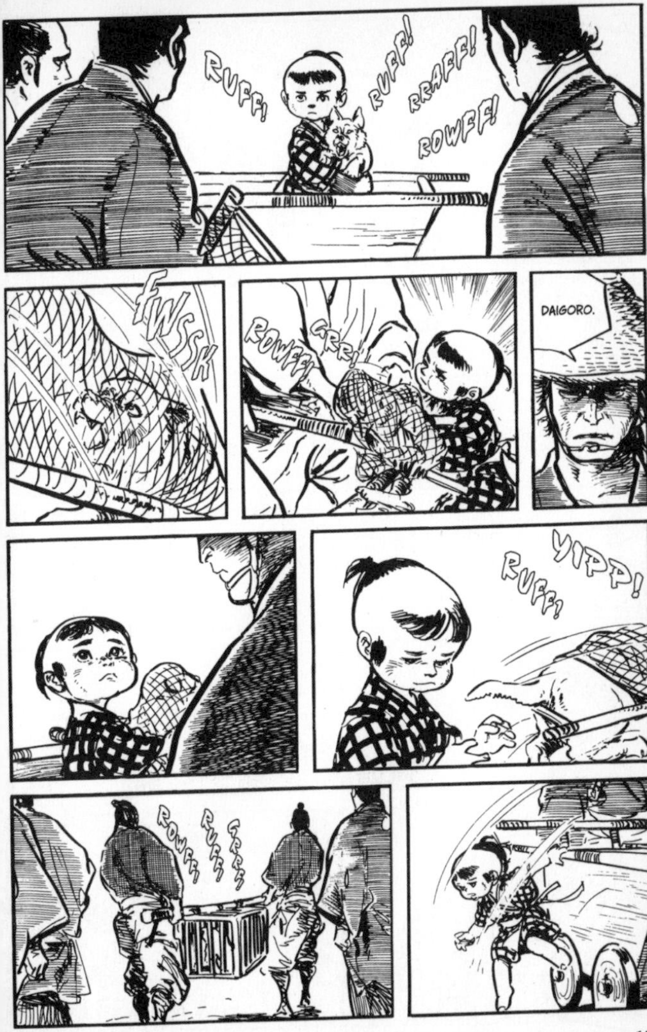
RUFF!
RUFF!
RRAFF!
ROWFF!
FWSSK
ROWFF!
GRR!
DAIGORO.
YIPP!
RUFF!
ROWFF!
RUFF!
GRRR!

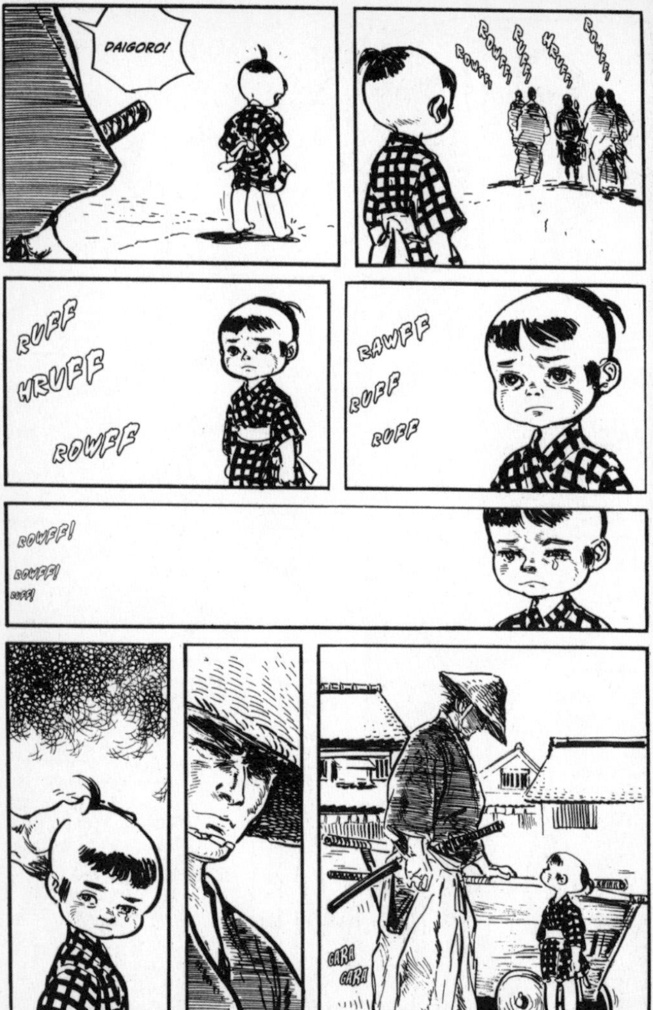
DAIGORO!
ROWFF,
ROWFF,
RUFF,
HRUFF,
ROWFF,
RUFF
HRUFF
ROWFF
RAWFF
RUFF
RUFF
ROWFF!
ROWFF!
RUFF!
GARA
GARA

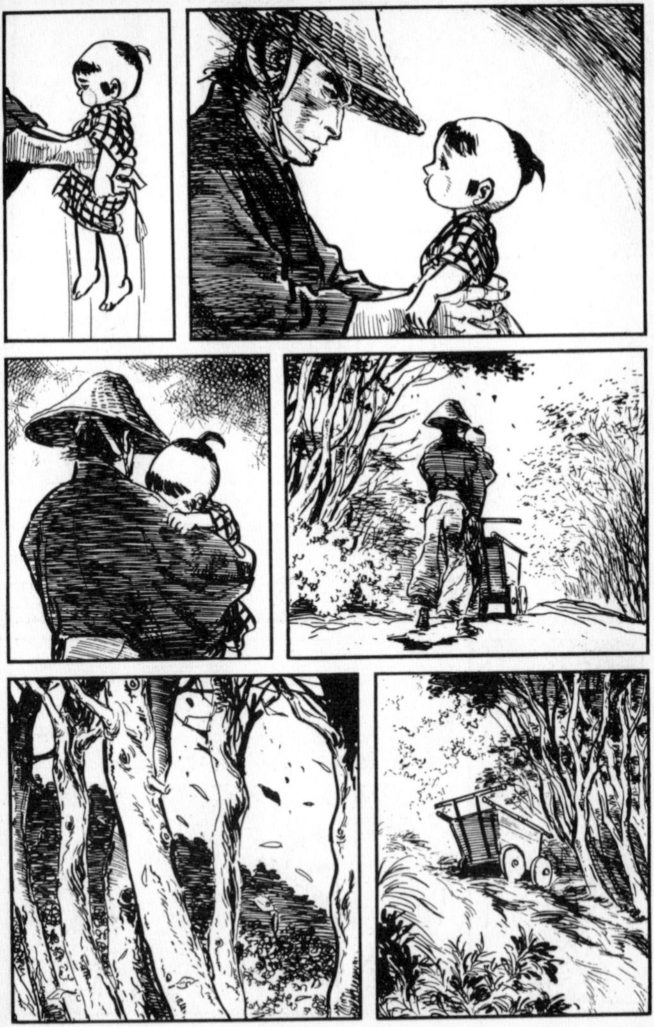

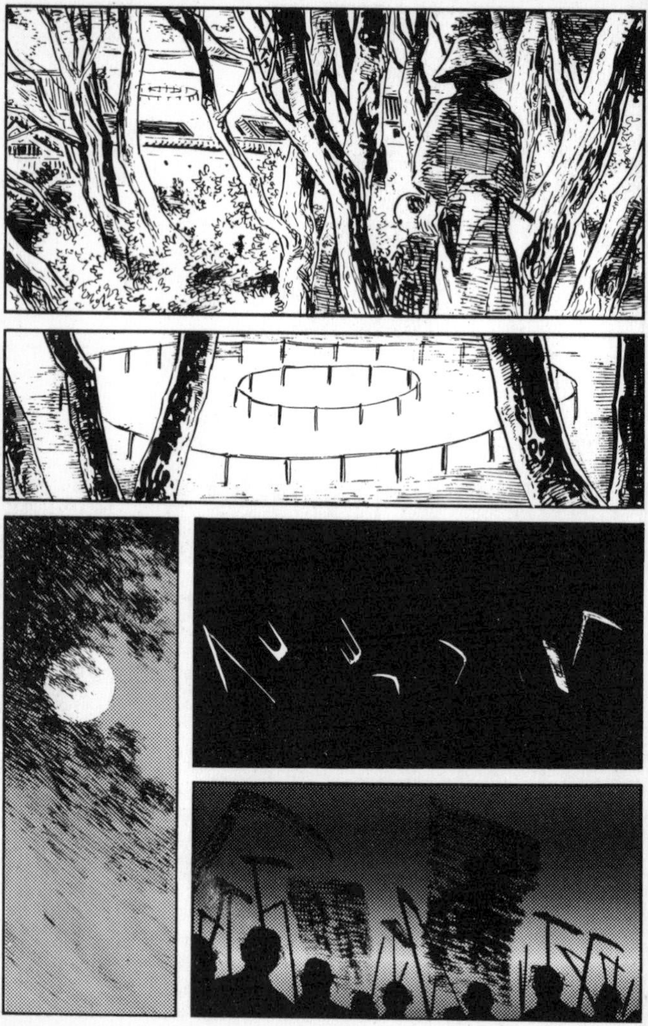

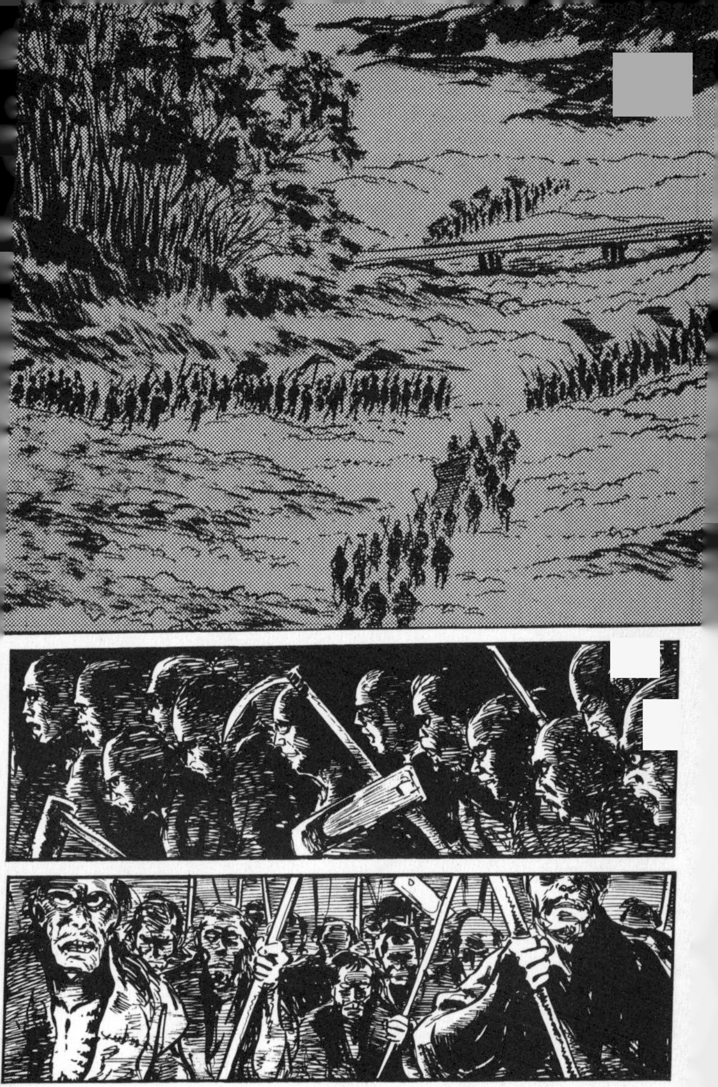

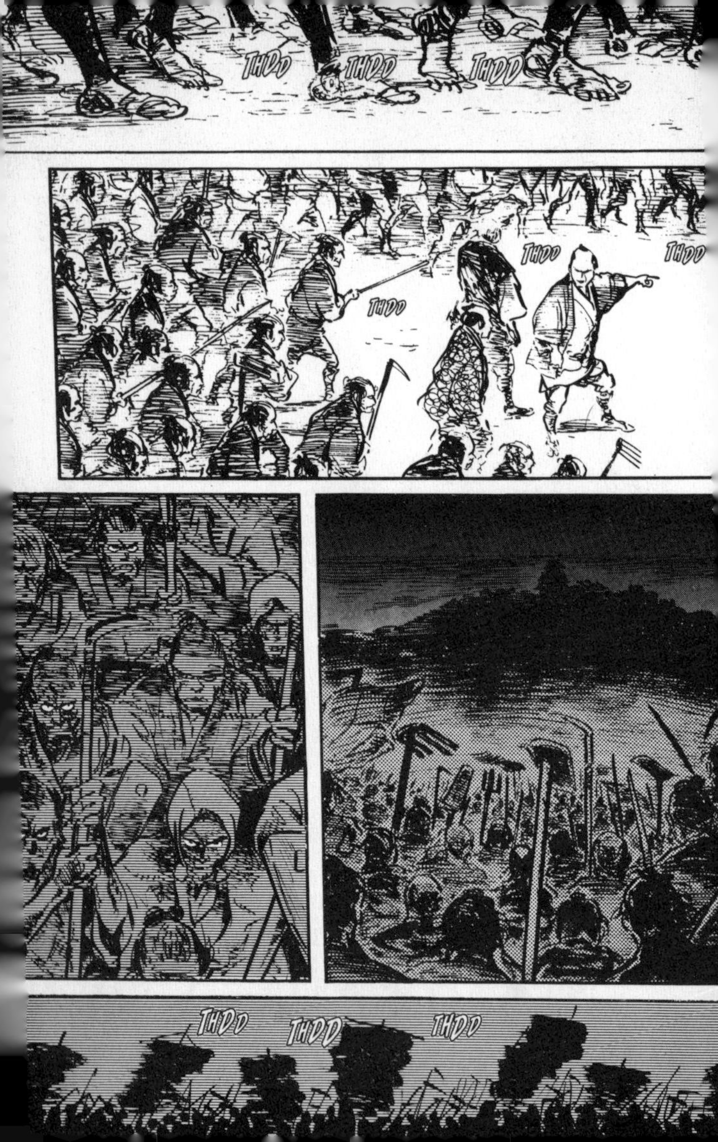
THDD
THDD
THDD
THDD
THDD
THDD
THDD
THDD
THDD

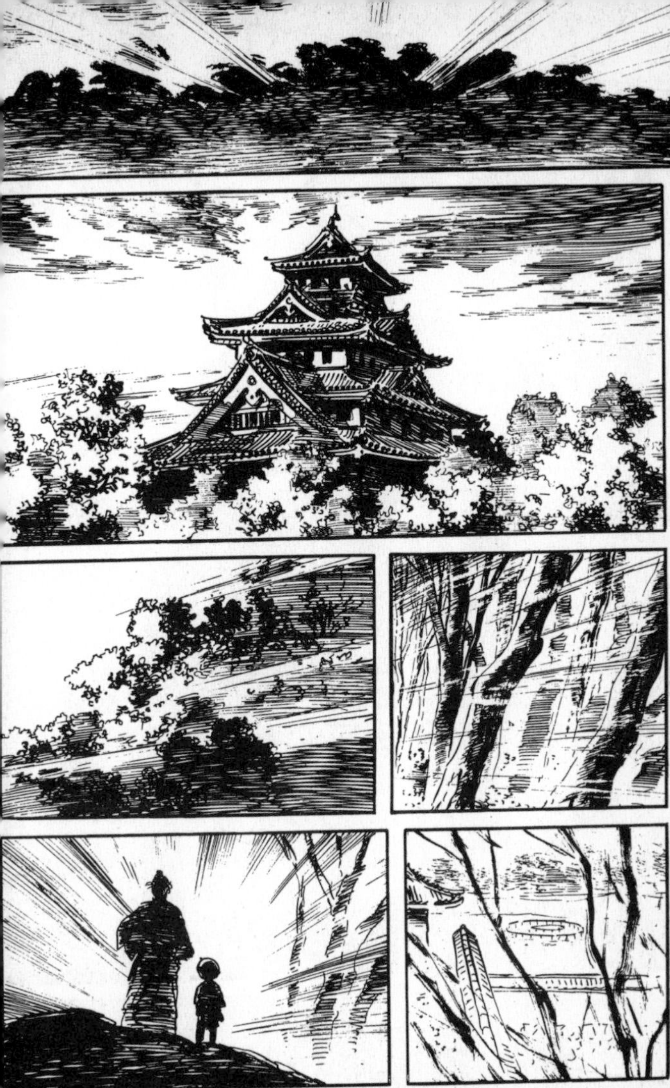

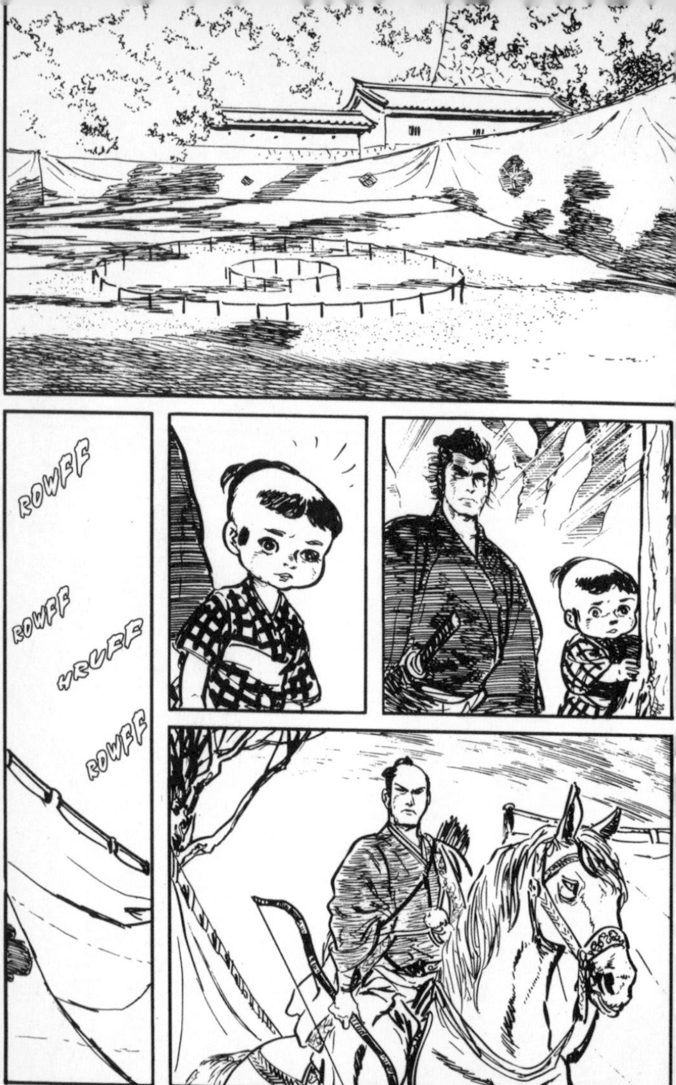
ROWFF
ROWFF
HRUFF
ROWFF

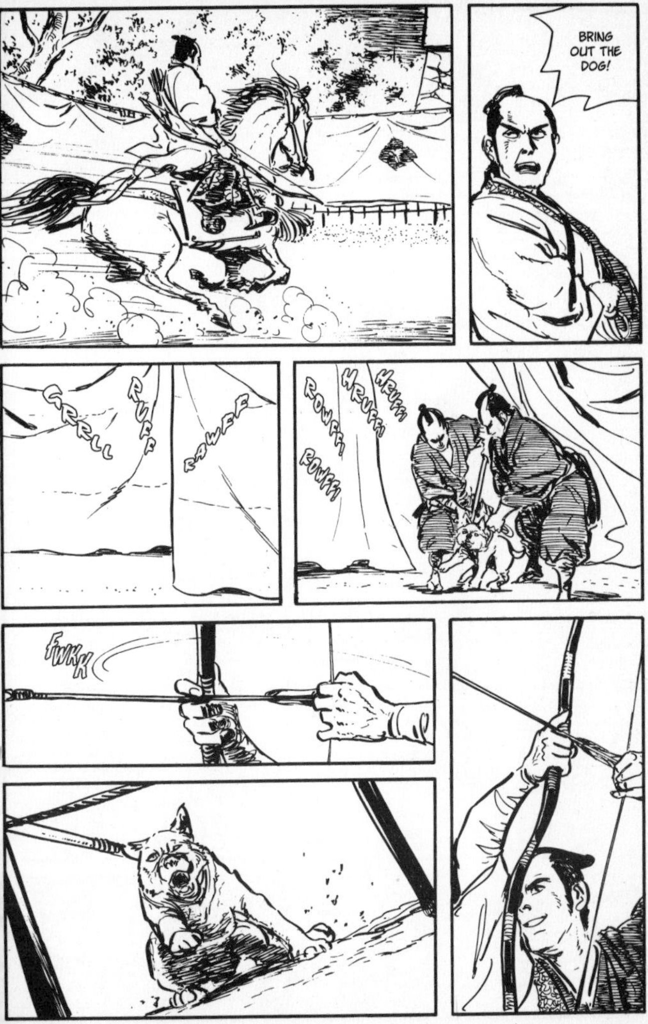
BRING OUT THE DOG!
GRRLL
RUFF
RAWFF
HRUFF!
HRUFF!
ROWFF!
ROWFF!
FWKK

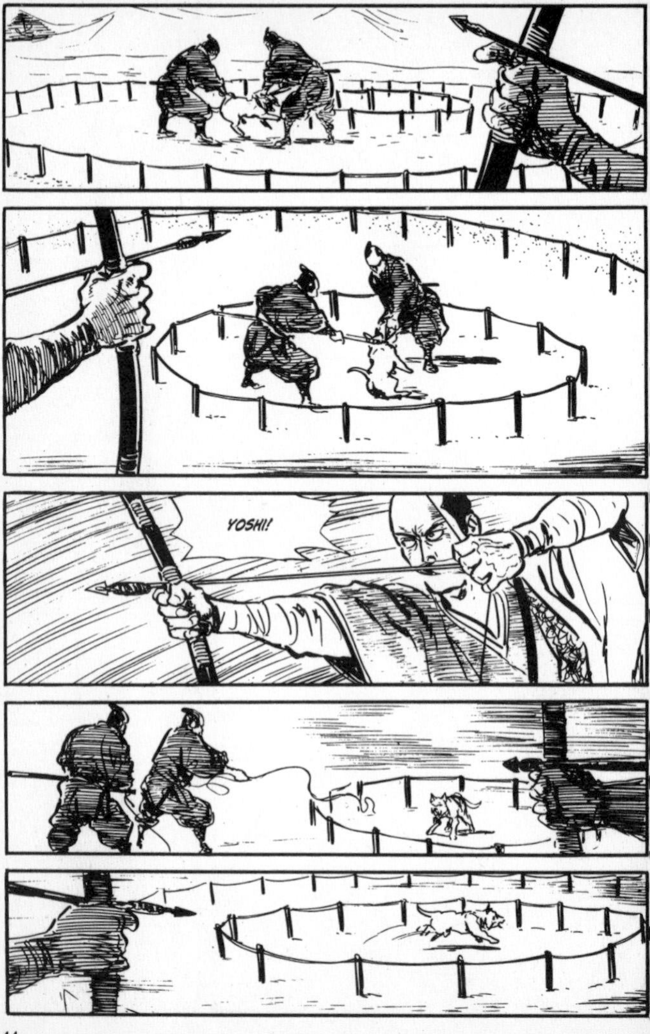
YOSHI!

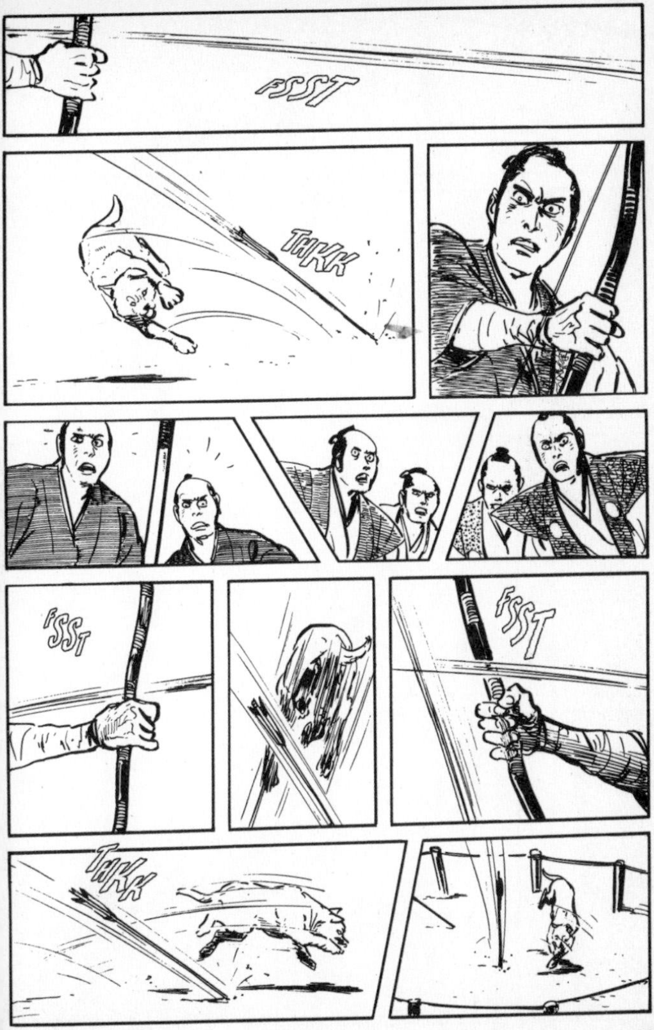
FSST
THKK
FSST
FSST
THKK

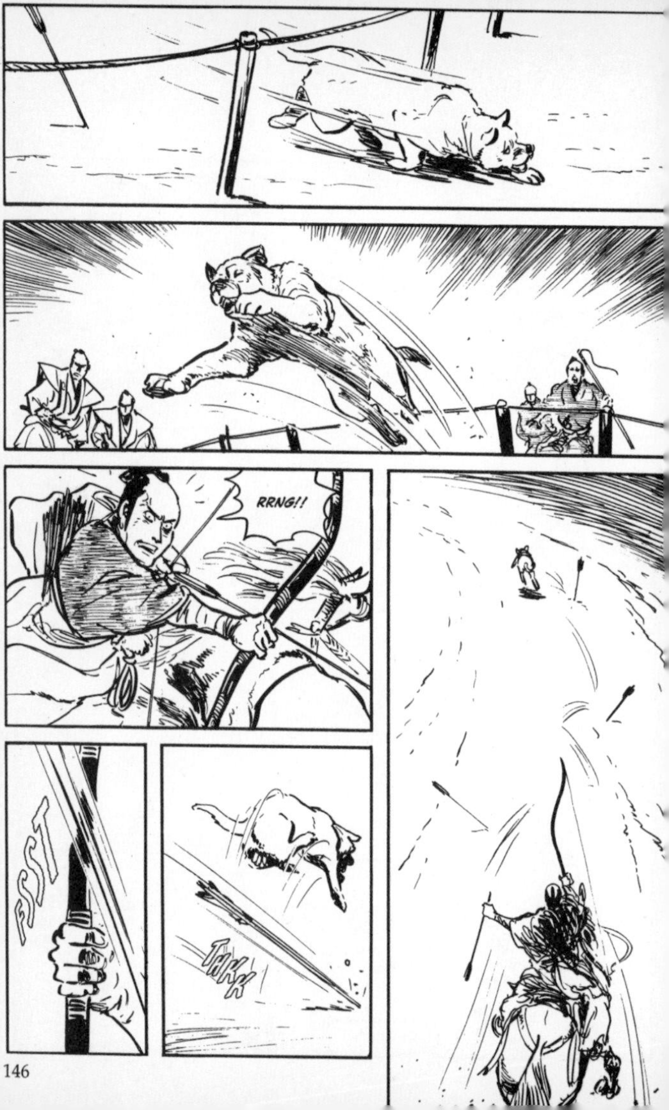
RRNG!!
FSST
THKK

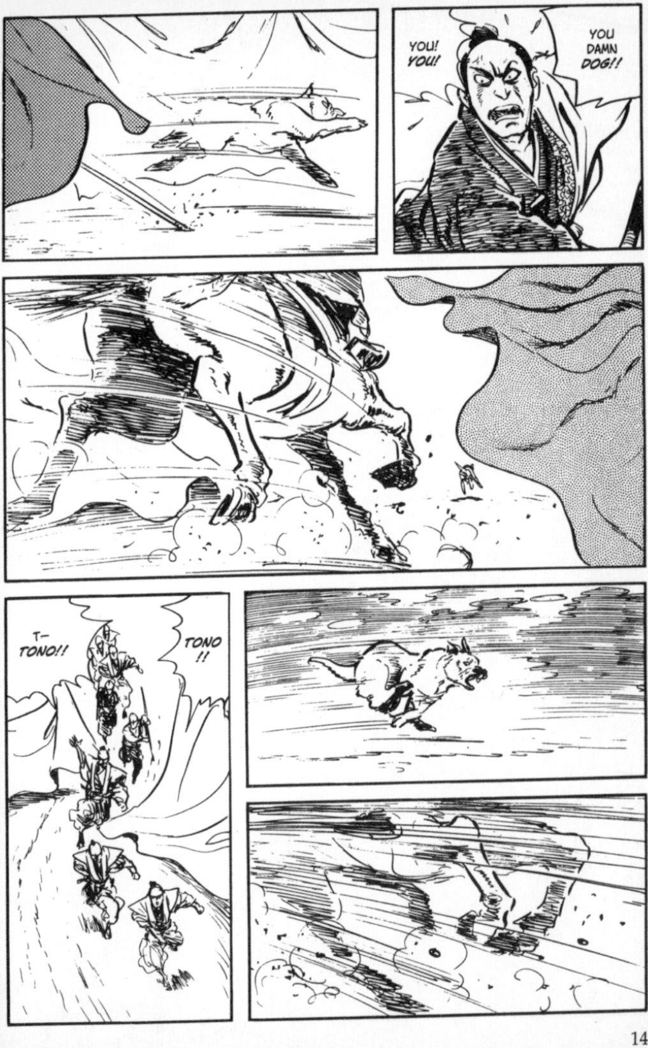
YOU! YOU!
YOU DAMN DOG!!
T—TONO!!
TONO!!

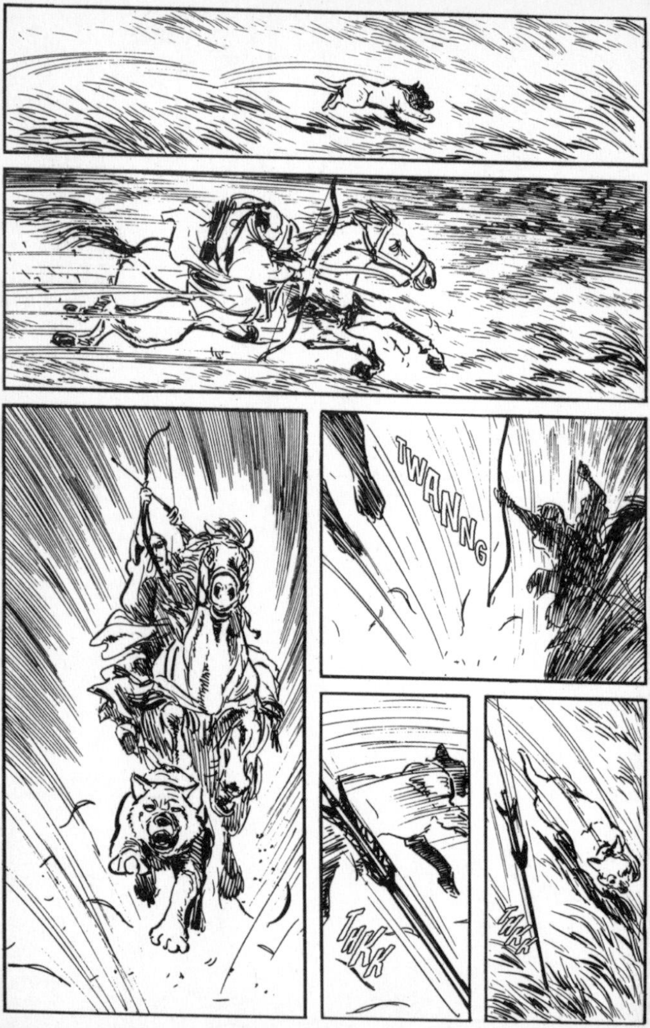
TWANNNG
THKK
THKK

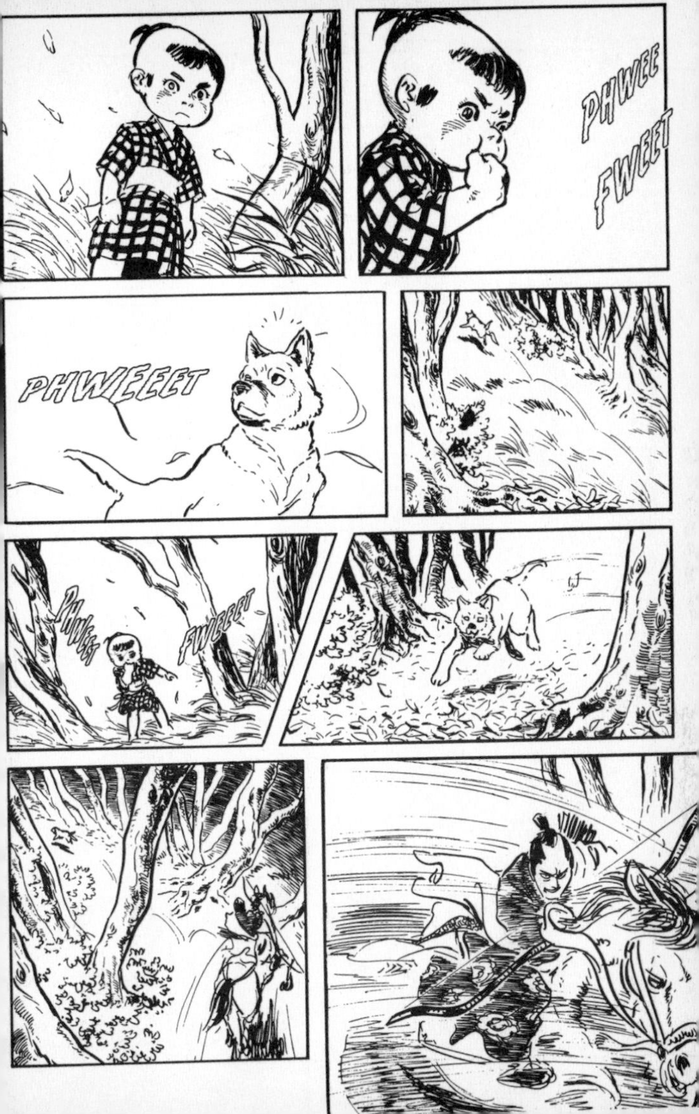
PHWEE
FWEET
PHWEEEET
PHWEET
FWEEEET

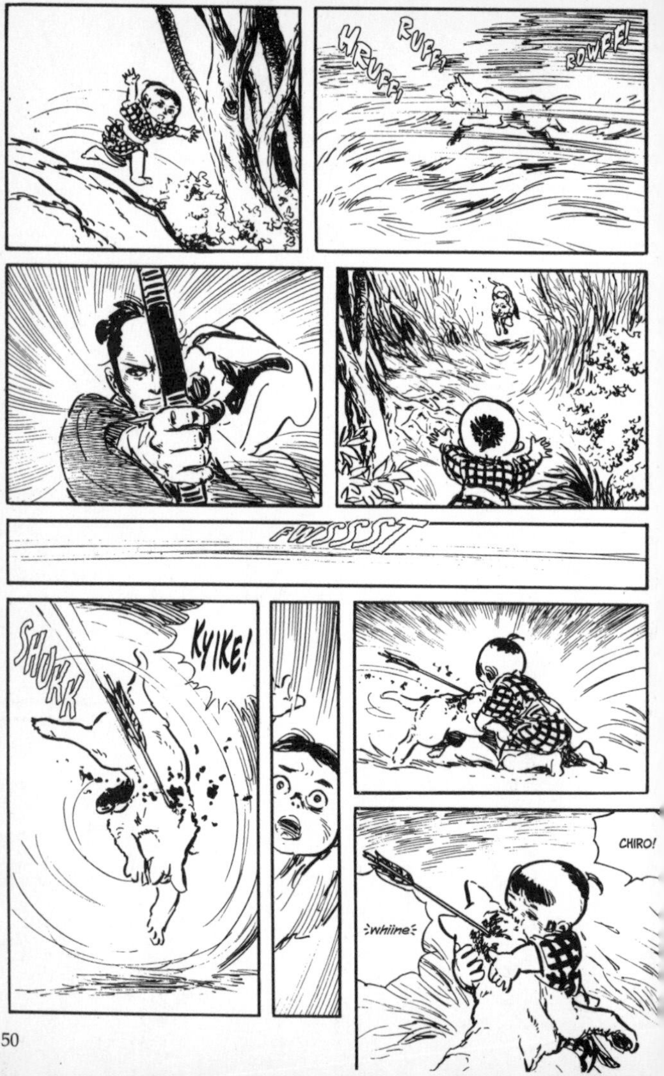
HRUFF!
RUFF!
ROWFF!
FWSSST
SHUKK
KYIKE!
CHIRO!
whiine

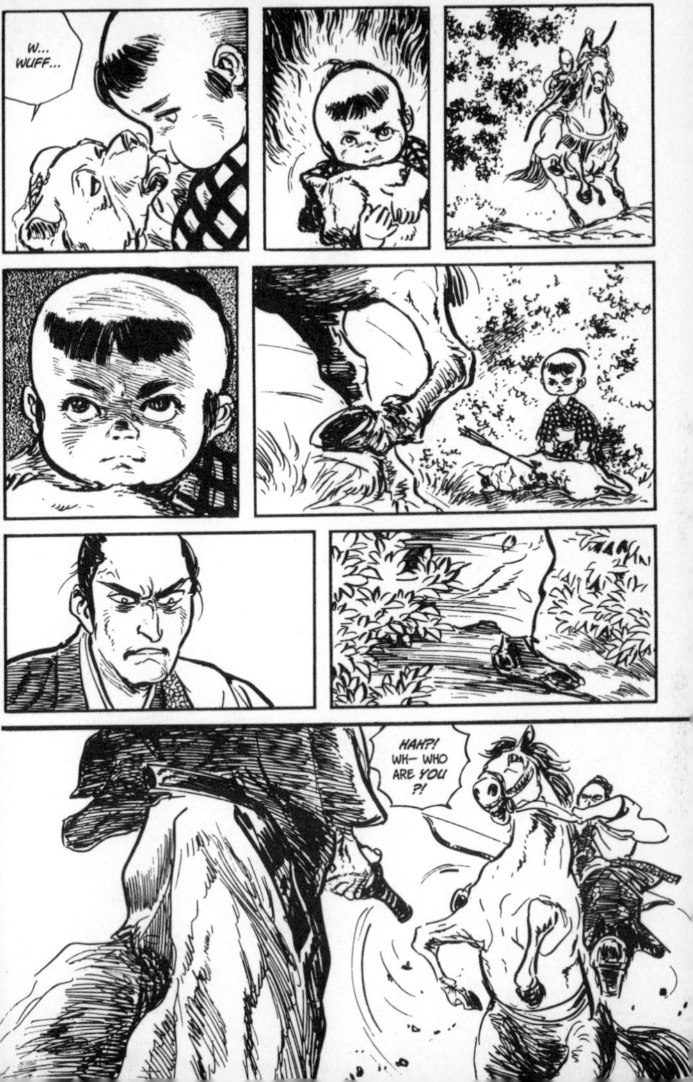
W... WUFF...
HAH?! WH- WHO ARE YOU ?!

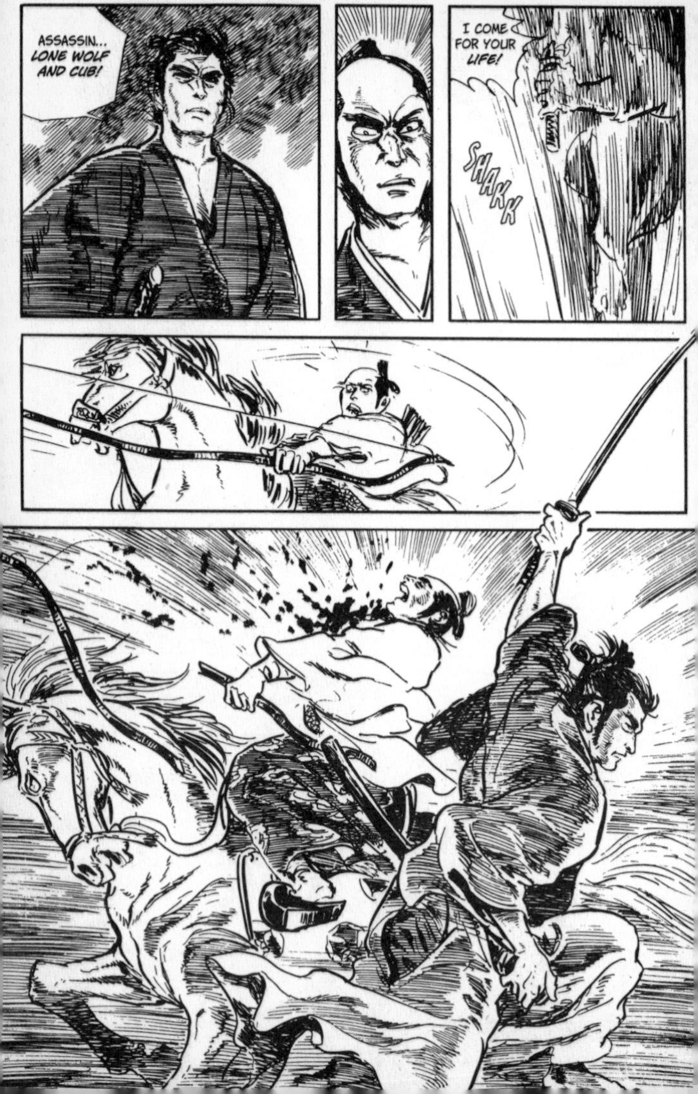
ASSASSIN... LONE WOLF AND CUB!
I COME FOR YOUR LIFE!
SHAKK

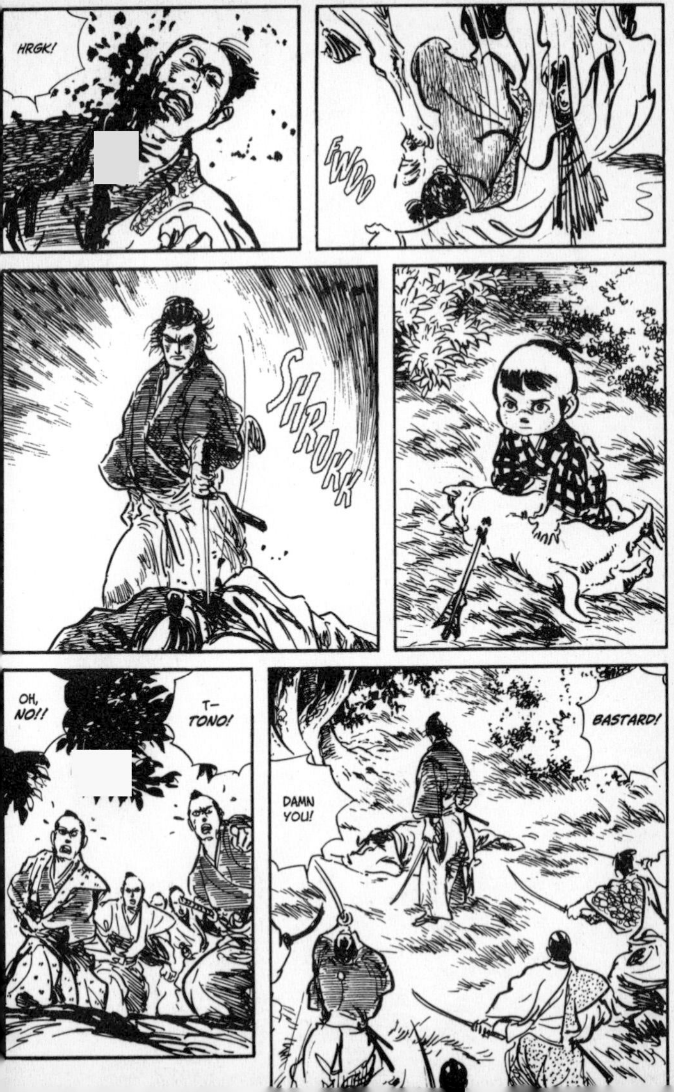
HRGK!
FWOO
SHRUKK
OH, NO!!
T-TONO!
BASTARD!
DAMN YOU!

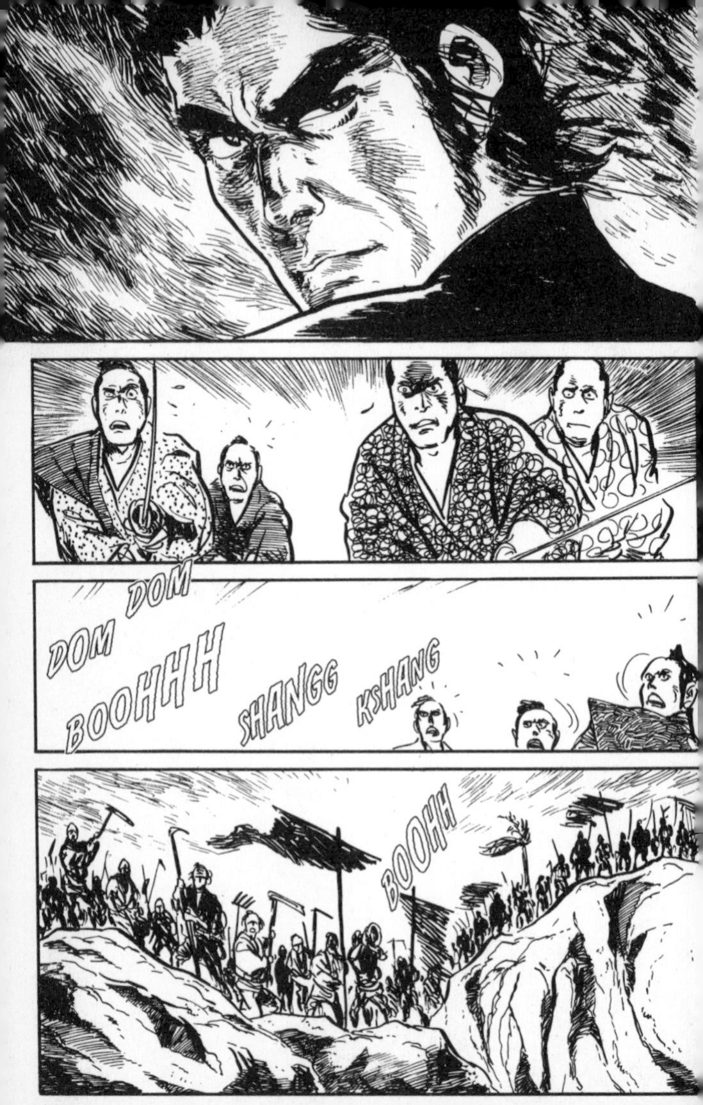
DOM
DOM
BOOHHH
SHANGG
KSHANG
BOOHH

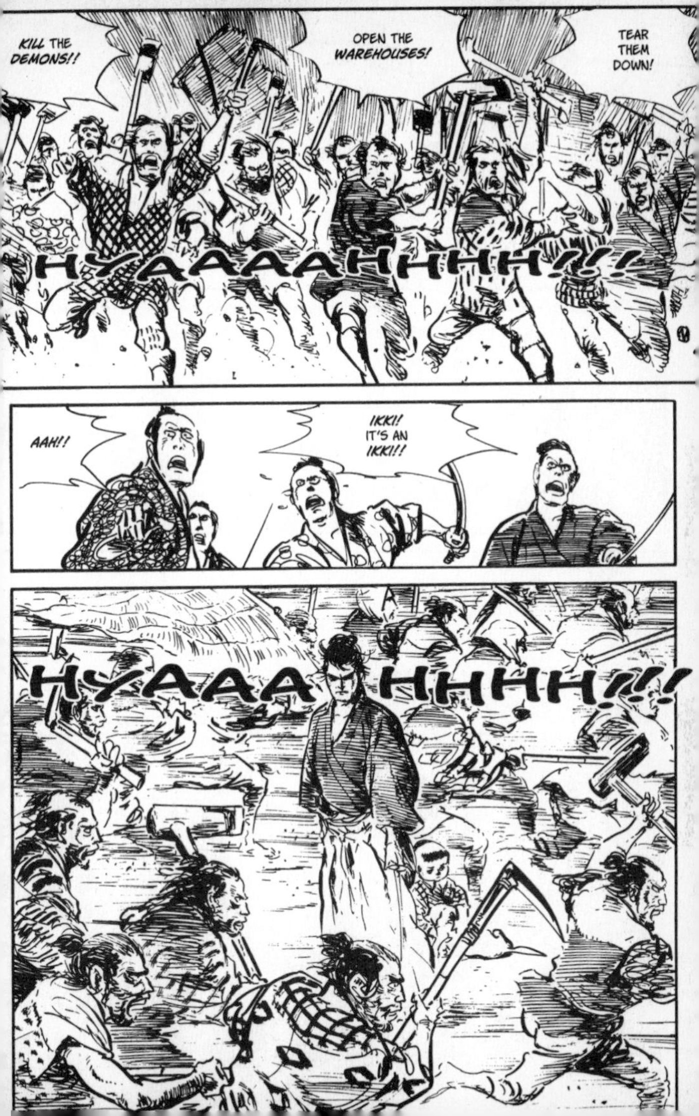
KILL THE DEMONS!!
OPEN THE WAREHOUSES!
TEAR THEM DOWN!
HYAAAAHHHH!!!
AAH!!
IKKI! IT'S AN IKKI!!
HYAAA HHHH!!!

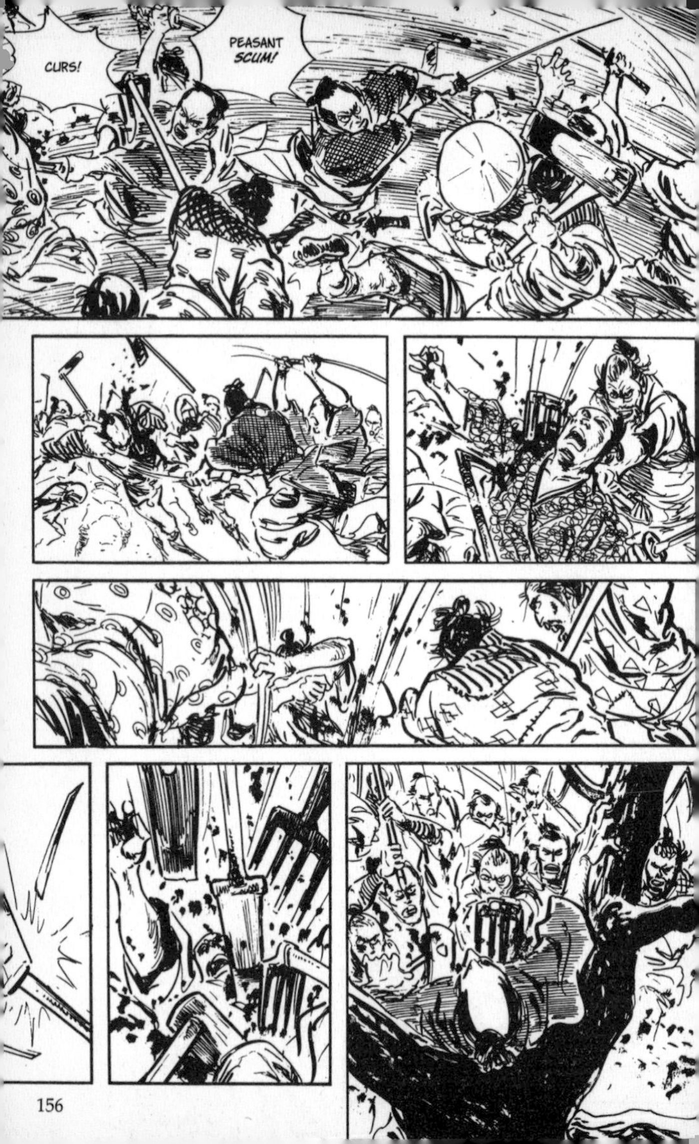
CURS!
PEASANT SCUM!

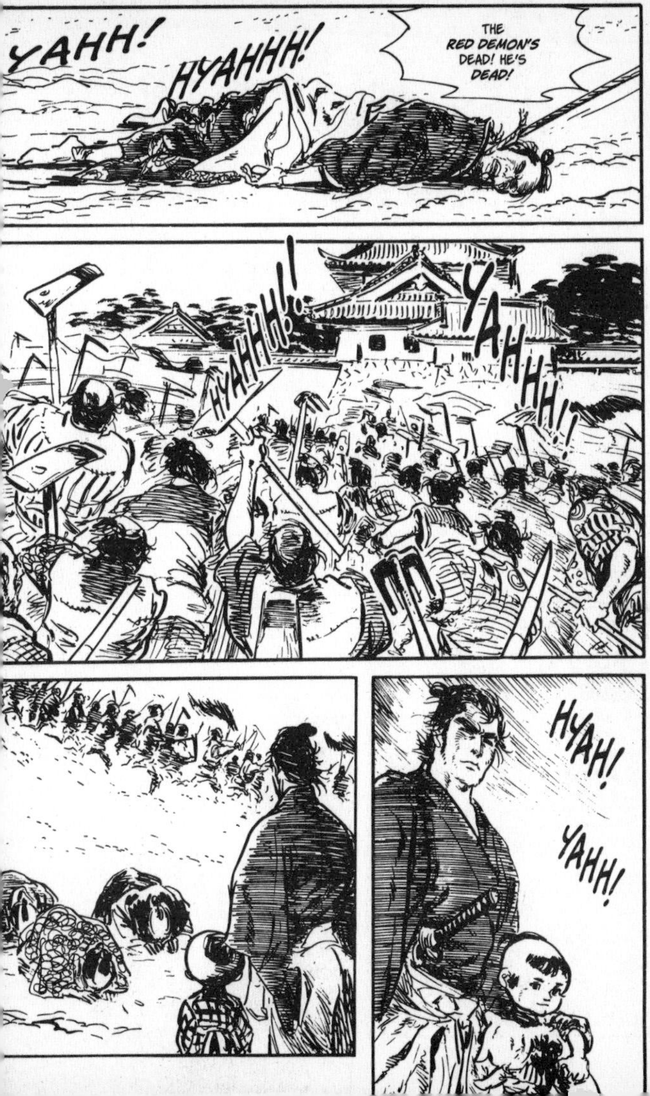
YAHH!
HYAHHH!
THE RED DEMON'S DEAD! HE'S DEAD!
HYAHHH!!
YAHHHH!!
HYAH!
YAHH!

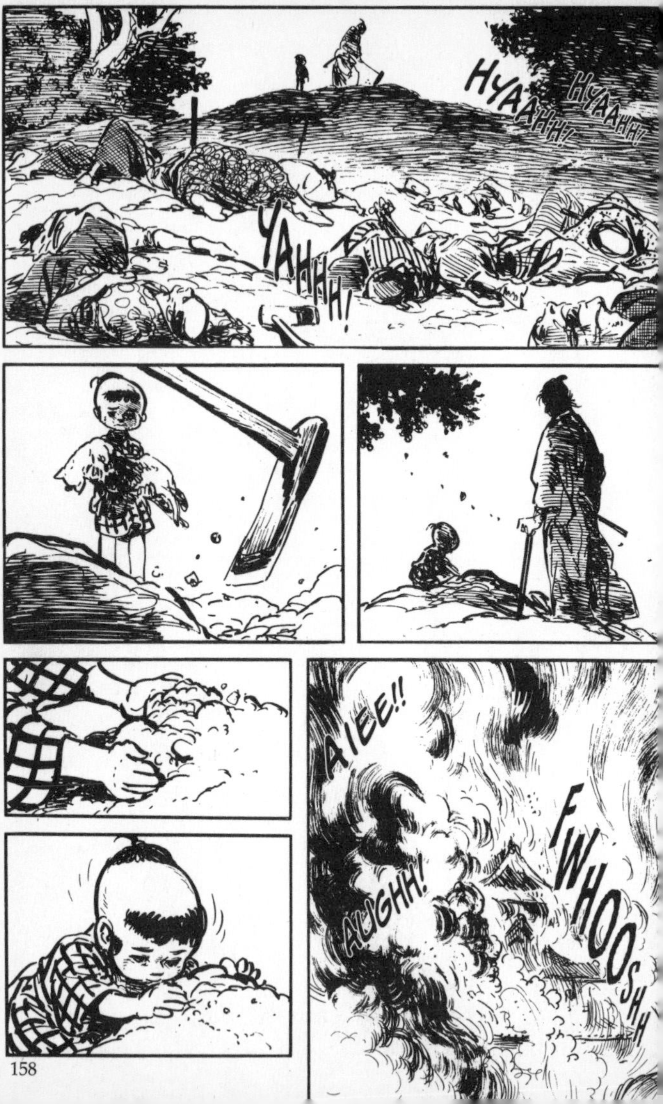
HYAAAHH!
HYAAAHH!
YAHHHH!
AIEE!!
AUGHH!
FWHOOSHH

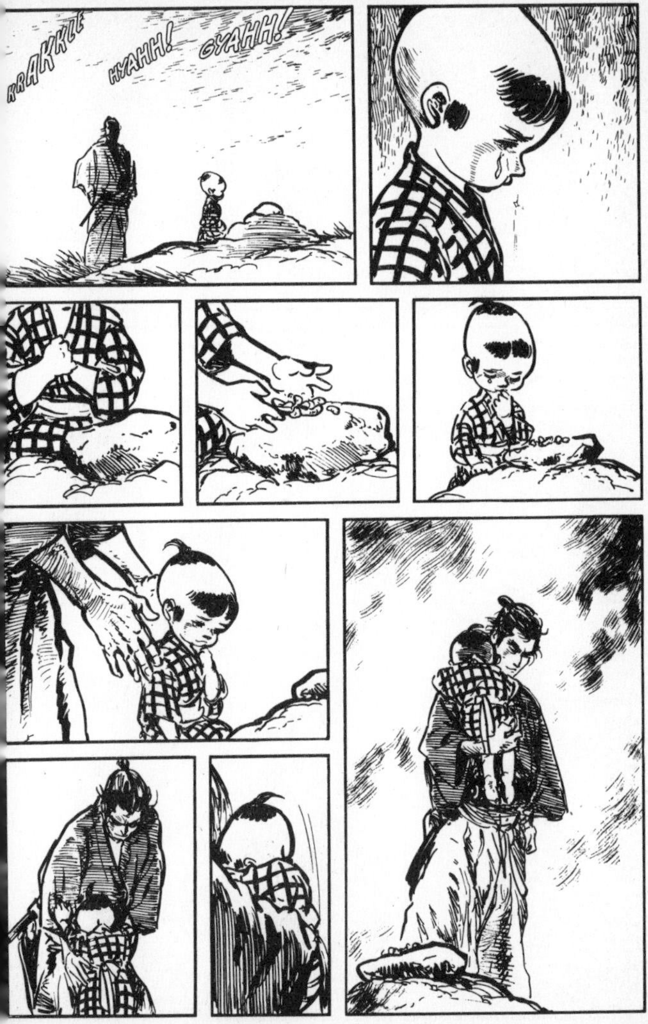
KRAKKLE
HYAHH!
GYAHH!

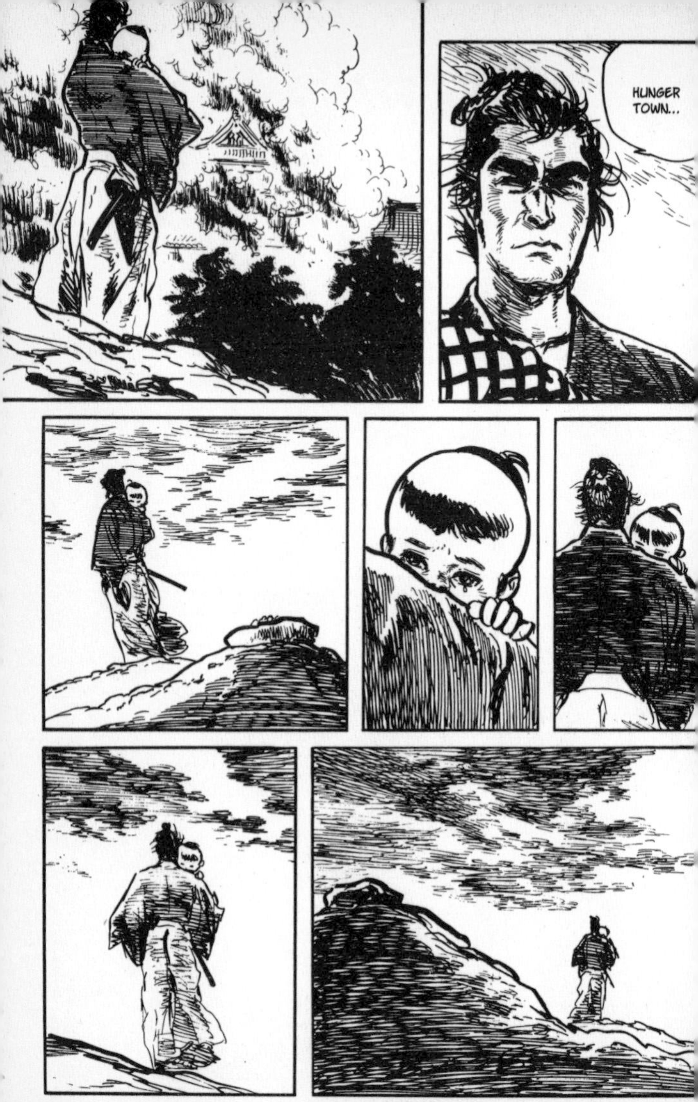
HUNGER TOWN...

the thirty-second

The Soldier is the Castle

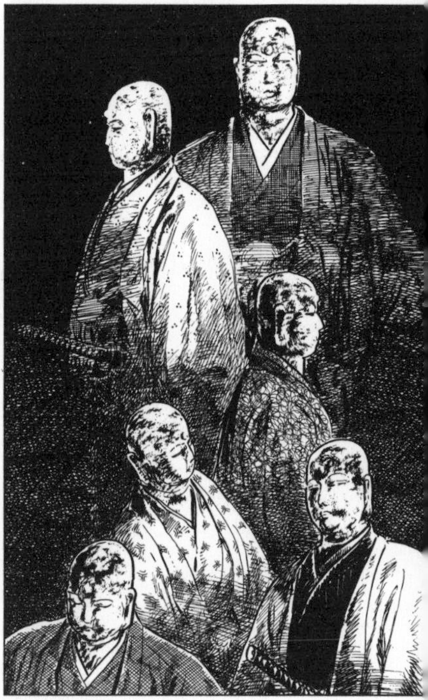

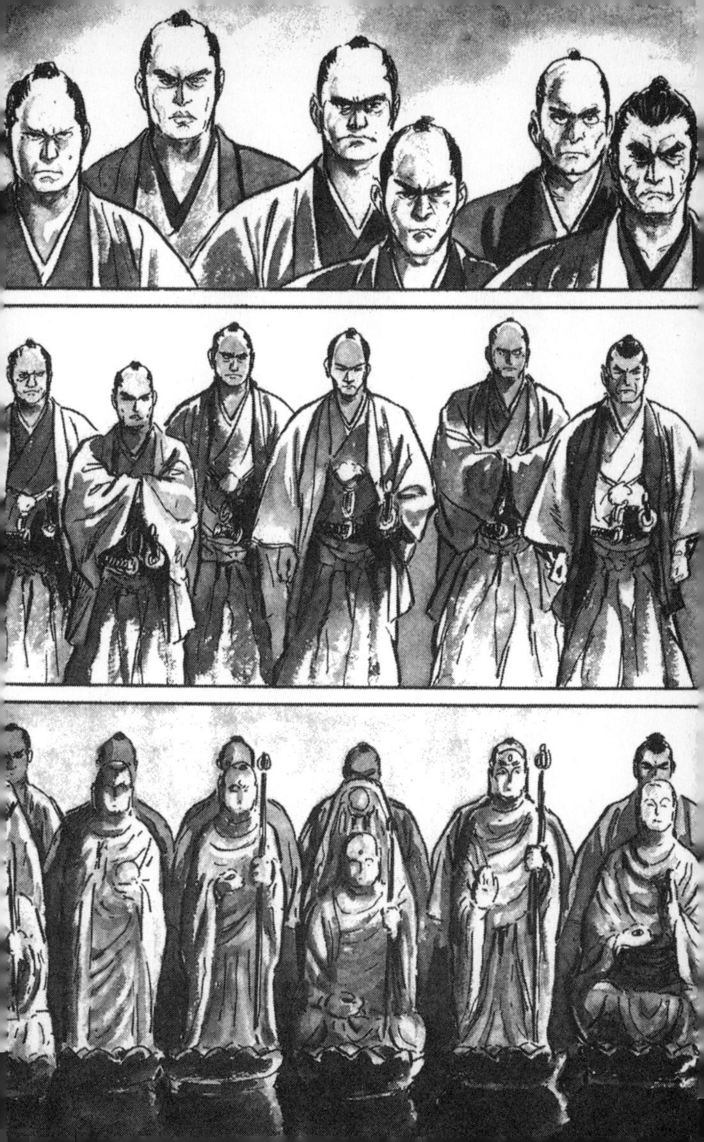

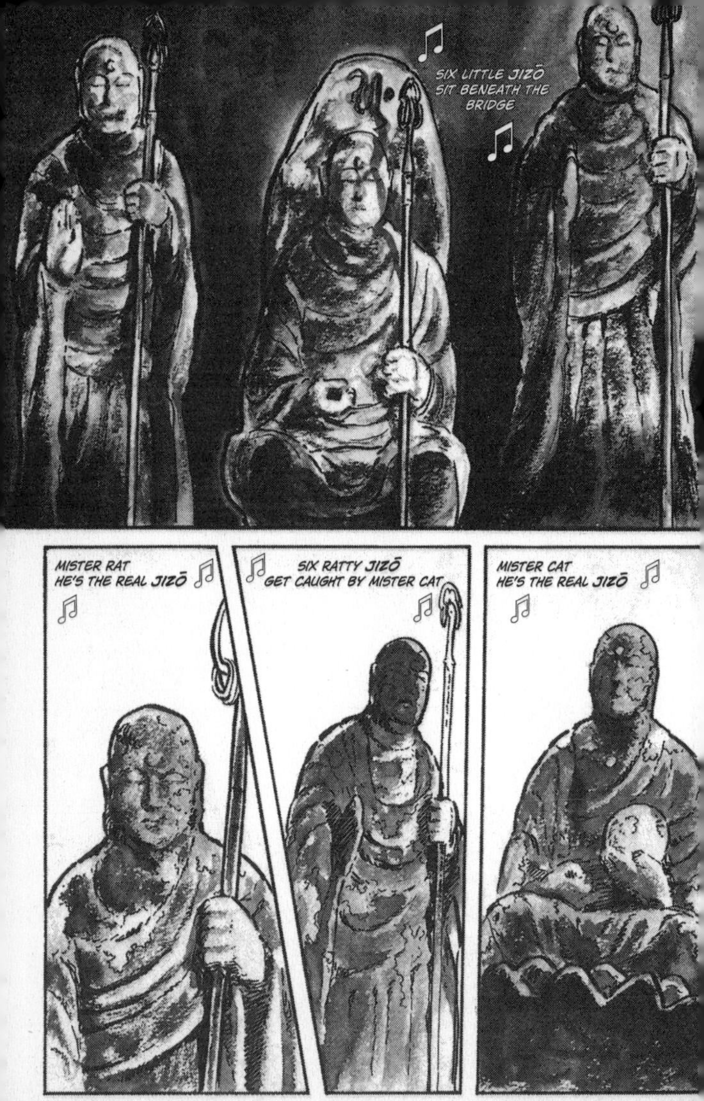
SIX LITTLE JIZŌ
SIT BENEATH THE
BRIDGE
MISTER RAT
HE'S THE REAL JIZŌ
SIX RATTY JIZŌ
GET CAUGHT BY MISTER CAT
MISTER CAT
HE'S THE REAL JIZŌ

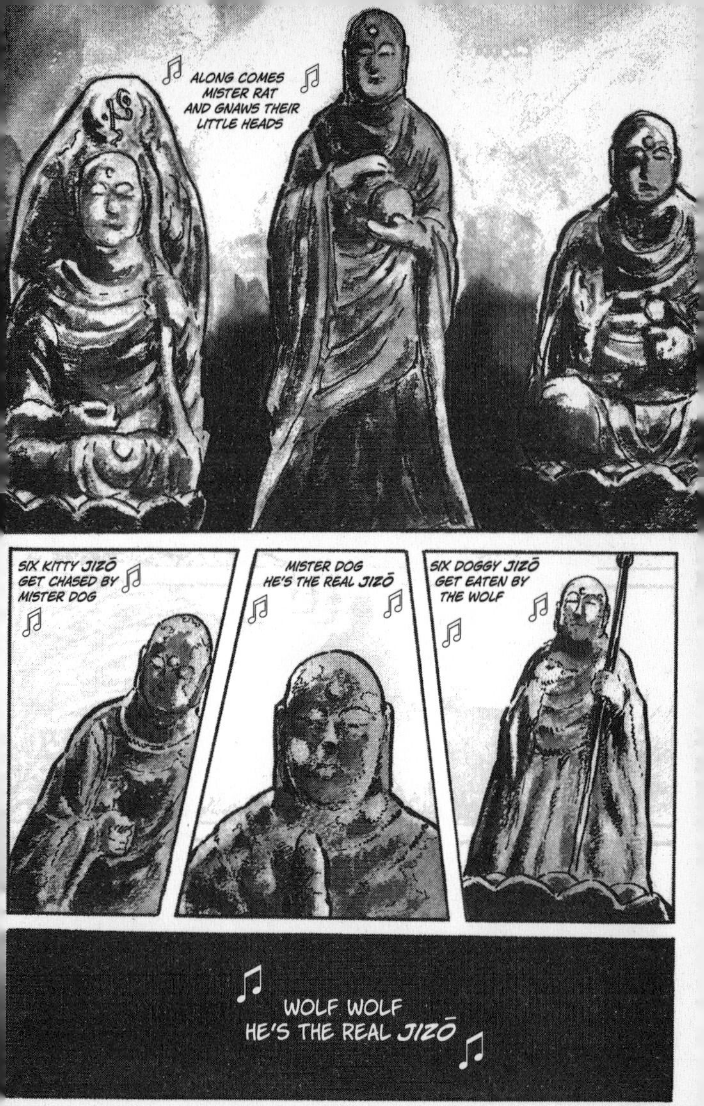
ALONG COMES MISTER RAT AND GNAWS THEIR LITTLE HEADS
SIX KITTY JIZŌ GET CHASED BY MISTER DOG
MISTER DOG HE'S THE REAL JIZŌ
SIX DOGGY JIZŌ GET EATEN BY THE WOLF
WOLF WOLF HE'S THE REAL JIZŌ

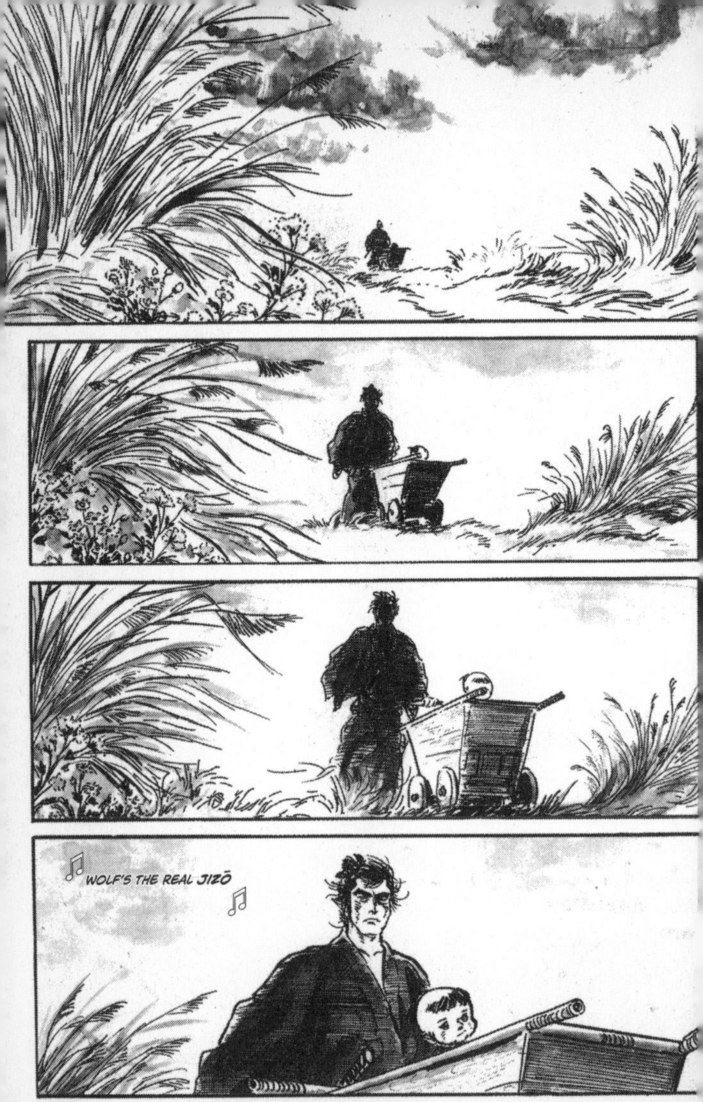
WOLF'S THE REAL JIZŌ

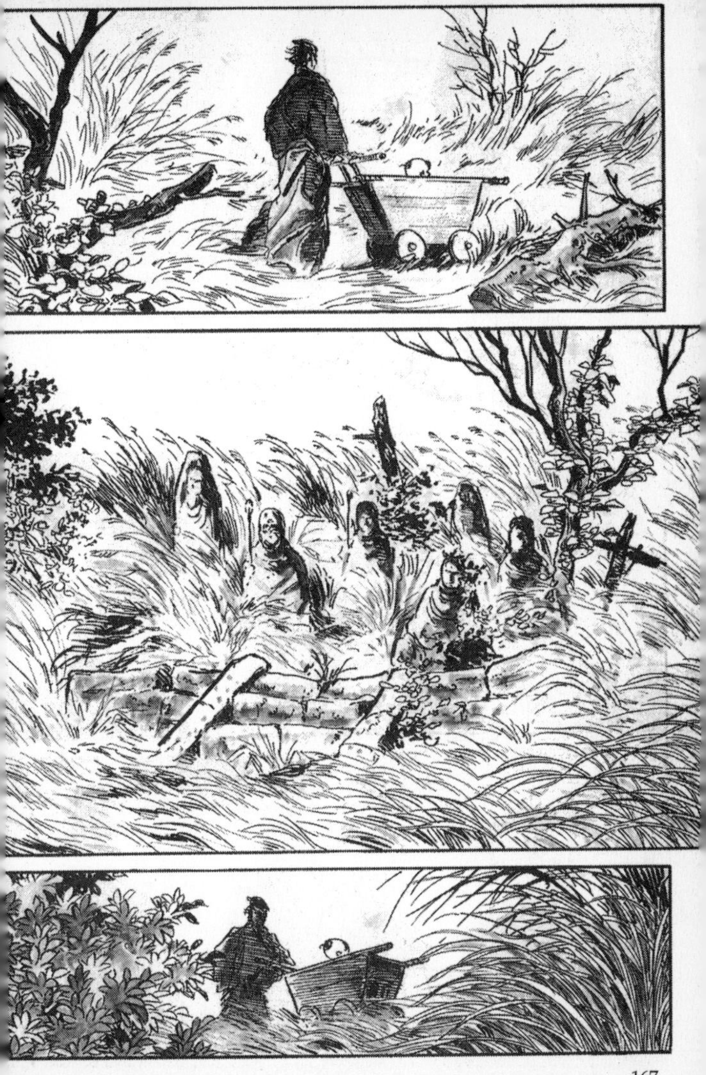

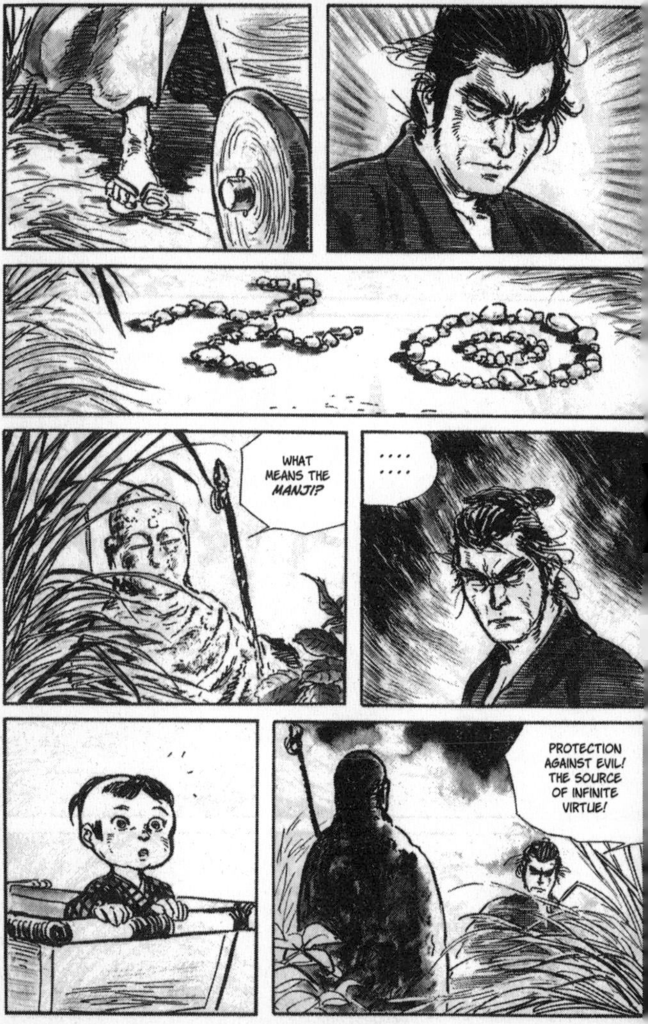
WHAT MEANS THE MANJI!?
....
....
PROTECTION AGAINST EVIL! THE SOURCE OF INFINITE VIRTUE!

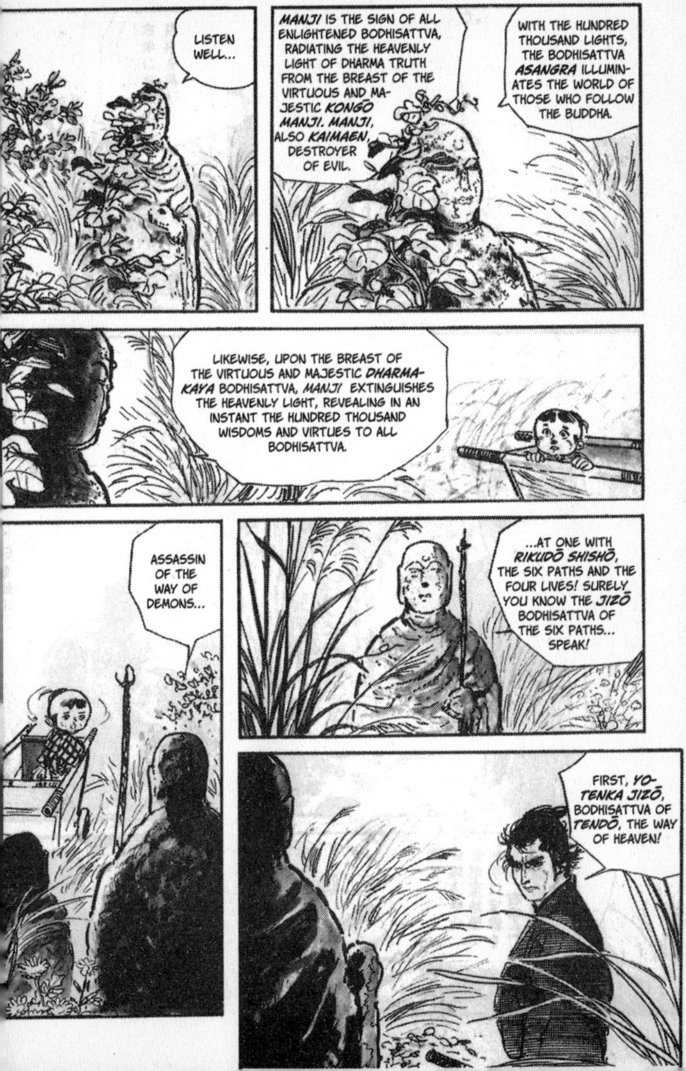
LISTEN WELL...
MANJI IS THE SIGN OF ALL ENLIGHTENED BODHISATTVA, RADIATING THE HEAVENLY LIGHT OF DHARMA TRUTH FROM THE BREAST OF THE VIRTUOUS AND MAJESTIC KONGŌ MANJI. MANJI, ALSO KAIMAEN, DESTROYER OF EVIL.
WITH THE HUNDRED THOUSAND LIGHTS, THE BODHISATTVA ASANGRA ILLUMINATES THE WORLD OF THOSE WHO FOLLOW THE BUDDHA.
LIKEWISE, UPON THE BREAST OF THE VIRTUOUS AND MAJESTIC DHARMAKAYA BODHISATTVA, MANJI EXTINGUISHES THE HEAVENLY LIGHT, REVEALING IN AN INSTANT THE HUNDRED THOUSAND WISDOMS AND VIRTUES TO ALL BODHISATTVA.
ASSASSIN OF THE WAY OF DEMONS...
...AT ONE WITH RIKUDŌ SHISHŌ, THE SIX PATHS AND THE FOUR LIVES! SURELY YOU KNOW THE JIZŌ BODHISATTVA OF THE SIX PATHS... SPEAK!
FIRST, YOTENKA JIZŌ, BODHISATTVA OF TENDŌ, THE WAY OF HEAVEN!

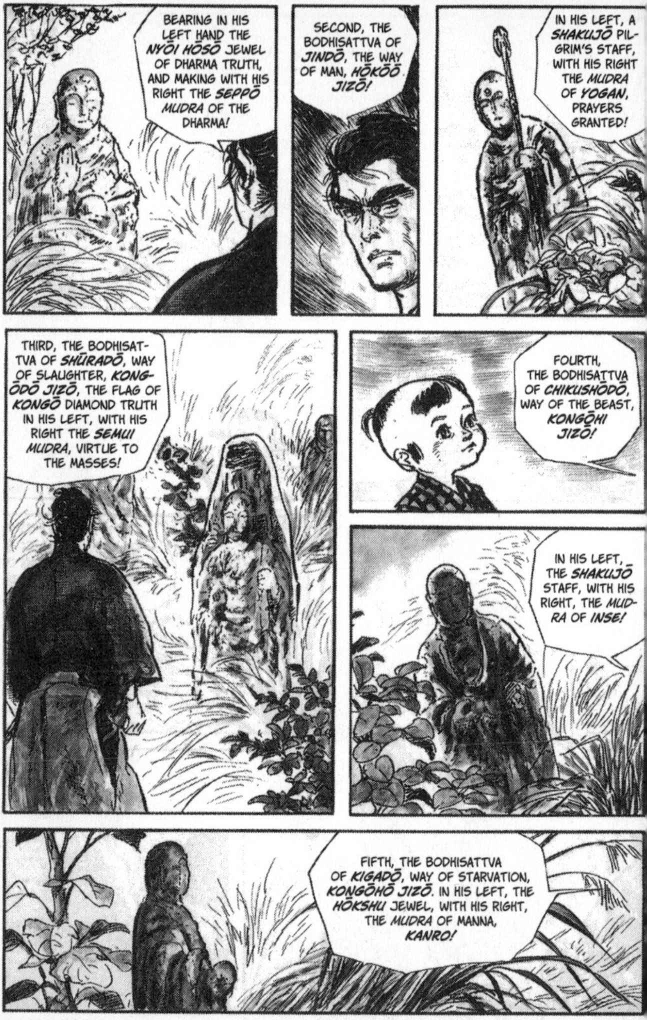

BEARING IN HIS LEFT HAND THE NYŌI HŌSŌ JEWEL OF DHARMA TRUTH, AND MAKING WITH HIS RIGHT THE SEPPŌ MUDRA OF THE DHARMA!
SECOND, THE BODHISATTVA OF JINDŌ, THE WAY OF MAN, HŌKŌŌ JIZŌ!
IN HIS LEFT, A SHAKUJŌ PILGRIM'S STAFF, WITH HIS RIGHT THE MUDRA OF YOGAN, PRAYERS GRANTED!
THIRD, THE BODHISATTVA OF SHŪRADŌ, WAY OF SLAUGHTER, KONGŌDŌ JIZŌ, THE FLAG OF KONGŌ DIAMOND TRUTH IN HIS LEFT, WITH HIS RIGHT THE SEMUI MUDRA, VIRTUE TO THE MASSES!
FOURTH, THE BODHISATTVA OF CHIKUSHŌDŌ, WAY OF THE BEAST, KONGŌHI JIZŌ!
IN HIS LEFT, THE SHAKUJŌ STAFF, WITH HIS RIGHT, THE MUDRA OF INSE!
FIFTH, THE BODHISATTVA OF KIGADŌ, WAY OF STARVATION, KONGŌHŌ JIZŌ. IN HIS LEFT, THE HŌKSHU JEWEL, WITH HIS RIGHT, THE MUDRA OF MANNA, KANRO!

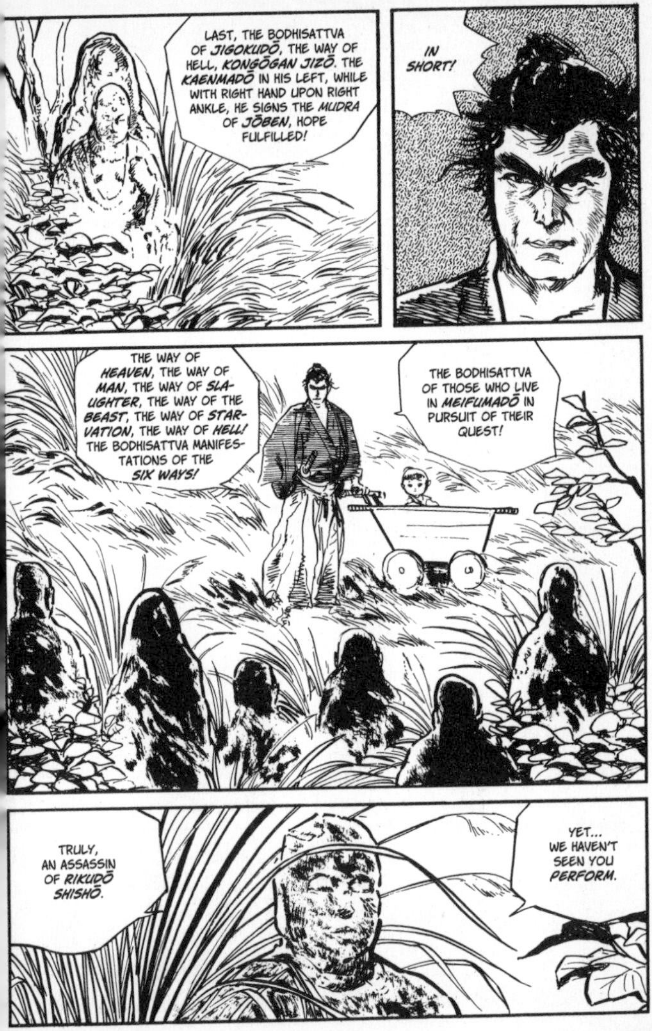

LAST, THE BODHISATTVA OF *JIGOKUDŌ*, THE WAY OF HELL, *KONGŌGAN JIZŌ*. THE *KAENMADŌ* IN HIS LEFT, WHILE WITH RIGHT HAND UPON RIGHT ANKLE, HE SIGNS THE *MUDRA* OF *JŌBEN*, HOPE FULFILLED!
IN SHORT!
THE WAY OF *HEAVEN*, THE WAY OF *MAN*, THE WAY OF *SLAUGHTER*, THE WAY OF THE *BEAST*, THE WAY OF *STARVATION*, THE WAY OF *HELL!* THE BODHISATTVA MANIFESTATIONS OF THE *SIX WAYS!*
THE BODHISATTVA OF THOSE WHO LIVE IN *MEIFUMADŌ* IN PURSUIT OF THEIR QUEST!
TRULY, AN ASSASSIN OF *RIKUDŌ SHISHŌ*.
YET... WE HAVEN'T SEEN YOU *PERFORM*.

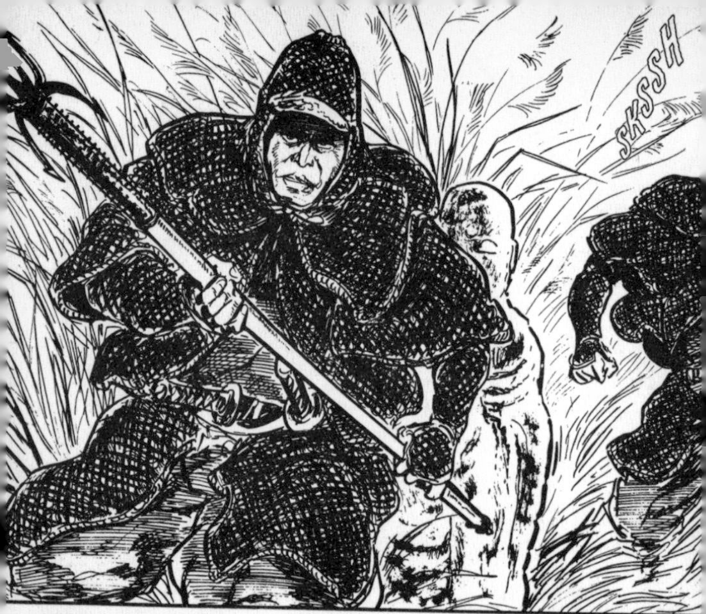
SKSSH
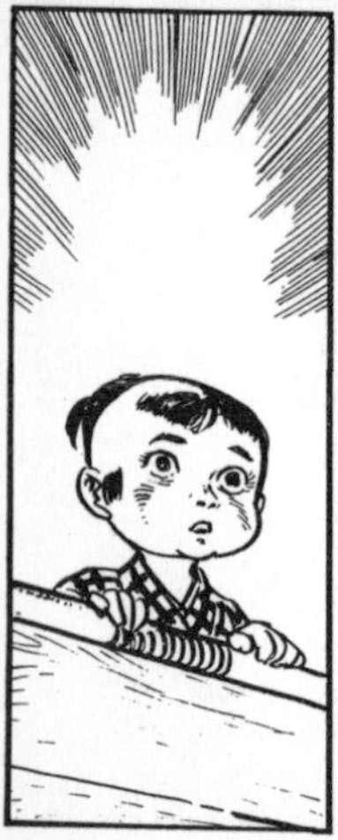
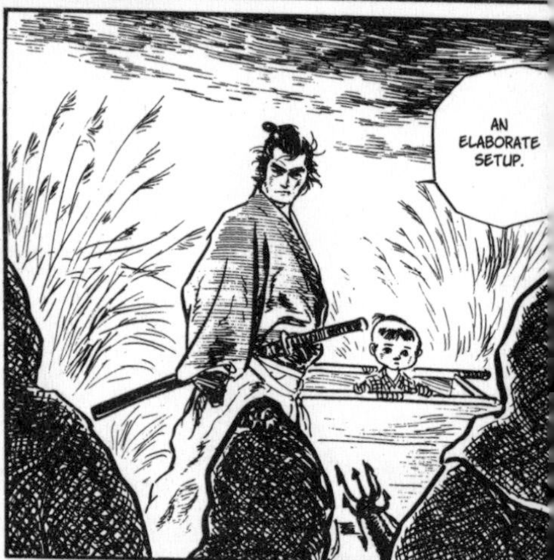
AN ELABORATE SETUP.

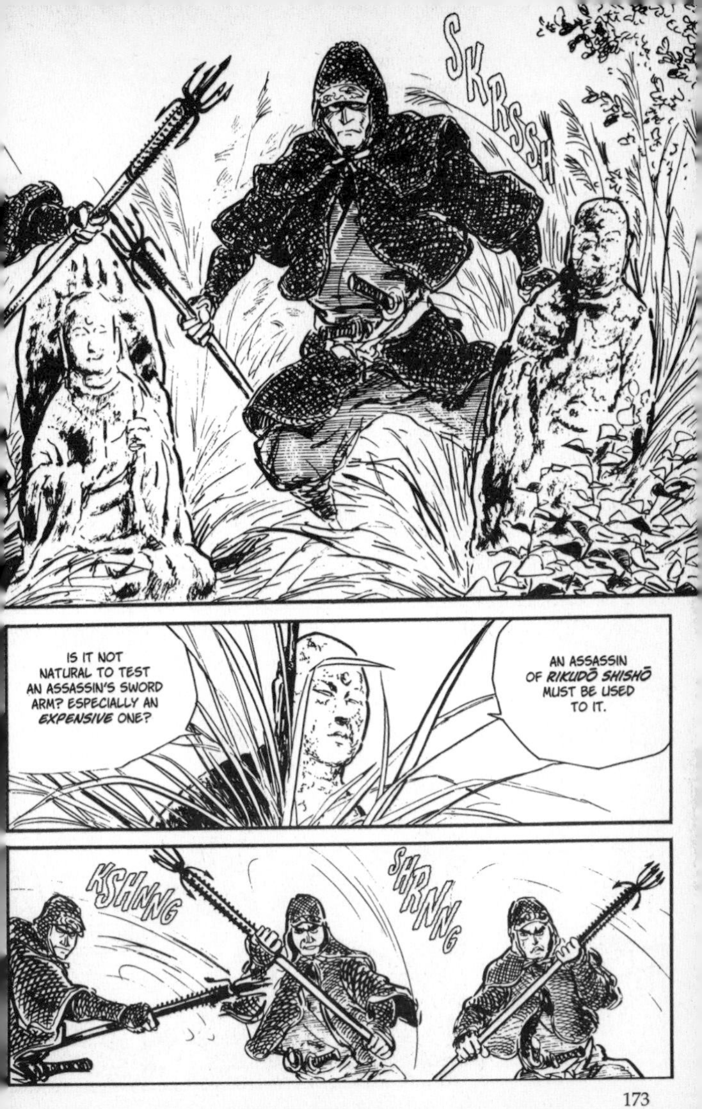
SKRSSSH
IS IT NOT NATURAL TO TEST AN ASSASSIN'S SWORD ARM? ESPECIALLY AN *EXPENSIVE* ONE?
AN ASSASSIN OF *RIKUDŌ SHISHŌ* MUST BE USED TO IT.
KSHNNG
SHRNNG

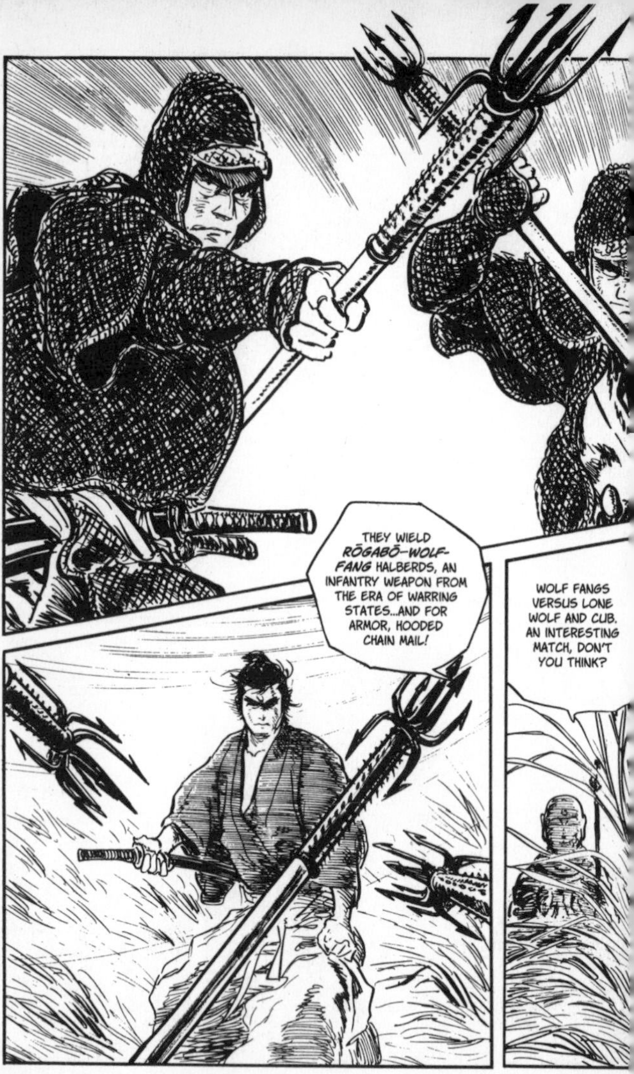
THEY WIELD *RŌGABŌ—WOLF-FANG* HALBERDS, AN INFANTRY WEAPON FROM THE ERA OF WARRING STATES...AND FOR ARMOR, HOODED CHAIN MAIL!
WOLF FANGS VERSUS LONE WOLF AND CUB. AN INTERESTING MATCH, DON'T YOU THINK?

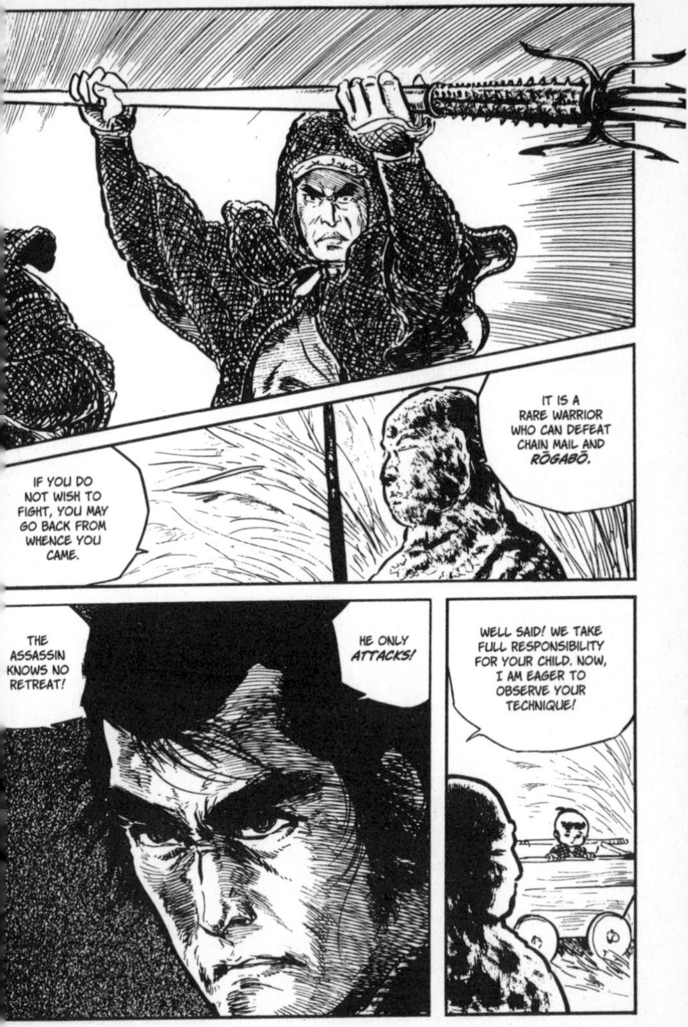
IT IS A RARE WARRIOR WHO CAN DEFEAT CHAIN MAIL AND RŌGABŌ.
IF YOU DO NOT WISH TO FIGHT, YOU MAY GO BACK FROM WHENCE YOU CAME.
THE ASSASSIN KNOWS NO RETREAT!
HE ONLY ATTACKS!
WELL SAID! WE TAKE FULL RESPONSIBILITY FOR YOUR CHILD. NOW, I AM EAGER TO OBSERVE YOUR TECHNIQUE!

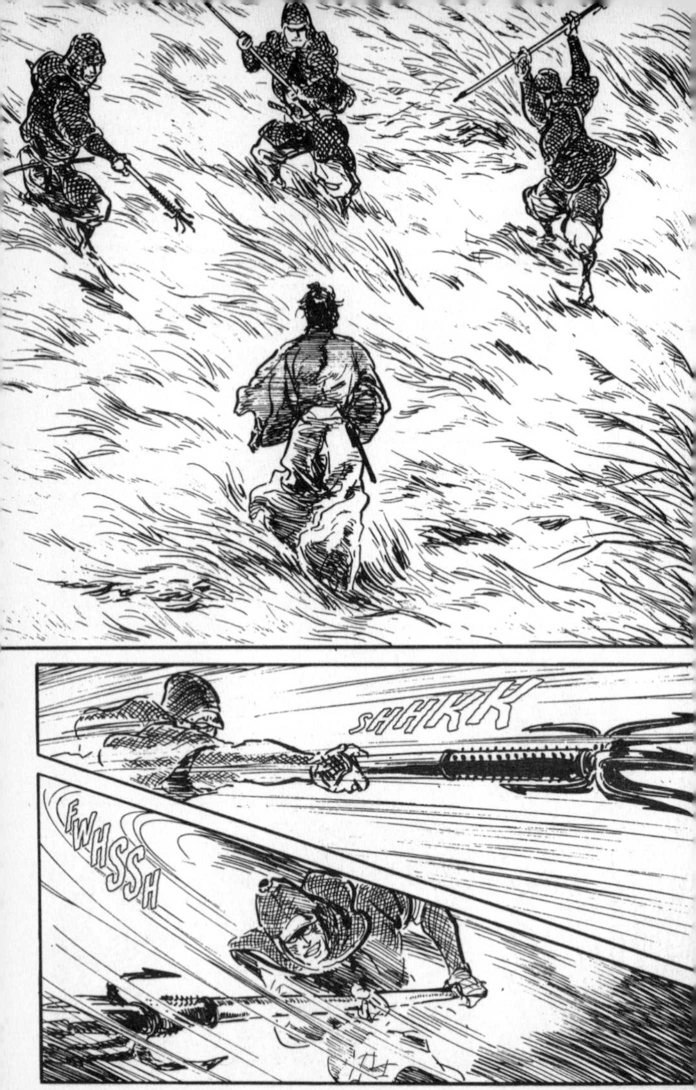
SHHKK
FWHSSH

SHNNG

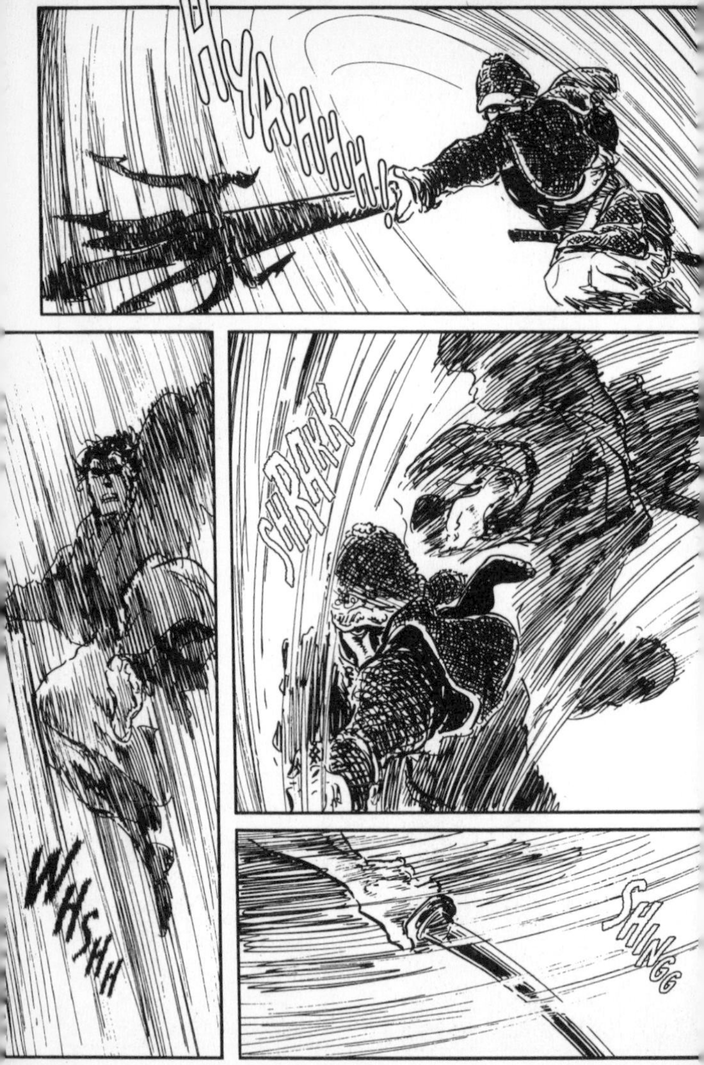
HIYAAHHH!
WHSHH
SHRAKK
SHINGG

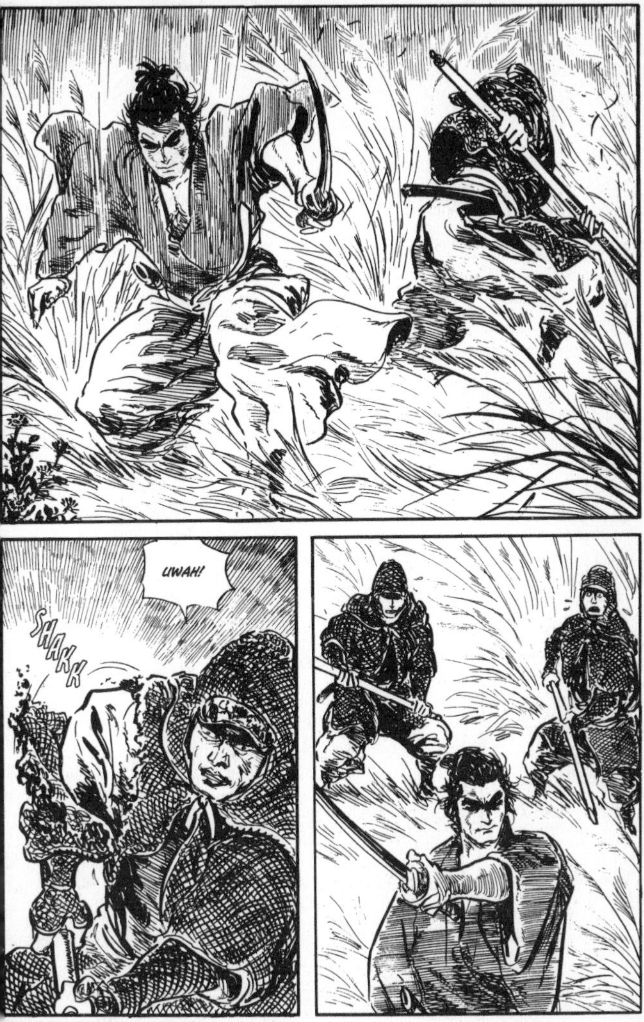
UWAH!
SHAKK

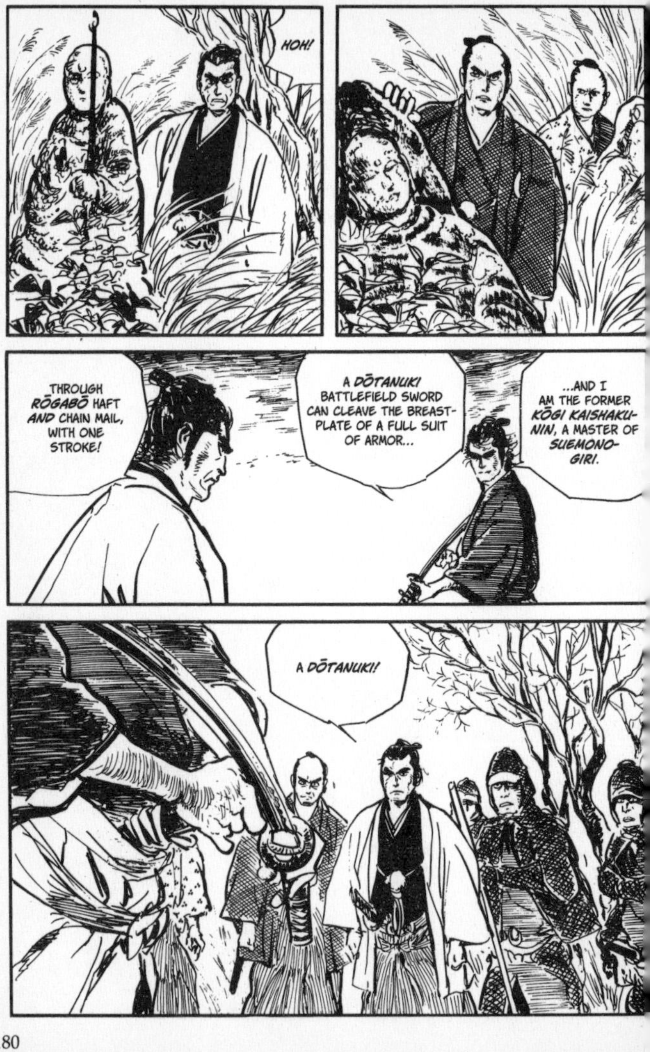
HOH!
THROUGH RŌGABŌ HAFT AND CHAIN MAIL, WITH ONE STROKE!
A DŌTANUKI BATTLEFIELD SWORD CAN CLEAVE THE BREAST-PLATE OF A FULL SUIT OF ARMOR...
...AND I AM THE FORMER KŌGI KAISHAKU-NIN, A MASTER OF SUEMONO-GIRI.
A DŌTANUKI!

AND SUCH INCREDIBLE SKILL! YOUR REPUTATION IS DESERVED!

I'M OVERWHELMED!

FORGIVE OUR IMPROPRIETY.

TELL ME THE STORY.

JIZŌ GENBA, JŌDAI CASTLE WARDEN OF IWAKIDAIRA HAN.

JIZŌ GYŌBU, METSUKE INSPECTOR.

COMMANDER OF THE GUARDS, JIZŌ KIKEN.

HOME COMMISSIONER, JIZŌ HEIDAI.

JIZŌ YAJIRŌ, INSPECTOR OF THE GUARDS.

FORGIVE MY EARLIER AFFRONT.

JIZŌ KOSHIRŌ, HAN STOREHOUSE MANAGER.

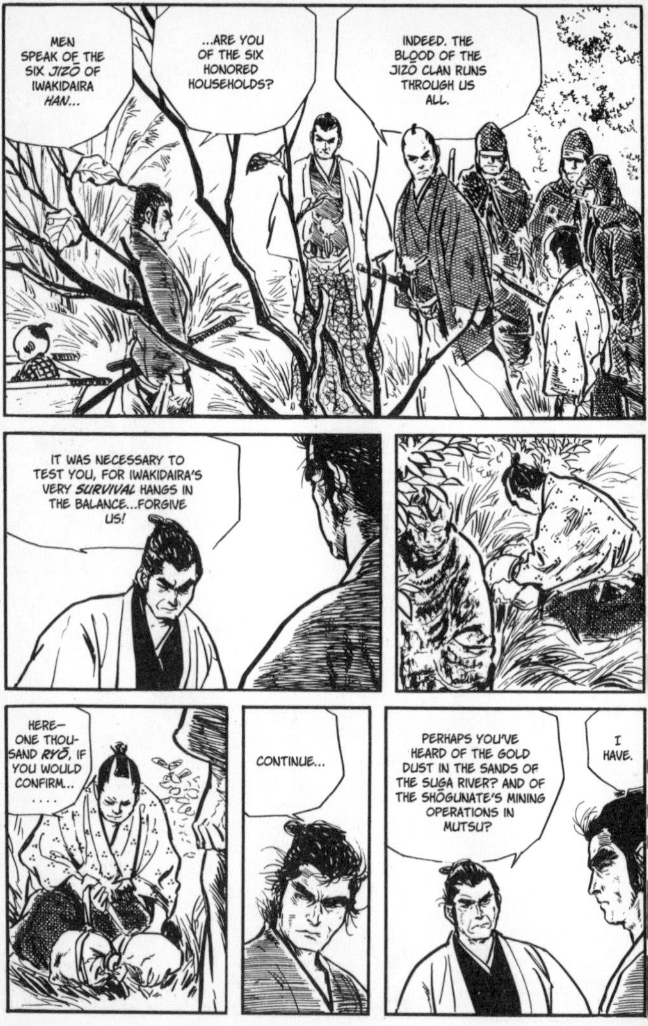
MEN SPEAK OF THE SIX *JIZŌ* OF IWAKIDAIRA *HAN*...
...ARE YOU OF THE SIX HONORED HOUSEHOLDS?
INDEED. THE BLOOD OF THE JIZŌ CLAN RUNS THROUGH US ALL.
IT WAS NECESSARY TO TEST YOU, FOR IWAKIDAIRA'S VERY *SURVIVAL* HANGS IN THE BALANCE...FORGIVE US!
HERE— ONE THOUSAND *RYŌ*, IF YOU WOULD CONFIRM..
....
CONTINUE...
PERHAPS YOU'VE HEARD OF THE GOLD DUST IN THE SANDS OF THE SUGA RIVER? AND OF THE SHŌGUNATE'S MINING OPERATIONS IN MUTSU?
I HAVE.

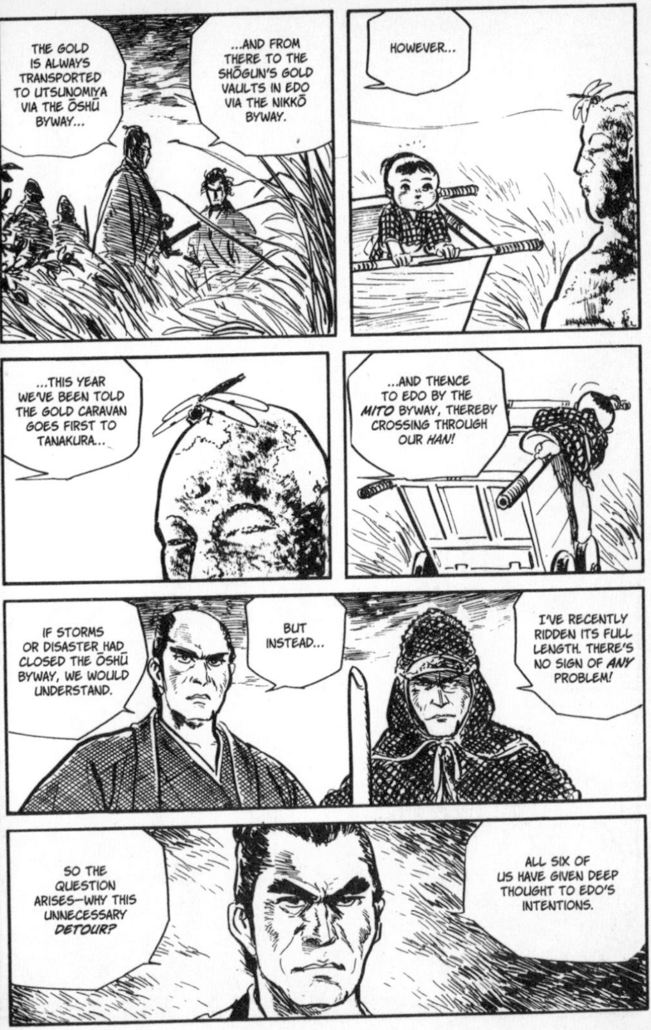
THE GOLD IS ALWAYS TRANSPORTED TO UTSUNOMIYA VIA THE ŌSHŪ BYWAY...
...AND FROM THERE TO THE SHŌGUN'S GOLD VAULTS IN EDO VIA THE NIKKŌ BYWAY.
HOWEVER...
...THIS YEAR WE'VE BEEN TOLD THE GOLD CARAVAN GOES FIRST TO TANAKURA...
...AND THENCE TO EDO BY THE *MITO* BYWAY, THEREBY CROSSING THROUGH OUR *HAN!*
IF STORMS OR DISASTER HAD CLOSED THE ŌSHŪ BYWAY, WE WOULD UNDERSTAND.
BUT INSTEAD...
I'VE RECENTLY RIDDEN ITS FULL LENGTH. THERE'S NO SIGN OF *ANY* PROBLEM!
SO THE QUESTION ARISES—WHY THIS UNNECESSARY *DETOUR?*
ALL SIX OF US HAVE GIVEN DEEP THOUGHT TO EDO'S INTENTIONS.

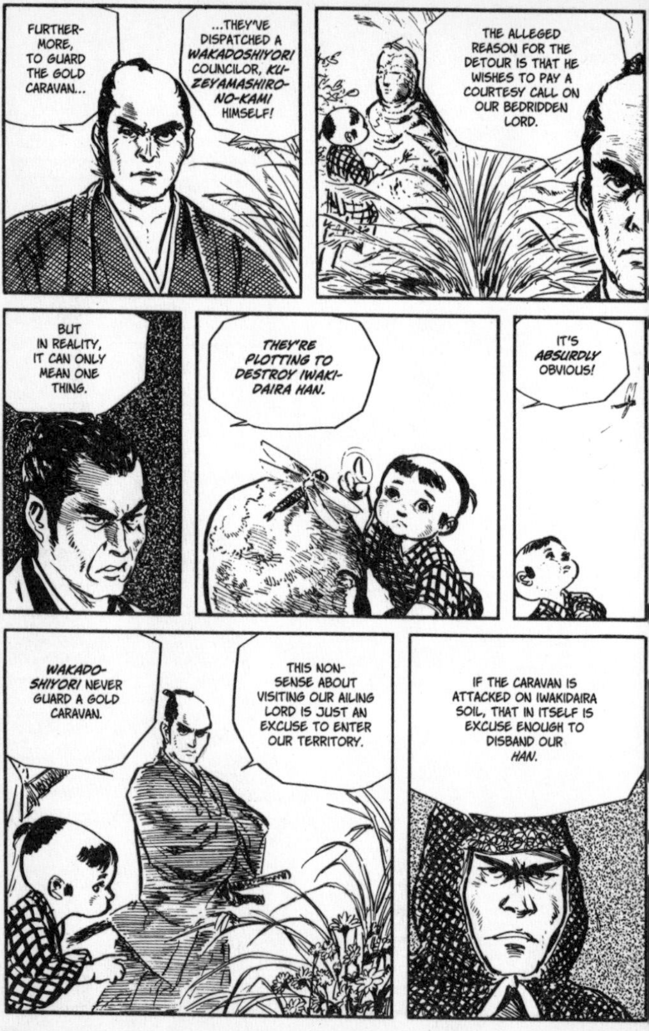
FURTHER-MORE, TO GUARD THE GOLD CARAVAN...
...THEY'VE DISPATCHED A *WAKADOSHIYORI* COUNCILOR, *KUZEYAMASHIRO-NO-KAMI* HIMSELF!
THE ALLEGED REASON FOR THE DETOUR IS THAT HE WISHES TO PAY A COURTESY CALL ON OUR BEDRIDDEN LORD.
BUT IN REALITY, IT CAN ONLY MEAN ONE THING.
THEY'RE PLOTTING TO DESTROY IWAKIDAIRA HAN.
IT'S *ABSURDLY* OBVIOUS!
WAKADOSHIYORI NEVER GUARD A GOLD CARAVAN.
THIS NONSENSE ABOUT VISITING OUR AILING LORD IS JUST AN EXCUSE TO ENTER OUR TERRITORY.
IF THE CARAVAN IS ATTACKED ON IWAKIDAIRA SOIL, THAT IN ITSELF IS EXCUSE ENOUGH TO DISBAND OUR *HAN*.

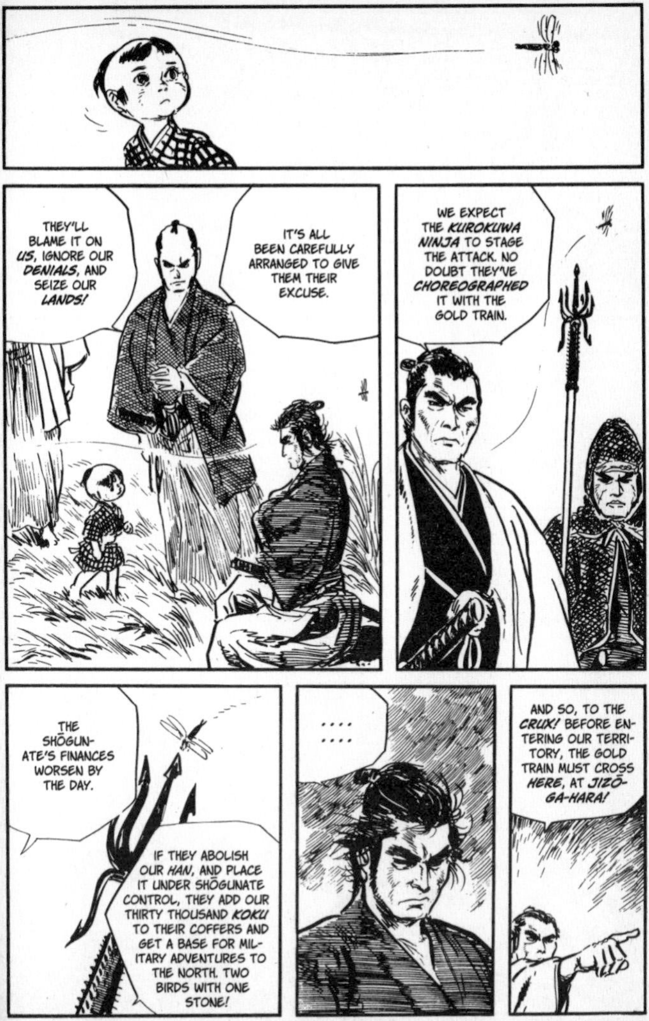
THEY'LL BLAME IT ON US, IGNORE OUR DENIALS, AND SEIZE OUR LANDS!
IT'S ALL BEEN CAREFULLY ARRANGED TO GIVE THEM THEIR EXCUSE.
WE EXPECT THE KUROKUWA NINJA TO STAGE THE ATTACK. NO DOUBT THEY'VE CHOREOGRAPHED IT WITH THE GOLD TRAIN.
THE SHŌGUNATE'S FINANCES WORSEN BY THE DAY.
IF THEY ABOLISH OUR HAN, AND PLACE IT UNDER SHŌGUNATE CONTROL, THEY ADD OUR THIRTY THOUSAND KOKU TO THEIR COFFERS AND GET A BASE FOR MILITARY ADVENTURES TO THE NORTH. TWO BIRDS WITH ONE STONE!
....
AND SO, TO THE CRUX! BEFORE ENTERING OUR TERRITORY, THE GOLD TRAIN MUST CROSS HERE, AT JIZŌ-GA-HARA!

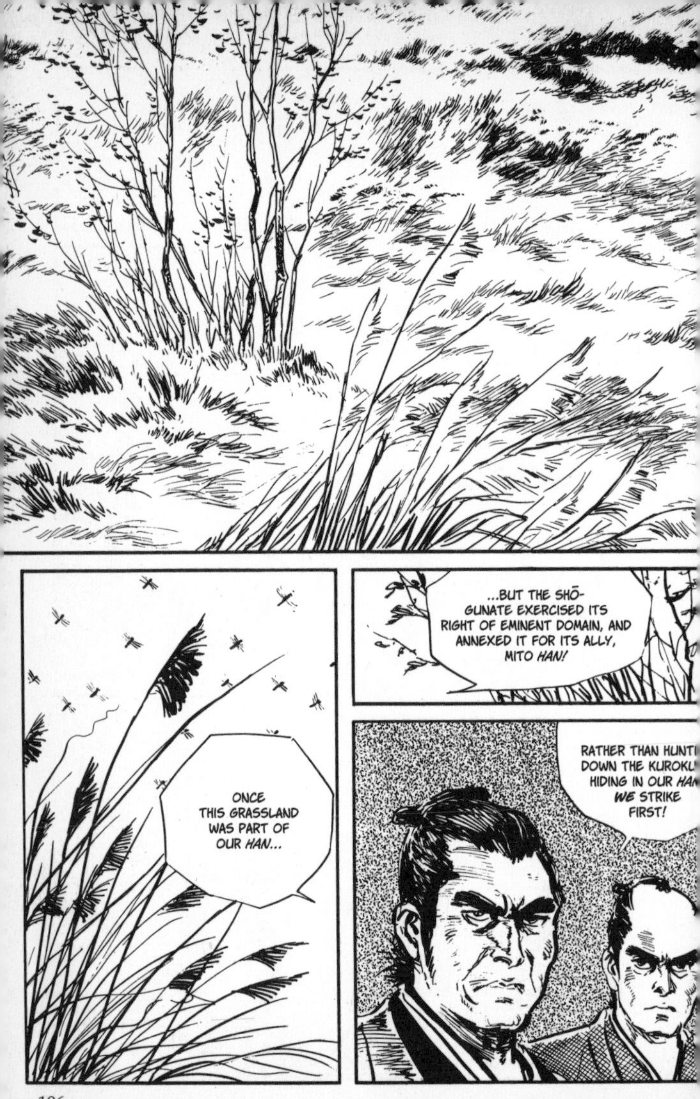
ONCE THIS GRASSLAND WAS PART OF OUR *HAN*...
...BUT THE SHŌ-GUNATE EXERCISED ITS RIGHT OF EMINENT DOMAIN, AND ANNEXED IT FOR ITS ALLY, MITO *HAN!*
RATHER THAN HUNTI DOWN THE KUROKU HIDING IN OUR *HA* ***WE*** STRIKE FIRST!

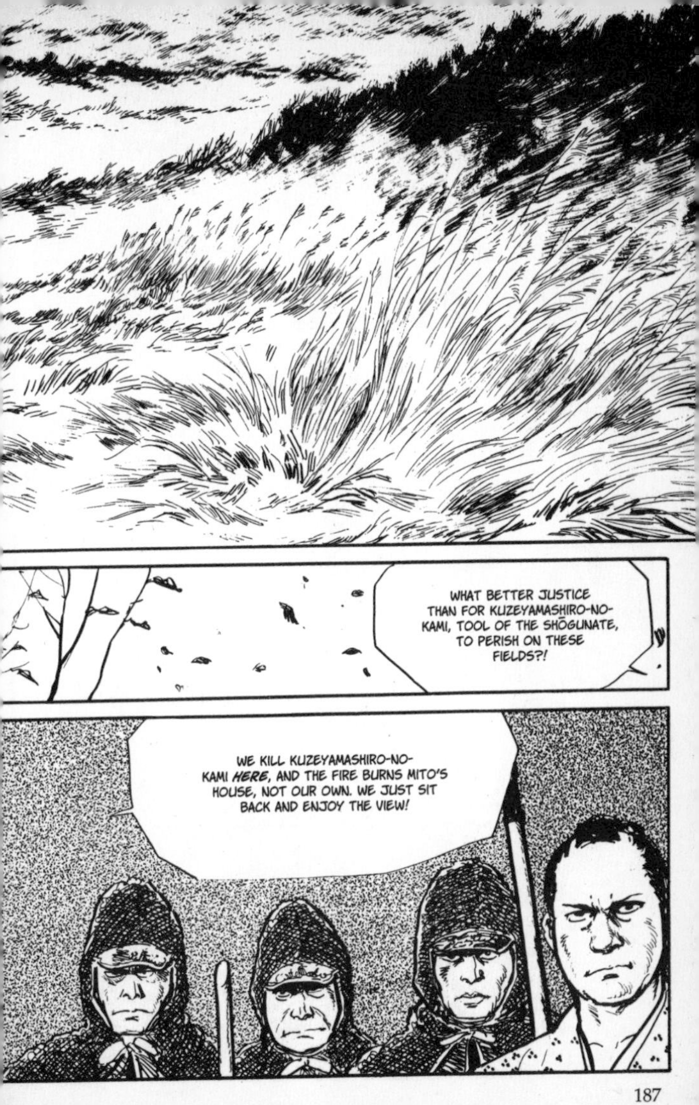
WHAT BETTER JUSTICE THAN FOR KUZEYAMASHIRO-NO-KAMI, TOOL OF THE SHŌGUNATE, TO PERISH ON THESE FIELDS?!
WE KILL KUZEYAMASHIRO-NO-KAMI *HERE*, AND THE FIRE BURNS MITO'S HOUSE, NOT OUR OWN. WE JUST SIT BACK AND ENJOY THE VIEW!

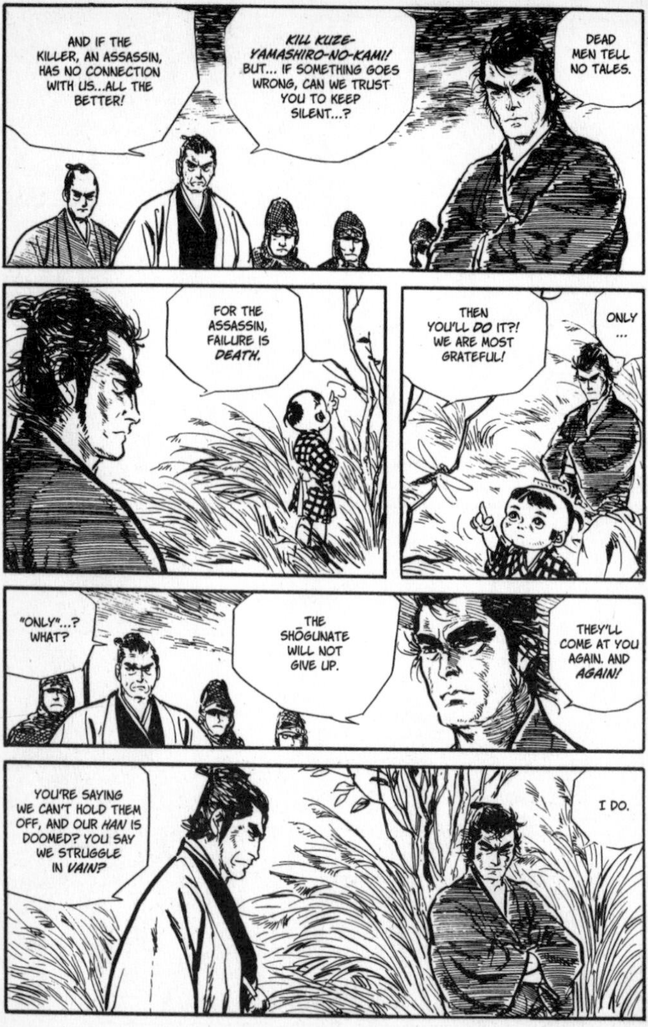
AND IF THE KILLER, AN ASSASSIN, HAS NO CONNECTION WITH US...ALL THE BETTER!
KILL KUZE-YAMASHIRO-NO-KAMI! BUT... IF SOMETHING GOES WRONG, CAN WE TRUST YOU TO KEEP SILENT...?
DEAD MEN TELL NO TALES.
FOR THE ASSASSIN, FAILURE IS DEATH.
THEN YOU'LL DO IT?! WE ARE MOST GRATEFUL!
ONLY ...
"ONLY"...? WHAT?
THE SHŌGUNATE WILL NOT GIVE UP.
THEY'LL COME AT YOU AGAIN. AND AGAIN!
YOU'RE SAYING WE CAN'T HOLD THEM OFF, AND OUR HAN IS DOOMED? YOU SAY WE STRUGGLE IN VAIN?
I DO.

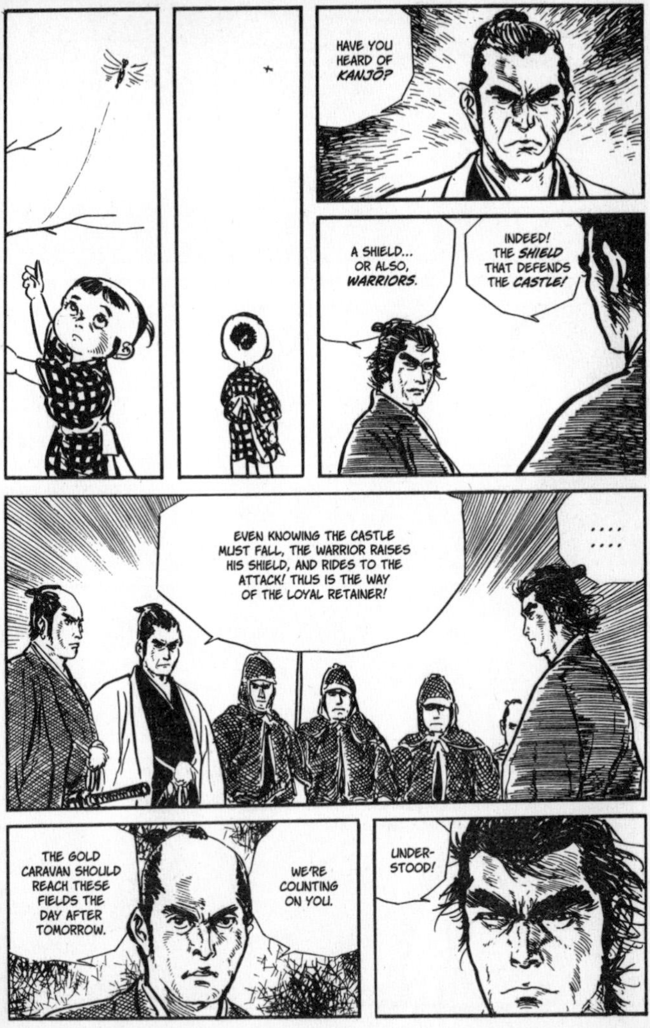
HAVE YOU HEARD OF *KANJŌ*?
A SHIELD... OR ALSO, ***WARRIORS***.
INDEED! THE ***SHIELD*** THAT DEFENDS THE ***CASTLE!***
EVEN KNOWING THE CASTLE MUST FALL, THE WARRIOR RAISES HIS SHIELD, AND RIDES TO THE ATTACK! THUS IS THE WAY OF THE LOYAL RETAINER!
....
THE GOLD CARAVAN SHOULD REACH THESE FIELDS THE DAY AFTER TOMORROW.
WE'RE COUNTING ON YOU.
UNDER-STOOD!

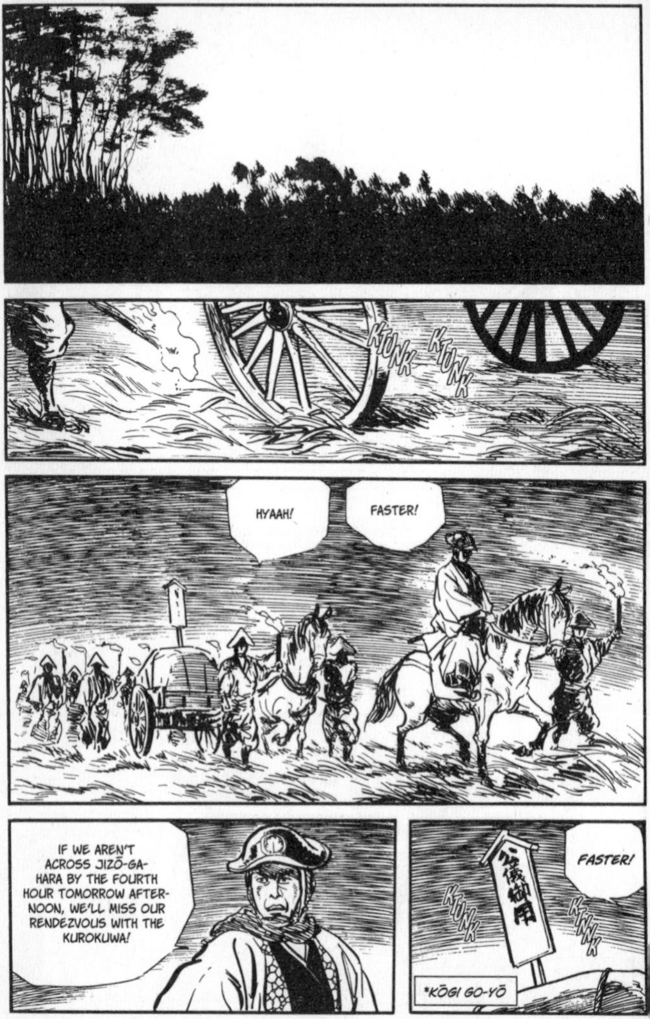
KTUNK
KTUNK
HYAAH!
FASTER!
IF WE AREN'T ACROSS JIZŌ-GA-HARA BY THE FOURTH HOUR TOMORROW AFTER-NOON, WE'LL MISS OUR RENDEZVOUS WITH THE KUROKUWA!
公儀御用
KTUNK
FASTER!
KTUNK
*KŌGI GO-YŌ

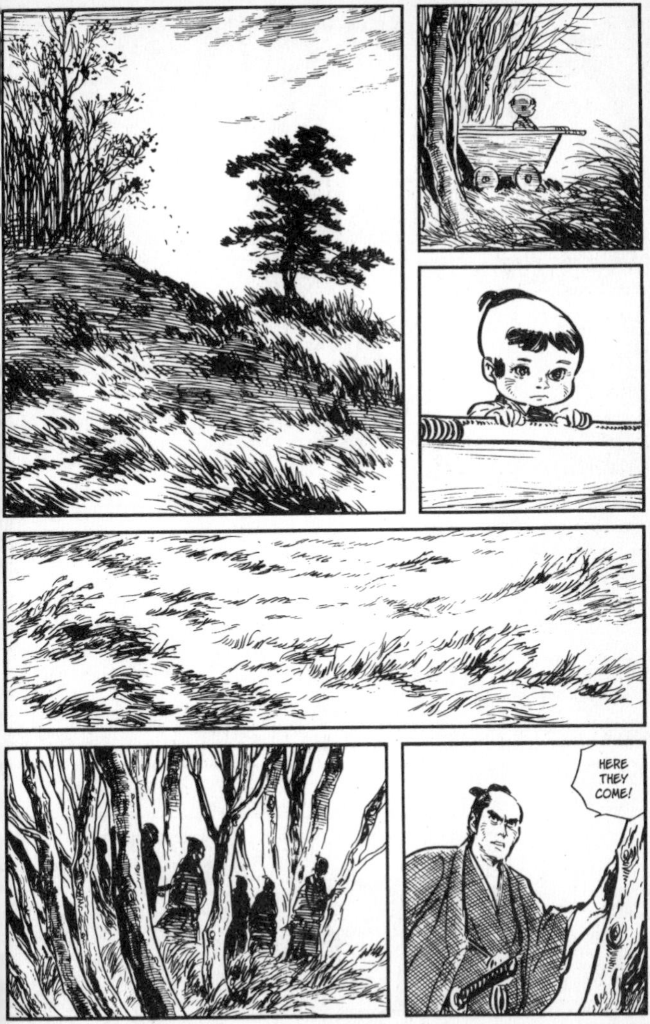
HERE THEY COME!

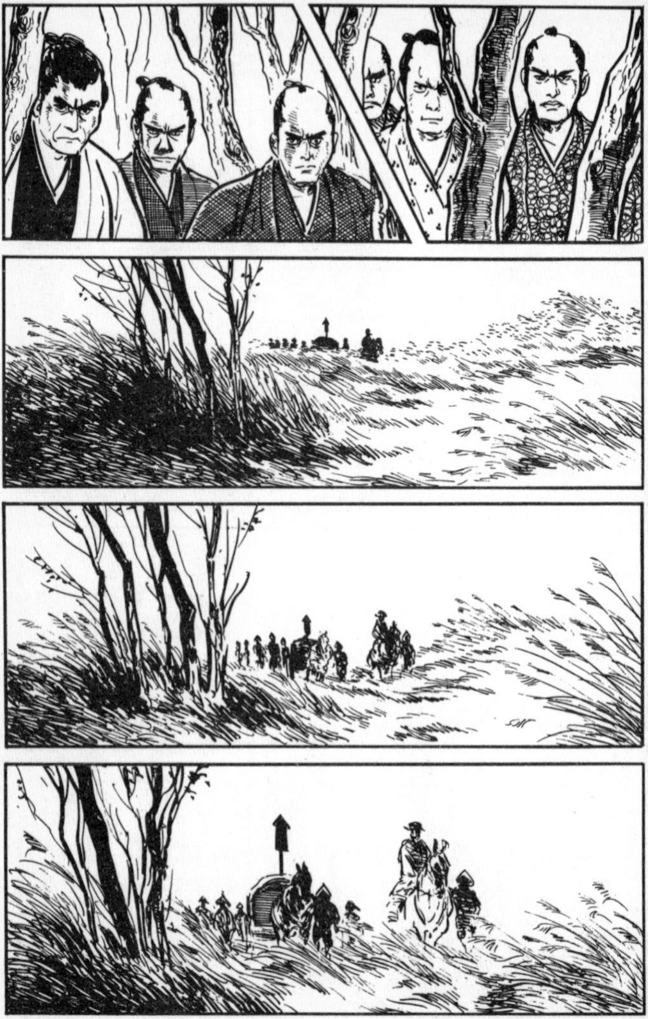

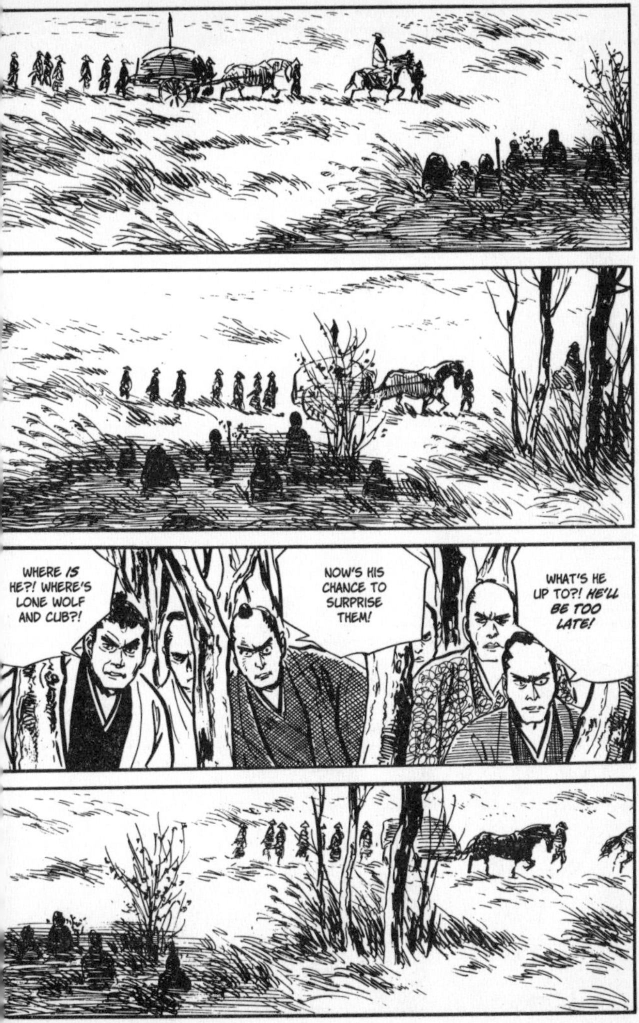
WHERE *IS* HE?! WHERE'S LONE WOLF AND CUB?!
NOW'S HIS CHANCE TO SURPRISE THEM!
WHAT'S HE UP TO?! *HE'LL BE TOO LATE!*

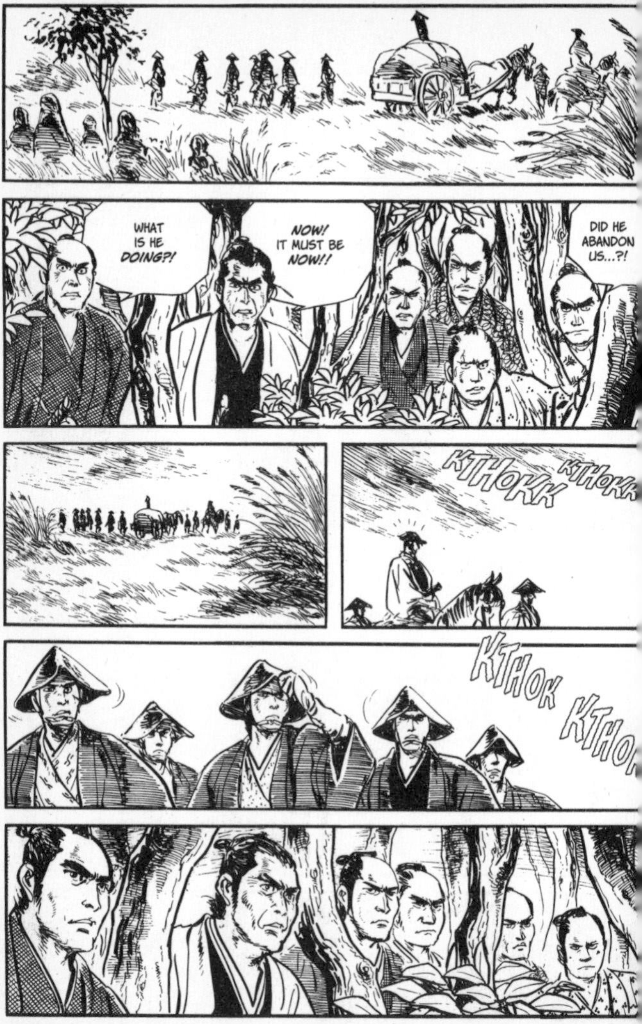
WHAT IS HE DOING?!
NOW! IT MUST BE NOW!!
DID HE ABANDON US...?!
KTHOKK KTHOKK
KTHOK KTHO

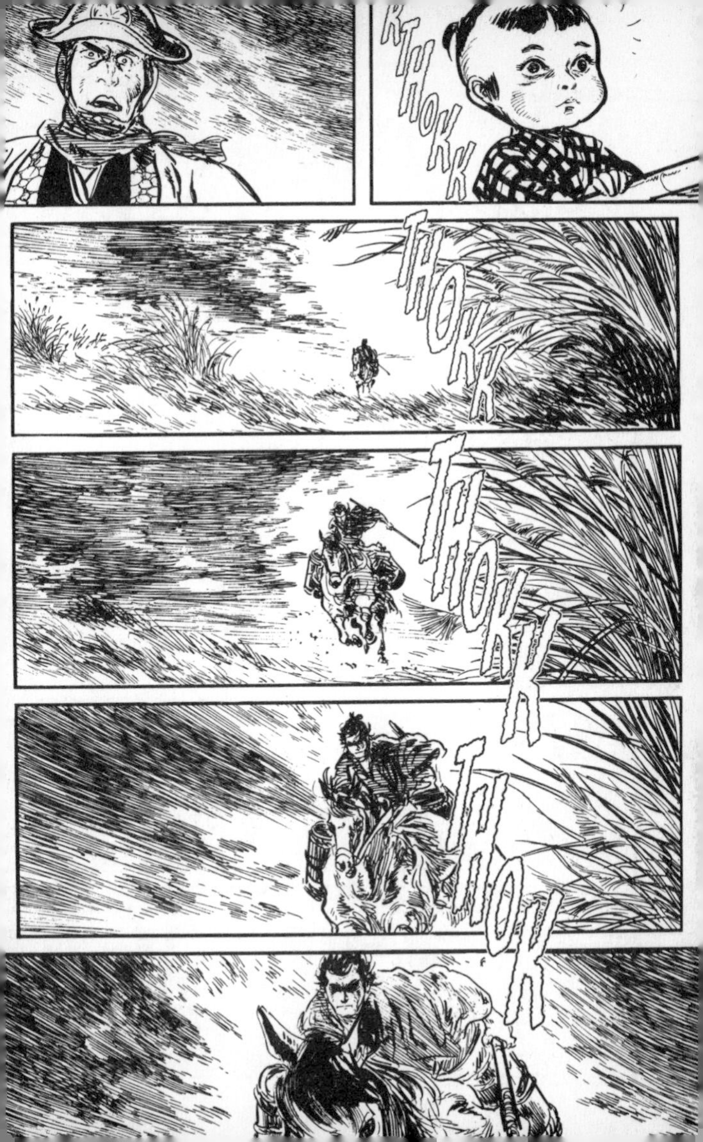

RTHOKK
THOKK
THOKK
THOK

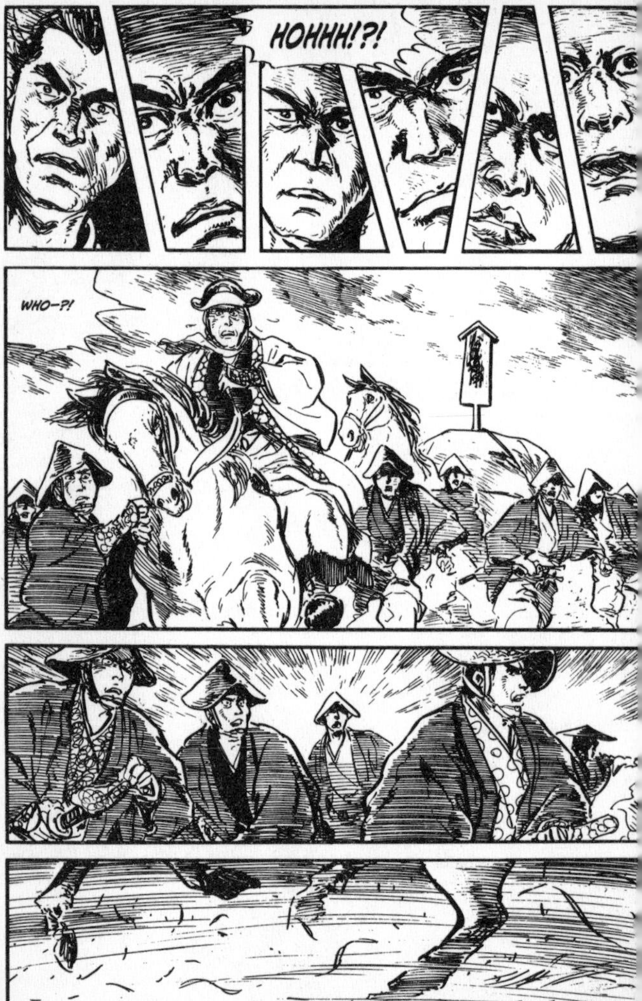
HOHHH!?!
WHO-?!

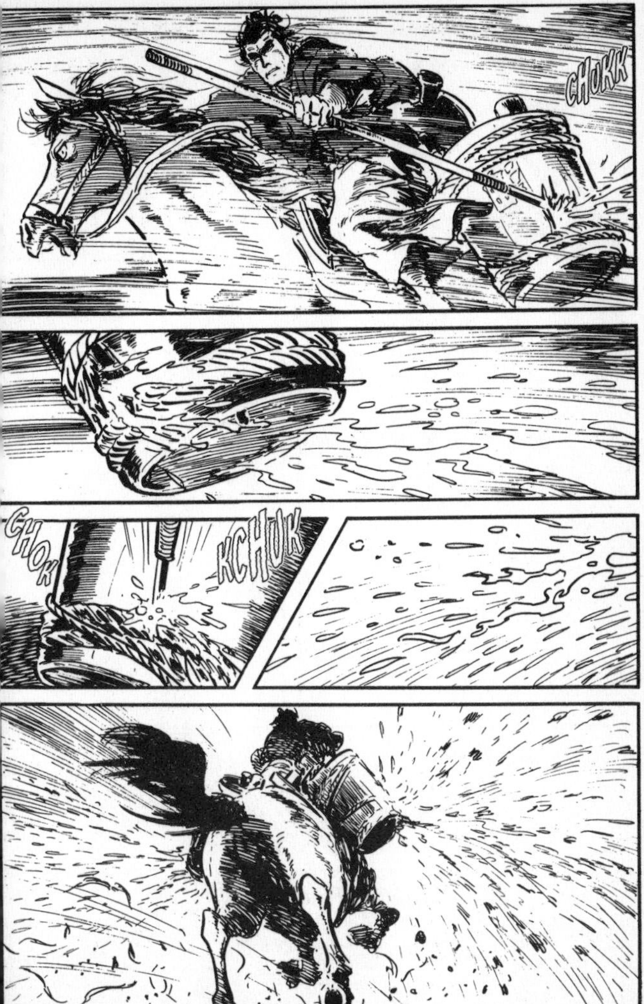
CHUKK
CHOK
KCHUK

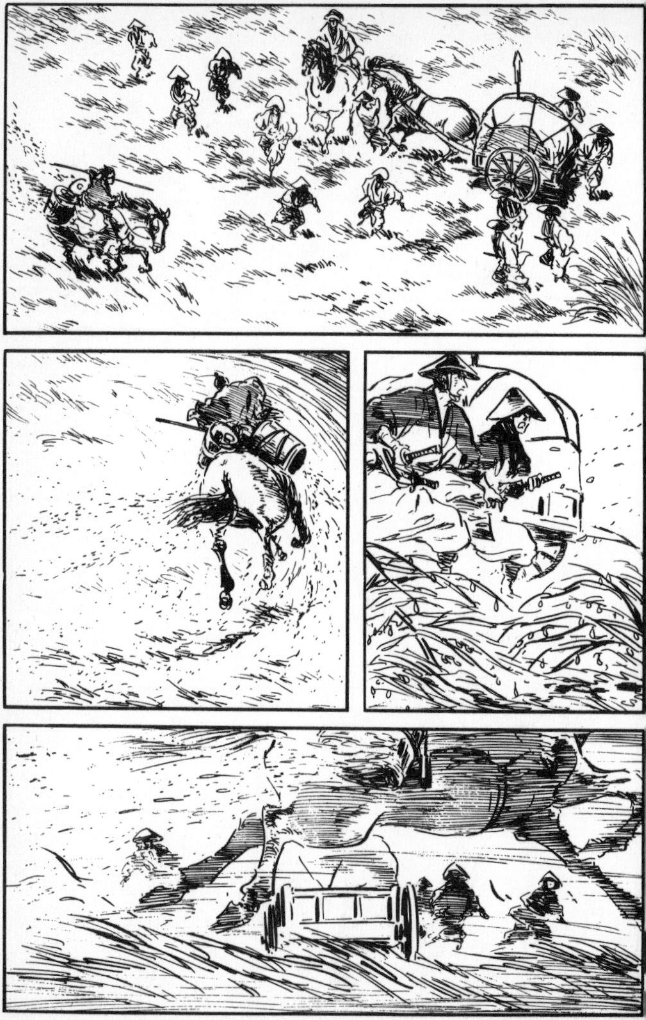

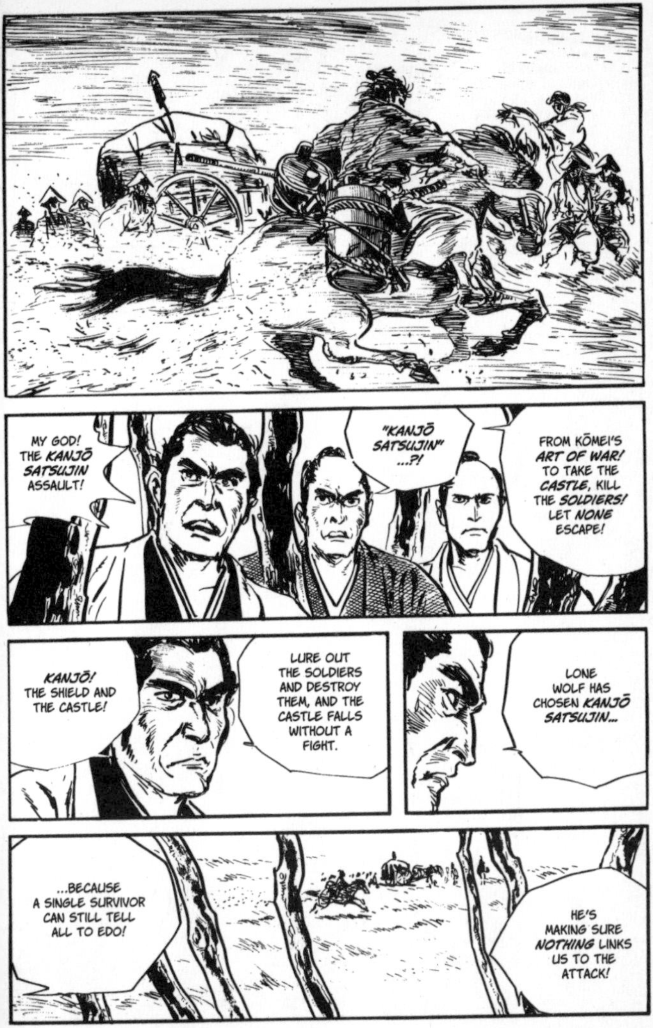
MY GOD! THE KANJŌ SATSUJIN ASSAULT!
"KANJŌ SATSUJIN" ...?!
FROM KŌMEI'S ART OF WAR! TO TAKE THE CASTLE, KILL THE SOLDIERS! LET NONE ESCAPE!
KANJŌ! THE SHIELD AND THE CASTLE!
LURE OUT THE SOLDIERS AND DESTROY THEM, AND THE CASTLE FALLS WITHOUT A FIGHT.
LONE WOLF HAS CHOSEN KANJŌ SATSUJIN...
...BECAUSE A SINGLE SURVIVOR CAN STILL TELL ALL TO EDO!
HE'S MAKING SURE NOTHING LINKS US TO THE ATTACK!

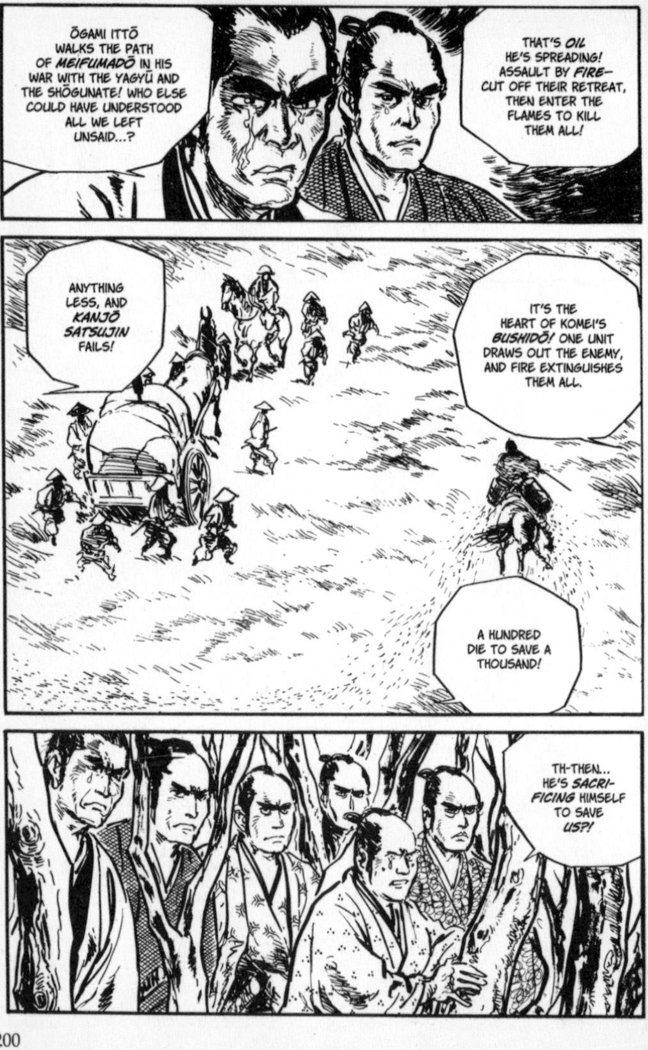
ŌGAMI ITTŌ WALKS THE PATH OF *MEIFUMADŌ* IN HIS WAR WITH THE YAGYŪ AND THE SHŌGUNATE! WHO ELSE COULD HAVE UNDERSTOOD ALL WE LEFT UNSAID...?
THAT'S *OIL* HE'S SPREADING! ASSAULT BY *FIRE*—CUT OFF THEIR RETREAT, THEN ENTER THE FLAMES TO KILL THEM ALL!
ANYTHING LESS, AND *KANJŌ SATSUJIN* FAILS!
IT'S THE HEART OF KOMEI'S *BUSHIDŌ!* ONE UNIT DRAWS OUT THE ENEMY, AND FIRE EXTINGUISHES THEM ALL.
A HUNDRED DIE TO SAVE A THOUSAND!
TH-THEN... HE'S *SACRIFICING* HIMSELF TO SAVE *US?!*

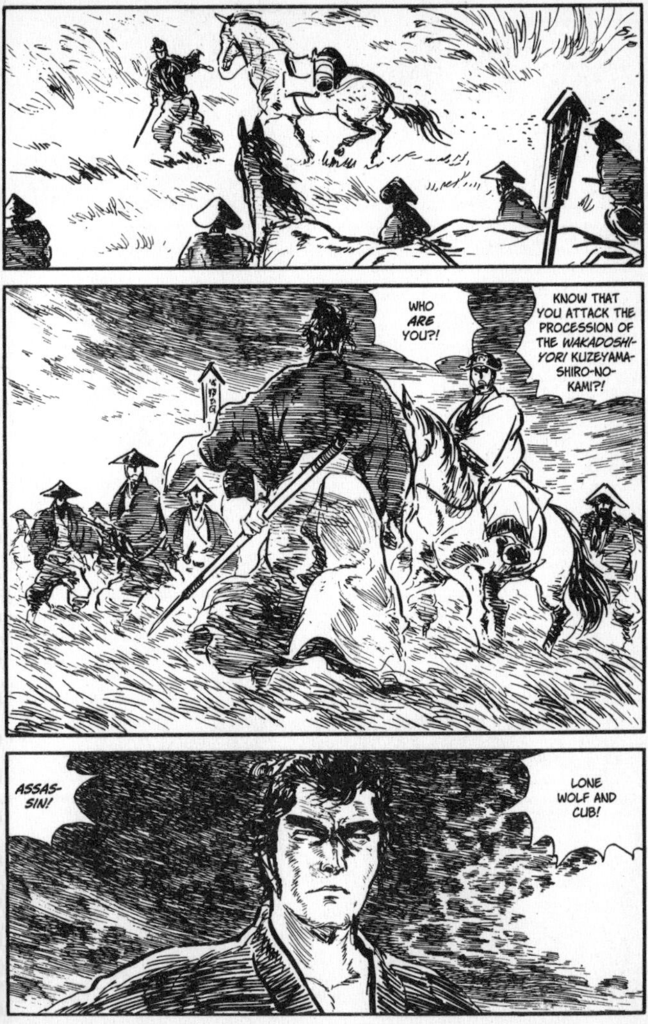

WHO *ARE* YOU?!
KNOW THAT YOU ATTACK THE PROCESSION OF THE *WAKADOSHIYORI* KUZEYAMA-SHIRO-NO-KAMI?!
ASSASSIN!
LONE WOLF AND CUB!

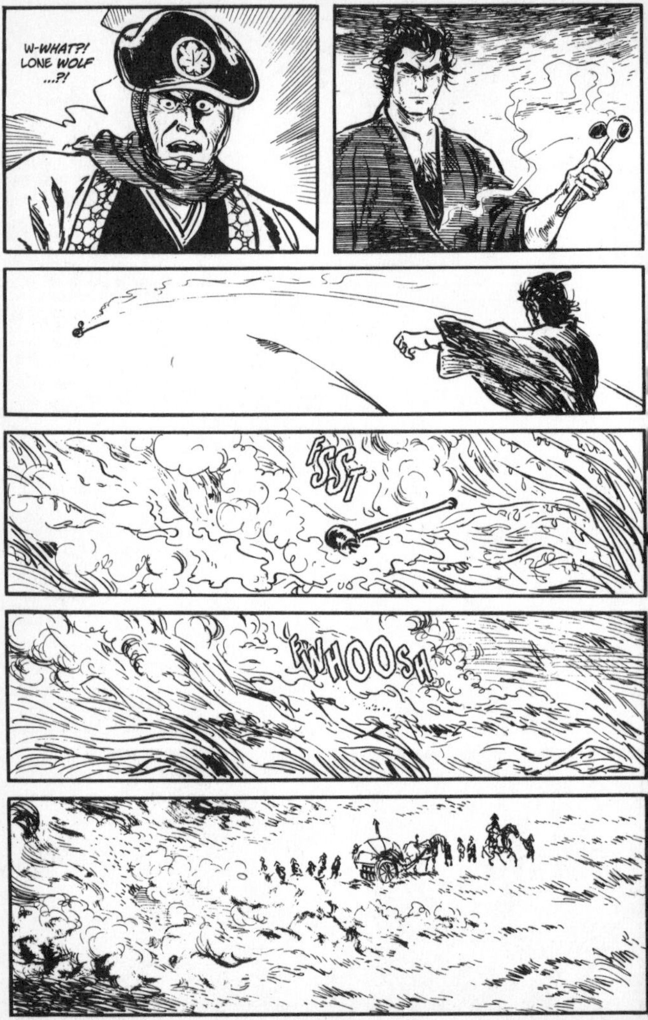
W-WHAT?! LONE WOLF ...?!
FSST
FWHOOSH

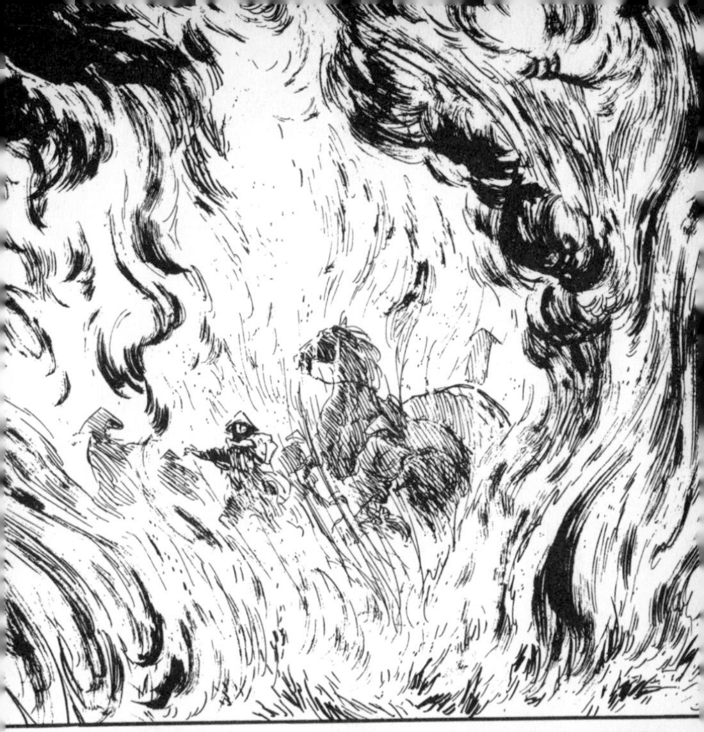

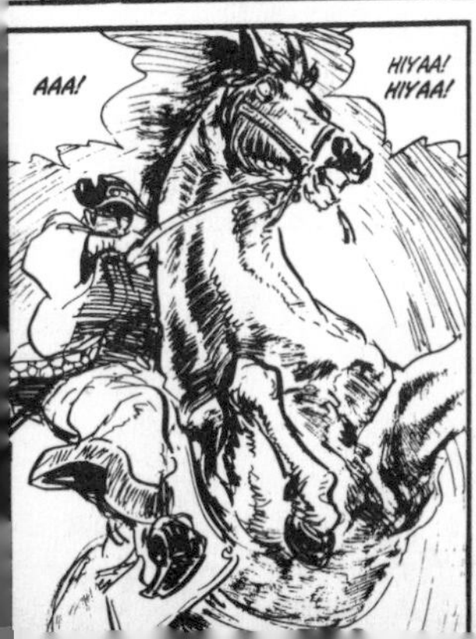
AAA!
HIYAA! HIYAA!

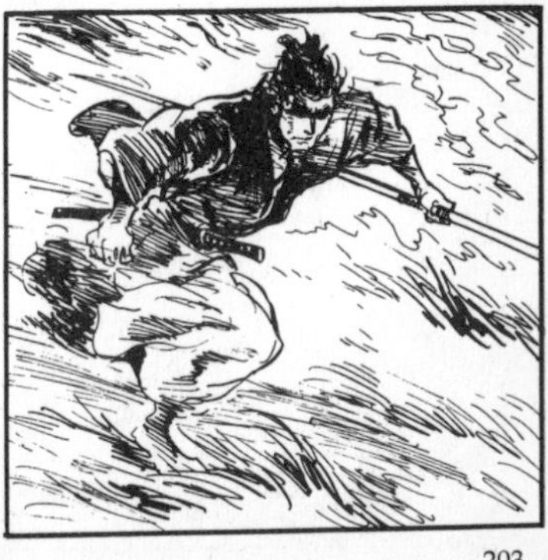

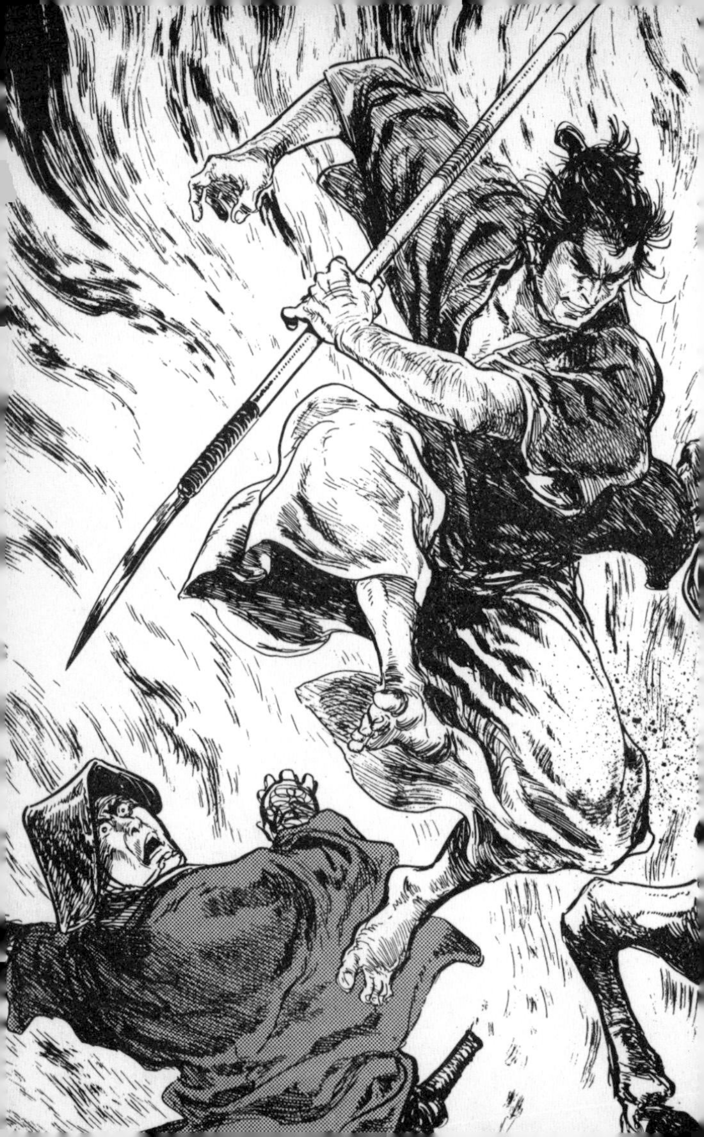

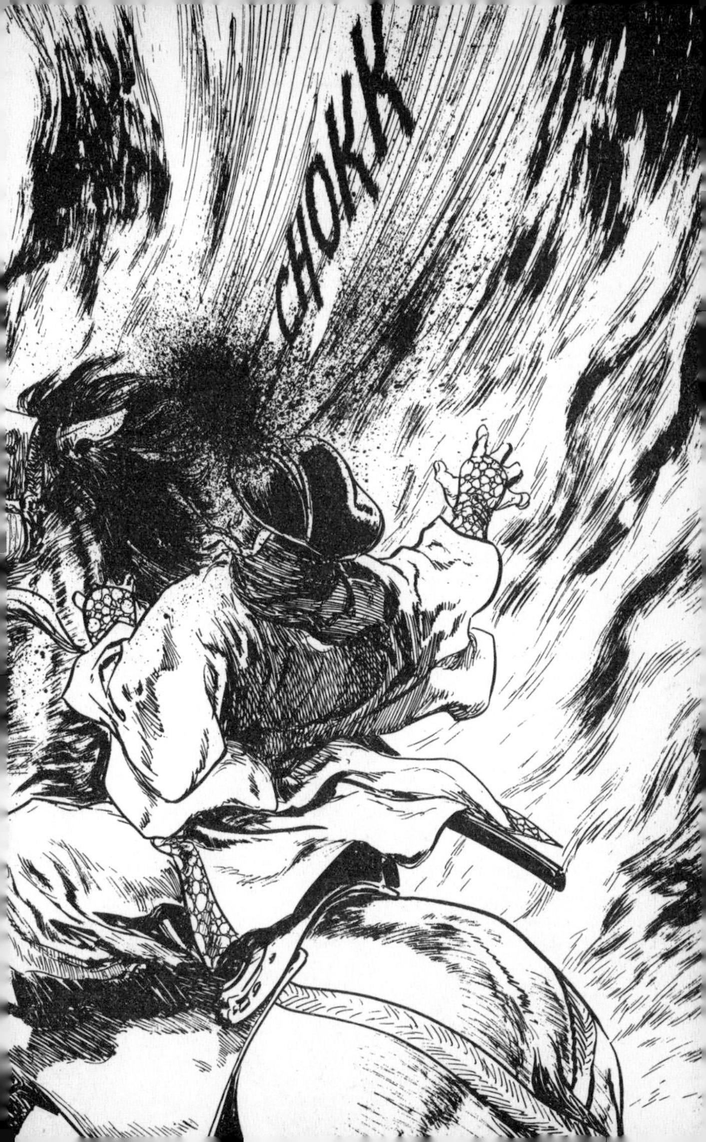
CHOKK

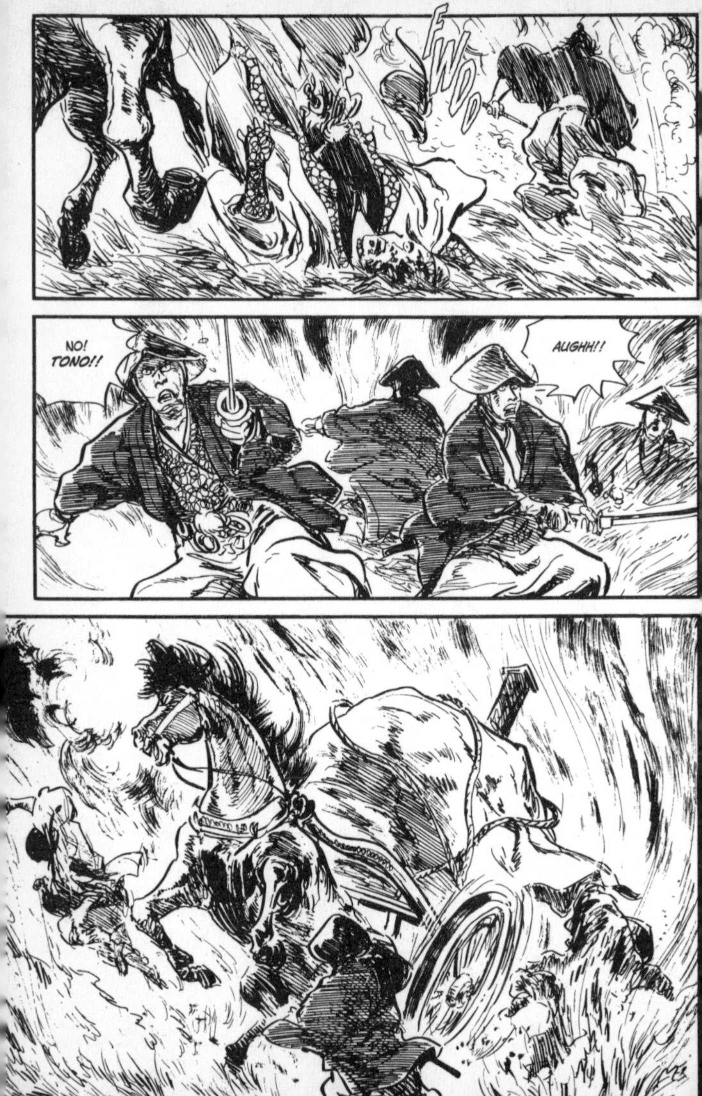
FWOOO
NO! TONO!!
AUGHH!!

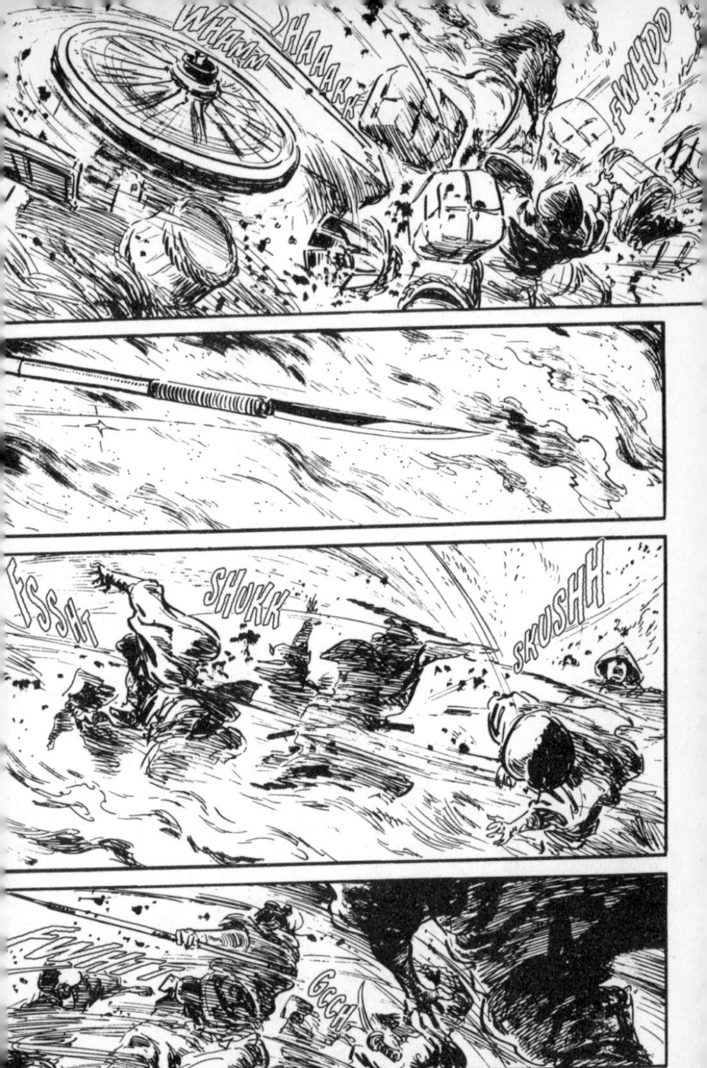
WHAMM
HAAAKK
FWHDD
FSSHT
SHUKK
SKUSHH
GCCH

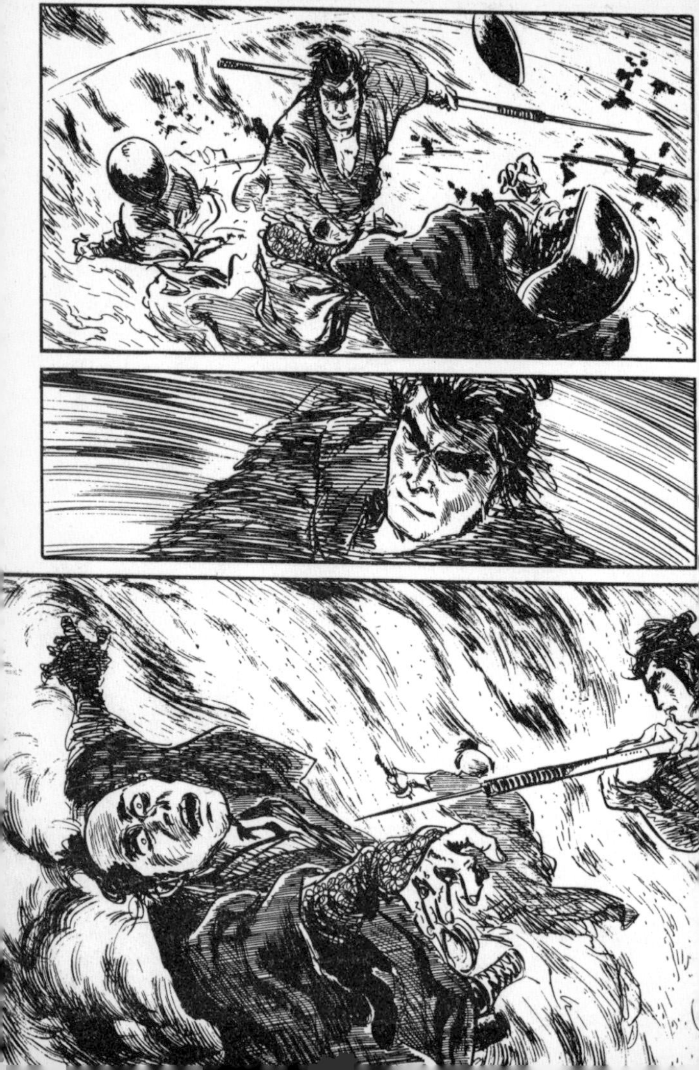

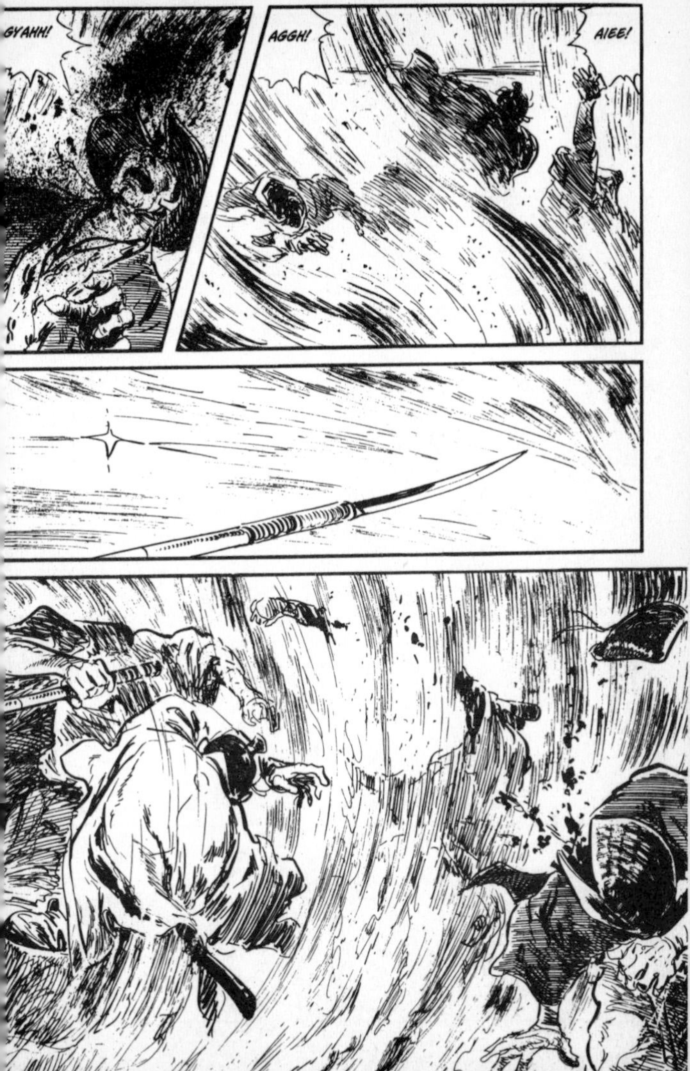
GYAHH!
AGGH!
AIEE!

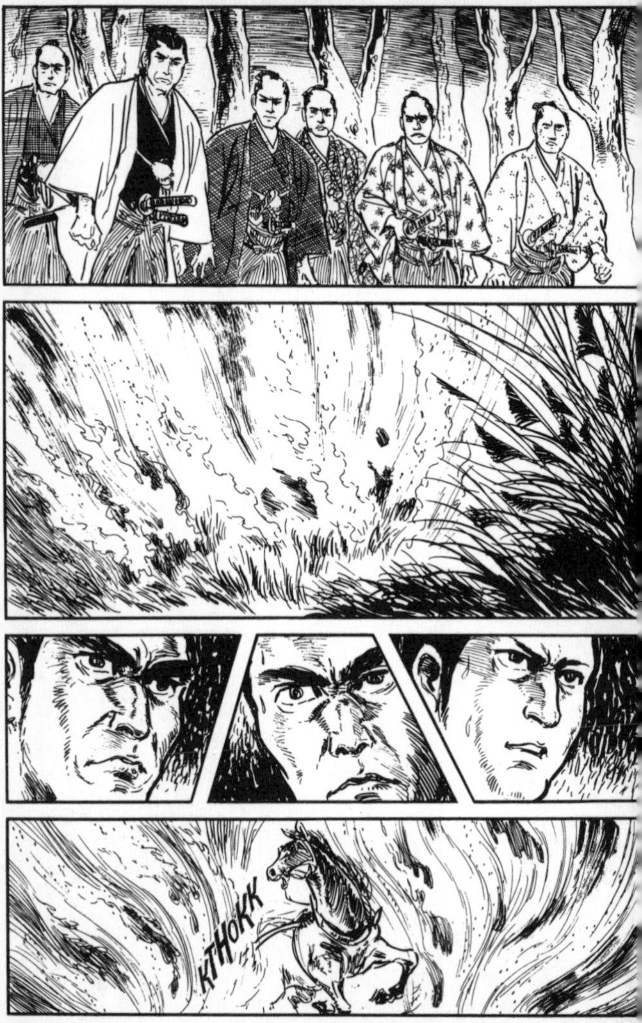
KTHOKK

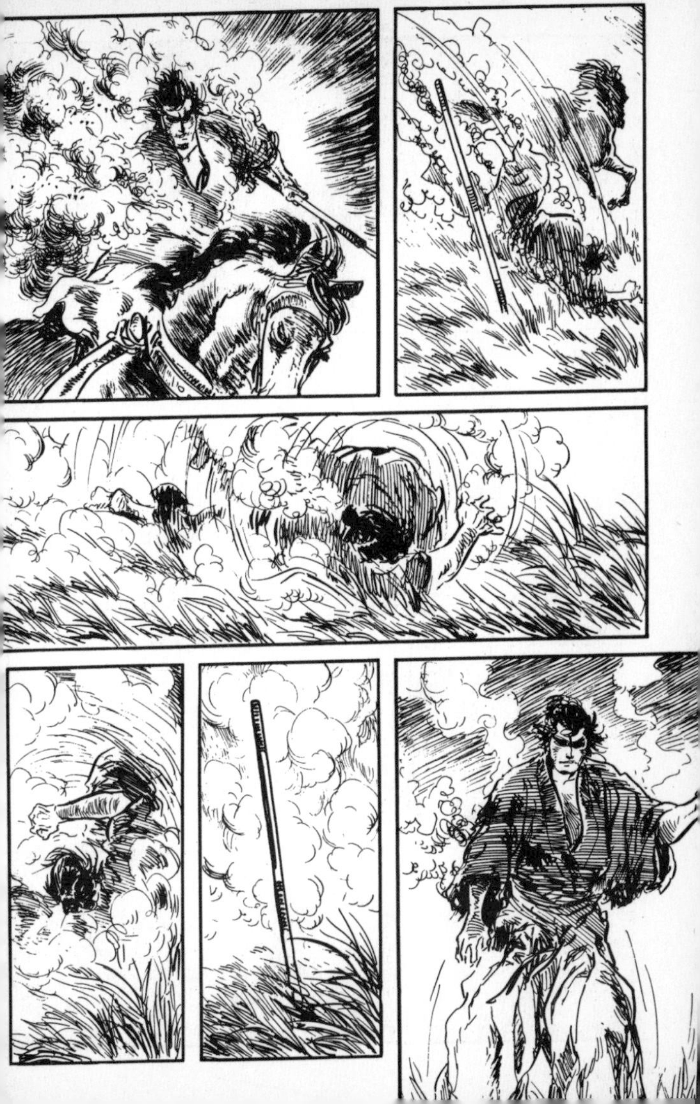

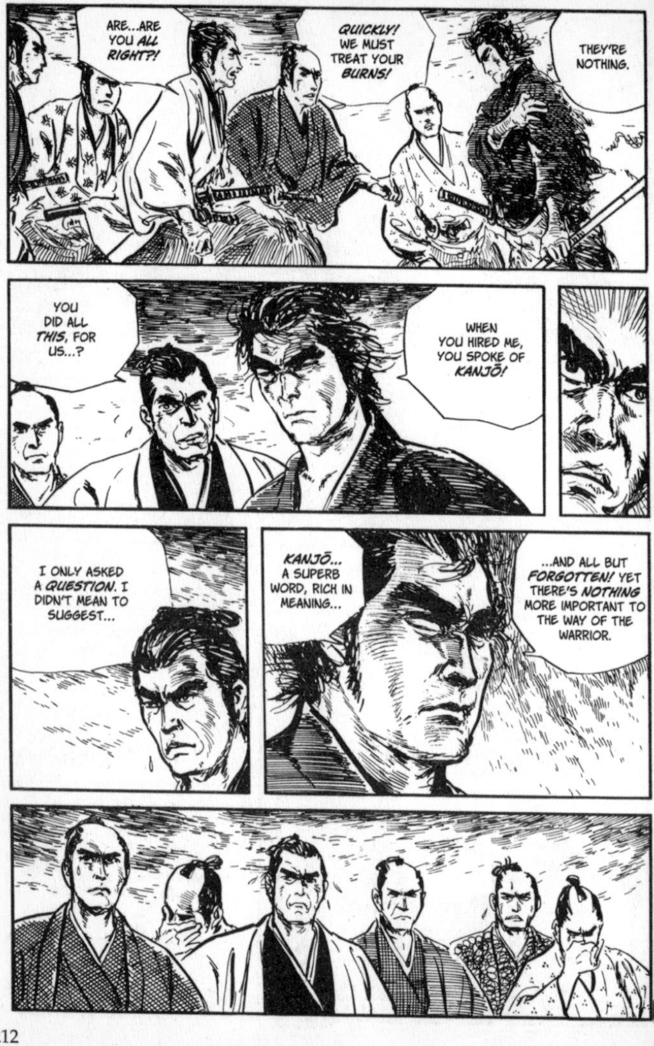
ARE...ARE YOU ALL RIGHT?!
QUICKLY! WE MUST TREAT YOUR BURNS!
THEY'RE NOTHING.
YOU DID ALL THIS, FOR US...?
WHEN YOU HIRED ME, YOU SPOKE OF KANJŌ!
I ONLY ASKED A QUESTION. I DIDN'T MEAN TO SUGGEST...
KANJŌ... A SUPERB WORD, RICH IN MEANING...
...AND ALL BUT FORGOTTEN! YET THERE'S NOTHING MORE IMPORTANT TO THE WAY OF THE WARRIOR.

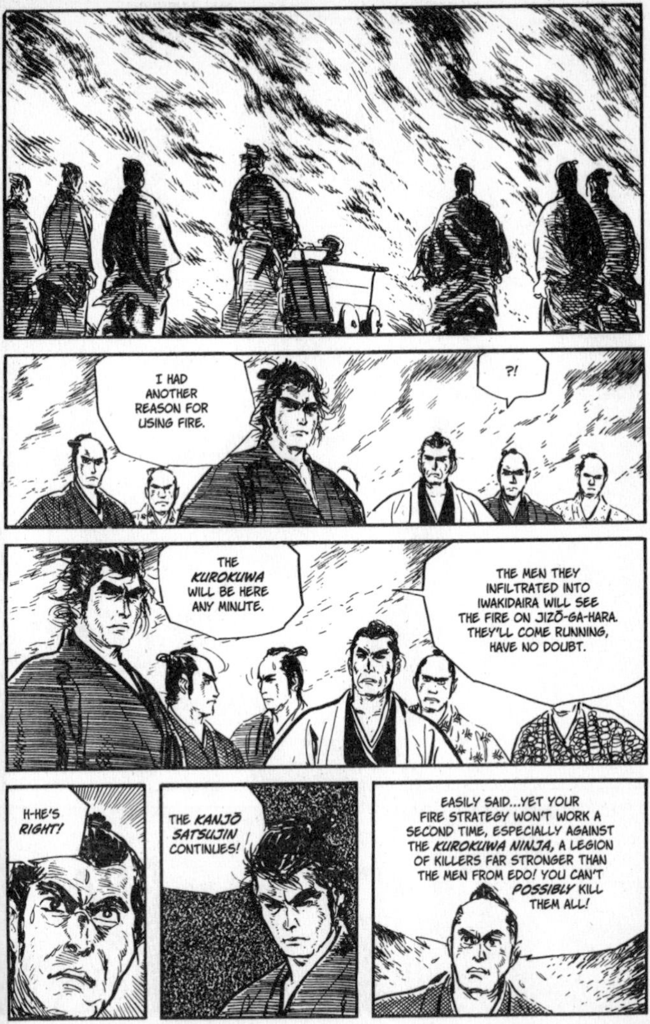
I HAD ANOTHER REASON FOR USING FIRE.
?!
THE *KUROKUWA* WILL BE HERE ANY MINUTE.
THE MEN THEY INFILTRATED INTO IWAKIDAIRA WILL SEE THE FIRE ON JIZŌ-GA-HARA. THEY'LL COME RUNNING, HAVE NO DOUBT.
H-HE'S *RIGHT!*
THE *KANJŌ SATSUJIN* CONTINUES!
EASILY SAID...YET YOUR FIRE STRATEGY WON'T WORK A SECOND TIME, ESPECIALLY AGAINST THE *KUROKUWA NINJA,* A LEGION OF KILLERS FAR STRONGER THAN THE MEN FROM EDO! YOU CAN'T *POSSIBLY* KILL THEM ALL!

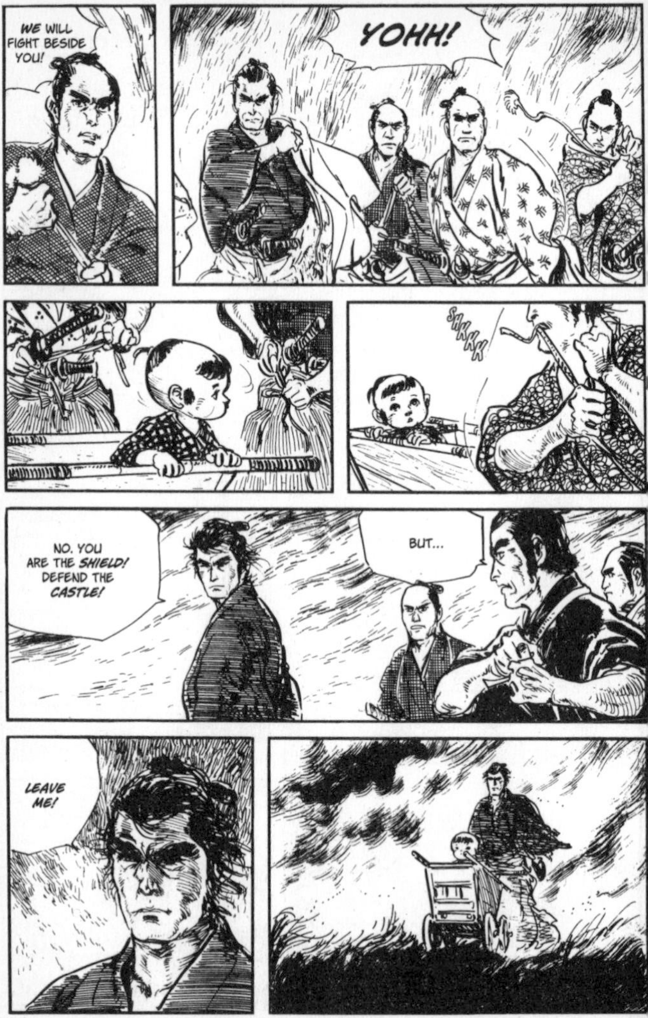

WE WILL FIGHT BESIDE YOU!
YOHH!
SHKKK
NO. YOU ARE THE SHIELD! DEFEND THE CASTLE!
BUT...
LEAVE ME!

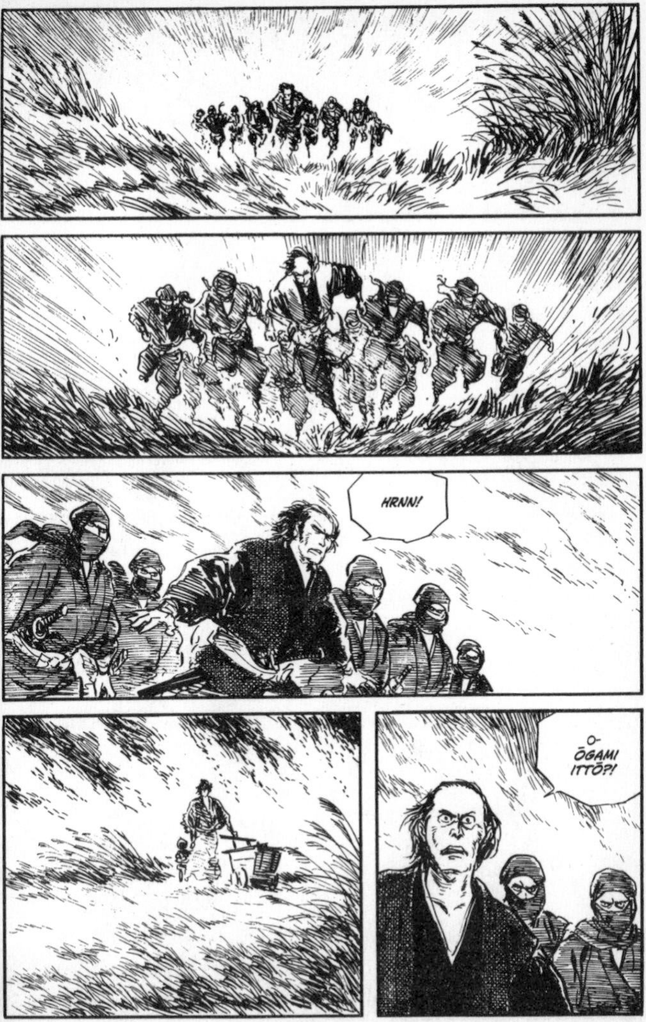
HRNN!
O-
ŌGAMI
ITTŌ?!

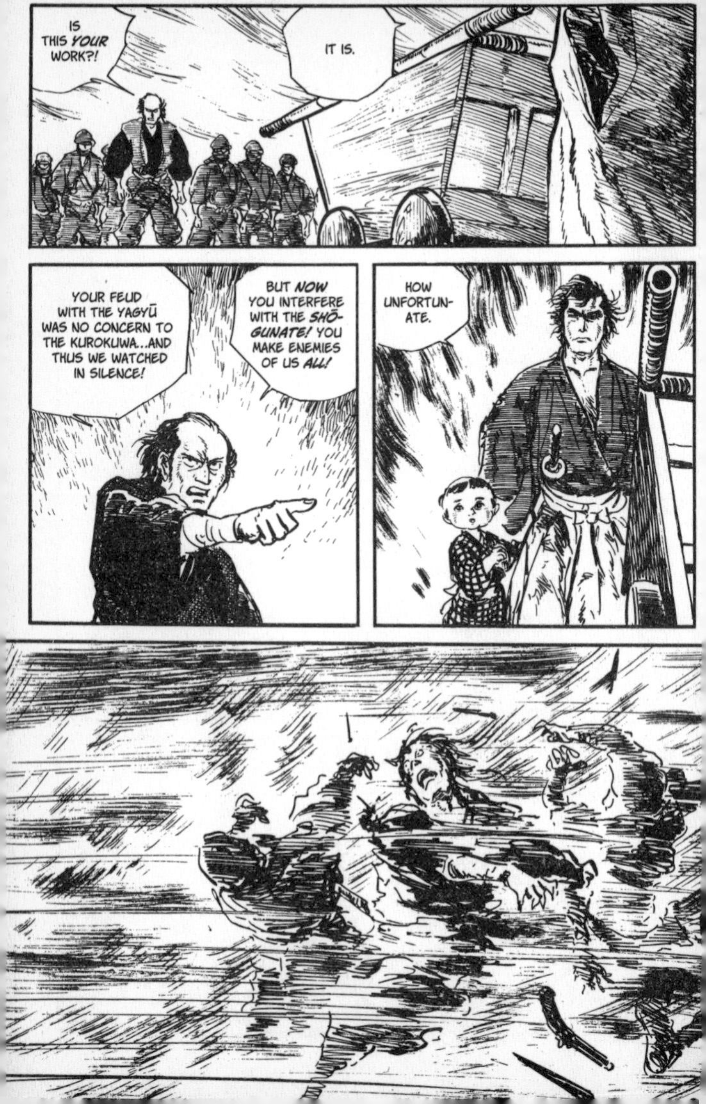
IS THIS *YOUR* WORK?!
IT IS.
YOUR FEUD WITH THE YAGYŪ WAS NO CONCERN TO THE KUROKUWA...AND THUS WE WATCHED IN SILENCE!
BUT *NOW* YOU INTERFERE WITH THE *SHŌGUNATE!* YOU MAKE ENEMIES OF US *ALL!*
HOW UNFORTUNATE.

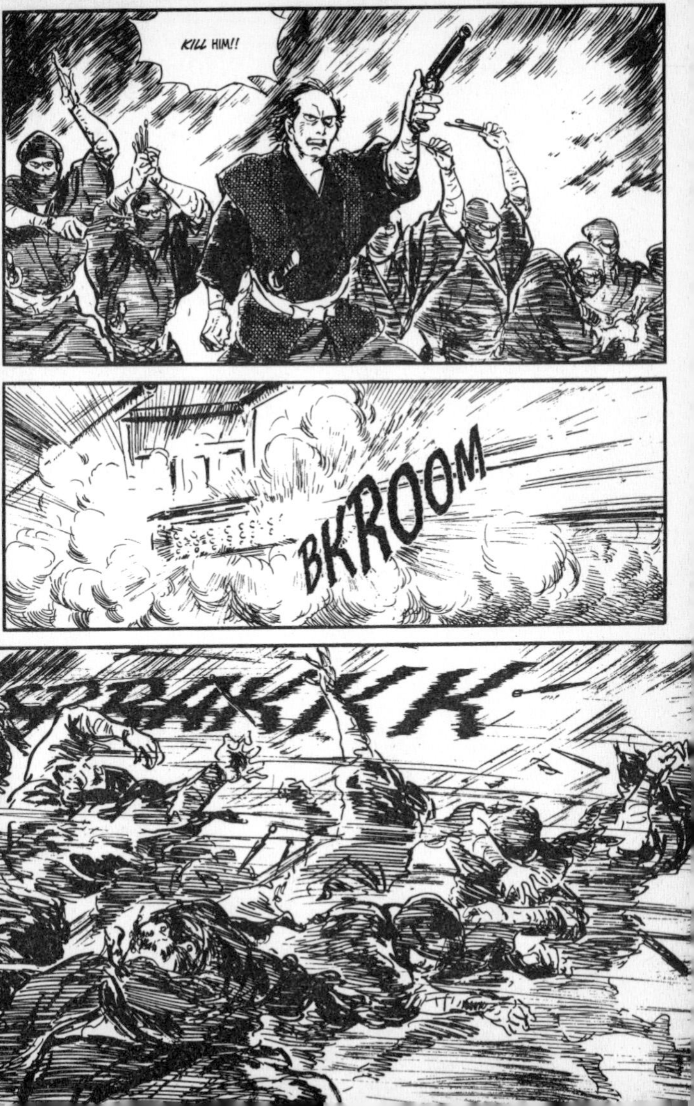
KILL HIM!!
BKROOM

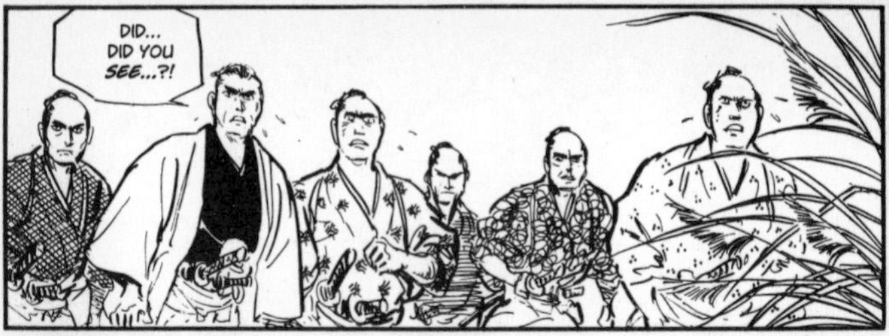
DID... DID YOU SEE...?!

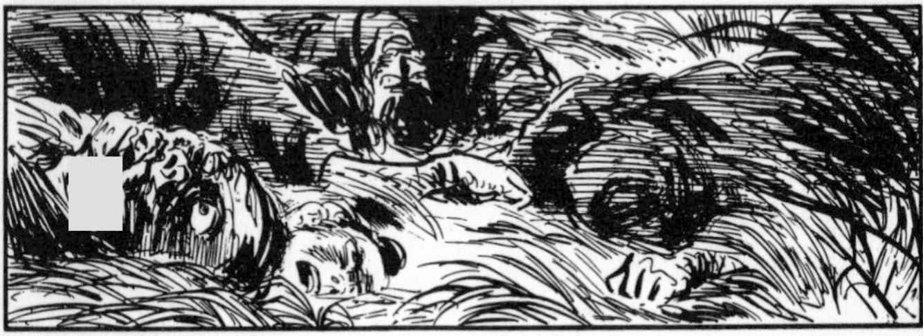

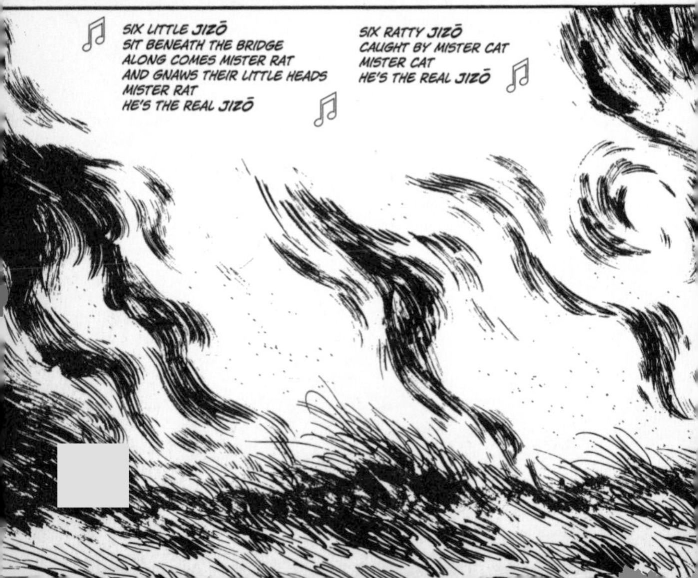
SIX LITTLE JIZŌ
SIT BENEATH THE BRIDGE
ALONG COMES MISTER RAT
AND GNAWS THEIR LITTLE HEADS
MISTER RAT
HE'S THE REAL JIZŌ
SIX RATTY JIZŌ
CAUGHT BY MISTER CAT
MISTER CAT
HE'S THE REAL JIZŌ

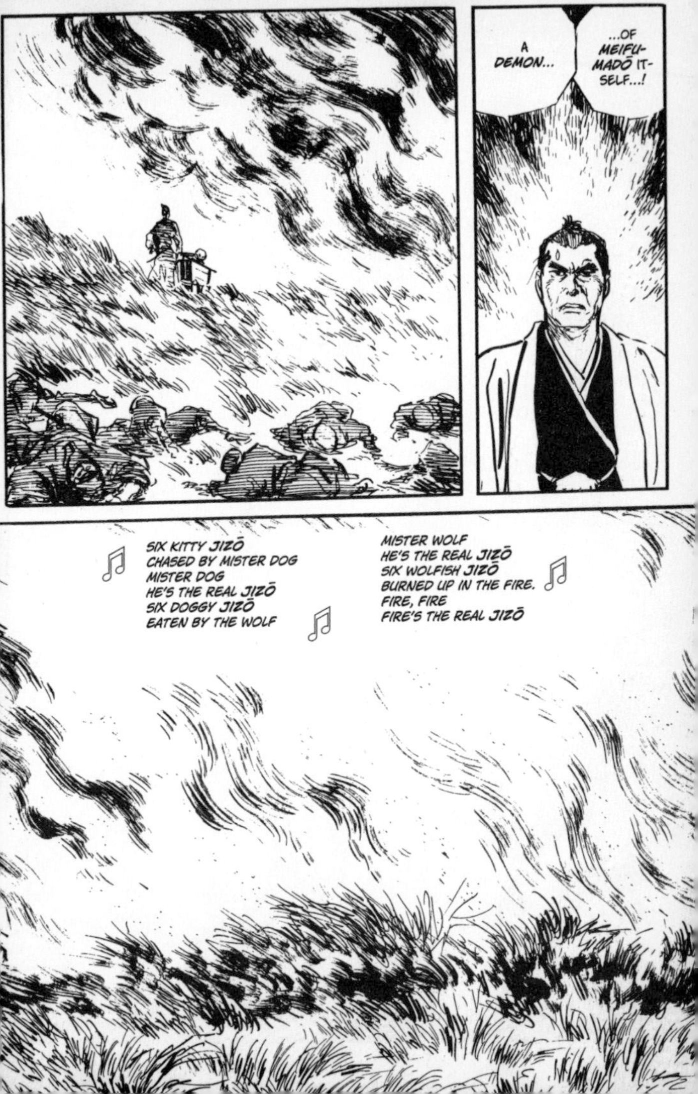
A DEMON...
...OF MEIFUMADŌ ITSELF...!
SIX KITTY JIZŌ
CHASED BY MISTER DOG
MISTER DOG
HE'S THE REAL JIZŌ
SIX DOGGY JIZŌ
EATEN BY THE WOLF
MISTER WOLF
HE'S THE REAL JIZŌ
SIX WOLFISH JIZŌ
BURNED UP IN THE FIRE.
FIRE, FIRE
FIRE'S THE REAL JIZŌ

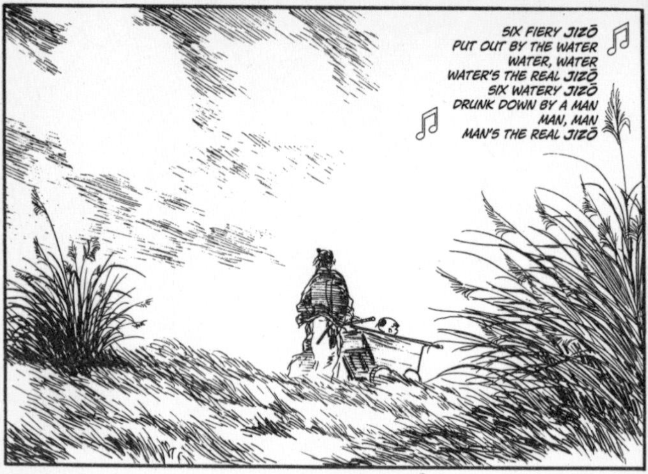
SIX FIERY JIZŌ
PUT OUT BY THE WATER
WATER, WATER
WATER'S THE REAL JIZŌ
SIX WATERY JIZŌ
DRUNK DOWN BY A MAN
MAN, MAN
MAN'S THE REAL JIZŌ
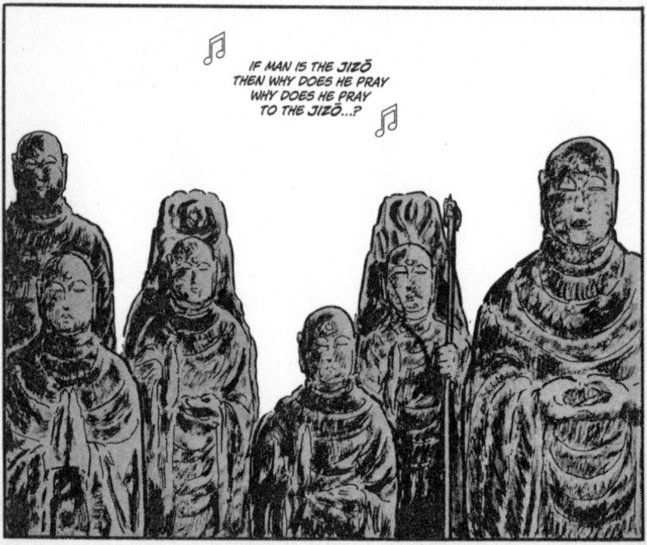
IF MAN IS THE JIZŌ
THEN WHY DOES HE PRAY
WHY DOES HE PRAY
TO THE JIZŌ...?

the thirty-third

One Stone Bridge

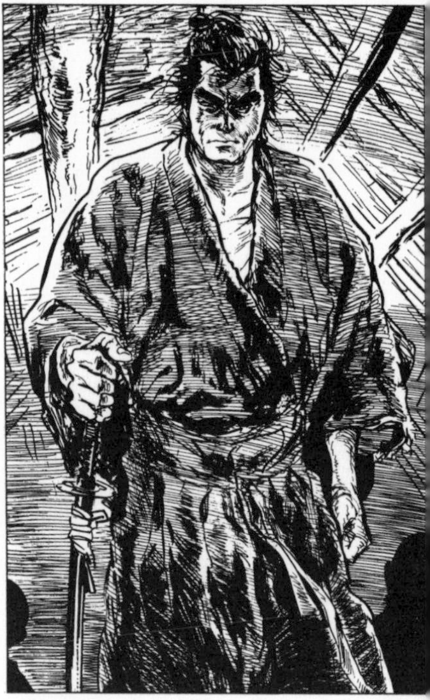

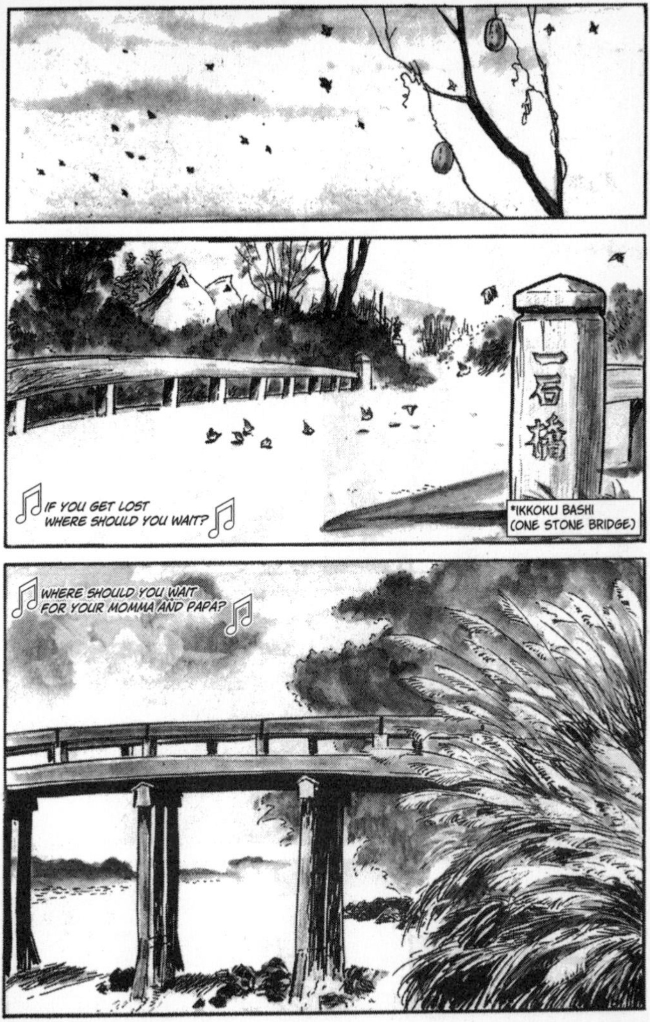

IF YOU GET LOST
WHERE SHOULD YOU WAIT?
一石橋
*IKKOKU BASHI
(ONE STONE BRIDGE)
WHERE SHOULD YOU WAIT
FOR YOUR MOMMA AND PAPA?

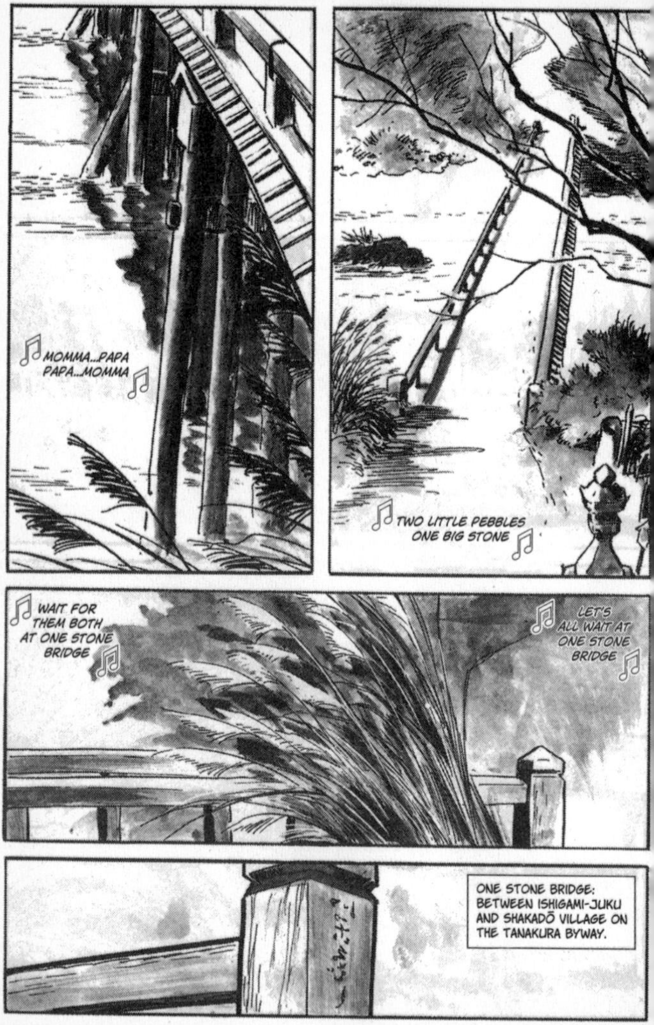
MOMMA...PAPA PAPA...MOMMA
TWO LITTLE PEBBLES ONE BIG STONE
WAIT FOR THEM BOTH AT ONE STONE BRIDGE
LET'S ALL WAIT AT ONE STONE BRIDGE
ONE STONE BRIDGE: BETWEEN ISHIGAMI-JUKU AND SHAKADŌ VILLAGE ON THE TANAKURA BYWAY.

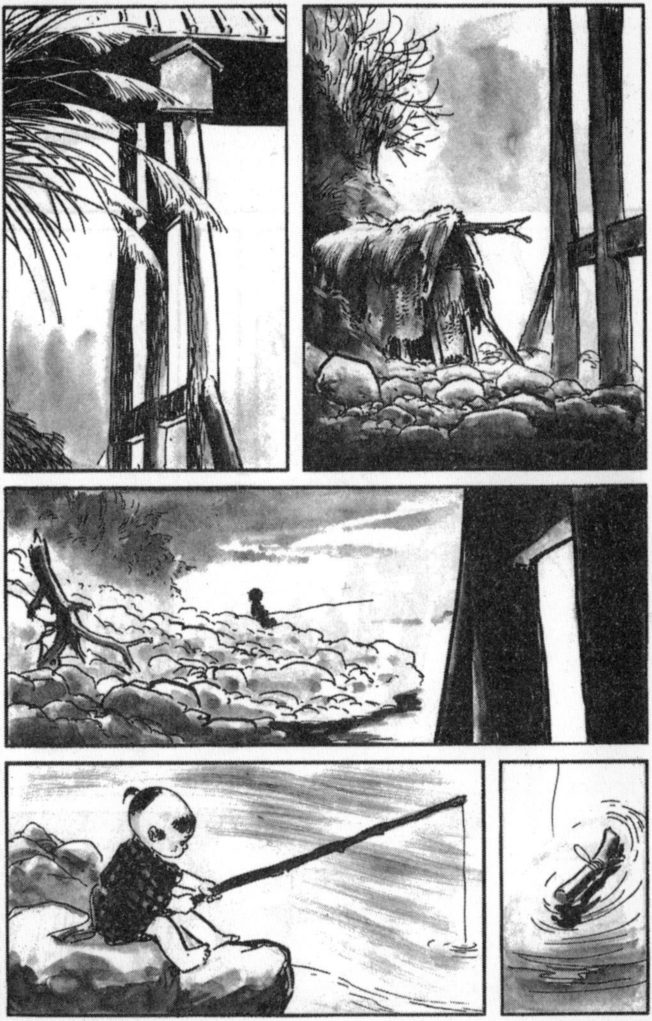

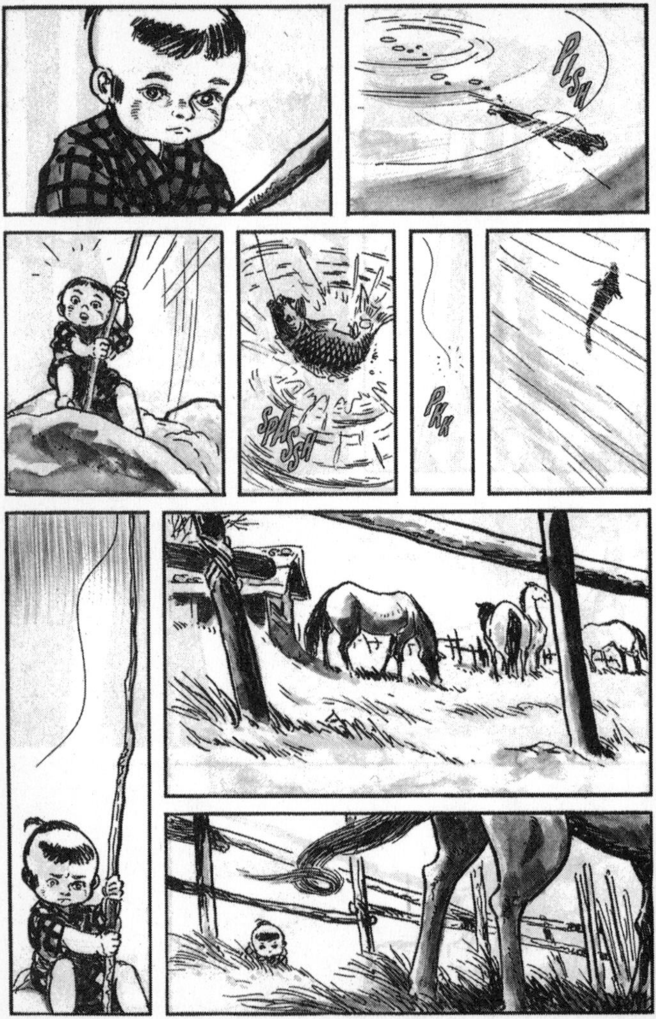
PLSH
SPASSH
PKK

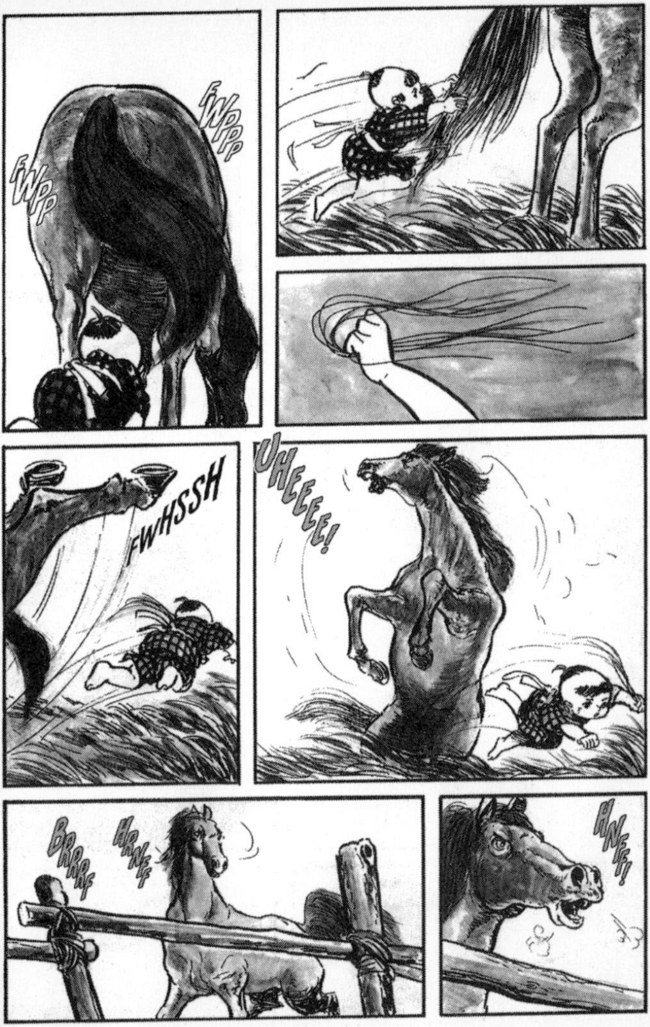
FWPPP
FWPP
FWHSSH
UHEEEE!
BRRRF
HRNFF
HNFF!

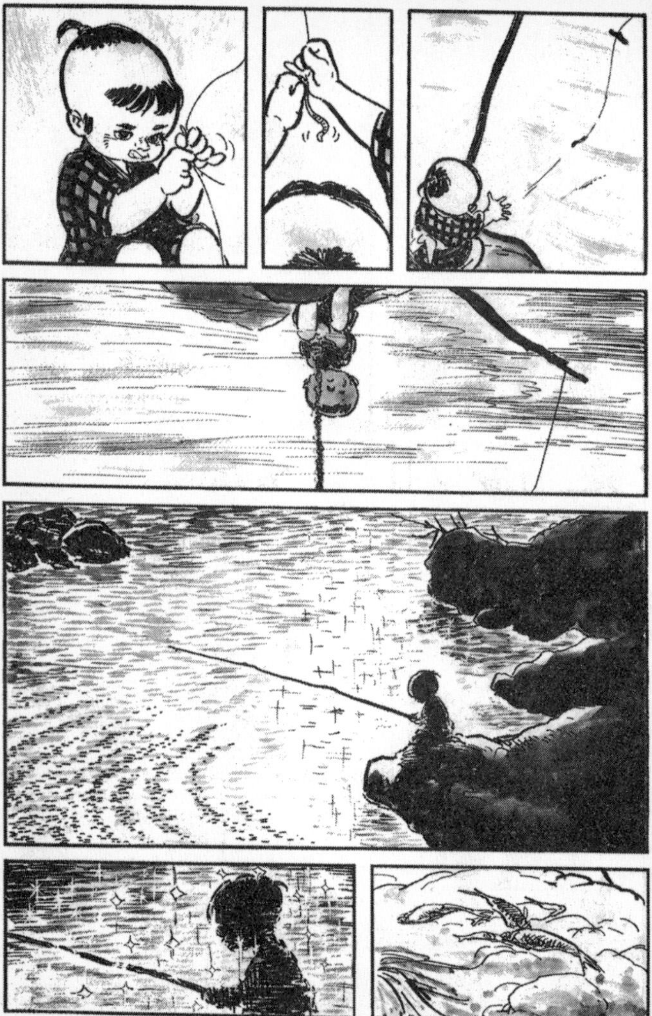

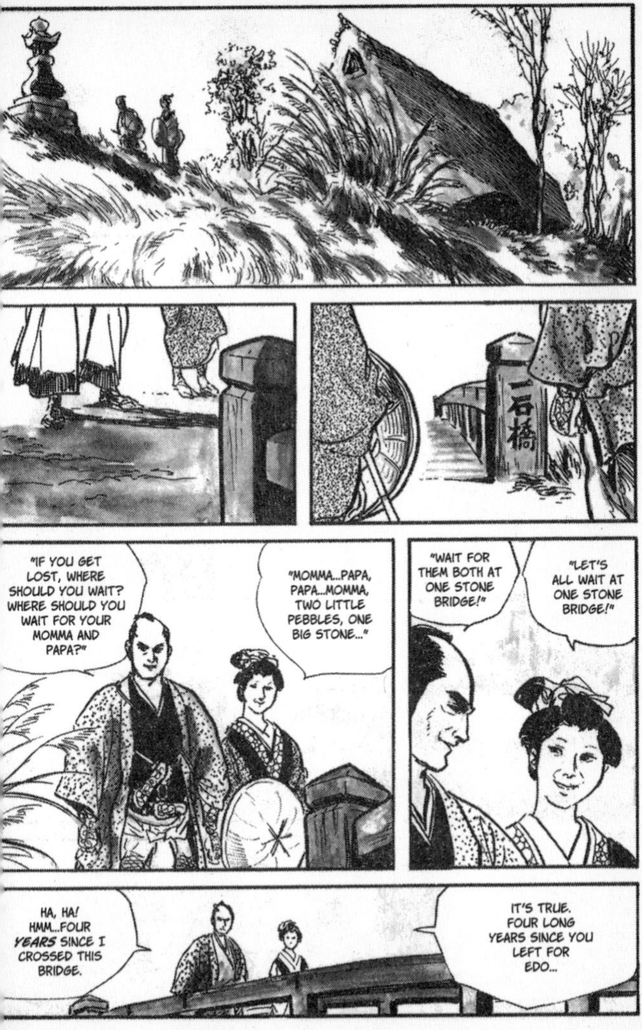
一石橋
"IF YOU GET LOST, WHERE SHOULD YOU WAIT? WHERE SHOULD YOU WAIT FOR YOUR MOMMA AND PAPA?"
"MOMMA...PAPA, PAPA...MOMMA, TWO LITTLE PEBBLES, ONE BIG STONE..."
"WAIT FOR THEM BOTH AT ONE STONE BRIDGE!"
"LET'S ALL WAIT AT ONE STONE BRIDGE!"
HA, HA! HMM...FOUR *YEARS* SINCE I CROSSED THIS BRIDGE.
IT'S TRUE. FOUR LONG YEARS SINCE YOU LEFT FOR EDO...

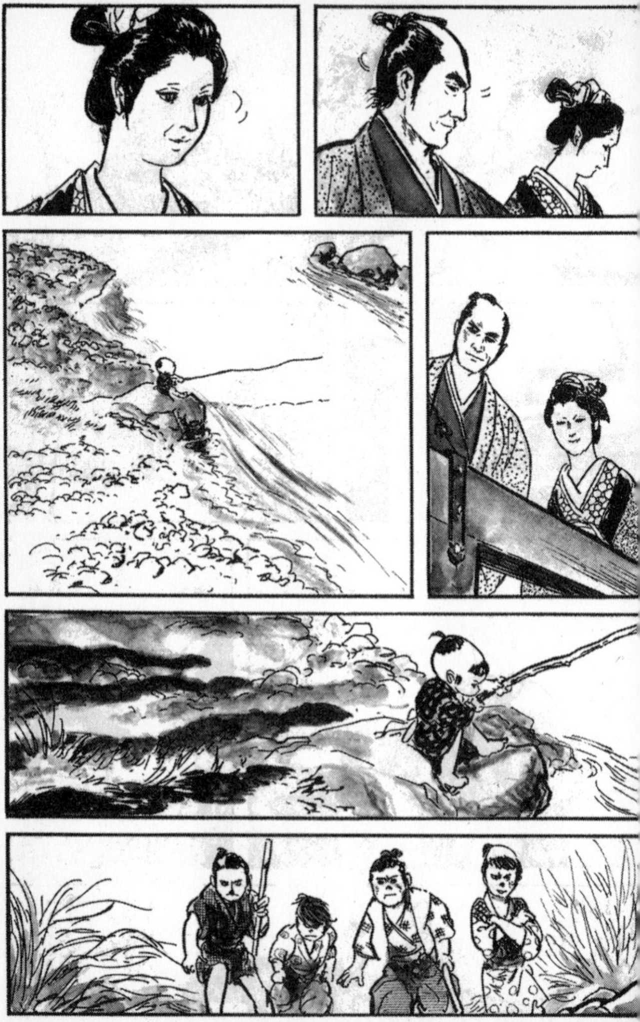

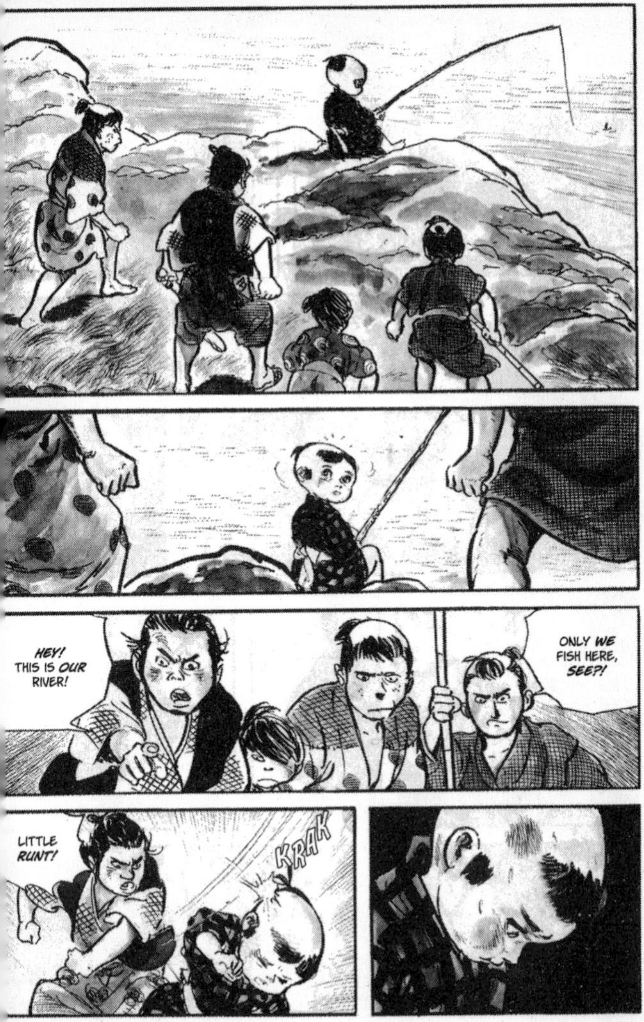
HEY! THIS IS OUR RIVER!
ONLY WE FISH HERE, SEE?!
LITTLE RUNT!
KRAK

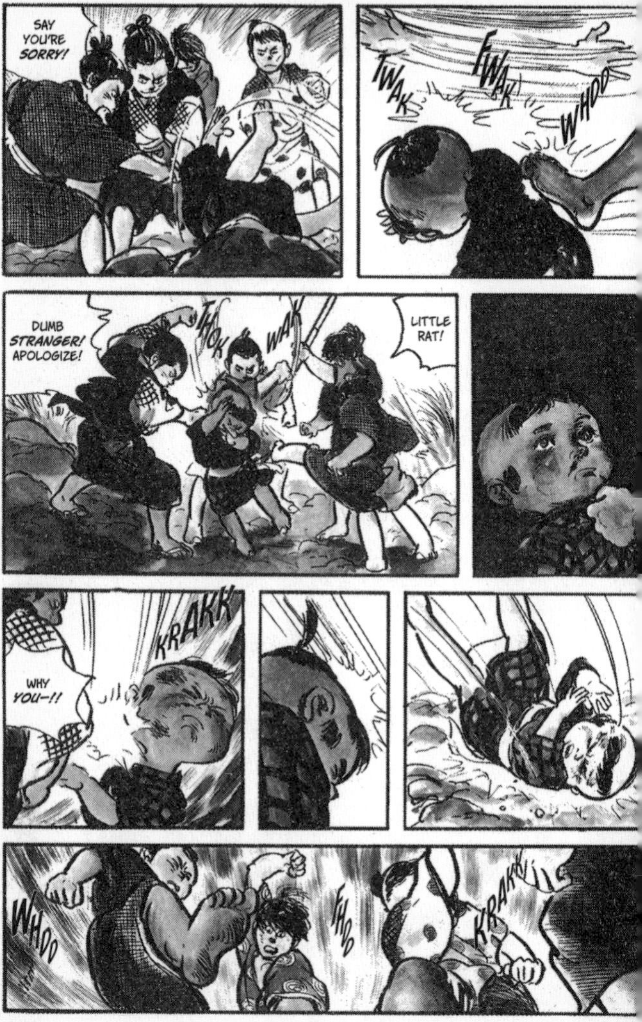
SAY YOU'RE SORRY!
TWAK
FWAK
WHOO
DUMB STRANGER! APOLOGIZE!
THOK
WAK
LITTLE RAT!
KRAKK
WHY YOU-!!
WHOO
FHOO
KRAKK

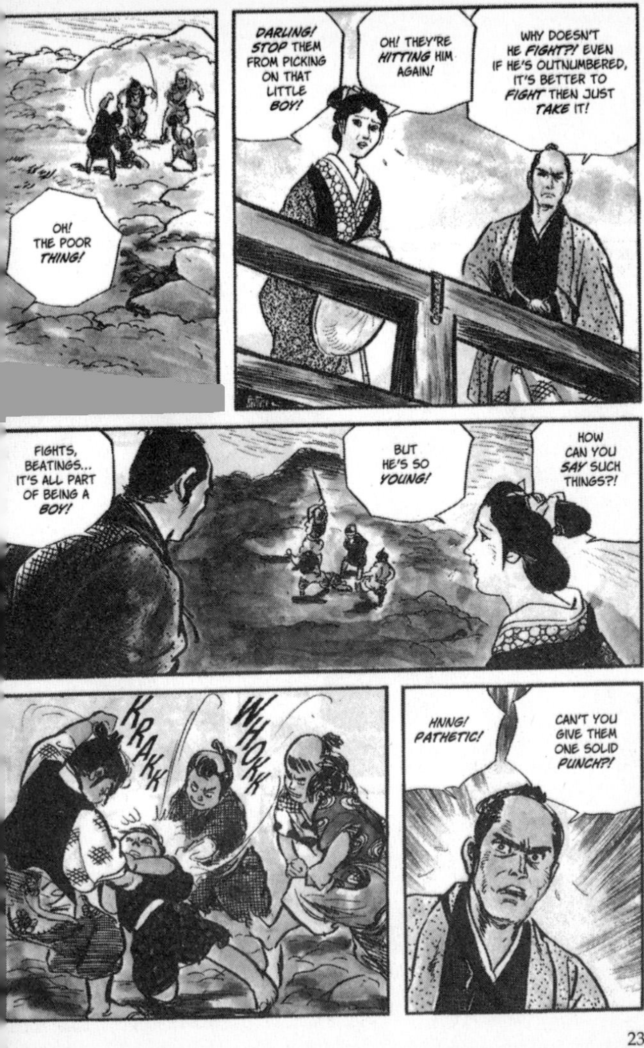
OH! THE POOR THING!
DARLING! STOP THEM FROM PICKING ON THAT LITTLE BOY!
OH! THEY'RE HITTING HIM AGAIN!
WHY DOESN'T HE FIGHT?! EVEN IF HE'S OUTNUMBERED, IT'S BETTER TO FIGHT THEN JUST TAKE IT!
FIGHTS, BEATINGS... IT'S ALL PART OF BEING A BOY!
BUT HE'S SO YOUNG!
HOW CAN YOU SAY SUCH THINGS?!
KRAKK
WHOKK
HNNG! PATHETIC!
CAN'T YOU GIVE THEM ONE SOLID PUNCH?!

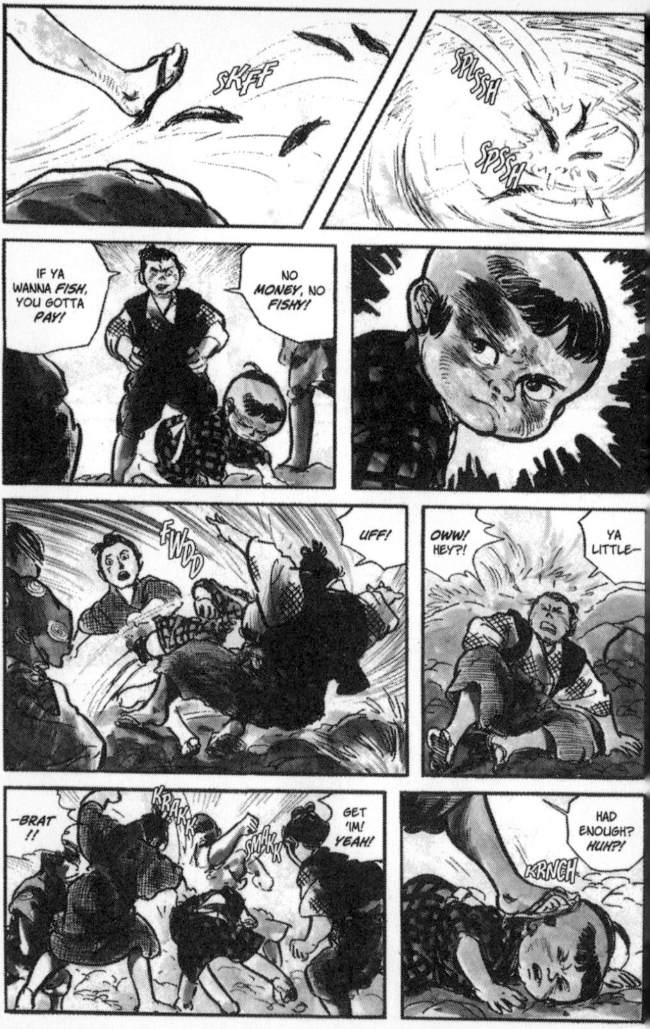
SKFF
SPLSSH
SPSSH
IF YA WANNA FISH, YOU GOTTA PAY!
NO MONEY, NO FISHY!
FWDD
UFF!
OWW! HEY?!
YA LITTLE—
—BRAT !!
KRAKK
SMAKK
GET 'IM! YEAH!
HAD ENOUGH? HUH?!
KRNCH

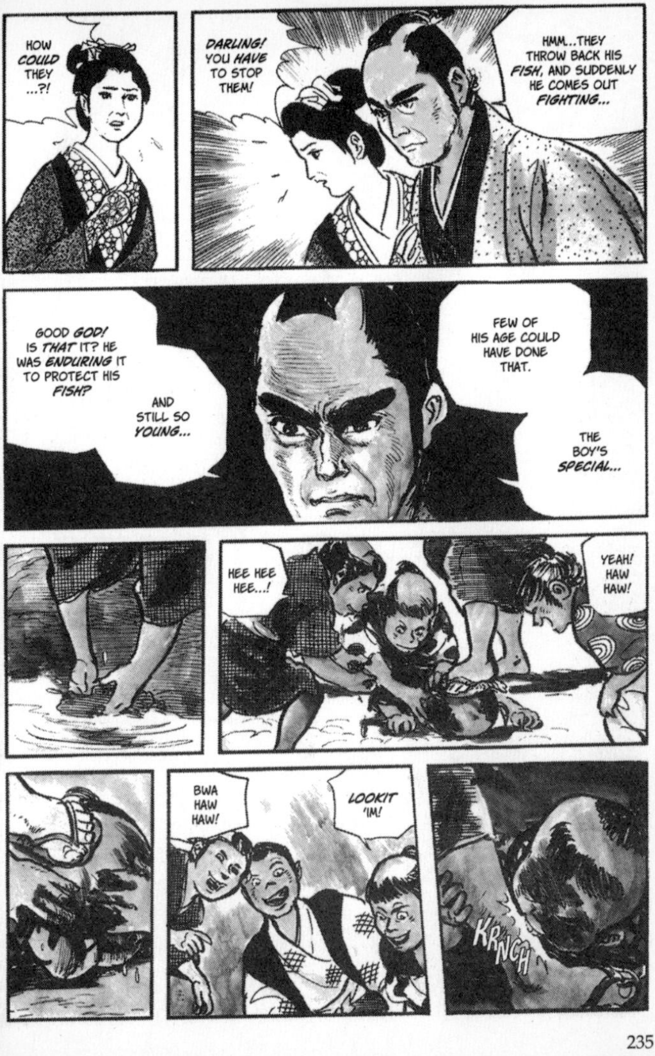
HOW COULD THEY ...?!
DARLING! YOU HAVE TO STOP THEM!
HMM...THEY THROW BACK HIS FISH, AND SUDDENLY HE COMES OUT FIGHTING...
GOOD GOD! IS THAT IT? HE WAS ENDURING IT TO PROTECT HIS FISH?
AND STILL SO YOUNG...
FEW OF HIS AGE COULD HAVE DONE THAT.
THE BOY'S SPECIAL...
HEE HEE HEE...!
YEAH! HAW HAW!
BWA HAW HAW!
LOOKIT 'IM!
KRNCH

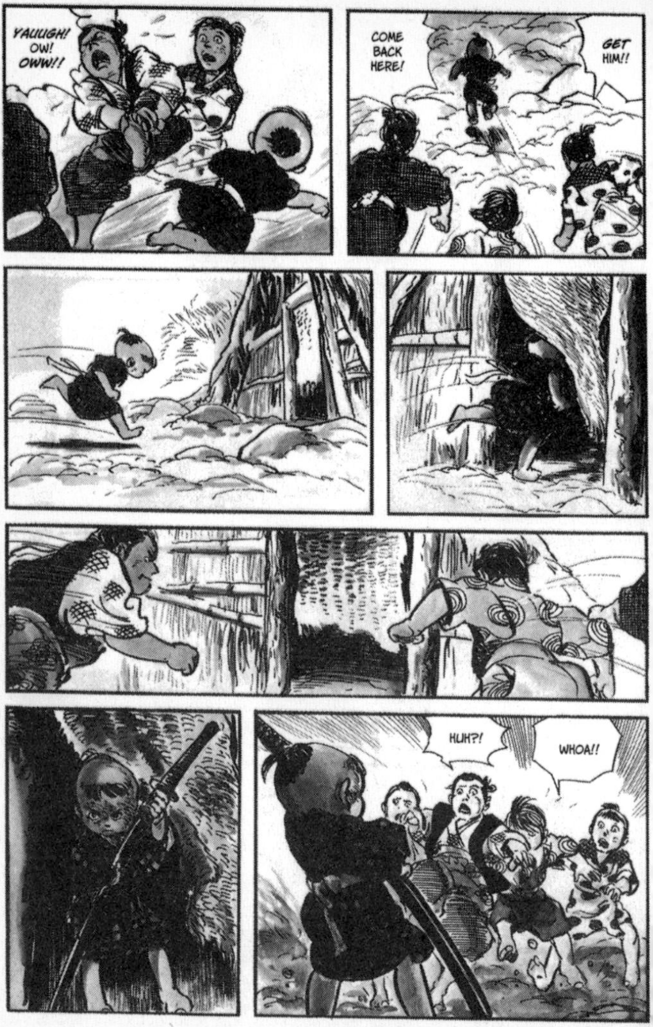
YAUUGH! OW! OWW!!
COME BACK HERE!
GET HIM!!
HUH?!
WHOA!!

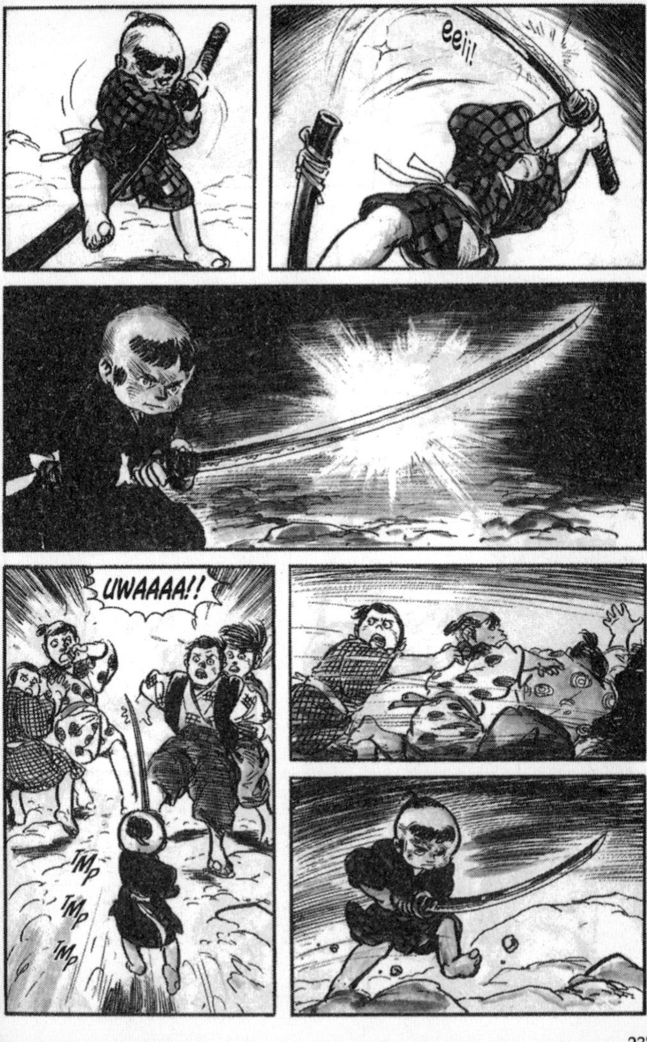
eeii!
UWAAAA!!
TMP
TMP
TMP

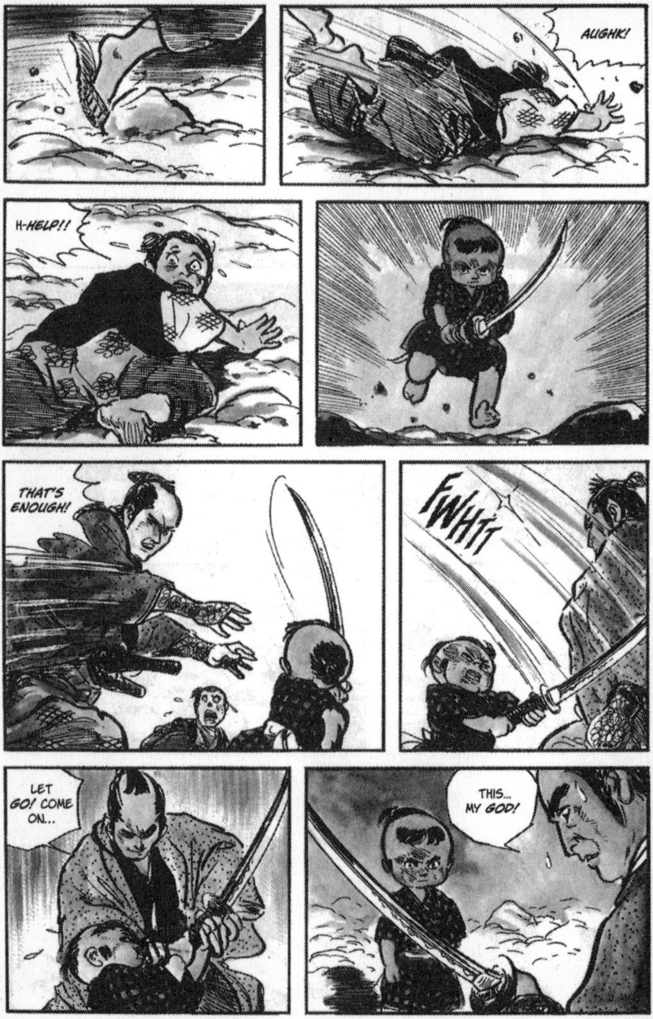
AUGHK!
H-HELP!!
THAT'S ENOUGH!
FWHT
LET GO! COME ON...
THIS... MY GOD!

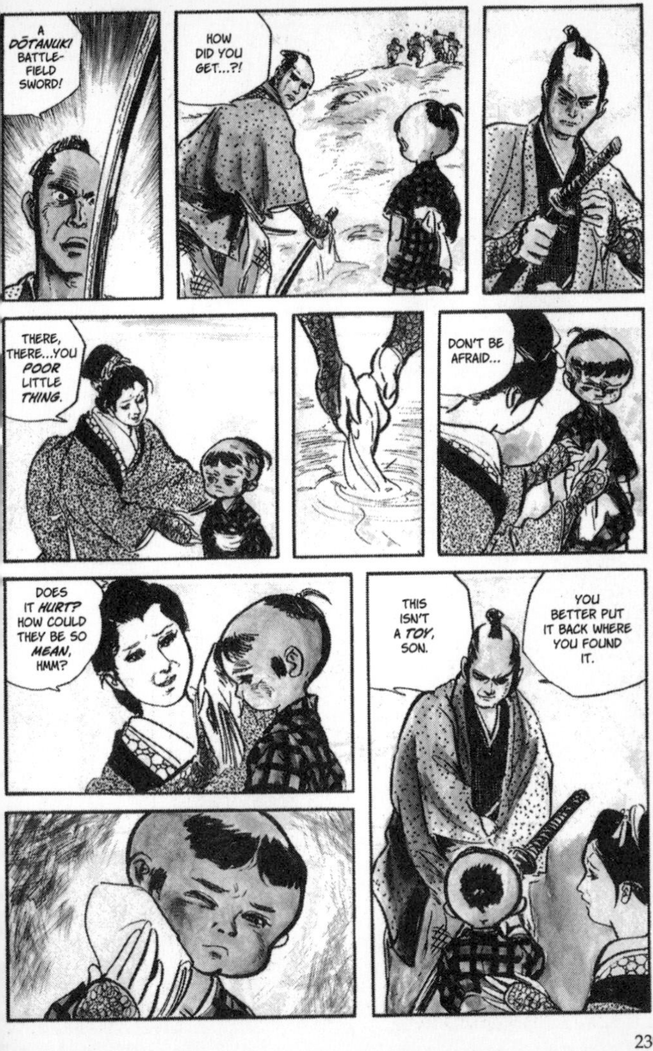
A DŌTANUKI BATTLE-FIELD SWORD!
HOW DID YOU GET...?!
THERE, THERE...YOU POOR LITTLE THING.
DON'T BE AFRAID...
DOES IT HURT? HOW COULD THEY BE SO MEAN, HMM?
THIS ISN'T A TOY, SON.
YOU BETTER PUT IT BACK WHERE YOU FOUND IT.

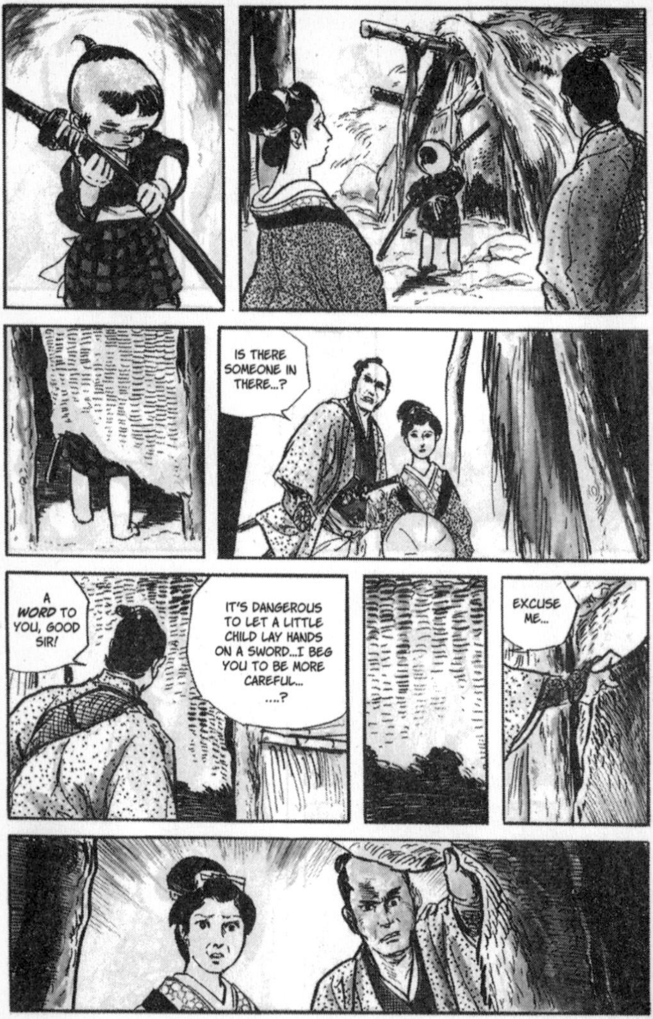
IS THERE SOMEONE IN THERE...?
A *WORD* TO YOU, GOOD SIR!
IT'S DANGEROUS TO LET A LITTLE CHILD LAY HANDS ON A SWORD...I BEG YOU TO BE MORE CAREFUL... ....?
EXCUSE ME...

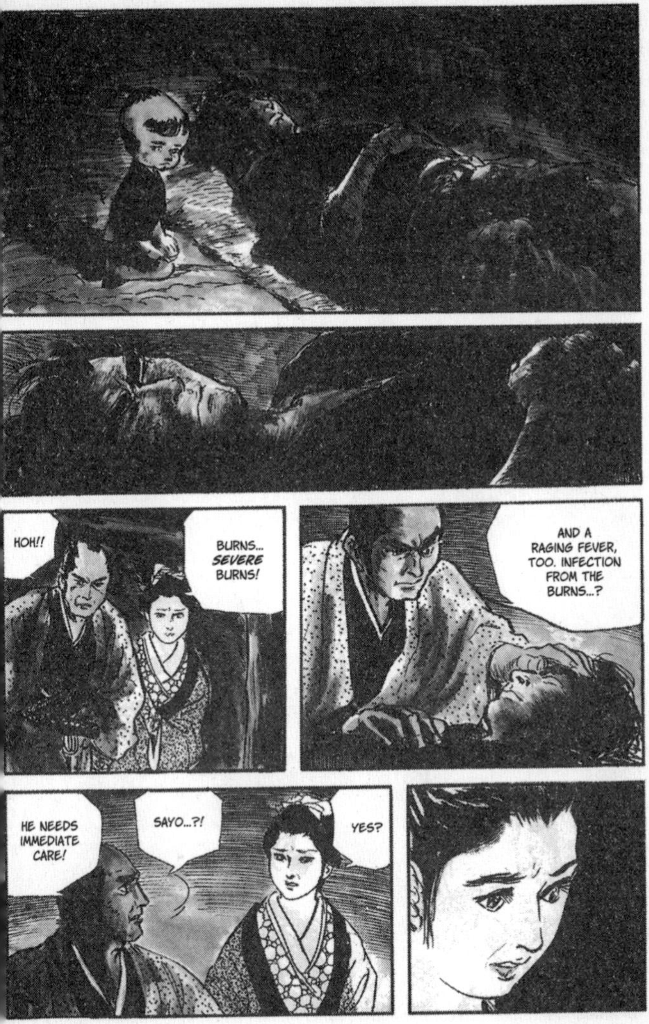
HOH!!
BURNS... *SEVERE* BURNS!
AND A RAGING FEVER, TOO. INFECTION FROM THE BURNS...?
HE NEEDS IMMEDIATE CARE!
SAYO...?!
YES?

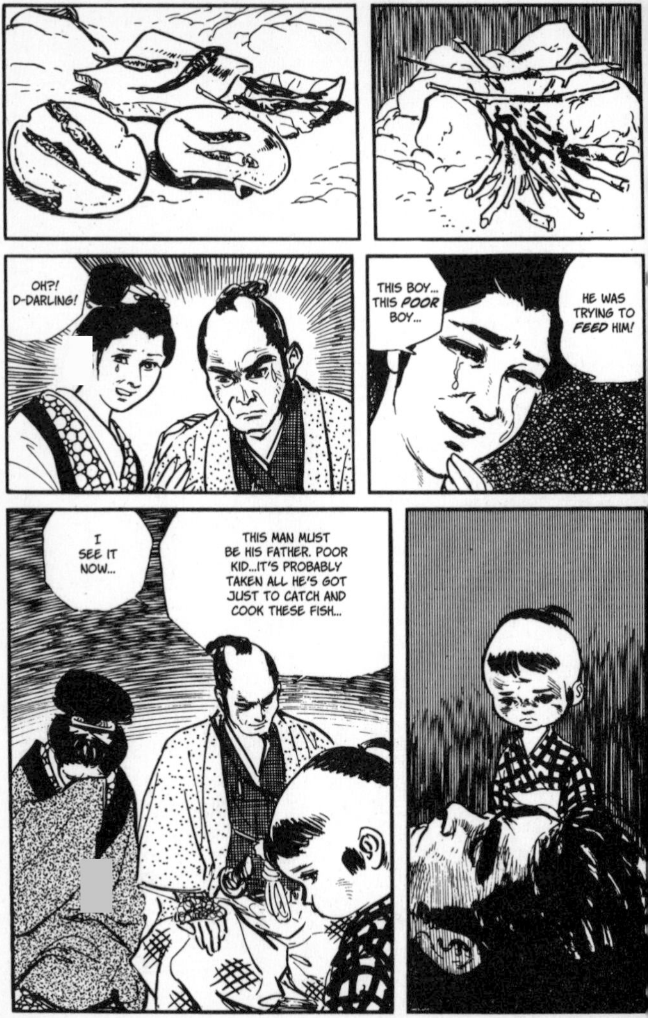
OH?! D-DARLING!
THIS BOY... THIS POOR BOY...
HE WAS TRYING TO FEED HIM!
I SEE IT NOW...
THIS MAN MUST BE HIS FATHER. POOR KID...IT'S PROBABLY TAKEN ALL HE'S GOT JUST TO CATCH AND COOK THESE FISH...

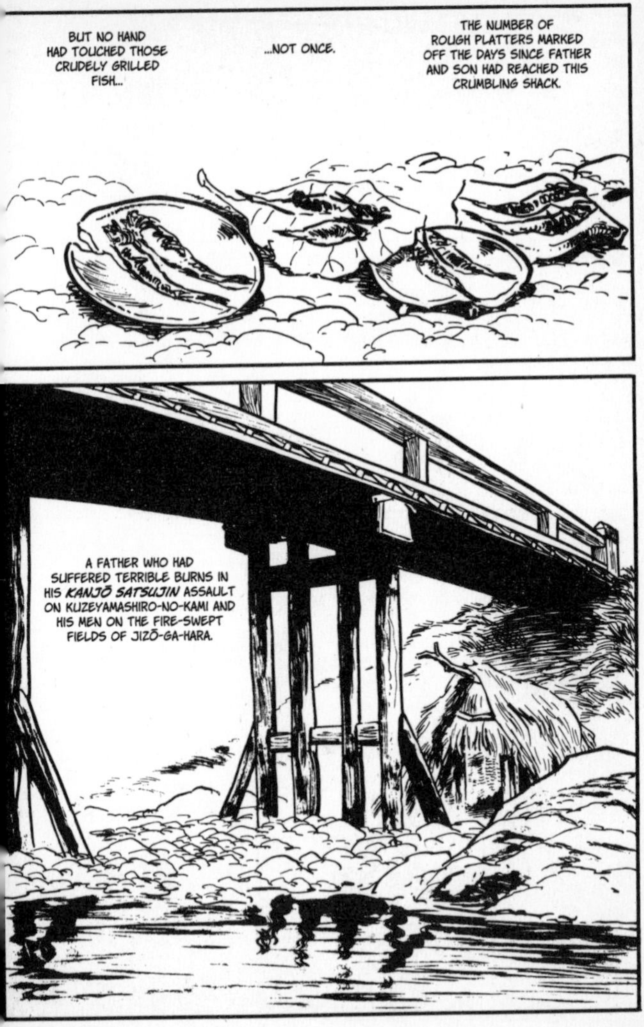
BUT NO HAND HAD TOUCHED THOSE CRUDELY GRILLED FISH...
...NOT ONCE.
THE NUMBER OF ROUGH PLATTERS MARKED OFF THE DAYS SINCE FATHER AND SON HAD REACHED THIS CRUMBLING SHACK.
A FATHER WHO HAD SUFFERED TERRIBLE BURNS IN HIS *KANJŌ SATSUJIN* ASSAULT ON KUZEYAMASHIRO-NO-KAMI AND HIS MEN ON THE FIRE-SWEPT FIELDS OF JIZŌ-GA-HARA.

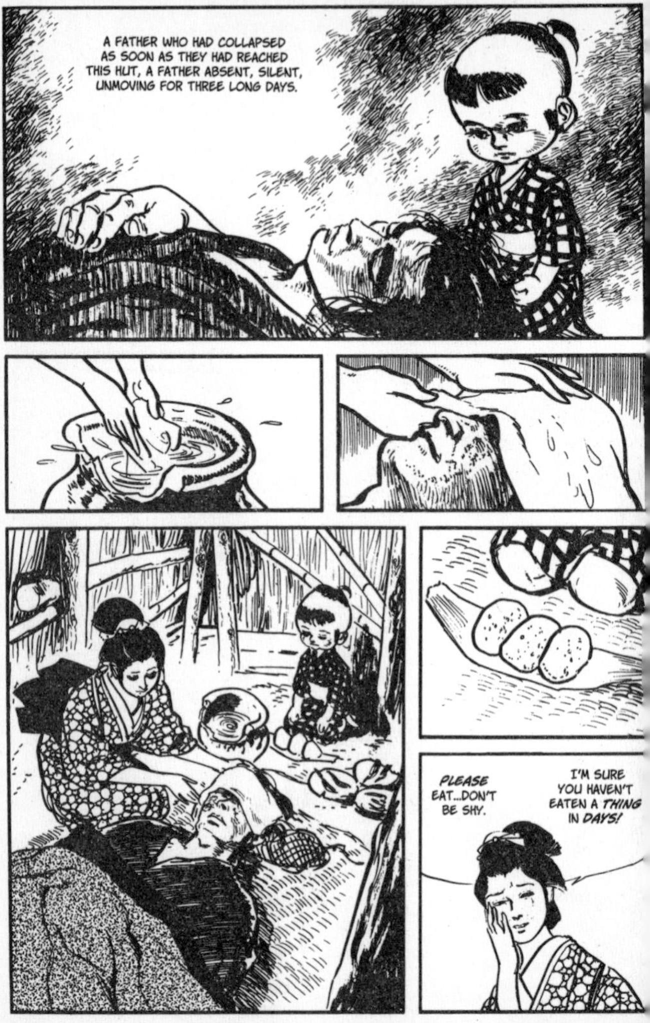
A FATHER WHO HAD COLLAPSED AS SOON AS THEY HAD REACHED THIS HUT, A FATHER ABSENT, SILENT, UNMOVING FOR THREE LONG DAYS.
PLEASE EAT...DON'T BE SHY.
I'M SURE YOU HAVEN'T EATEN A *THING* IN *DAYS!*

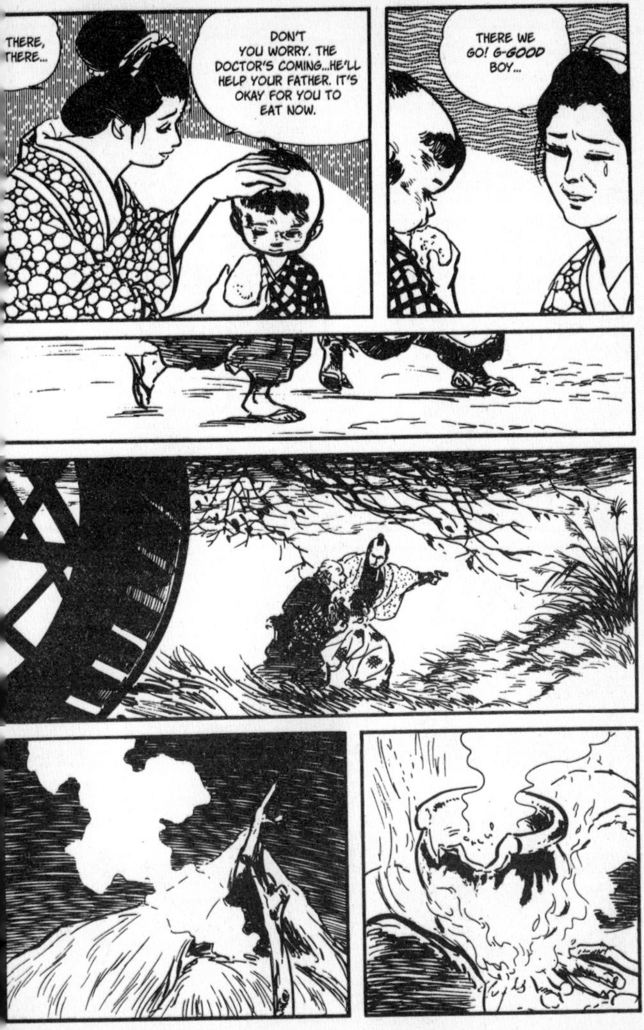
THERE, THERE...
DON'T YOU WORRY. THE DOCTOR'S COMING...HE'LL HELP YOUR FATHER. IT'S OKAY FOR YOU TO EAT NOW.
THERE WE GO! G-GOOD BOY...

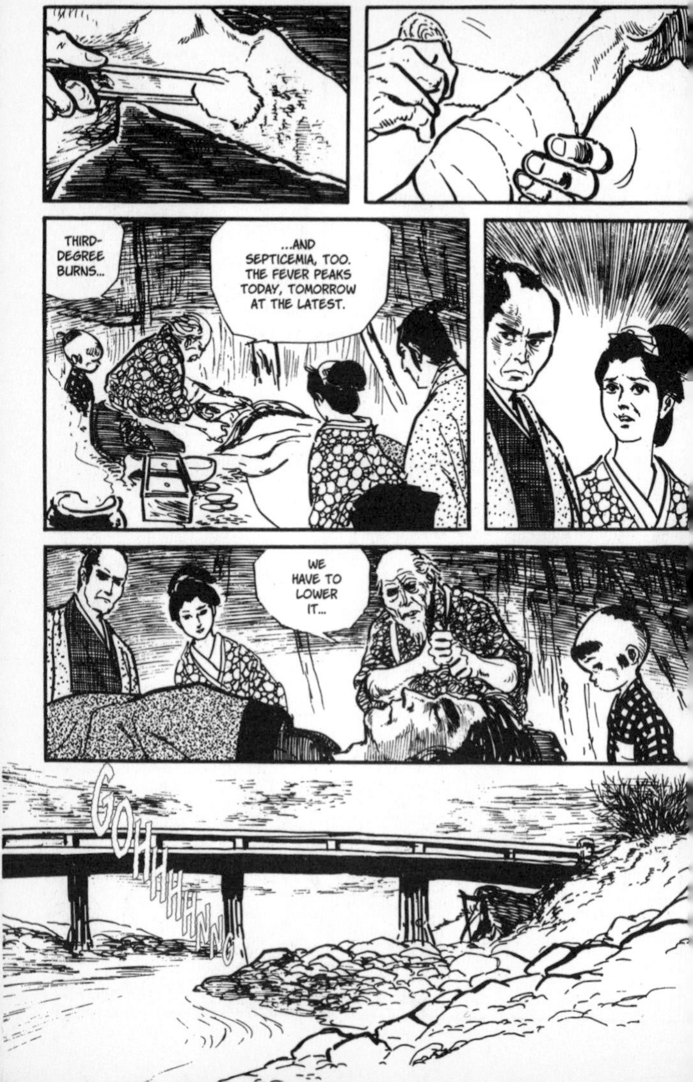
THIRD-DEGREE BURNS...
...AND SEPTICEMIA, TOO. THE FEVER PEAKS TODAY, TOMORROW AT THE LATEST.
WE HAVE TO LOWER IT...
GOHHHHHNNG

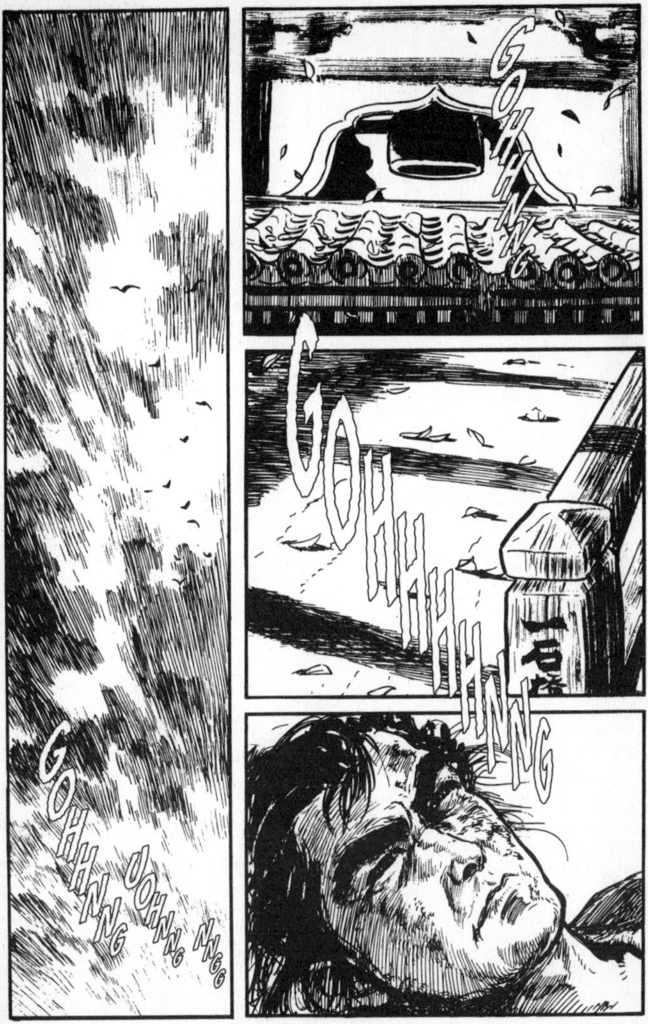
GOHHNNG
UOHHNNG
NNGG
GOHHNNG
GOHHHHNNG

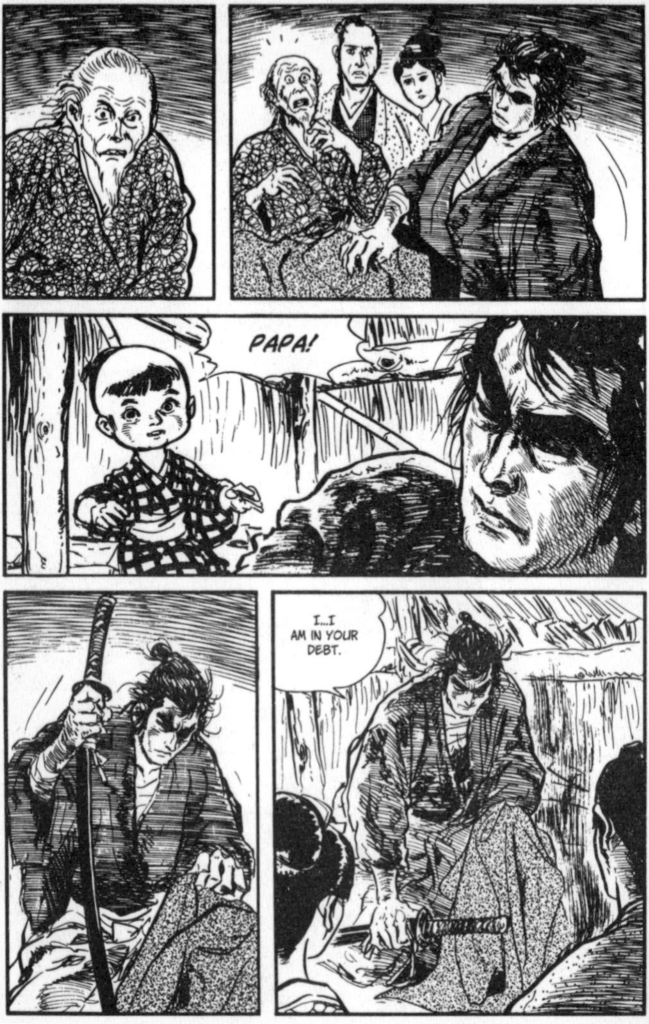
PAPA!
I...I AM IN YOUR DEBT.

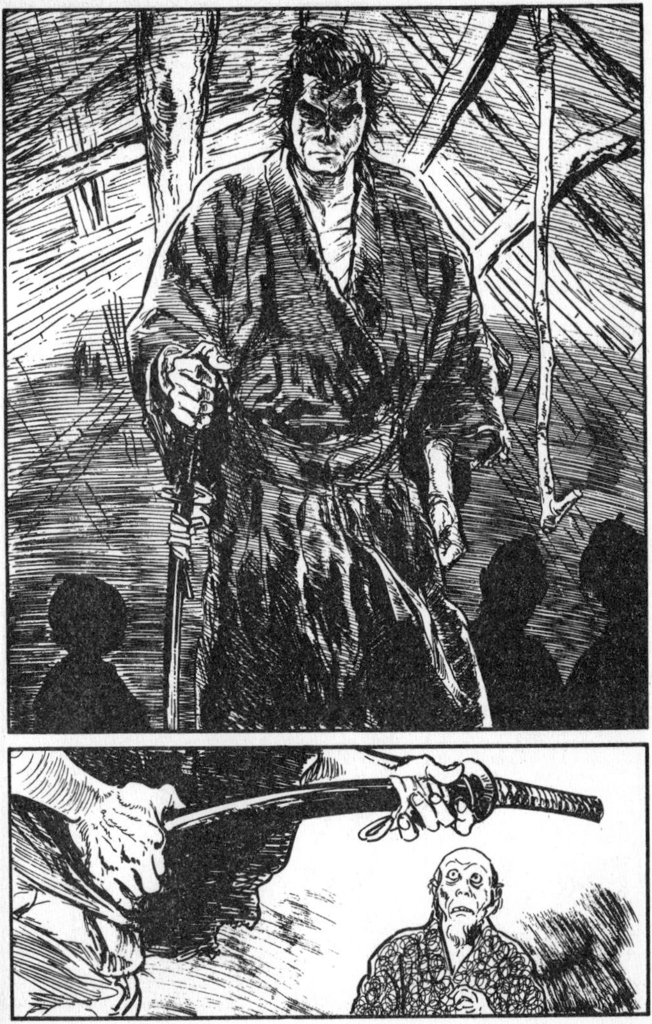

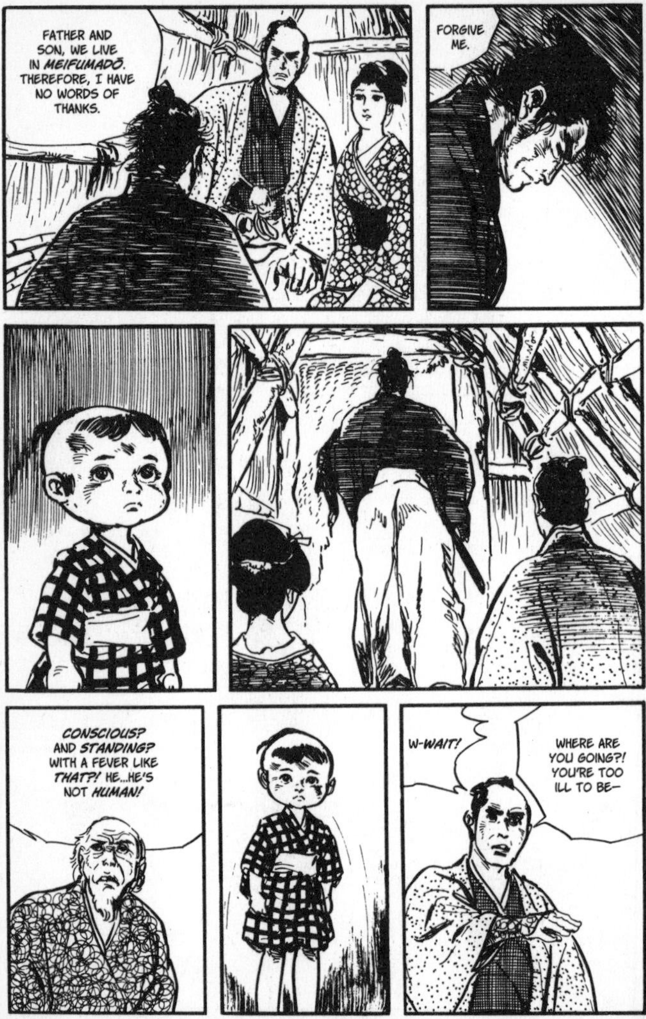
FATHER AND SON, WE LIVE IN *MEIFUMADŌ*. THEREFORE, I HAVE NO WORDS OF THANKS.
FORGIVE ME.
CONSCIOUS? AND *STANDING?* WITH A FEVER LIKE *THAT?!* HE...HE'S NOT *HUMAN!*
W-*WAIT!*
WHERE ARE YOU GOING?! YOU'RE TOO ILL TO BE—

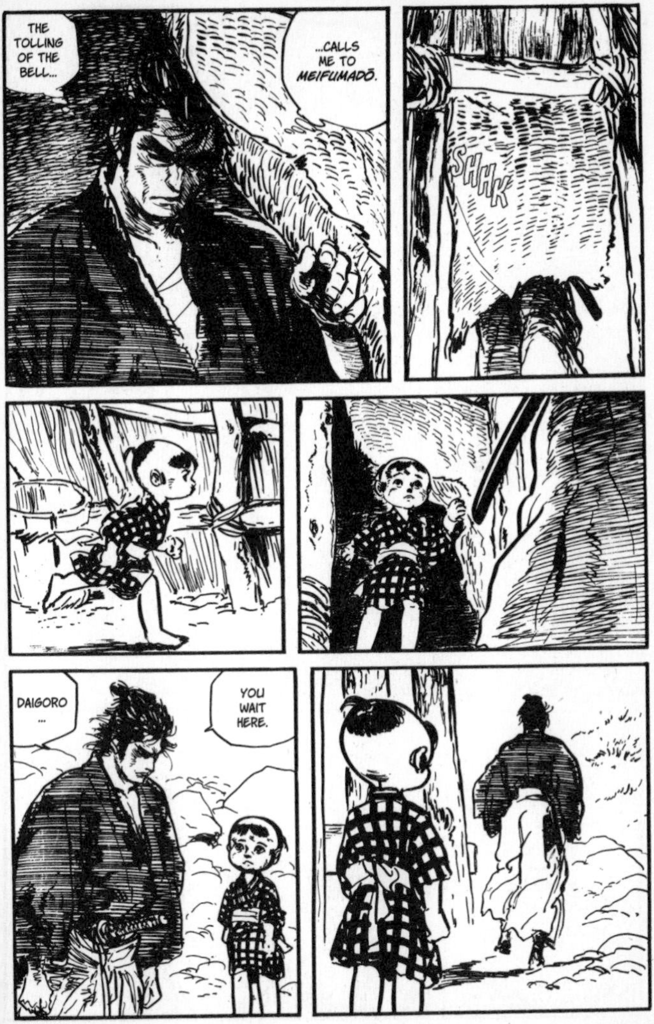
THE TOLLING OF THE BELL...
...CALLS ME TO MEIFUMADŌ.
SHHK
DAIGORO ...
YOU WAIT HERE.

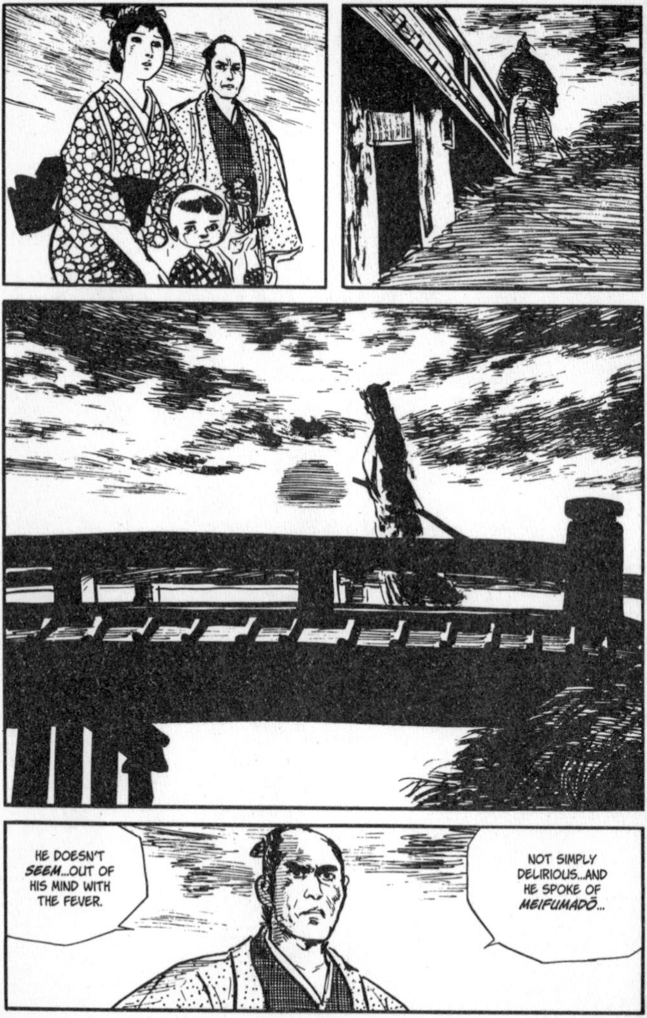
HE DOESN'T SEEM...OUT OF HIS MIND WITH THE FEVER.
NOT SIMPLY DELIRIOUS...AND HE SPOKE OF MEIFUMADŌ...

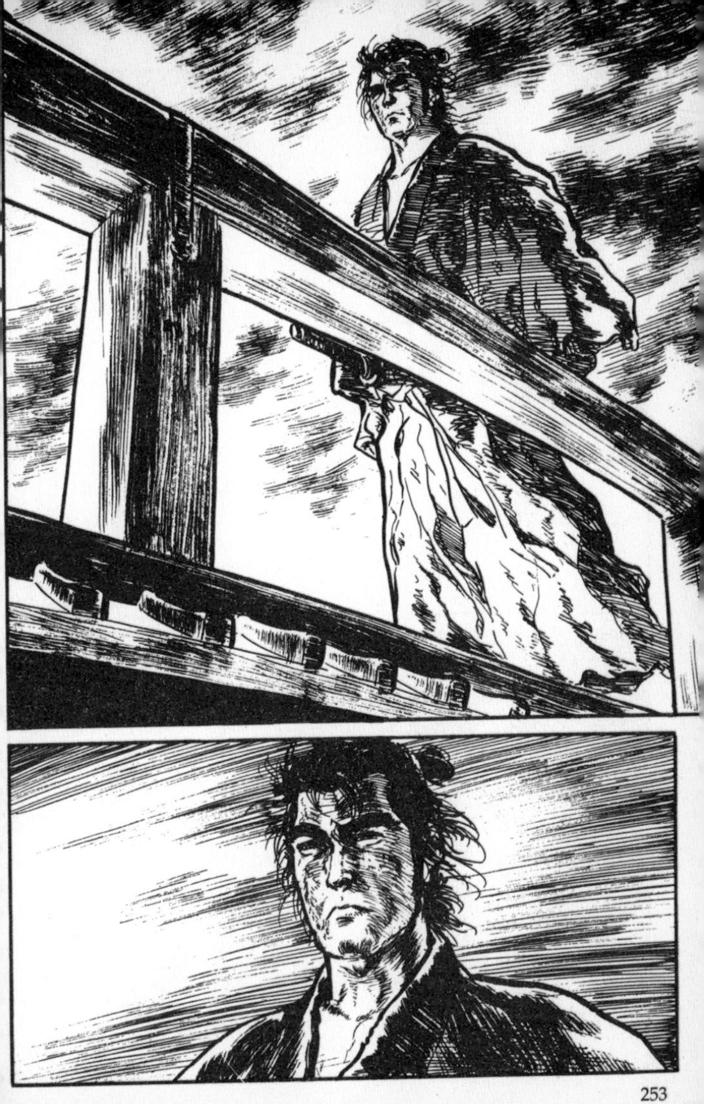

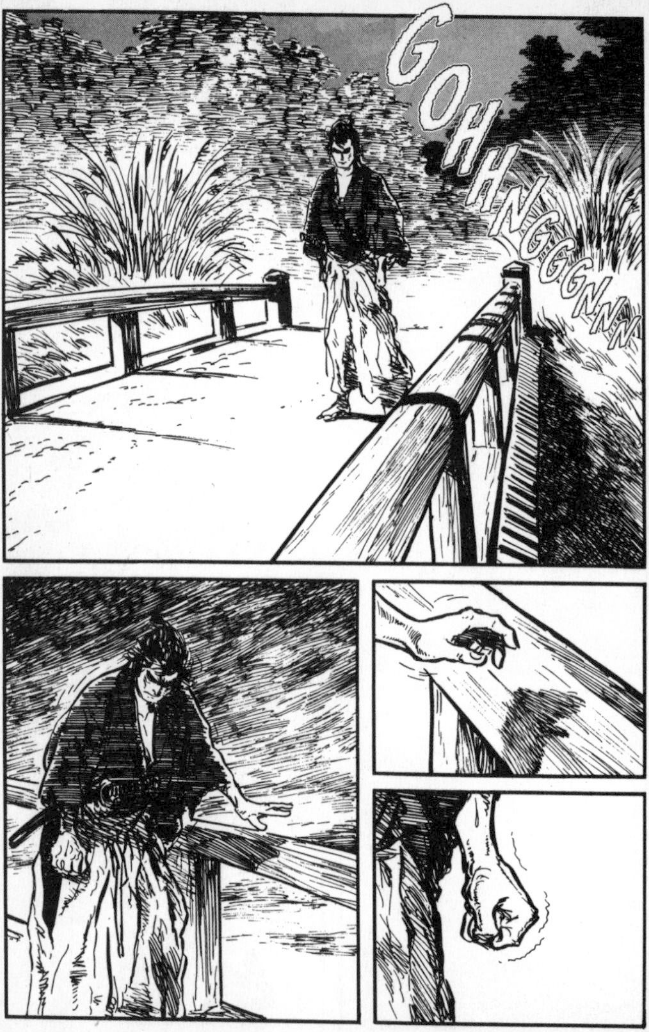
GOHHNGGGNNN

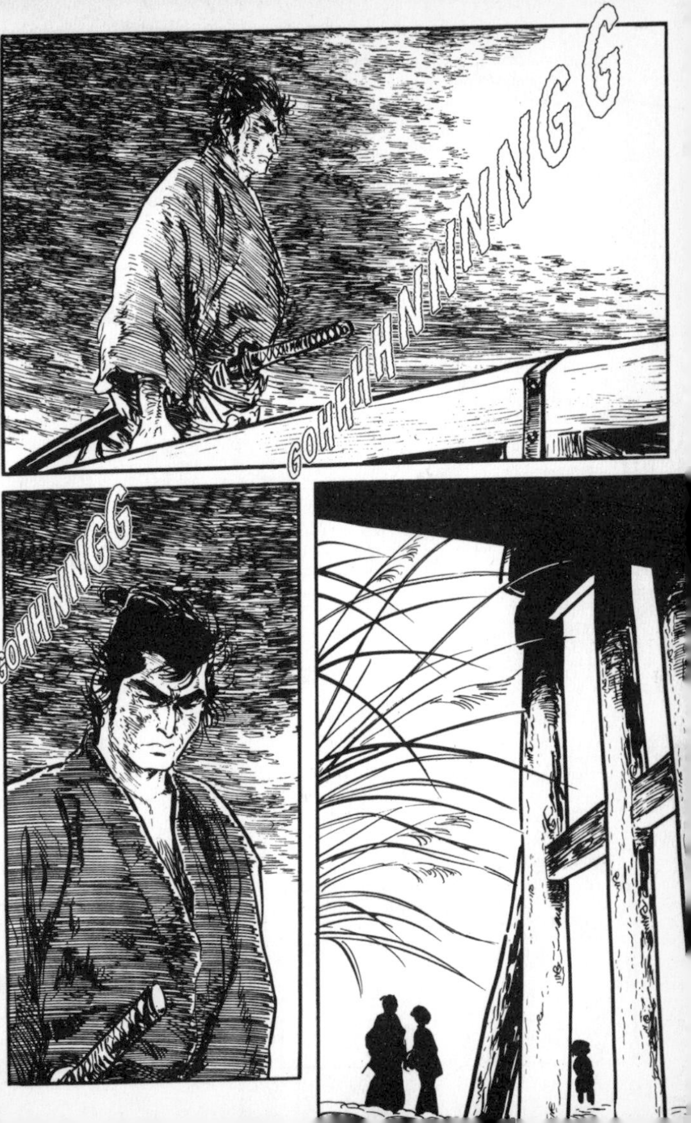
GOHHHHNNNNNGG
GOHHNNGG

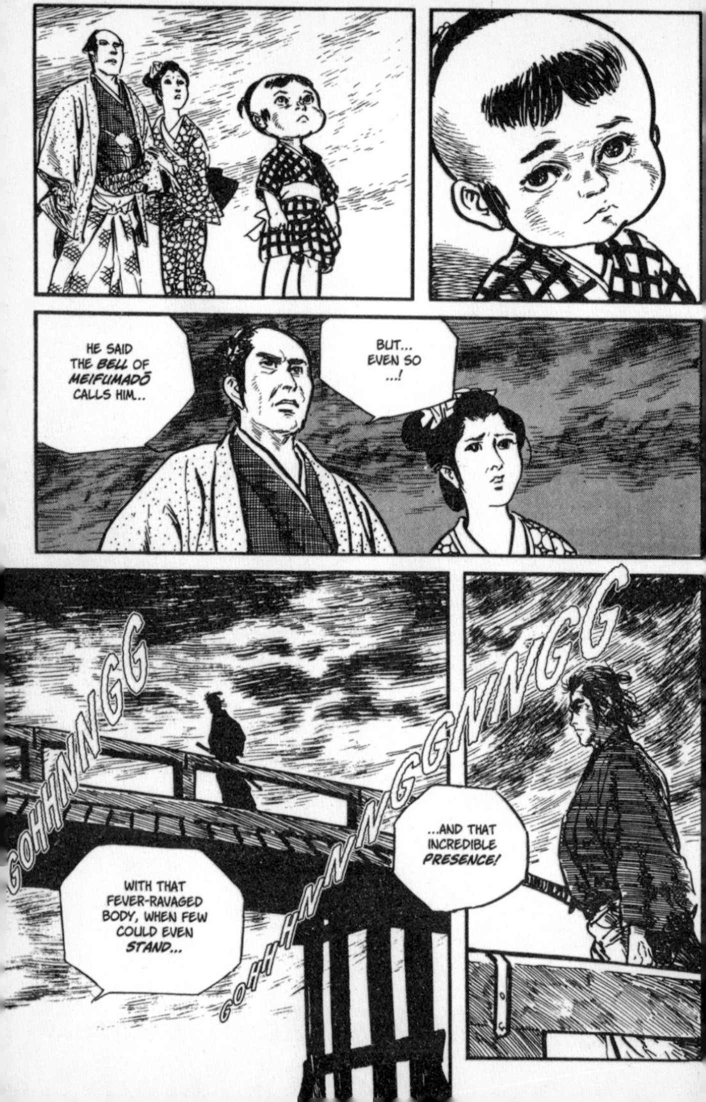
HE SAID THE BELL OF MEIFUMADŌ CALLS HIM...
BUT... EVEN SO ...!
GOHHNNGG
WITH THAT FEVER-RAVAGED BODY, WHEN FEW COULD EVEN STAND...
GOHHHNNNNGGNNGG
...AND THAT INCREDIBLE PRESENCE!

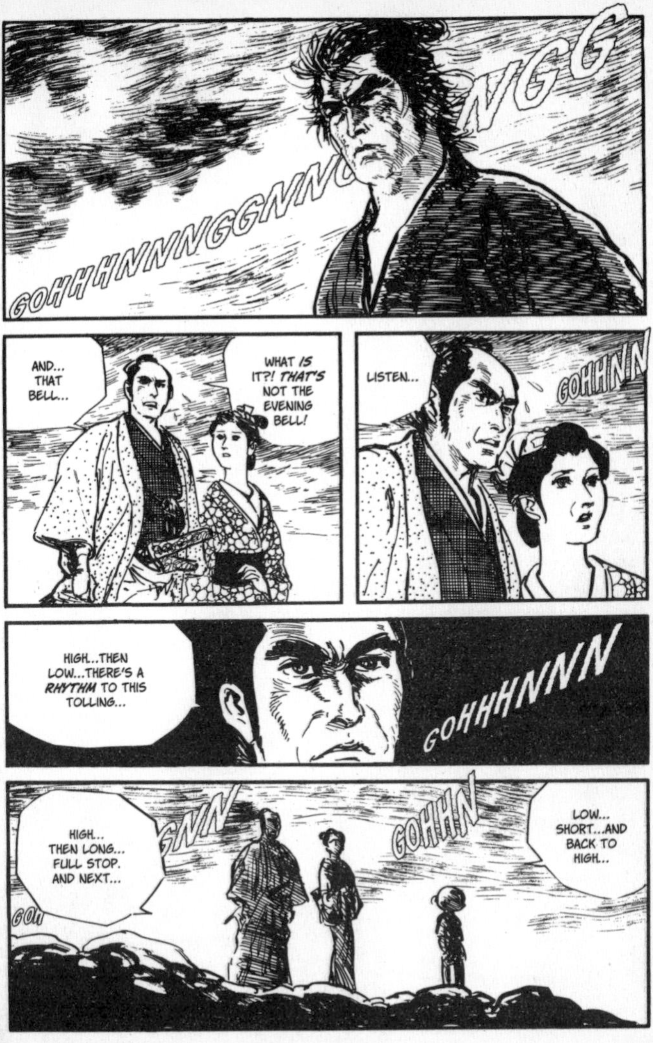
GOHHHNNNNGGNNNGG
AND... THAT BELL...
WHAT *IS* IT?! *THAT'S* NOT THE EVENING BELL!
LISTEN...
GOHHNN
HIGH...THEN LOW...THERE'S A *RHYTHM* TO THIS TOLLING...
GOHHHNNNN
HIGH... THEN LONG... FULL STOP. AND NEXT...
GO
GNN
GOHHN
LOW... SHORT...AND BACK TO HIGH...

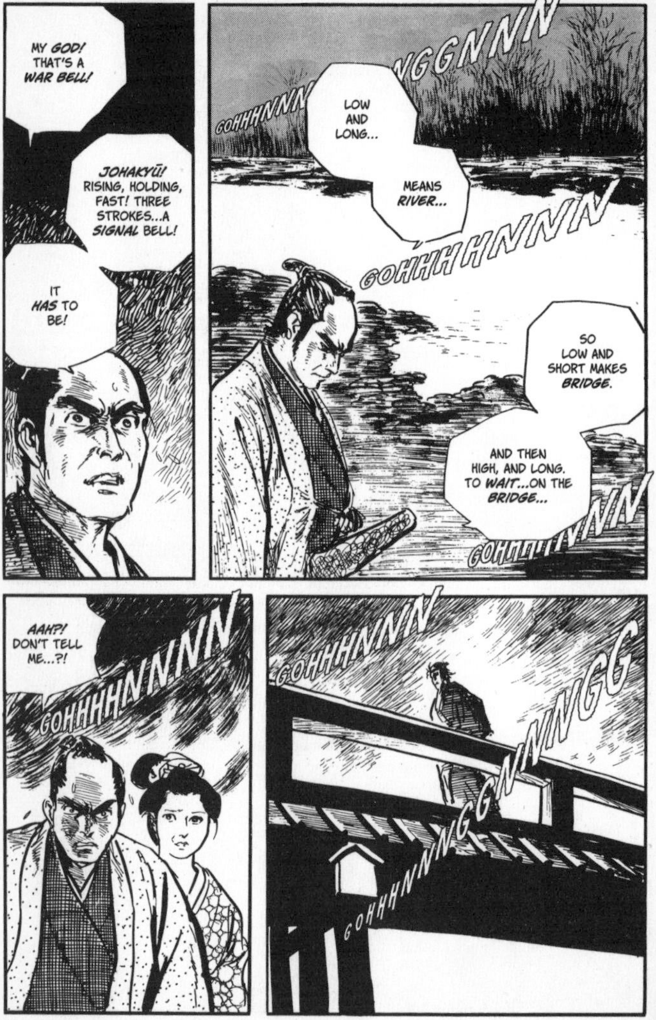
MY GOD! THAT'S A WAR BELL!
JOHAKYŪ! RISING, HOLDING, FAST! THREE STROKES...A SIGNAL BELL!
IT HAS TO BE!
GOHHHNNN
NGGNNN
LOW AND LONG...
MEANS RIVER...
GOHHHHNNNN
SO LOW AND SHORT MAKES BRIDGE.
AND THEN HIGH, AND LONG. TO WAIT...ON THE BRIDGE...
AAH?! DON'T TELL ME...?!
GOHHHHNNNNN
GOHHHNNNN
GOHHHNNNNGGNNNNGG

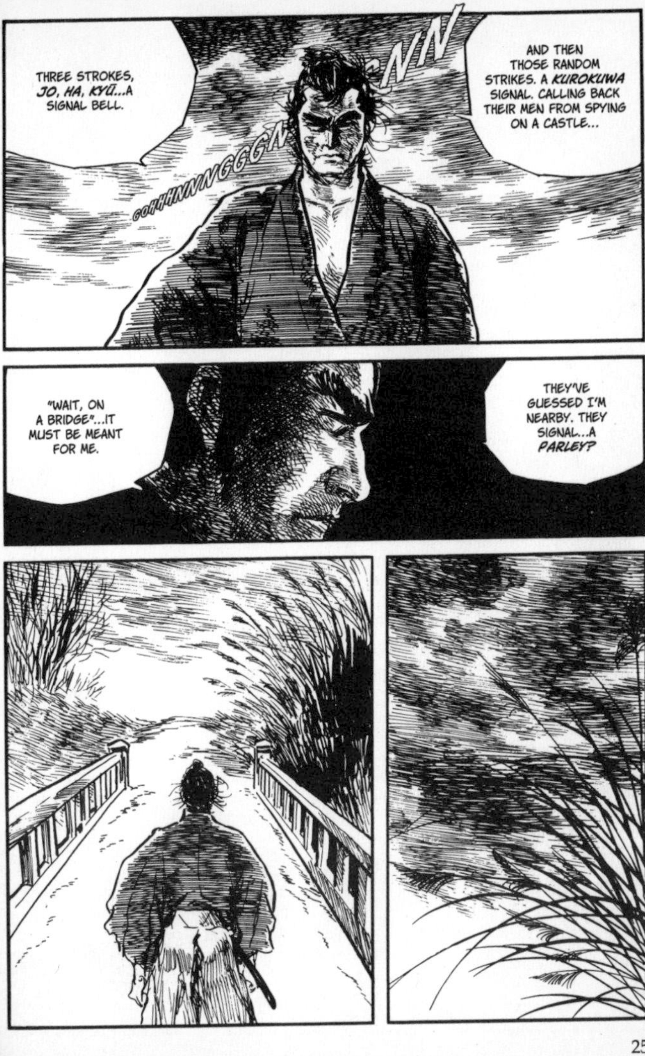
THREE STROKES, JO, HA, KYŪ...A SIGNAL BELL.
GOHHHNNNGGGN
NN
AND THEN THOSE RANDOM STRIKES. A KUROKUWA SIGNAL. CALLING BACK THEIR MEN FROM SPYING ON A CASTLE...
"WAIT, ON A BRIDGE"...IT MUST BE MEANT FOR ME.
THEY'VE GUESSED I'M NEARBY. THEY SIGNAL...A PARLEY?

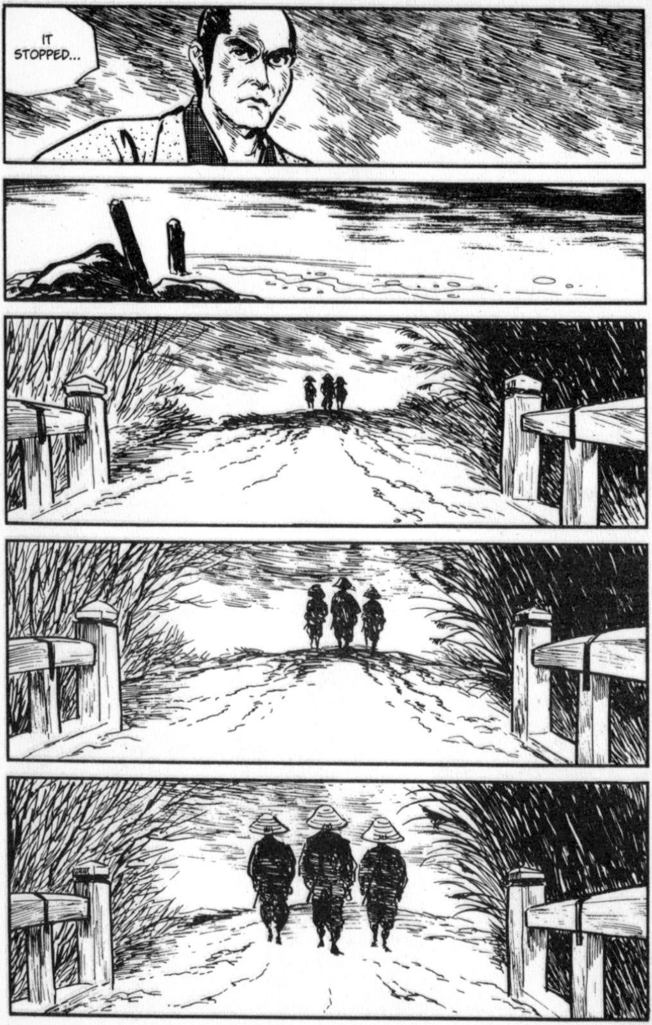
IT STOPPED...

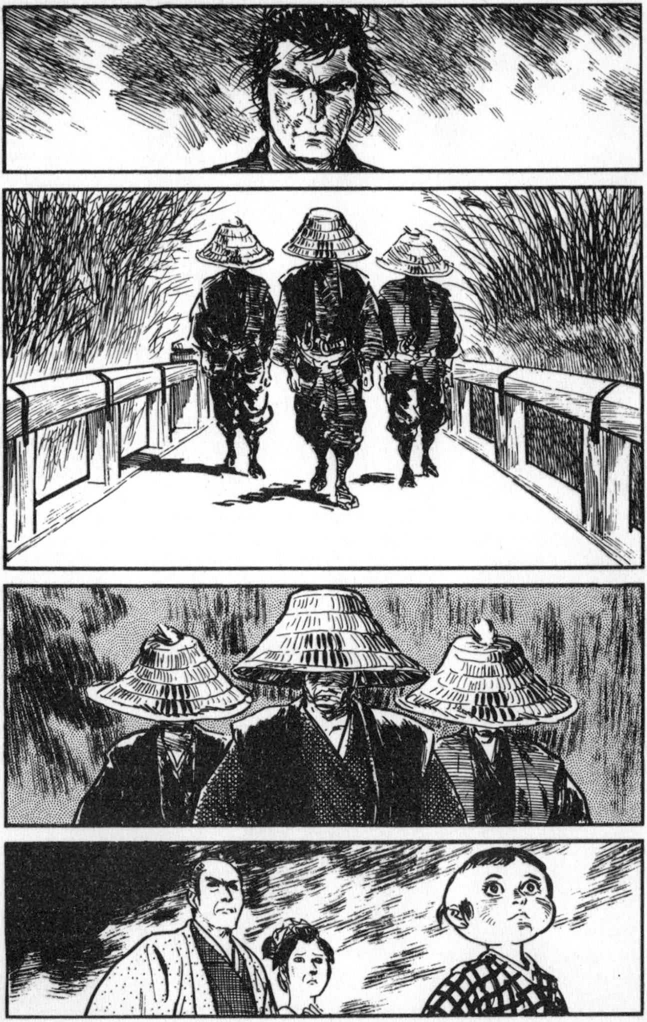

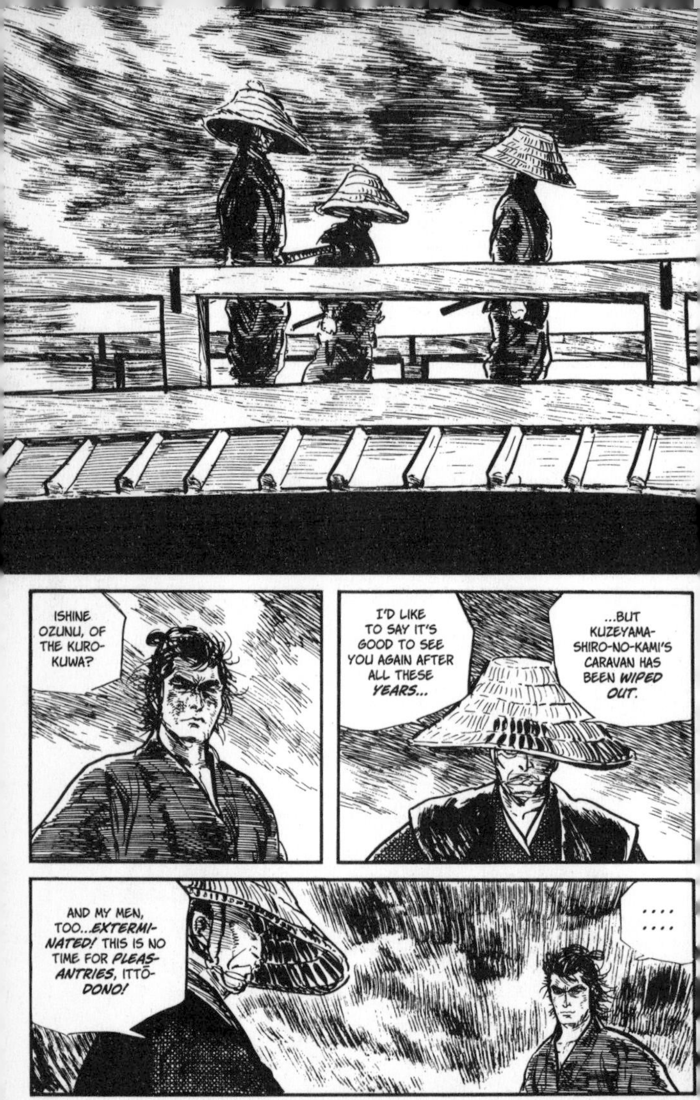
ISHINE OZUNU, OF THE KURO-KUWA?
I'D LIKE TO SAY IT'S GOOD TO SEE YOU AGAIN AFTER ALL THESE *YEARS...*
...BUT KUZEYAMA-SHIRO-NO-KAMI'S CARAVAN HAS BEEN *WIPED OUT*.
AND MY MEN, TOO...*EXTERMI-NATED!* THIS IS NO TIME FOR *PLEAS-ANTRIES*, ITTŌ-*DONO!*
....
....

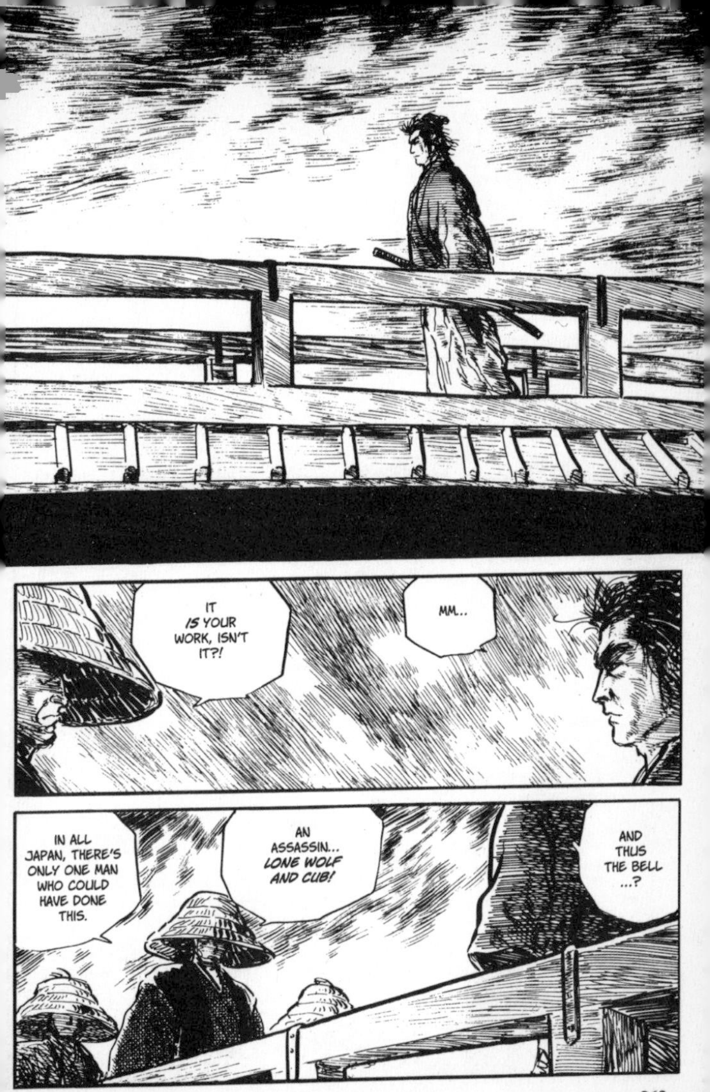
IT *IS* YOUR WORK, ISN'T IT?!
MM..
IN ALL JAPAN, THERE'S ONLY ONE MAN WHO COULD HAVE DONE THIS.
AN ASSASSIN... *LONE WOLF AND CUB!*
AND THUS THE BELL ...?

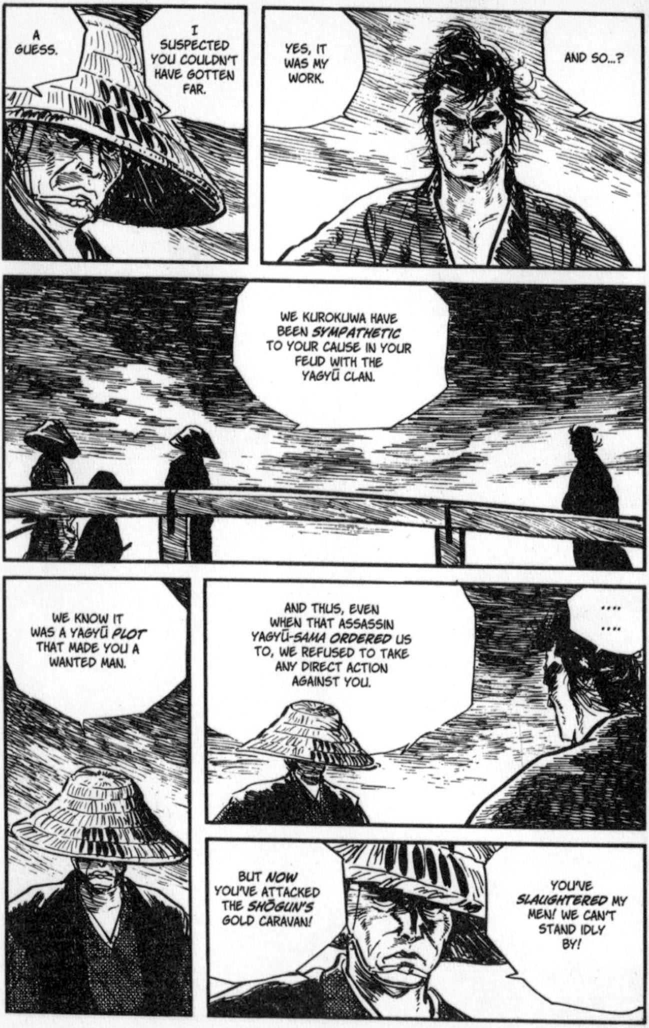
A GUESS.
I SUSPECTED YOU COULDN'T HAVE GOTTEN FAR.
YES, IT WAS MY WORK.
AND SO...?
WE KUROKUWA HAVE BEEN *SYMPATHETIC* TO YOUR CAUSE IN YOUR FEUD WITH THE YAGYŪ CLAN.
WE KNOW IT WAS A YAGYŪ *PLOT* THAT MADE YOU A WANTED MAN.
AND THUS, EVEN WHEN THAT ASSASSIN YAGYŪ-*SAMA ORDERED* US TO, WE REFUSED TO TAKE ANY DIRECT ACTION AGAINST YOU.
....
....
BUT *NOW* YOU'VE ATTACKED THE *SHŌGUN'S* GOLD CARAVAN!
YOU'VE *SLAUGHTERED* MY MEN! WE CAN'T STAND IDLY BY!

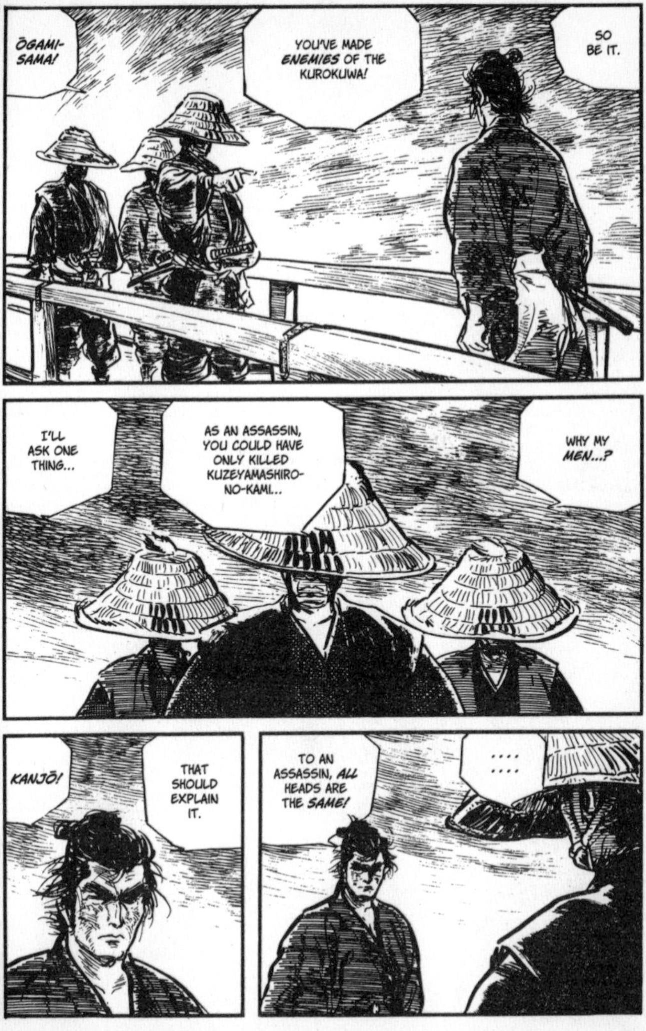
ŌGAMI-SAMA!
YOU'VE MADE ENEMIES OF THE KUROKUWA!
SO BE IT.
I'LL ASK ONE THING...
AS AN ASSASSIN, YOU COULD HAVE ONLY KILLED KUZEYAMASHIRO-NO-KAMI...
WHY MY MEN...?
KANJŌ!
THAT SHOULD EXPLAIN IT.
TO AN ASSASSIN, ALL HEADS ARE THE SAME!
....
....

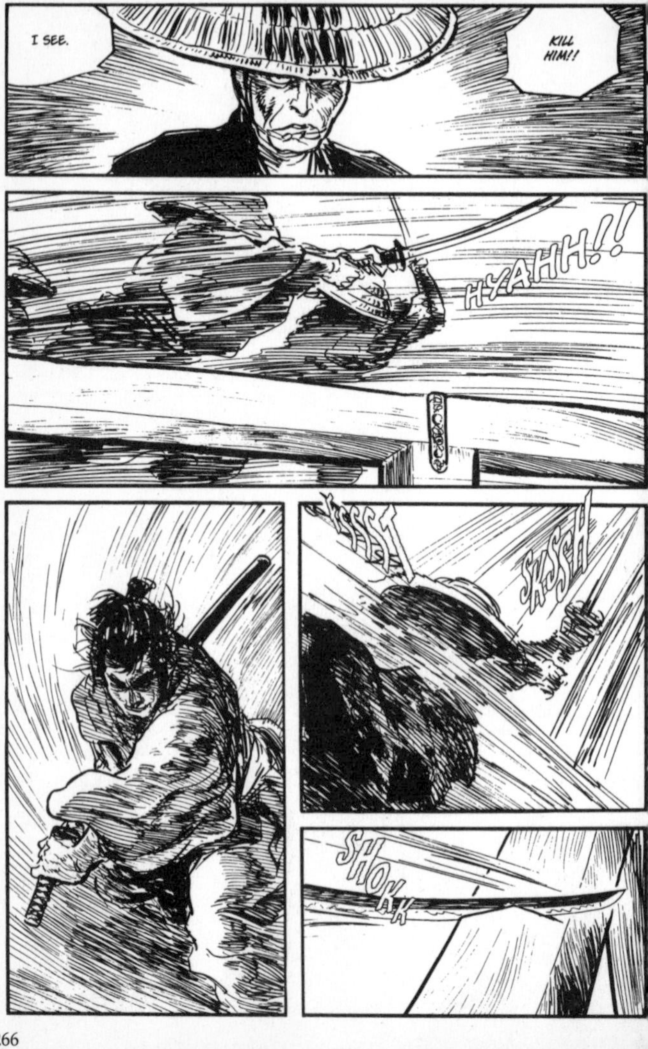
I SEE.
KILL HIM!!
HYAHH!!
SKSST
SKSSH
SHOKK

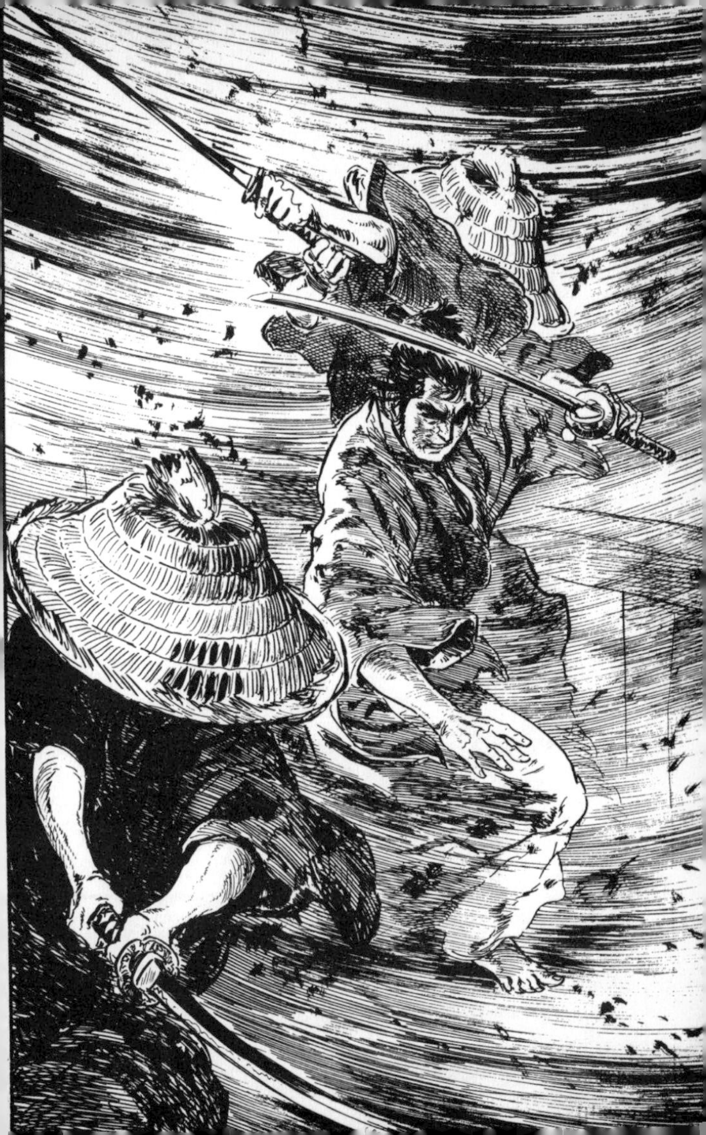

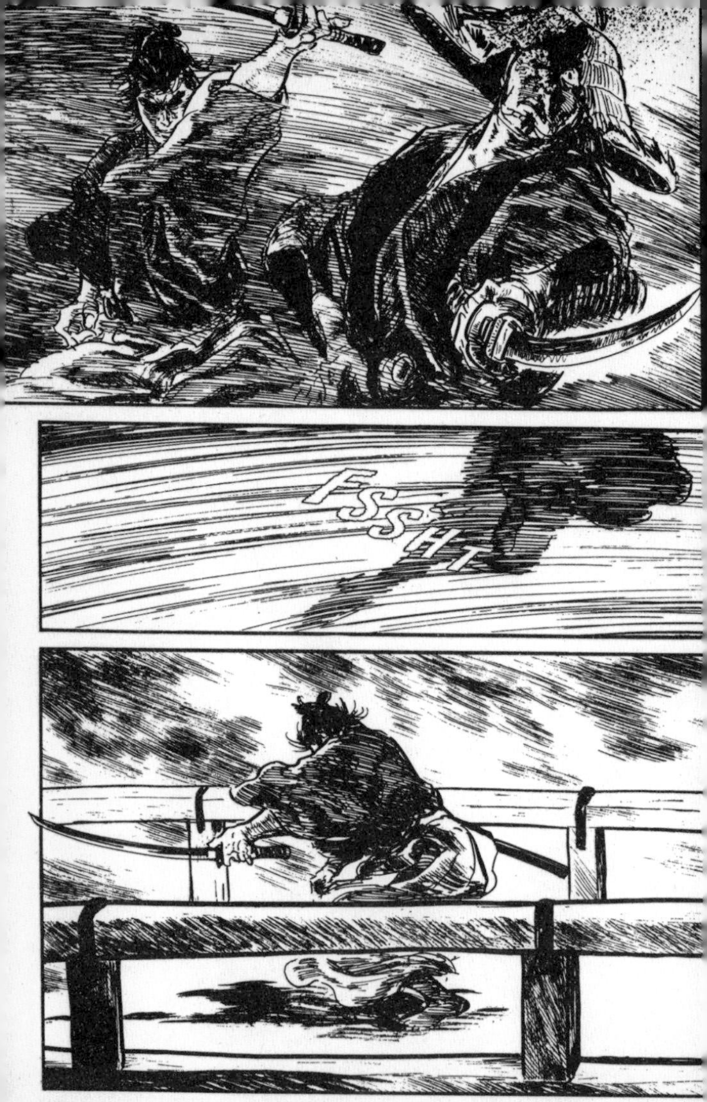
FSSHT

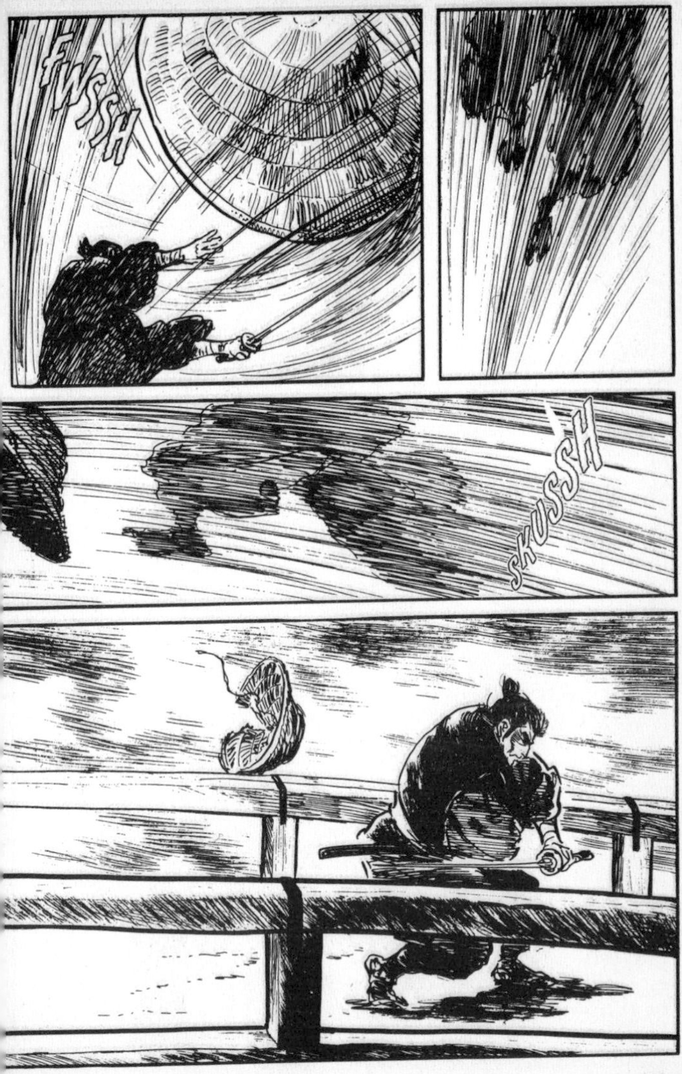
FWSSH
SKUSSH

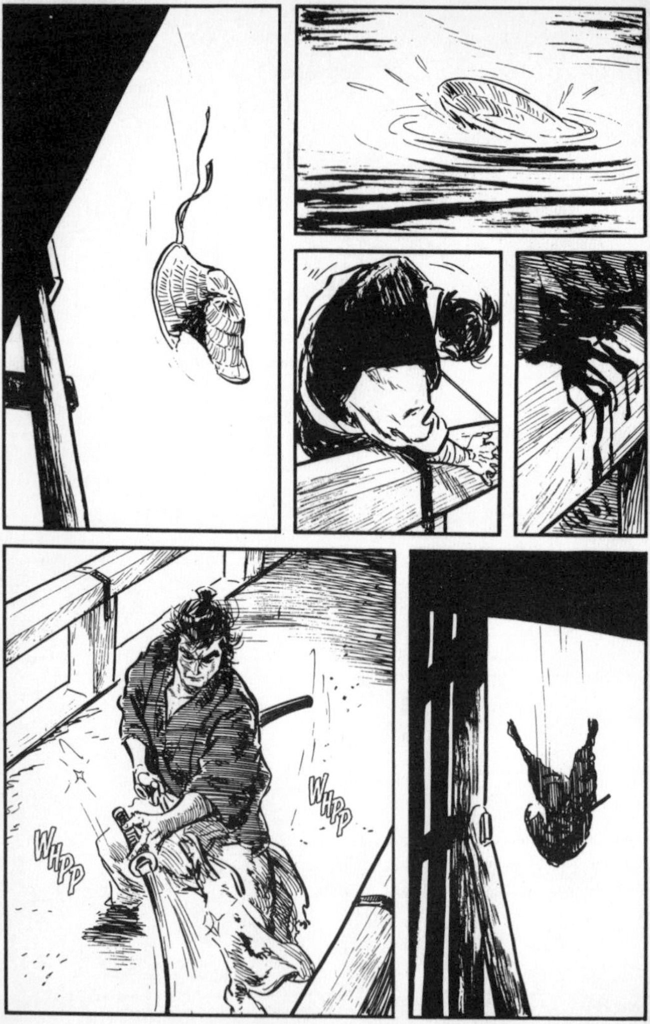
WHPP
WHPP

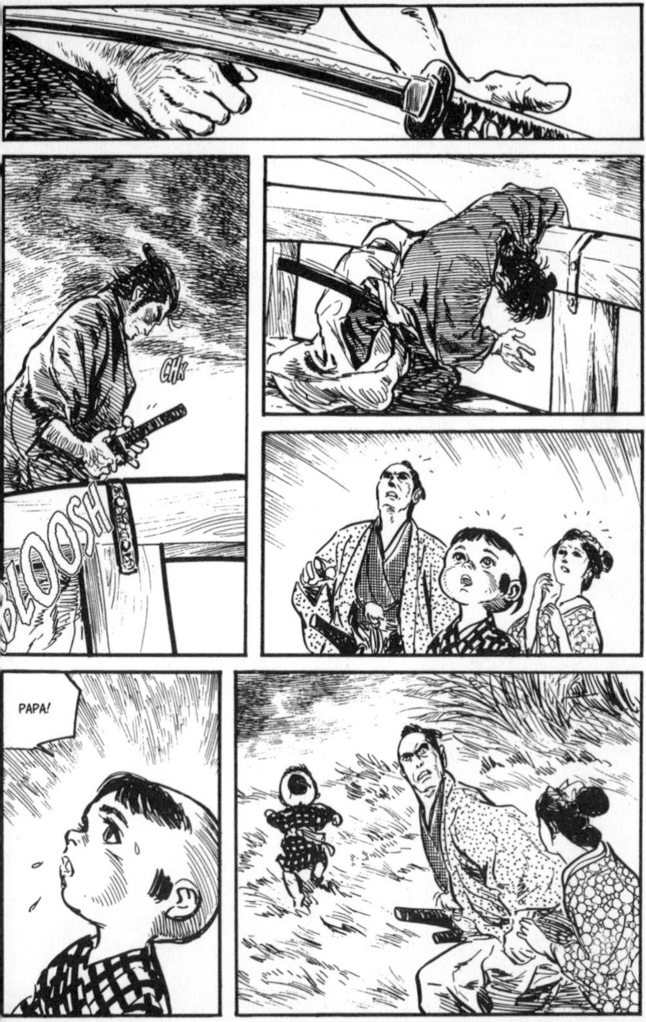
CHK
BLOOSH
PAPA!

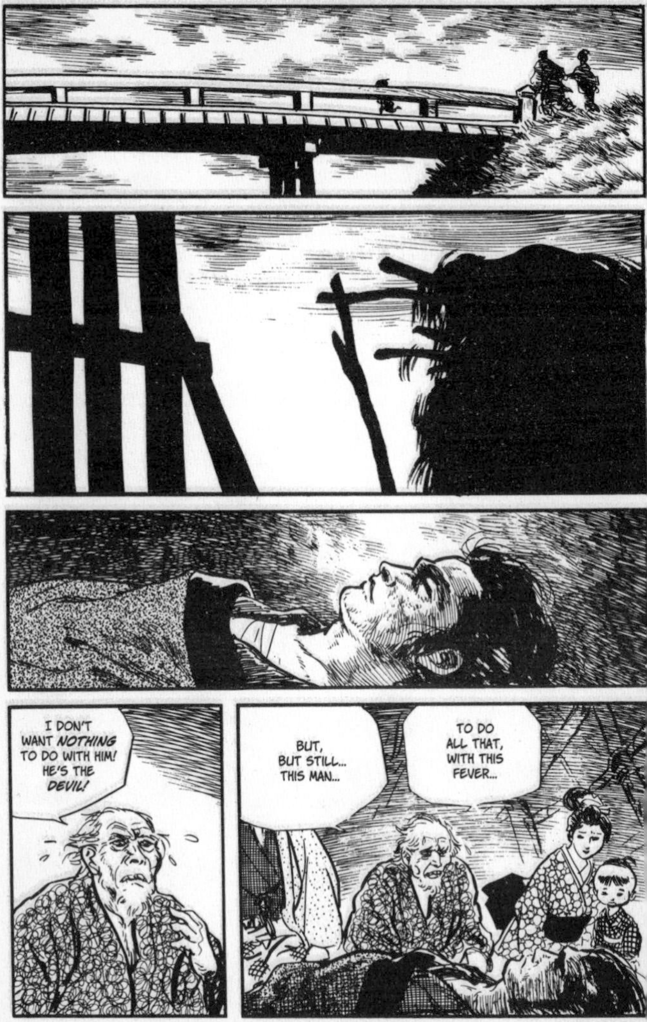
I DON'T WANT NOTHING TO DO WITH HIM! HE'S THE DEVIL!
BUT, BUT STILL... THIS MAN...
TO DO ALL THAT, WITH THIS FEVER...

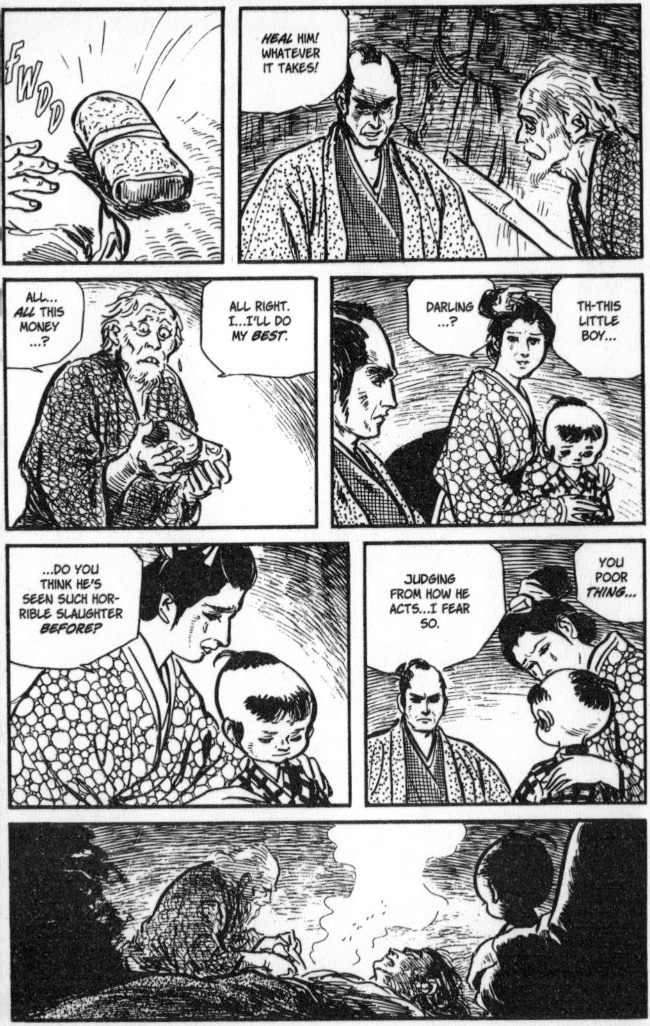
FWDD
HEAL HIM! WHATEVER IT TAKES!
ALL... ALL THIS MONEY ...?
ALL RIGHT. I...I'LL DO MY BEST.
DARLING ...?
TH-THIS LITTLE BOY...
...DO YOU THINK HE'S SEEN SUCH HORRIBLE SLAUGHTER BEFORE?
JUDGING FROM HOW HE ACTS...I FEAR SO.
YOU POOR THING...

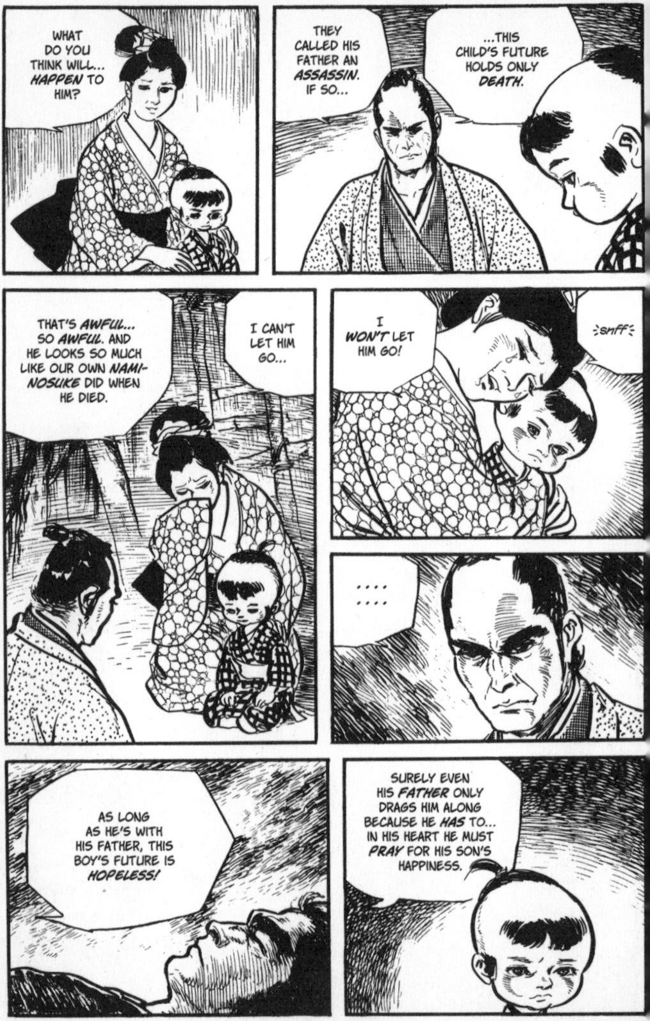
WHAT DO YOU THINK WILL... HAPPEN TO HIM?
THEY CALLED HIS FATHER AN ASSASSIN. IF SO...
...THIS CHILD'S FUTURE HOLDS ONLY DEATH.
THAT'S AWFUL... SO AWFUL. AND HE LOOKS SO MUCH LIKE OUR OWN NAMI-NOSUKE DID WHEN HE DIED.
I CAN'T LET HIM GO...
I WON'T LET HIM GO!
snff
....
....
AS LONG AS HE'S WITH HIS FATHER, THIS BOY'S FUTURE IS HOPELESS!
SURELY EVEN HIS FATHER ONLY DRAGS HIM ALONG BECAUSE HE HAS TO... IN HIS HEART HE MUST PRAY FOR HIS SON'S HAPPINESS.

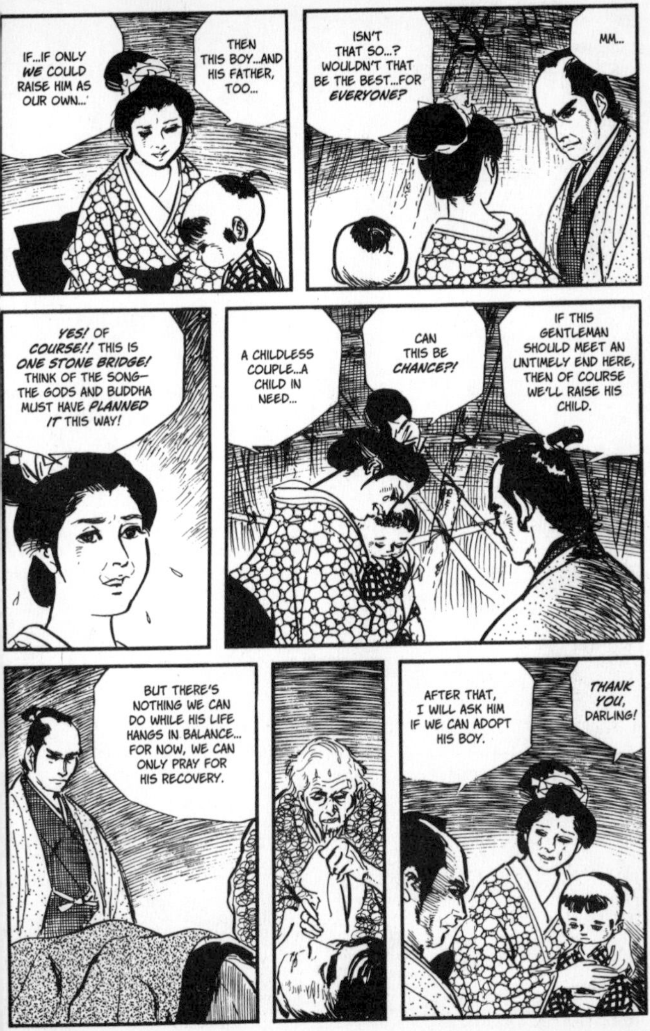
IF...IF ONLY WE COULD RAISE HIM AS OUR OWN...'
THEN THIS BOY...AND HIS FATHER, TOO...
ISN'T THAT SO...? WOULDN'T THAT BE THE BEST...FOR EVERYONE?
MM...
YES! OF COURSE!! THIS IS ONE STONE BRIDGE! THINK OF THE SONG— THE GODS AND BUDDHA MUST HAVE PLANNED IT THIS WAY!
A CHILDLESS COUPLE...A CHILD IN NEED...
CAN THIS BE CHANCE?!
IF THIS GENTLEMAN SHOULD MEET AN UNTIMELY END HERE, THEN OF COURSE WE'LL RAISE HIS CHILD.
BUT THERE'S NOTHING WE CAN DO WHILE HIS LIFE HANGS IN BALANCE... FOR NOW, WE CAN ONLY PRAY FOR HIS RECOVERY.
AFTER THAT, I WILL ASK HIM IF WE CAN ADOPT HIS BOY.
THANK YOU, DARLING!

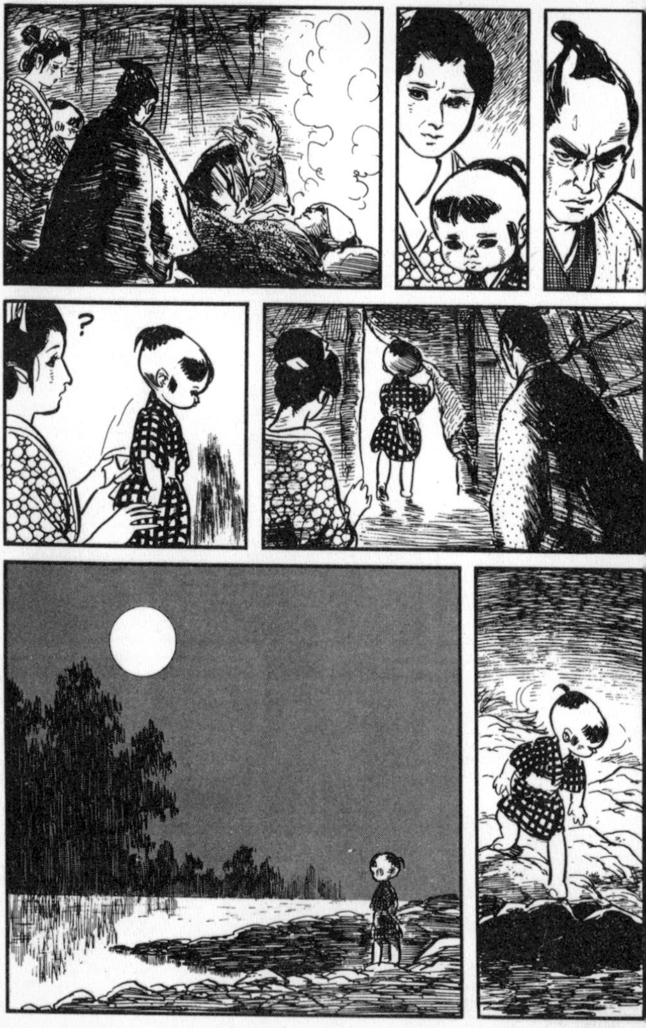
?

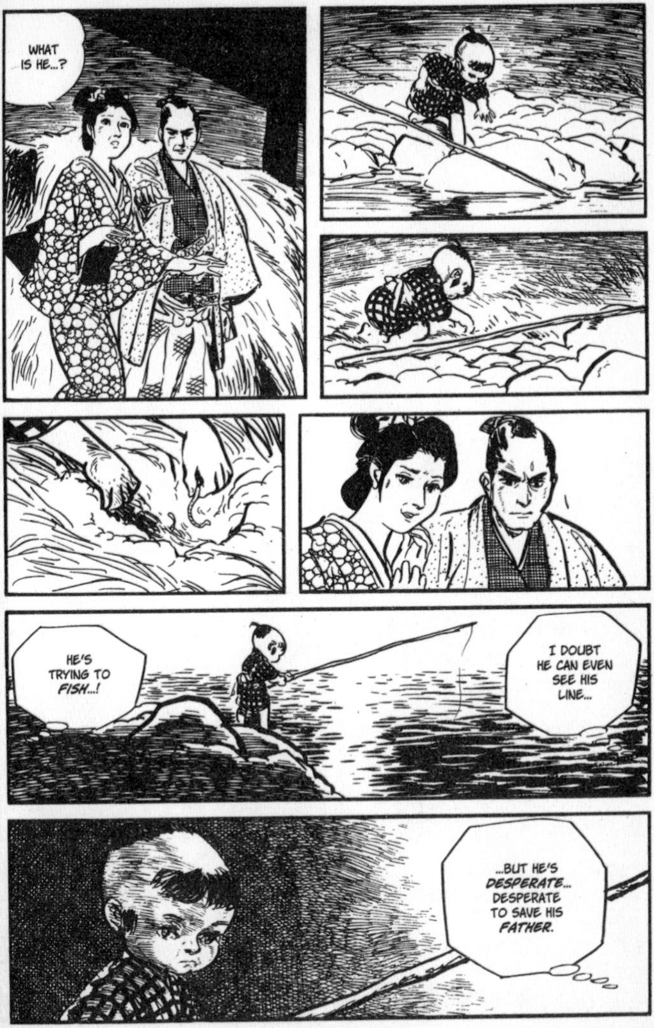
WHAT IS HE...?
HE'S TRYING TO *FISH*...!
I DOUBT HE CAN EVEN SEE HIS LINE...
...BUT HE'S *DESPERATE*... DESPERATE TO SAVE HIS *FATHER*.

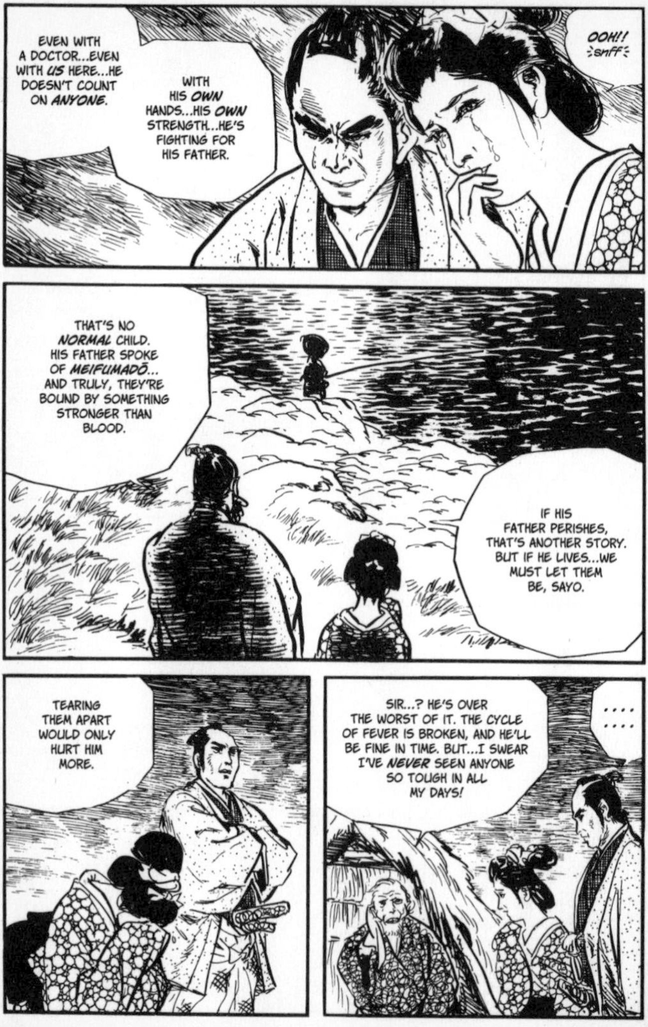
EVEN WITH A DOCTOR...EVEN WITH *US* HERE...HE DOESN'T COUNT ON *ANYONE*.
WITH HIS *OWN* HANDS...HIS *OWN* STRENGTH...HE'S FIGHTING FOR HIS FATHER.
OOH!!
snff
THAT'S NO *NORMAL* CHILD. HIS FATHER SPOKE OF *MEIFUMADŌ*... AND TRULY, THEY'RE BOUND BY SOMETHING STRONGER THAN BLOOD.
IF HIS FATHER PERISHES, THAT'S ANOTHER STORY. BUT IF HE LIVES...WE MUST LET THEM BE, SAYO.
TEARING THEM APART WOULD ONLY HURT HIM MORE.
SIR...? HE'S OVER THE WORST OF IT. THE CYCLE OF FEVER IS BROKEN, AND HE'LL BE FINE IN TIME. BUT...I SWEAR I'VE *NEVER* SEEN ANYONE SO TOUGH IN ALL MY DAYS!
....
....

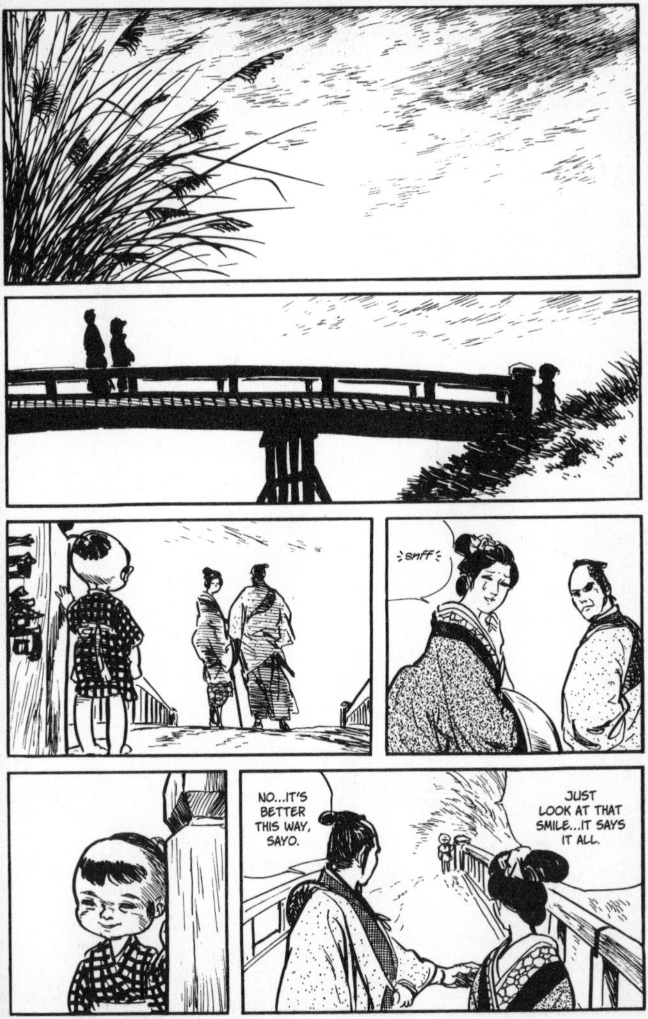
snff
NO...IT'S BETTER THIS WAY, SAYO.
JUST LOOK AT THAT SMILE...IT SAYS IT ALL.

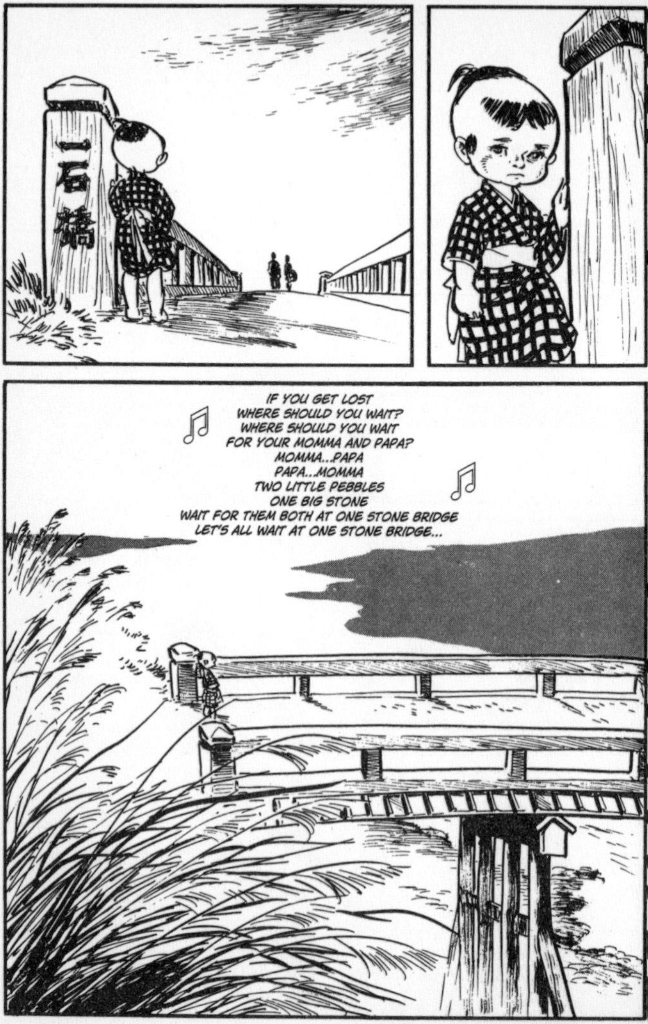
一石橋
IF YOU GET LOST
WHERE SHOULD YOU WAIT?
WHERE SHOULD YOU WAIT
FOR YOUR MOMMA AND PAPA?
MOMMA...PAPA
PAPA...MOMMA
TWO LITTLE PEBBLES
ONE BIG STONE
WAIT FOR THEM BOTH AT ONE STONE BRIDGE
LET'S ALL WAIT AT ONE STONE BRIDGE...

LONE WOLF AND CUB BOOK SIX: THE END
TO BE CONTINUED

GLOSSARY

currency

bu – A small coin, worth 1/4th of a *ryō*.

mon – A copper coin.

kan – A bundle of 1,000 *mon*.

monme – A silver piece.

ryō – A gold piece, worth 60 *monme* or 4 *kan*.

shu – Edo-period coin. Worth 1/16th of a *ryō*.

deiri

A fight between rival *yakuza* gangs.

dōtanuki

A battle sword. Literally, "sword that cuts through torsos."

Edo

The capital of medieval Japan and the seat of the shōgunate. The site of modern-day Tokyo.

go-inkyo

A wealthy, retired gentleman. (*"Go"* is an honorific.)

han

A feudal domain.

honorifics

Japan is a class and status society, and proper forms of address are critical. Common markers of respect are the prefixes *o* and *go*, and a wide range of suffixes. Some of the suffixes you will encounter in *Lone Wolf and Cub*:

chan – for children, young women, and close friends

dono – archaic; used for higher-ranked or highly respected figures

sama – used for superiors

san – the most common, used among equals or near-equals

sensei – used for teachers, masters, respected entertainers, and politicians

ikki

A peasant revolt. Japan's downtrodden peasants had almost no recourse in the Edo period. Peasants could travel to Edo to petition the government for relief, but the emissaries and their families would be put to death for their insolence, even when their pleas were accepted. No wonder then that the peasants frequently took matters into their own hands.

jin

Five *shaku*. Approximately 1.7 yards.

jingi

The traditional world of the *yakuza* was bounded by elaborate codes of behavior and duty. Improper greetings, rude speech, and other violations of the code could escalate into bloody feuds.

jizō

Folk expression of Kshitigarbha, a *bodhisattva* comforting the common man. Over time, the rough-hewn *jizō* figures came to be worshipped as guardian saints of travelers, children, women, and the weak and ailing.

jō

Ten *shaku*. Approximately 3.3 yards.

jōdai

Castle warden. The ranking *han* official in charge of a *daimyō's* castle when the *daimyō* was spending his obligatory years in Edo.

johakyū

The fundamental rhythm of Japanese music, composition, and performance art. A sustained buildup, a heightened pause, and a rapid rush to denouement.

kōgi go-yō

The shōgun's business.

kōgi kaishakunin

The shōgun's own second, who performed executions ordered by the shōgun.

koku

A bale of rice. The traditional measure of a *han's* wealth, a measure of its agricultural land and productivity.

kyōjō-mochi

To have a murder rap. *Yakuza* often cooperated with the local authorities during the Edo period in keeping the peace, but when they committed a serious crime like murder, they were expected to pack up and leave town until the dust settled. They traveled with their faces covered by wide hats.

manji

The Buddhist symbol of prosperity and good fortune, the *svastika* in Sanskrit. The clockwise "swastika," a solar symbol in many mystic traditions, was adopted by the Nazi regime as the "hakenkreuz." The Japanese Buddhist tradition, however, uses the "sauvastika," or counter-clockwise sign, dating back more than a thousand years. Here it is seen alongside the *dōchūjin* trail marker for "encampment."

meifumadō

The Buddhist Hell. The way of demons and damnation.

metsuke

Inspector. A post combining the functions of chief of police and chief intelligence officer.

mudra

A sign representing one of the virtues of the Buddha; frequently found in Buddhist art.

Nagashi-tōrō

In this traditional festival, tōrō mounted on small boats are released in rivers, carrying the souls of the dead.

oyabun

Literally, "father status," the boss of a *yakuza* gang. His underlings were known as *kobun*, or children.

rōnin

A masterless samurai. Literally, "one adrift on the waves." Members of the samurai caste who have lost their masters through the dissolution of *han*, expulsion for misbehavior, or other reasons. Prohibited from working as farmers or merchants under the strict Confucian caste system imposed by the Tokugawa shōgunate, many impoverished *rōnin* became "hired guns" for whom the code of the samurai was nothing but empty words.

sakazuki

A *sake* cup. As part of the traditional initiation rites into a *yakuza* gang, a *kobun* accepts a drink from the *oyabun*, and keeps the cup as a sign of loyalty.

sanshita

Lowest rank of *yakuza*.

"shikii-uchi gomen kōmurimasu"

"We beg your pardon for intruding upon your house." *Yakuza* had distinctive speech patterns that further separated them from the general population.

suemono-giri

Cutting through a stationary object.

tono

Lord, *daimyō*. Sometimes used as a form of address, as in *tono-sama*.

tōrō

Lanterns. The *mandō* lanterns are simple constructions of wood and paper for festivals.

wakadoshiyori

Junior councilors. The Tokugawa shōgunate was a hybrid government, both a national government empowered by the emperor to govern the nation as a whole, and a *daimyō* government like that of any *han*, concerned with protecting the interests of the Tokugawa clan itself. The council of *wakadoshiyori* junior councilors was the highest advisory body to the shōgun on matters affecting the clan, rather than the nation as a whole.

yakuza

Japan's criminal syndicates. In the Edo period, *yakuza* were a common part of the landscape, running houses of gambling and prostitution. As long as they did not overstep their bounds, they were tolerated by the authorities, a tradition little changed in modern Japan.

KAZUO KOIKE

Though widely respected as a powerful writer of graphic fiction, Kazuo Koike has spent a lifetime reaching beyond the bounds of the comics medium. Aside from co-creating and writing the successful *Lone Wolf and Cub* and *Crying Freeman* manga, Koike has hosted television programs; founded a golf magazine; produced movies; written popular fiction, poetry, and screenplays; and mentored some of Japan's best manga talent.

Lone Wolf and Cub was first serialized in Japan in 1970 (under the title *Kozure Okami*) in *Manga Action* magazine and continued its hugely popular run for many years, being collected as the stories were published, and reprinted worldwide. Koike collected numerous awards for his work on the series throughout the next decade. Starting in 1972, Koike adapted the popular manga into a series of six films, the *Baby Cart Assassin* saga, garnering widespread commercial success and critical acclaim for his screenwriting.

This wasn't Koike's only foray into film and video. In 1996, Crying Freeman, the manga Koike created with artist Ryoichi Ikegami, was produced in Hollywood and released to commercial success in Europe and is currently awaiting release in America.

And to give something back to the medium that gave him so much, Koike started the *Gekiga Sonjuku*, a college course aimed at helping talented writers and artists — such as *Ranma 1/2* creator Rumiko Takahashi — break into the comics field.

The driving focus of Koike's narrative is character development, and his commitment to character is clear: "Comics are carried by characters. If a character is well created, the comic becomes a hit." Kazuo Koike's continued success in comics and literature has proven this philosophy true.

GOSEKI KOJIMA

Goseki Kojima was born on November 3, 1928, the very same day as the godfather of Japanese comics, Osamu Tezuka. While just out of junior high school, the self-taught Kojima began painting advertising posters for movie theaters to pay his bills.

In 1950, Kojima moved to Tokyo, where the postwar devastation had given rise to special manga forms for audiences too poor to buy the new manga magazines. Kojima created art for *kami-shibai*, or "paper-play" narrators, who would use manga story sheets to present narrated street plays. Kojima moved on to creating works for the *kashi-bon* market, bookstores that rented out books, magazines, and manga to mostly low-income readers. He soon became highly popular among *kashi-bon* readers.

In 1967, Kojima broke into the magazine market with his series *Dojinki*. As the manga magazine market grew and diversified, he turned out a steady stream of popular series.

In 1970, in collaboration with Kazuo Koike, Kojima began the work that would seal his reputation, *Kozure Okami* (*Lone Wolf and Cub*). Before long the story had become a gigantic hit, eventually spinning off a television series, six motion pictures, and even theme song records. Koike and Kojima were soon dubbed the "golden duo" and produced success after success on their way to the pinnacle of the manga world.

When *Manga Japan* magazine was launched in 1994, Kojima was asked to serve as consultant, and he helped train the next generation of manga artists.

In his final years, Kojima turned to creating original graphic novels based on the movies of his favorite director, Akira Kurosawa. Kojima passed away on January 5, 2000 at the age of 71.

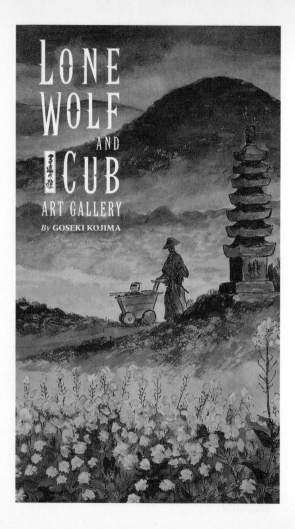

LONE WOLF AND CUB

子連れ狼

ART GALLERY

By GOSEKI KOJIMA

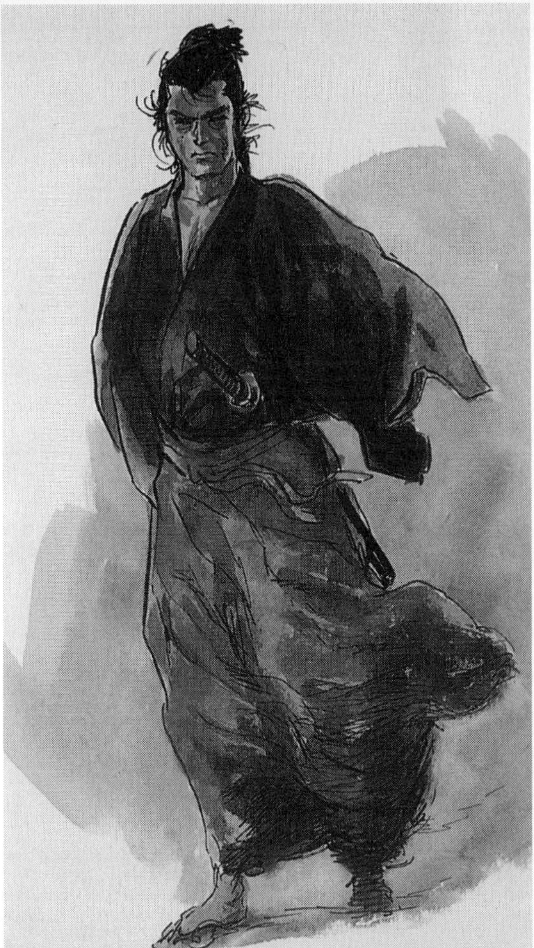

The legend of Lone Wolf and Cub continu
to grow, chronicling the wanderings of
cunning assassin and his infant son durir
the deadliest era of feudal Japan. In th
volume, the Lone Wolf battles the mo
dangerous killer in the countryside, foi
the plans of a deceptive gambling troup
tricks an evil lord into exposing his wea
underbelly, and pits himself against th
Shogun's deadly ninja! In print for decad
in its native Japan, the basis of numerou
popular Japanese films, and the inspiratio
of writers and artists worldwide, *Lone Wc
and Cub* is undeniably a masterpiece
graphic storytelling.

*"Period authenticity and pure artistry (combin
with) bizarre and moving studies of human natu
and the bond between parent and child... it's a drea
come true!"*

— *Animerica* onli

Published for the first time in America in th
Japanese format.

DARK HORSE COMICS®

STUDIO PROTEUS

子連れ狼

Front cover illustration
by FRANK MILLER
and LYNN VARLEY

$9.95 U.S., $14.95 CANADA

ISBN 1-56971-507-6
50995>
9 781569 715079

www.darkhorse.com